Complete Curriculum

Grade 2

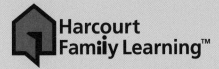
Harcourt
Family Learning™

© 2006 by Flash Kids
Adapted from *Comprehension Skills Complete Classroom Library*
by Linda Ward Beech, Tara McCarthy, and Donna Townsend;
© 2001 by Harcourt Achieve • Adapted from *Steck-Vaughn Spelling: Linking Words to Meaning, Level 2*, by John R. Pescosolido;
© 2002 by Harcourt Achieve • Adapted from Steck-Vaughn *Working with Numbers, Level B*; © 2001 by Harcourt Achieve • Adapted from
Language Arts, Grade 2; © 2003 by Harcourt Achieve • Adapted from *Experiences with Writing Styles Grade 2*; © 1998 by Steck-Vaughn
Company • Adapted from *Test Best for Test Prep, Level B*; © 1999 by Harcourt Achieve
Licensed under special arrangement with Harcourt Achieve.

For more information, please visit www.flashkids.com
Please submit all inquiries to Flashkids@sterlingpublishing.com

ISBN 978-1-4114-9883-9

Manufactured in China

Lot#:
24   23
10/18

New York

Dear Parent,

Beginning a new grade is a milestone for your child, and each new subject is bound to present some challenges that may require some attention out of the classroom. With this comprehensive second-grade workbook at hand, you and your child can work together on any skill that he or she is finding difficult to master. Here to help are hundreds of fun, colorful pages for learning and practicing reading, spelling, math, language arts, writing, and test preparation.

In the reading section, the wide range of high-interest stories will hold your child's attention and help develop his or her proficiency in reading. Each of the six units focuses on a different reading comprehension skill: finding facts, detecting a sequence, learning new vocabulary through context, identifying the main idea, drawing conclusions, and making inferences. Mastering these skills will ensure that your child has the necessary tools for a lifetime love of reading.

Lessons in the spelling section present second-grade words in lists grouped by vowel sound, suffix, or related forms, like plurals and contractions. This order will clearly show your child the different ways that similar sounds can be spelled. Your child will learn to sort words, recognize definitions, synonyms, and base words, as well as use capitalization and punctuation. Each lesson also features a short passage containing spelling and grammar mistakes that your child will proofread and correct.

The math section starts with basics like place value and counting, followed by addition and subtraction with and without regrouping. You'll also find sections on money, time, geometry, and measurement. Throughout each unit, your child will be given ample opportunity to estimate, compare, find patterns, and use logic. Exercises like these help your child develop important thinking and problem-solving skills. They are also the foundation upon which your child will build more complex math skills.

More than 100 lessons in the language arts section provide clear examples of and exercises in language skills such as parts of speech, sentences, mechanics, vocabulary and usage, writing, and research skills. Grammar lessons range from using nouns and verbs to constructing better sentences. Writing exercises include the friendly letter and the book report. These skills will help your child improve his or her communication abilities, excel in all academic areas, and increase his or her scores on standardized tests.

Each of the six units in the writing section focuses on a unique type of writing: sentence about a picture, personal story, friendly letter, paragraph that describes, story, and how-to paragraph. The first half of each unit reinforces writing aspects such as putting pictures into sentences and using descriptive words, in addition to providing fun, inspirational writing ideas for your child to explore alone or with a friend. In the second half of each unit, your child will read a practice paragraph, analyze it, prepare a writing plan for his or her own paper or paragraph, and then write and revise.

Lastly, the test prep section applies your child's knowledge in reading, math, and language to the basic standardized test formats that your child will encounter throughout his or her school career. Each unit in the first half of this section teaches specific test strategies for areas such as word study skills, reading comprehension, and mathematics. The second half of the section allows your child to apply these test-taking skills in a realistic testing environment. By simulating the experience of taking standardized tests, these practice tests can lessen feelings of intimidation during school tests.

As your child works through the test prep section, help him or her keep in mind these four important principles of test-taking:

1. Using Time Wisely

All standardized tests are timed, so your child should learn to work rapidly but comfortably. He or she should not spend too much time on any one question, and mark items to return to if possible. Use any remaining time to review answers. Most importantly, use a watch to keep on track!

2. Avoiding Errors

When choosing the correct answers on standardized tests, your child should pay careful attention to directions, determine what is being asked, and mark answers in the appropriate place. He or she should then check all answers and not make stray marks on the answer sheet.

3. Reasoning

To think logically toward each answer, your child should read the entire question or passage and all the answer choices before answering a question. It may be helpful to restate questions or answer choices in his or her own words.

4. Guessing

When the correct answer is not clear right away, your child should eliminate answers that he or she knows are incorrect. If that is not possible, skip the question. Then your child should compare the remaining answers, restate the question, and then choose the answer that seems most correct.

An answer key at the back of this workbook allows you and your child to check his or her work in any of the subject sections. Remember to give praise and support for each effort. Also, learning at home can be accomplished at any moment—you can ask your child to read aloud to you, write grocery lists, keep a journal, or measure the ingredients for a recipe. Use your imagination! With help from you and this workbook, your child is well on the way to completing the second grade with flying colors!

TABLE OF CONTENTS

READING SKILLS

SPELLING SKILLS

MATH SKILLS

Language Arts

Writing Skills

Test Prep

Answer Key

Reading
Skills

What Are Facts?

Facts are things you know are true. Everything you read has facts in it. Read this:

Bob was smiling. At last it was spring.

Bob was smiling. That is a fact. The time of year was spring. That is also a fact. There is one more fact you know. You know the person's name.

Try It!

Read this story. It has facts about what people used to think a long time ago.

The Earth and the Sun

Long ago a man was thinking about the sky. He had been watching the Sun for days. He began to see it in a new way. "Earth is going around the Sun," he said. At that time most people thought the Sun went around Earth. They thought Earth was the biggest and best thing in the sky.

The man said, "I must write a book. It might make people angry. But I must tell the truth." The man did write a book, but he never saw it printed. He died in 1543. The book was printed later that year.

People were angry when they read the book. They wanted to think that everything went around Earth. Today people know that the man was right.

How to Find Facts

Try to find the facts in the story. Write the facts on the lines below.

Fact 1: The man had been watching the _____ for days. (Moon, Earth, Sun)

Fact 2: The man died in the year _____. (1543, 1453, 1457)

Fact 3: The man said, "I must write a _____." (letter, story, book)

- To find facts you must know what to look for. For Fact 1 you must look for a thing the man watched. For Fact 2 you must look for a date. For Fact 3 you must look for what the man said. Read the story again. Draw a line under the words *Sun* and *book*, and under the number *1543*. They are the right answers for Facts 1, 3, and 2.

- To find the facts, read the story very carefully. If you cannot remember the facts, read the story again.

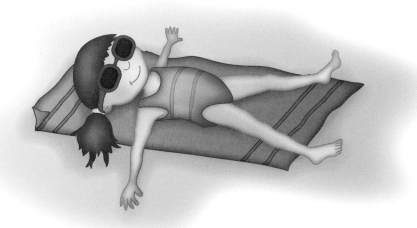

Read each story. After each story you will answer questions about the facts in the story. Remember, a fact is something that you know is true.

Seashells

Seashells come in many different shapes, sizes, and colors. Some shells grow as big as 4 feet long. Some shells are smaller than ½ inch long. Some shells have two sides that open like wings. Other shells are shaped like a curling tube. Shells come in all colors: white, black, brown, yellow, green, red, orange, and pink. They are like a rainbow in the ocean.

Many seashells are named for other things we know. The spider shell is one example. The spider shell has long points that look like spider legs. The comb shell has points, too. Its points are straight and close together, just like those in a comb.

_____ **1.** Some shells grow
    A. rainbows
    B. 4 feet long
    C. butterfly wings

_____ **3.** Some shells are named for
    A. people who found them
    B. other things we know
    C. where they are found

_____ **2.** The smallest shells are
    A. ½ foot long
    B. 2 inches wide
    C. smaller than ½ inch long

_____ **4.** Some seashells have
    A. arms
    B. points
    C. homes

There are two kinds of bear shells. One is called the little bear. It is a small shell. The bear-paw shell is different. It is a big shell with two parts. Each half looks like an animal foot.

Some names of shells do not make any sense. The apple shell doesn't look like an apple at all. And the dog shell doesn't look like a dog. The butterfly shell is very plain. Many other shells look more like a butterfly than that one does! But the heart shell does have the shape of a heart. Not all heart shells are red. Some are yellow. Others have brown spots.

_____ **5.** There are
- **A.** two kinds of bear shells
- **B.** three types of butterflies
- **C.** two kinds of apple shells

_____ **6.** The bear-paw shell has
- **A.** one part
- **B.** two parts
- **C.** three parts

_____ **7.** The dog shell
- **A.** looks like an animal foot
- **B.** doesn't look like a dog
- **C.** is yellow or red

_____ **8.** Sometimes the heart shell has
- **A.** brown spots
- **B.** a butterfly shape
- **C.** three points

Good Foods, Poor Names

Some foods have names that make good sense. Take an orange, for example. Its color is orange. So it seems only right to call the fruit by that name.

But what about the peanut? True, it is a kind of pea. Like other peas, a peanut grows in a shell, or pod. But a peanut is not a nut. It might seem like a nut. After all, it is small, round, and hard. But a peanut is not part of the nut family. So the name *peanut* is really not the best name for the food! Can you think of a better name for the peanut?

_____ **1.** An orange gets its
name because
   A. it is a round fruit
   B. it is juicy inside
   C. its color is orange

_____ **2.** A peanut is a kind of
   A. pea
   B. nut
   C. pea and nut

_____ **3.** A peanut grows in a
   A. shell
   B. pit
   C. skin

_____ **4.** A peanut is
   A. long and soft
   B. small and round
   C. flat and square

Did you ever eat a pineapple? You might have liked its taste. But how good is its name? A pineapple is neither a pine nor an apple. It looks like a large pinecone. But it is not in the pine family. It is not in the apple family, either. What may be a better name for a pineapple?

You may enjoy grapefruit. But its name is not the best. Yes, it is a fruit. But it is not in the grape family. Grapes grow on vines. Grapefruit grow on trees. What does all this prove? The names of foods can be food for thought!

_____ **5.** A pineapple is
   A. both a pine and an apple
   B. not a pine or an apple
   C. a pine but not an apple

_____ **6.** A pineapple looks like
   A. a big pine cone
   B. a big apple
   C. a big grape

_____ **7.** A grapefruit is
   A. a grape but not a fruit
   B. both a grape and a fruit
   C. a fruit but not a grape

_____ **8.** Grapefruit grow on
   A. vines
   B. trees
   C. pines

Our Amazing Skin

Our skin is like a bag that we live in. Inside the bag our bodies are mostly water. Our water is like the water in the sea. It is very salty. Also, like the ocean, we can lose our water. The wind and the sun could take it away. Our bag of skin keeps our body's ocean from drying up.

Our skin keeps out sunshine. Too much sun can hurt us. Skin also keeps out dirt. That's important because some kinds of dirt can make us sick. Our skin feels things. It feels warm things, cold things, things it touches, and things that hurt it. A campfire feels warm. A snowball thrown in our face feels cold and hurts. A hug is the touch of another person's skin on our own.

_____ **1.** Our bodies are mostly
   A. salt
   B. water
   C. skin

_____ **2.** Our skin keeps our body's water from
   A. drying up
   B. getting cold
   C. smelling bad

_____ **3.** Skin keeps out
   A. dirt
   B. food
   C. water

_____ **4.** Our skin helps us
   A. read
   B. feel
   C. dream

Our hair is a special kind of covering. It helps keep things out of our eyes, ears, and nose. Hair is also good for keeping us warm. When we get goose bumps, our body hairs stand up. Then the hairs hold air close to our skin like a thin blanket. Hair keeps animals warm, too. Some animals have more hair than others, so they have a better blanket for cold weather.

Our nails are like very hard skin. They help keep our fingers and toes from getting hurt. Our nails aren't as strong or sharp as the nails that animals have. But they are good for scratching backs and picking up coins.

_____ **5.** Hair helps keep things out of our
     A. fingers and toes
     B. mouth and ears
     C. eyes, ears, and nose

_____ **6.** Hair is good for
     A. keeping us clean
     B. helping us stay warm
     C. keeping us from getting hurt

_____ **7.** Nails are like
     A. flat hair
     B. hard skin
     C. thin blankets

_____ **8.** Nails help keep our
     A. toes sharp
     B. fingers from getting loose
     C. toes from getting hurt

Crazy Town, U.S.A.

Towns get their names in many ways. One town in Wyoming is called Ten Sleep. People there had their own way of telling how far away a place was. They would tell how many nights one had to sleep on a trip there. This town was ten nights from three other places.

Ong's Hat, New Jersey, got its name in a funny way. A man named Jacob Ong lived in this village. He liked three things: dancing, women, and his fancy hat. One night he was at a big dance. One woman thought that he should dance with her more. Finally she grabbed his fancy hat and threw it on the floor. Then she danced all over his hat.

_____ **1.** One town in Wyoming is called
   A. Three Sheep
   B. Ong's Hat
   C. Ten Sleep

_____ **2.** Ten Sleep got its name from the
   A. name of a man who lived there
   B. way people told how far to travel
   C. river that ran through the town

_____ **3.** Jacob Ong had a village named after his
   A. dance
   B. hat
   C. mother

_____ **4.** Ong got into trouble when he was
   A. at a big dance
   B. telling a funny story
   C. talking to a man

In New Mexico there is a place called Pie Town. A man started making little fruit pies to sell at his gas station. Then the people who owned the food store got the same idea. They started selling big pies. One day a cowboy passed through town. He said, "This sure is a pie town." Pie Town became the new name.

Midnight, Mississippi, got its name from a card game. The farmers would get together to play cards. Late one night a player lost all his money. Then he bet his land, but he lost that, too. The winner looked at his watch. "It's midnight," he said. "That's what I'll call my new land!"

_____ **5.** A man sold fruit pies at his
   A. friend's house
   B. pie shop
   C. gas station

_____ **6.** Pie Town was named by
   A. a cowboy who passed through
   B. the owner of the gas station
   C. the state of New Mexico

_____ **7.** In Mississippi the farmers would
   A. make pies and sell them
   B. work for many days and nights
   C. get together to play cards

_____ **8.** The winner of the card game
   A. named his land Pie Town
   B. won at midnight
   C. lived in Alaska

An Amazing Life

Helen Keller became ill while she was still a baby. The illness caused her to lose her sight and hearing. Because she could not see or hear, she did not know how to speak. Helen was shut off from the rest of the world.

At age seven Helen was given a private teacher. Her name was Anne Sullivan. Anne was nearly blind as a child. She knew how it felt not to see. Anne taught Helen through touch. She spelled out letters on Helen's hand. The letters spelled the names of things. Anne placed those things in Helen's hand. Soon Helen knew how to spell words.

_____ **1.** Helen's illness caused her to
  A. lose her taste
  B. lose her touch
  C. lose her sight and hearing

_____ **2.** As a child, Helen
  A. could only whisper
  B. spoke normally
  C. was not able to speak

_____ **3.** Anne Sullivan taught Helen
  A. by phone
  B. through music
  C. through touch

_____ **4.** Anne spelled letters on Helen's
  A. throat
  B. hand
  C. eyes

Helen wanted to learn more. At age 10 she began to learn to speak. Her teacher spoke to her. Helen placed a finger on the speaker's lips and throat. By age 16 Helen could speak pretty well. She went to college and made top grades.

After college Helen worked to help other people who were blind. She taught them to have hope and to be brave. She wrote many books about her life. She gave speeches all over the world. She raised lots of money for those who were blind. Helen Keller became a hero to people everywhere.

_____ **5.** At age 10 Helen started to learn
     A. to speak
     B. to sing
     C. to write

_____ **6.** Helen felt a speaker's
     A. nose and ears
     B. eyes and hands
     C. throat and lips

_____ **7.** Helen wrote books about
     A. famous people
     B. her own life
     C. how the brain works

_____ **8.** Helen helped people who were blind by
     A. raising money for them
     B. letting Anne teach them
     C. becoming a doctor

Bicycles

People who rode the first bicycles worked hard. They had to push their feet against the ground to make their bikes move. These bikes, called hobby horses, had four wheels.

Later, people began to make bikes with two wheels. The bikes were not like those seen on the streets today. People sat above the front wheel of the bikes. As they rode, their feet turned the wheel. Bicycle makers tried making big front wheels and small front wheels. They learned that bikes with larger front wheels could move faster. So they started making bikes with large front wheels and small back wheels.

_____ **1.** Hobby horses had
   A. big wheels
   B. two wheels
   C. four wheels

_____ **2.** On later bikes people
   A. sat above the front wheel
   B. pushed their feet against the ground
   C. rode a long way without stopping

_____ **3.** Bicycle makers tried making
   A. no wheels at all
   B. small front wheels
   C. rubber wheels

_____ **4.** Bikes with larger front wheels were
   A. slower
   B. faster
   C. safer

Soon the streets were filled with bikes with huge front wheels. Some bikes had wheels that were 5 feet tall. Many people were hurt when they fell off these bikes.

Later, people in England made a bike with smaller wheels. The two wheels on the new bike were almost the same size. People sat between the wheels, and their feet pushed two pedals. The two pedals moved a chain that turned the back wheel. The new bike was called a safety bike. People could ride on it without falling 5 feet to the ground. This safe bike became the model for today's bikes.

_____ **5.** The streets were filled with bikes with
    A. huge front wheels
    B. five pedals
    C. small seats

_____ **6.** In England people made a bike with
    A. two wheels of the same size
    B. three wheels on the back
    C. no handles

_____ **7.** The new bike's back wheel turned with a
    A. chain
    B. brake
    C. pedal

_____ **8.** The safety bike became a model for
    A. model trains
    B. new cars
    C. today's bikes

Working Worms

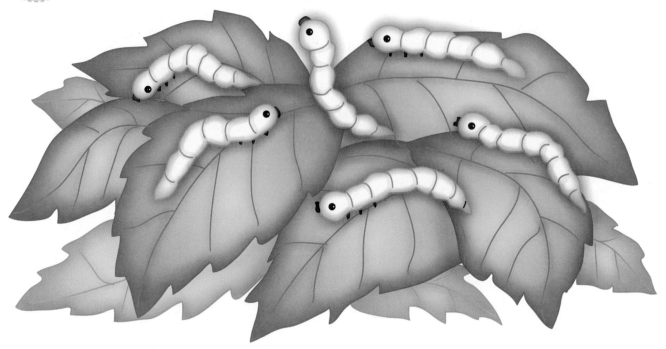

Many people think that silk is the finest cloth of all. Just touching silk can be a surprise because it is so soft. Even more surprising is the fact that silk is made by special worms.

If you visited a silk farm, you would see two things: worms and trees. Silkworms eat only the leaves of mulberry trees. So rows and rows of these trees grow on silk farms. On some farms the leaves are picked by hand. Workers gather leaves from whole branches at once. In other places machines do this work. The farmers chop the leaves. Then they feed them to their worms.

_____ **1.** Silk is a type of very fine
    A. worm
    B. tree
    C. cloth

_____ **2.** At a silk farm, there are worms and
    A. spiders
    B. cows
    C. trees

_____ **3.** Silkworms eat only
    A. silk cloth
    B. mulberry leaves
    C. apple trees

_____ **4.** On some farms the leaves are
    A. picked by hand
    B. cooked in pots
    C. left on trees

Silkworms do nothing but sleep and eat. They grow very quickly. As the worms grow, they shed their skin four times. The old skin splits and falls off.

After so much work, the worms are ready to change into moths. Each worm spins a single long thread around and around itself. This new home is called a cocoon. The thread of each cocoon is as thin as a spiderweb. The farmers steam and dry the cocoons. Then the dry cocoons go to a silk-making plant. There the threads are spun into silk yarn. The yarn will be made into soft cloth that feels like a cloud.

_____ **5.** A silkworm grows
    A. slowly
    B. smaller
    C. quickly

_____ **6.** A silkworm's skin splits and
    A. gets smaller
    B. comes off
    C. becomes wet

_____ **7.** The thread of each cocoon is
    A. thin
    B. fat
    C. red

_____ **8.** Silk cloth is very
    A. rough
    B. tight
    C. soft

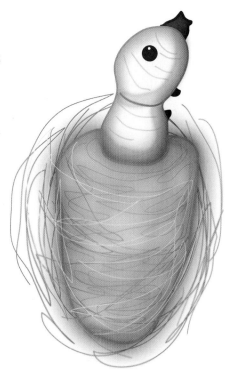

Tears and More Tears

Sometimes people cry when they are sad. Other times people cry tears of joy. But your eyes make tears all the time, whether you are crying or not. Did you know that tears help keep your eyes healthy? They keep your eyes from drying out. A special area of the eye drips all the time. It keeps the eye damp.

If you look in a mirror, you can see tiny holes in the corners of your eyes. Each hole leads to a small tube that runs to your nose. Tears run slowly into this tube drip by drip. Day and night the holes drain the tears away. If they didn't, you would always look as if you were crying!

_____ **1.** Your eyes make tears
    A. all the time
    B. only at night
    C. only when you are sad

_____ **3.** In the corners of your eyes, there are
    A. short brushes
    B. small hairs
    C. tiny holes

_____ **2.** Tears keep your eyes from
    A. blinking
    B. drying out
    C. opening

_____ **4.** Each hole leads to
    A. another hole
    B. your ear
    C. a tube

If you begin to cry, there are many more tears. The holes can't drain all of them. The extra tears spill out onto your face.

Tears help keep your eyes safe. If there is something harmful in the air, the eyes fill with tears. These tears coat your eyes. They keep the harmful air out.

Contact lenses can make the eyes too dry. Some people have to add tears to their eyes. They buy bottles of eye drops to keep their eyes damp.

_____ **5.** When you cry, there are many more
      A. tears
      B. holes
      C. drains

_____ **6.** If there are harmful things in the air,
      A. the eyes will fill with tears
      B. you will never know it
      C. most people close their eyes

_____ **7.** Tears will
      A. coat your eyes
      B. put you to sleep
      C. open your eyes

_____ **8.** Contact lenses can make the eyes too
      A. weak
      B. old
      C. dry

Writing Roundup

Read the story below. Think about the facts. Then answer the questions in complete sentences.

Today we know many facts about the Moon. Humans have traveled to the Moon and back. They have brought back soil to study.

The Moon's soil is made of rock and glass. Some of the rock is small and ground up. Other rock is in large chunks. The glass on the Moon is very tiny. Each bit is about as small as the period at the end of this sentence. In the future more trips to the Moon will be made. Then we will learn even more facts about its soil.

1. How do we know facts about the Moon today?

_____

_____

2. What is the Moon's soil made of?

_____

_____

3. How small is the glass on the Moon?

_____

_____

Prewriting

Think of an idea you might write about, such as a place you visited or an item you found. Write the idea in the center of the idea web below. Then fill out the rest of the web with facts.

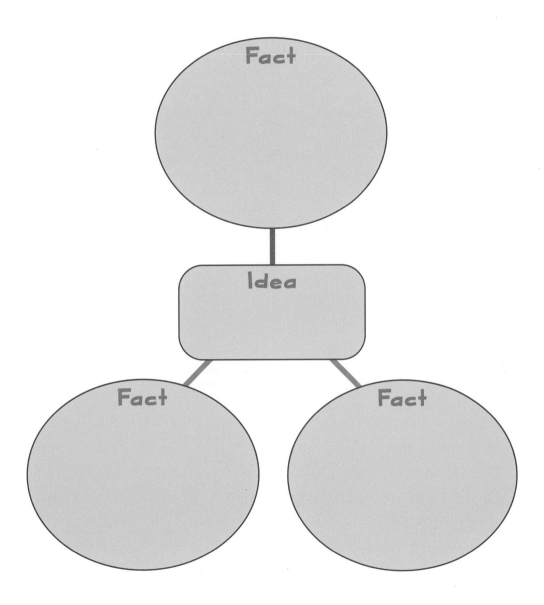

On Your Own

Now use another sheet of paper to write a story about your idea. Use the facts from your idea web.

unit 2

What Is Sequence?

Sequence means *time order*. When things happen in a story, they happen in a sequence. Something happens first. Then other things happen. Then something happens last. How can you find the sequence in a story? Just look for clue words, like these:

today	Monday	then
first	after	June

Try It!

Here is a story about apples. See whether you can follow the sequence. Circle all the clue words.

Apples

People have liked apples for many years. But the New World has not always had apple trees. People carried the trees to America about 400 years ago. At first people planted trees only in the East. Later, travelers carried them west. Now apples grow in most states. We use them in pies and jellies. But most of all, we just like to eat them raw.

How to Find Sequence

Try to follow the sequence in the story about apples. On this page there are two sentences about the story. Write the number **1** on the line by the sentence that tells what happened first. Write the number **2** by the sentence that tells what happened next.

_____ Travelers carried apple trees west.

_____ People planted apple trees in the East.

- Read all the words in the two sentences above. Now read the story about apples again. Try to find the words in the two sentences that are in the story. Did you find the words *travelers* and *East* in the story? Draw a line under these two words.

- After you find the words *travelers* and *East*, find the clue words that are close by. The clue words that go with *East* are *at first*. The clue word that goes with *travelers* is *later*. The clue words tell you how to put things in a sequence. *At first* tells you that something happened at the very beginning. *Later* tells you that something happened after something else.

- If you still cannot find the sequence, try this. Look at the sentences in the story. One sentence is first. Another sentence is second, and another one is third. The sentences are in order. The action in the first sentence happened first, and the action in the second sentence happened second.

Read each story. After each story you will answer questions about the sequence of events in the story. Remember, sequence is the order of things.

King of the Worms

Jody Gerard was 10 years old when he decided he needed a job. He thought it might be fun to raise worms. He could sell them to farmers and people who fished. So in the spring, he bought many worms. Jody put the worms in clean dirt. He gave them water, leaves, and corn all summer. The worms got fat, and Jody sold many of them. But that winter he did not put them in a warm place. The cold weather killed all the worms.

The next spring Jody tried again. He bought more worms. He took good care of them. Many people bought Jody's worms. When winter came Jody took the worms inside so they would stay warm.

One day when Jody was 12, he got a letter. It was from the state of New York, where he lived. The letter said, "Everyone who sells things has to pay taxes!" Jody made only 50¢ per day selling worms. But he still had to pay part of that money to the state. Jody told many people in his town what had happened. Soon some people from a television station came to Jody's house. He told them about his problem. They showed a film on television of their talk with Jody. Many people saw it. The people began to write letters to the state. The letters said that the law was unfair. Finally the law was changed. Children like Jody can now sell things without paying money to the state.

1. Put these events in the order that they happened. What happened first? Write the number **1** on the line by that sentence. Then write the number **2** by the sentence that tells what happened next.

_____ Jody had to pay money to the state.

_____ Television people came to Jody's house.

_____ **2.** When did Jody first sell worms?
    A. when he was 10
    B. when he was 14
    C. when he was 12

_____ **3.** When did all of Jody's worms die?
    A. in the summer
    B. in the spring
    C. in the winter

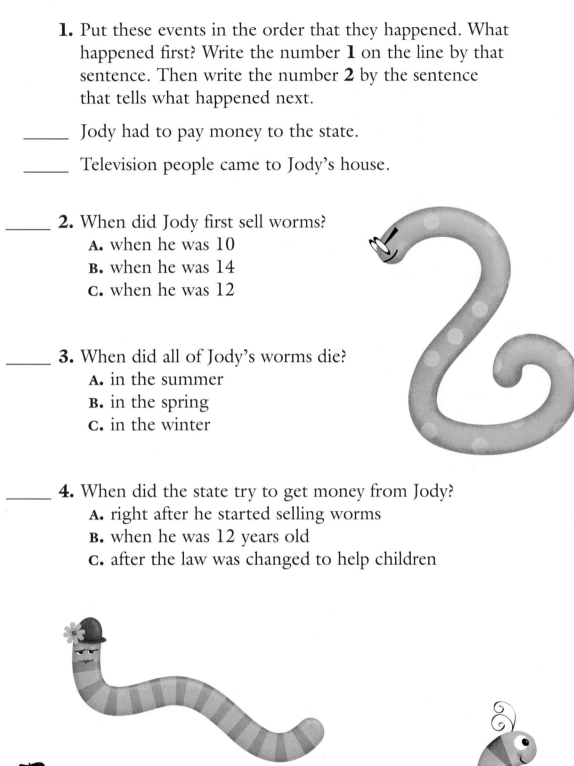

_____ **4.** When did the state try to get money from Jody?
    A. right after he started selling worms
    B. when he was 12 years old
    C. after the law was changed to help children

Making a Rose Necklace

Here is how you can make a necklace that smells like roses. First find roses that smell very sweet. Pick about four cups of rose flowers. Pick only the colored flowers. Be sure to keep the green parts out.

Then tear the flowers into very tiny pieces. Put the pieces into a bowl, and add 1/2 cup of cold water. Use a wooden spoon to mash the flower bits. Mash them into a smooth paste.

Next cook the rose paste in a big pot. You can use a pot made of glass or iron. Cook the paste on low heat. Watch it all the time. If the paste gets too hot and begins to boil, it will not smell good anymore. Stir the rose paste so it will not burn. The paste is ready when it sticks to the sides of the pot. Turn off the heat and let the paste cool.

When the paste has cooled, it's time to make rose beads. Squeeze the paste in your hands. It should be stiff and a little sticky. If it's still really wet, pat it with a soft paper towel. Now make little balls about 1 inch across. Then stick a big needle through each ball to make a hole. After you make the holes, put the beads on clean paper to dry. Drying them will take two or three days. Turn the beads over carefully each day. This helps them dry evenly. When the beads are dry, they are hard and black. Rub them well with a soft cloth to make them shine. Now string the beads on fishing line. The dark beads will smell of roses.

1. Put these events in the order that they happened. What happened first? Write the number **1** on the line by that sentence. Then write the number **2** by the sentence that tells what happened next.

_____ Rub the rose beads with a soft cloth.

_____ String the beads on fishing line.

_____ **2.** When do you add water to the rose flowers?
    A. before you pick them
    B. after you tear them into little pieces
    C. after the rose paste is cooked

_____ **3.** When do you cook the rose paste?
    A. before making rose beads
    B. after it is stiff
    C. while tearing the flowers into pieces

_____ **4.** When do you let the beads dry?
    A. after you put them on a string to wear
    B. after you put the needle through them
    C. before you make the little, round balls

Stunt Car Driving

A thief runs from the bank. He jumps into a waiting car and roars off. People run after him, but it's too late. He's gotten away. Or has he? Look! Another car is coming toward the thief. The car is not stopping. Crash!!! Suddenly the two cars are in flames. There's been a terrible accident.

Scenes like this in movies thrill people all the time. The accident looks real, but no one is really hurt. These scenes are done by actors called stunt people. They take the place of the regular actors in the dangerous parts.

A director hires stunt people to appear in a film. First the stunt people plan what will happen. This is called rigging the gag. They go over each part of the scene many times. The timing is very important. It may take many days to plan a stunt. The stunt people then check all the equipment. Everything must be in perfect working order.

Then it's time to begin. For a crash scene, the stunt people get into the cars. The cameras roll. At the moment of the crash, the two drivers jump from the cars. The stunt drivers are quick, and their escape does not show on the film.

The shells of two other cars are then towed to the scene. These shells look just like the cars that crashed. Dummy drivers are put into the cars. When the cars hit a trigger in the road, they burst into flames. These shells have no engines and they burn without exploding. The camera takes pictures of it all.

1. Put these events in the order that they happened. What happened first? Write the number **1** on the line by that sentence. Then write the number **2** by the sentence that tells what happened next.

_____ The thief jumped into a car.

_____ The thief ran from the bank.

_____ **2.** When do the stunt people rig the gag?
  A. before they do the stunt
  B. as they get in the cars
  C. at the moment of the crash

_____ **3.** When do stunt people check the equipment?
  A. after the shells arrive
  B. when they do the stunt
  C. after they plan the stunt

_____ **4.** When do the stunt people jump out of the cars?
  A. before they check the equipment
  B. during the crash
  C. after the shells are towed into place

Growing Tiny Popcorn

When Shelly Hoff was eight, a woman gave her three ears of popcorn. They were the smallest ears that Shelly had ever seen. They were about 3 inches long. That's about half as big as an ear of common corn.

Shelly wanted to grow popcorn. She took some of the seeds from the corn ears. When spring came she dug her garden. Then she put the corn seeds in water for one night. The next day she planted her corn. She put the seeds about 1 inch under the dirt.

Shelly watered her garden all summer, but she had made one mistake. She had planted the small popcorn too close to some common corn. Her new plants just grew big ears of corn.

The next year Shelly tried again. This time she made sure there wasn't any common corn nearby. The seeds came up, and the corn looked good. It didn't grow very fast. Her friends told her that corn is a hungry plant. It takes a lot of food out of the ground. So she put special food on the plants. That fall she picked a few ears of popcorn.

When spring came again, Shelly planted lots of popcorn. The corn had sun, food, and water all summer. By fall she had many small ears of corn.

Now Shelly sells her corn to flower shops. Farmers' markets and gift shops also buy it. She uses her corn money for clothes. She also saves money so she can go to college.

1. Put these events in the order that they happened. What happened first? Write the number **1** on the line by that sentence. Then write the number **2** by the sentence that tells what happened next.

_____ Shelly's plants grew big ears of corn.

_____ Shelly planted corn seeds.

_____ 2. When did a woman give popcorn to Shelly?
   A. when Shelly was eight
   B. when Shelly was three
   C. when Shelly was seven

_____ 3. When did Shelly put the seeds in water?
   A. before she put the seeds in the ground
   B. after she planted the seeds in the garden
   C. right before she sold the popcorn

_____ 4. What mistake did Shelly make the first year?
   A. planting too much popcorn
   B. not giving the popcorn enough food
   C. planting the popcorn too close to common corn

A Secret King

A king wanted to see what his people were really like. So he put on rags and went for a walk. After a while he got tired and hungry. When he asked people for food, they laughed and threw rocks at him. They did not know who the poor man was.

Then the king came to an old house. A poor old man and woman lived there. They asked the king to eat with them. They didn't know he was the king. They just wanted to help a tired, hungry man. The woman made a fire. Then she brought cool water for the king to drink. While she was doing this, the old man went outside. He picked some food from the tiny garden. Then he tried to catch a chicken for supper. But the chicken ran fast, and the old man was tired. So he chose some eggs instead.

The woman cooked supper for them. When the food was ready, she put it on the table. The king was given the best food. Suddenly there was a knock at the door. The old woman opened it and saw some neighbors.

"Great king, forgive us," they said. "We threw rocks because we did not recognize you." The king was angry. "I was tired and hungry. You gave me only rocks and bad words. Get out of here!" he shouted.

The poor man and woman were afraid. The king was used to nice food, but they had given him only bread and eggs. The king said, "You gave me the best you had. Because you were kind, I will give money and food to you for the rest of your lives."

1. Put these events in the order that they happened. What happened first? Write the number **1** on the line by that sentence. Then write the number **2** by the sentence that tells what happened next.

_____ The man and woman asked the king to dinner.

_____ The king put on rags and went for a walk.

_____ **2.** When did the people of the town throw rocks?
    A. after the king stopped at the old house
    B. when the king asked them for food
    C. when the king shouted, "Get out of here!"

_____ **3.** When did the old man get the food for supper?
    A. while the old woman made the fire
    B. before the people threw rocks
    C. after the neighbors knocked at the door

_____ **4.** When did the woman give water to the king?
    A. before he dressed in rags and went walking
    B. after the neighbors came by the house
    C. after she made a fire to cook supper

The Brothers Grimm

You know who Snow White is. You've heard of Hansel and Gretel. But have you heard of the Brothers Grimm? If not for them, you might never have heard these tales.

Jakob and Wilhelm Grimm were the oldest of six children. Jakob was born in 1785. Wilhelm was born the next year. They were the best of friends. The brothers lived and worked together for most of their lives.

In 1798, the Grimms moved to the town of Kassel. There they finished school. Then they found jobs in the king's library. Both men loved old stories. In their free time, they searched for old folktales and songs.

From 1807 to 1814, Jakob and Wilhelm collected tales from everyone they knew. Marie Muller was a nanny. She told them the tales of Snow White, Little Red Riding Hood, and Sleeping Beauty. One day the Grimms met Frau Viehmann. She came to their house many times. She drank coffee and ate rolls. She told the Grimms more than 20 tales. Cinderella was one of them.

In 1812, the Grimms' first book of fairy tales was published. The Grimms had meant the stories for grown-ups. They were surprised when children loved them, too. The brothers wanted to find more tales. This time it was much easier. Now people would bring stories to them. The next book of tales was published in 1814. The last book of Grimm's fairy tales was published in 1857.

1. Put these events in the order that they happened. What happened first? Write the number **1** on the line by that sentence. Then write the number **2** by the sentence that tells what happened next.

_____ The brothers finished school.

_____ The brothers collected tales.

_____ **2.** When was Wilhelm Grimm born?
    A. the year before Jakob was born
    B. in 1785
    C. the year after Jakob was born

_____ **3.** When did the brothers collect tales from friends?
    A. from 1807 to 1814
    B. in 1798
    C. when they were children

_____ **4.** When was the Grimms' first book of fairy tales published?
    A. when the brothers were in school
    B. after they began working in the library
    C. from 1807 to 1814

Elephants

Elephants are the largest mammals on land. Long ago there were elephants in most countries. Now elephants live only in Africa and Asia. They are smart animals that live together and help each other.

Female elephants live in close family groups. The group is made of mothers and their babies. The young males stay with this group until they are about 14 years old. Then they leave to join a group of male elephants. The males travel in groups, but they are not as close as the family groups. Males often move from one herd to another.

A herd wakes up at 4:00 in the morning. The elephants want to start grazing before it gets too hot. They walk to a water hole and drink. The herd walks and eats about 16 hours per day. They eat grass, leaves, bark, and fruit. Sometimes they stop and take naps. At midnight the herd stops for the night. All the elephants lie down and sleep. Some of them snore.

Babies can be born at any time of the year. A baby weighs 250 pounds when it is born. It stands up 15 minutes after it's born. The herd moves slowly for the first few days. The young one walks between its mother and another female. If it gets tired, they hold it up with their trunks. By the third day, the baby can keep up with the herd. At first the little one doesn't know how to use its trunk. Sometimes it steps on it. Sometimes it even sucks its trunk like a human baby sucks its thumb.

1. Put these events in the order that they happened. What happened first? Write the number **1** on the line by that sentence. Then write the number **2** by the sentence that tells what happened next.

_____ Elephants live only in Africa and Asia.

_____ Elephants lived in most countries.

_____ **2.** When do young males join a male herd?
    A. when they are about 14
    B. in the early morning
    C. when their mothers tell them to

_____ **3.** When does a herd wake up?
    A. after it gets hot
    B. at midnight
    C. about 4:00 in the morning

_____ **4.** When are baby elephants born?
    A. in the spring
    B. during any season
    C. usually in the summer

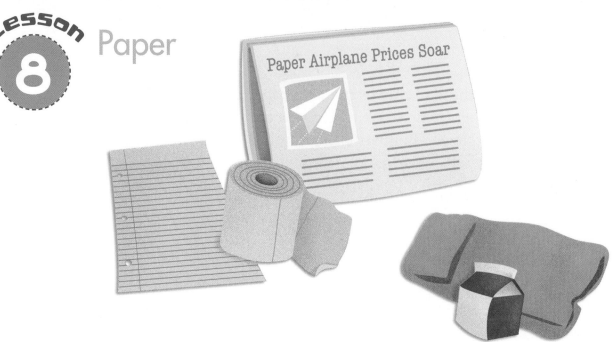

Paper has been around for a long time. It was invented by the Chinese about A.D. 105. In the 1400s the printing press was invented in Europe. For the first time, large numbers of books could be made. Many paper mills were built.

Now we use paper for lots of things. Most of the paper goods we take for granted haven't been in use for very long. There were no paper towels or tissues 100 years ago. Paper bags were rarely used. Children in school wrote on slates, not on paper.

Each person in a rich country uses about 350 pounds of paper a year! A person in a poor country uses about 40 pounds a year. This adds up to a lot of paper and a lot of trees! It takes more than 2 tons of wood to make 1 ton of paper. The more paper we use, the more trees have to be cut down. Luckily, many kinds of paper can be reused. Egg cartons and newspapers are now made from recycled paper.

Let's take a look at how paper is made. First, of course, the trees are cut down. The logs are carried by truck to a pulp mill. Pulp mills are often built near rivers. It takes a lot of water to make paper. The bark is cut off the logs. Then the logs are rolled into water and ground into chips. Chemicals are added, and the chips become pulp. The pulp is poured onto a moving screen. Water drains out of the pulp. A thin sheet of fibers is left. This sheet is heated and dried. Then it passes through rollers. At last it is paper!

1. Put these events in the order that they happened. What happened first? Write the number **1** on the line by that sentence. Then write the number **2** by the sentence that tells what happened next.

_____ Large numbers of books could be made.

_____ The printing press was invented.

_____ **2.** When was paper invented?
  A. in the 1400s
  B. 100 years ago
  C. before the printing press

_____ **3.** When is the bark cut off the logs?
  A. before the logs are rolled into water
  B. after the chemicals are added
  C. when a thin sheet of fibers is left

_____ **4.** When is the pulp poured onto a moving screen?
  A. when the sheet passes through rollers
  B. after the chips become pulp
  C. before egg cartons are recycled

Writing Roundup

Read the story below. Think about the sequence, or time order. Answer the questions in complete sentences.

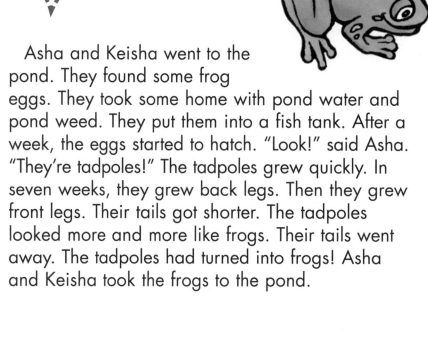

Asha and Keisha went to the pond. They found some frog eggs. They took some home with pond water and pond weed. They put them into a fish tank. After a week, the eggs started to hatch. "Look!" said Asha. "They're tadpoles!" The tadpoles grew quickly. In seven weeks, they grew back legs. Then they grew front legs. Their tails got shorter. The tadpoles looked more and more like frogs. Their tails went away. The tadpoles had turned into frogs! Asha and Keisha took the frogs to the pond.

1. When did the frog eggs start to hatch?

_____

_____

2. When did the tadpoles grow back legs?

_____

_____

3. When did the tadpoles grow front legs?

_____

_____

Prewriting

Think about something that you have done, such as making a sandwich, setting up a tent, or making your bed. Write the events in sequence below.

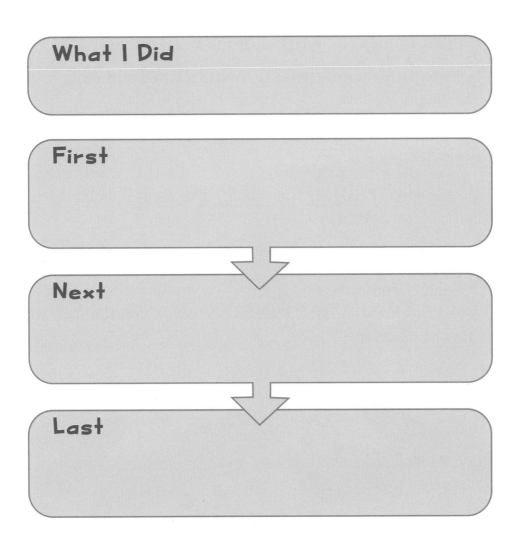

What I Did

First

Next

Last

On Your Own

Now use another sheet of paper to write a story about what you have done. Write the events in the order that they happened. Use time order words.

unit 3

What Is Context?

You can use context to learn new words. If you find a word you do not know, look at the words around it. These other words can help you guess what the word means.

Look at the words below. Choose a word and write it on the line.

Bats hunt at night and sleep during the _____.

Did you write *day*? Why did you write that word? Some words go together. *Day* goes with *night*. The context helped you choose the right word.

Try It!

Read the story below. It has a word you may not know. The word is printed in **dark letters**. See if you can find out what the new word means.

Chuck Berry Makes a Hit

The singer named Muddy Waters listened to the young man. He really liked to hear him sing. He **encouraged** Chuck to make a record. "You're really good!" he said. "Go ahead and try to make the big time." Chuck's first record had a new kind of music. It was called rock and roll. Today many people say that Chuck Berry is the father of rock and roll.

How to Use Context

If you don't know what **encouraged** means, look at the context. Remember, the context is all the other words in the story. Here are some of the other words in the story. They can help you find out what **encouraged** means.

1. "You're really good!"

2. "Go ahead and try to make the big time."

Find these words in the story about Chuck Berry. Draw a circle around them. What words do you think of when you read the clues? Write a few words on the line below:

_____

Did you write a word like *help*? To *encourage* someone is to *help* someone by what you say or do.

• To use context, read all the words in a story. If some words are too hard, don't stop reading! Read all the words you can. They may tell you something about the words you could not read.

• When you try to find out what new words mean, remember that some words go together. Think of a meaning that goes with the other words in the story.

Read the stories in this unit. If a word in a story is missing, choose the word that fits. If there is a word in **dark letters** in a story, figure out what that word means.

Read each passage. After each passage you will answer a question about context. Remember, context is a way to learn new words by thinking about the other words used in a story.

Juan Largo has spent seven years learning about black bears. He catches the bears. Then he puts little radios on them. He can track the bears and ___**1**___ down what they do. He even knows where they sleep during the winter. Sometimes he puts a tag on a bear's ear. Then he will know that bear when he sees it again.

_____ **1.** The word that best completes the sentence is

      A. back   **B.** write   **C.** sing

Many good baseball games have been played during the World Series. But one game had the fans on the edge of their seats. It was when the Yankees played the Dodgers. Don Larsen pitched a perfect game for the Yankees. No one on the Dodgers team ever hit the ball. No one got a walk, either. Not ___**2**___ Dodger got on base! Of course the Yankees won the game.

_____ **2.** The word that best completes the sentence is

      A. on   **B.** working   **C.** one

Mangrove trees grow in salt water. Most trees take in water with their roots. Then they let it out through their leaves. When mangroves take in water, they take in salt, too. They let the water and the salt out. After that, mangroves look as if someone ___**3**___ salt all over their leaves.

_____ **3.** The word that best completes the sentence is

      A. threw   **B.** liked   **C.** grew

A newt hatches from an egg under water. This small animal first lives in water. Later in life the newt grows lungs and moves to land. At this stage the newt is bright orange. Other animals can see it easily. But they do not __4__ it. They know that the newt's skin will make them sick.

_____ **4.** The word that best completes the sentence is
    A. bother   **B.** drive   **C.** iron

A beam of light from the Sun looks as if it's white. But it's really made up of many colors. These are the same colors you see in a __5__ after a storm. Light that goes from the Sun to Earth passes through the air first. Some light bounces off bits of dust in the air. The blue and purple beams in the light are the shortest and bounce the most. They bounce all over the sky. This is why the sky looks blue most of the time.

_____ **5.** The word that best completes the sentence is
    A. cup   **B.** rainbow   **C.** face

Scuba divers swim deep in the ocean. They use face masks to see better. They wear fins on their feet to help them swim. To breathe underwater, divers use air tanks. One or two tanks are __6__ onto their backs. Then divers can stay underwater for a long time. If the water is cold, they can wear wet suits to stay warm.

_____ **6.** The word that best completes the sentence is
    A. imagined   **B.** lost   **C.** strapped

At first Sandra was a lawyer. Later she worked as a judge. The president looked at Sandra's work. He saw that she treated people __1__ in her court. He asked her to be a judge on the Supreme Court. Sandra Day O'Connor is the first woman ever to hold this job.

_____ **1.** The word that best completes the sentence is

    A. poorly   **B.** fairly   **C.** wrongly

A ladybug is a type of small beetle. It has a small, round body. It looks like half of a pea. The ladybug is bright red or yellow. It has black, yellow, red, or white spots on its back. People who grow fruit like this bug. It is helpful. It eats other insects that harm fruit __2__ .

_____ **2.** The word that best completes the sentence is

    A. crops   **B.** clouds   **C.** games

A river made a __3__ in Colorado. It's called Royal Gorge. People used to go through it to get to silver mines. Some people wanted to build a railroad through the deep valley. Two groups of people began to fight. Both of them wanted to build the railroad. Then one group sold out to the other. The railroad was finished.

_____ **3.** The word that best completes the sentence is

    A. fan   **B.** canyon   **C.** window

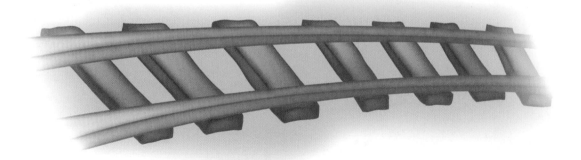

There was once a big fair in France. The Eiffel Tower was built for it. This tall tower was made of iron. Today people come from all over to see it. There is a great view from the top. You can even eat in a __4__ while you enjoy the view.

_____ **4.** The word that best completes the sentence is

    A. restaurant   **B.** book   **C.** garage

The Inuit people live in the far North. Life has changed for them through the years. Most Inuit once lived by the sea. In the summer they lived in tents. The tents were made of animal skins. In the __5__ they moved to new homes. They were made from blocks of dirt or ice. Now most Inuit live in towns.

_____ **5.** The word that best completes the sentence is

    A. water   **B.** afternoon   **C.** winter

You might have heard a cat purr when it came up to __6__ you. But have you ever wondered how it can make that sound? A cat purrs as it breathes in and out. When the air goes to and from the lungs, it passes through the cat's voice box. The cat can make the space in its voice box smaller. That changes the flow of air. The sound this makes is the cat's purr.

PURRRR

PURRRR

_____ **6.** The word that best completes the sentence is

    A. hold   **B.** greet   **C.** feed

The scorpion can be found in warm ___1___. It's a small animal. It has four pairs of legs. The scorpion has two large claws in front. It grabs and crushes its food with these claws. The scorpion has from six to twelve eyes. But it is best known for its tail. The scorpion stings with its tail. The sting is very painful, but it is usually not deadly.

_____ **1.** The word that best completes the sentence is
      A. shirts   **B.** countries   **C.** moons

There's a museum in Ohio. It's called the Cleveland Health Education Museum. People go there to learn how the human body works. There are huge models of an eye, an ear, and a tooth. The models are big enough for people to walk inside. People come from all over the ___2___ to see this museum.

_____ **2.** The word that best completes the sentence is
      A. turtle   **B.** engine   **C.** world

Light can pass through some objects, such as glass. You can see through these objects. But light can't pass through other objects. You cannot see through these. On the side of the object away from the source of light, there is a dark place on the ground. This shows where the light has been blocked. The dark spot is called a ___3___.

_____ **3.** The word that best completes the sentence is
      A. painting   **B.** baby   **C.** shadow

The day lily is a plant. It has ___4___ without leaves. At the end of each one is a group of flowers. These flowers are yellow or orange. During the summer two or three of them bloom each day. They bloom when the Sun comes up. Then they die when the Sun sets.

_____ **4.** The word that best completes the sentence is

    A. fences   **B.** stalks   **C.** apartments

There's a museum where you can learn about the desert. You can see plants and animals that live in the desert. Snakes, bobcats, and elf owls are just a few of these animals. There are many kinds of ___5___ plants. This museum is in an Arizona desert. It is called the Arizona-Sonora Desert Museum.

_____ **5.** The word that best completes the sentence is

    A. jolly   **B.** breakfast   **C.** cactus

A barnyard pig takes a bath in mud. This is not because it likes to be dirty. In fact it would like cool, clean water much better. But a pig must find a way to cool off. It can't ___6___ to stay cool the way people do. So it will lie in the mud to stay cool. The thick mud also helps the pig's skin. Insects can't bite it, and the sun won't burn it.

_____ **6.** The word that best completes the sentence is

    A. fly   **B.** sweat   **C.** kick

Trees are important. People make many things from trees. Trees are also helpful. They hold the dirt in place and help make the air we breathe. Trees are also homes for many creatures. So we need to be sure we __1__ the trees. When old trees are cut down, new ones must be planted.

_____ **1.** The word that best completes the sentence is

    A. forget   **B.** find   **C.** save

A cat's tongue feels rough. This is true for all cats. House cats, lions, and tigers all have rough tongues. A cat uses its tongue in many ways. It __2__ itself to brush its fur. The cat removes dirt and loose hair this way. The cat also uses its rough tongue to scrape meat from a bone. When the cat is through, the bone is clean.

_____ **2.** The word that best completes the sentence is

    A. paints   **B.** licks   **C.** frightens

Young people can join the 4-H Club. The goal of this club is to improve head, heart, hands, and health. Members have a chance to learn skills. They also find out about careers. Members try out jobs by working on __3__. These jobs may deal with plants, animals, food, or safety.

_____ **3.** The word that best completes the sentence is

    A. ice   **B.** moments   **C.** projects

Germs are living things. They are very small. They are so small that you need a microscope to see them. Germs can be found in all places. Many germs are harmless. Others can make you sick if they get inside your ___4___. There are ways you can keep safe from these germs. Be sure to wash your hands, keep cuts clean, and stay away from someone who has a cold.

_____ **4.** The word that best completes the sentence is

     A. body   **B.** glasses   **C.** homework

Alvin is the name of a small ship. People use *Alvin* to study the sea. The ship goes under the water. The people ride inside of it. The deep sea is very dark, so *Alvin* has big headlights. They light up parts of the sea. Then ___5___ take pictures. A long hook scoops up samples from the sea floor. Later, people study these pictures and samples.

_____ **5.** The word that best completes the sentence is

     A. cats   **B.** cameras   **C.** nails

The mimosa is a plant. It has parts that look like feathers. These parts are made from two rows of tiny leaves. When it rains, the leaves lie open. If an animal touches any of the leaves, they ___6___ up. The leaves open again the next time it rains.

_____ **6.** The word that best completes the sentence is

     A. sit   **B.** fold   **C.** dress

Some snakes have four eyes. They have eyes that see in the day. They also have two more eyes. These eyes can see heat. Snakes use these eyes to look for food. A snake **gazes** all around with its special eyes. Its eyes cannot see a plant. Plants do not give off any heat. But the eyes can see a mouse. A mouse is warm and makes a good meal for a snake.

_____ **1.** In this story the word **gazes** means

    A. stares   **B.** gives   **C.** adds

Deep inside, Earth is made of very hot rock. The rock is so hot that it can turn water into steam. In some places this steam comes out of cracks in the ground. In other places people pipe the steam up from deep in the ground. People use this steam **energy** to warm their homes.

_____ **2.** In this story the word **energy** means

    A. ice   **B.** power   **C.** stream

What is vegetable art? Ask Bob Spohn. For 50 years Spohn has **whittled** faces and animals out of large vegetables. He uses a knife to make the faces. Then he paints them. He once made a smiling face from a giant pumpkin. The pumpkin was almost 1 yard high and weighed 110 pounds!

_____ **3.** In this story the word **whittled** means

    A. drawn   **B.** shaken   **C.** cut

How do desert animals get water? Some catch it on their bodies. Some snakes, lizards, and bugs sleep in the open air. Cool winds blow during the night. These winds take water from the desert air. By morning small drops of this water have landed on the bodies of the animals. They drink the water by licking it. The wind and the water are **necessary** for desert animals. Without the wind they might die.

_____ **4.** In this story the word **necessary** means

    A. thanked   **B.** pitched   **C.** needed

One bird really can swim like a fish. It is called the loon. This bird has been found more than 100 feet below the water's **surface**. The bird can also fly, but it cannot walk. Its legs are very far back on its body. When it tries to stand up, it falls over.

_____ **5.** In this story the word **surface** means

    A. hole   **B.** top   **C.** ribbon

Doctors did a study on how some people stay thin. They found that nervous people use more energy. They walk back and forth. They tap their toes. They drum their fingers. In one day these people burn up the energy it takes to run 5 miles. This finding may lead to a new kind of exercise. People may **squirm** the pounds away!

_____ **6.** In this story the word **squirm** means

    A. wiggle   **B.** jump   **C.** run

Not all sharks are mean. Nurse sharks look bad, but they almost never hurt people. Instead they stay on the bottom of the ocean. They swim along, **sucking** in sand, crabs, snails, and tiny fish. They spit out the sand and eat the animals!

_____ **1.** In this story the word **sucking** means
      A. rolling   **B.** pulling   **C.** calling

People have loved amber for thousands of years. Amber looks like stone, but it really comes from the gum of trees. This gum fell to the ground long ago. It was covered with dirt and then became hard. There it stayed until it was found. Pieces of amber can be **polished** to make beads and rings. To do this you must rub the amber for a very long time.

_____ **2.** In this story the word **polished** means
      A. shined   **B.** missed   **C.** hidden

Some farmers in China were digging a well. They dug deeper and deeper. Suddenly a shovel struck something hard. A farmer bent down and pushed the dirt away. He found himself looking into a person's eyes. The person was made of clay. Scientists later dug up the area. Under the earth were 3,000 clay **warriors**. Some were on horses. Many carried spears and knives. All of them were as big as real people.

_____ **3.** In this story the word **warriors** means
      A. fighters   **B.** pots   **C.** animals

The sap from a poison ivy plant causes itchy bumps on your skin. It is best to know what this plant looks like. Poison ivy grows as a vine or a shrub. The leaves are always in groups of three on each stem. The color, size, and shape of the leaves can be different for each plant. Poison ivy **blooms** in the first part of summer. It has small blossoms that turn into berries.

_____ **4.** In this story the word **blooms** means
     A. flowers   **B.** cries   **C.** travels

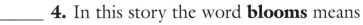

The Great Dane is a type of dog. It has a thick coat of short hair. Its hair can be black, tan, or white. The Great Dane is very large and strong. For this reason it can be used as a **guard** dog. But a Great Dane is also very gentle, so it makes a good pet, too.

_____ **5.** In this story the word **guard** means
     A. funny   **B.** lazy   **C.** watch

People wrote with secret codes long ago. Today many people still use secret codes. Two types of codes are used the most. In one kind of code, symbols take the place of letters. These symbols can be letters, numbers, or words. A code book is used to read the message. The other kind of code changes the **arrangement** of the letters. People must unscramble the letters to read the message.

_____ **6.** In this story the word **arrangement** means
     A. order   **B.** shape   **C.** face

The frostweed is a plant that grows in Texas. It grows best in the shade or in moist dirt. It is found under large trees and on the banks of creeks. This plant has a tall stem with a group of white flowers on the end. When the first freeze of the year comes, the plant's stem **splits**. Then sap leaks out. The sap freezes around the stem. It looks like ribbons or clusters of flowers.

_____ **1.** In this story the word **splits** means

    A. shuts   **B.** cracks   **C.** wanders

The first newspaper was a letter. It told the news. The letter was sent by messenger. It went to people who lived in far-off lands. Hundreds of years later, a news sheet was used. It was written by hand each day. Then it was **hung** up for all to read. Much later the Chinese carved wooden blocks. They printed a paper. Now the newspaper is a quick way to get the news.

_____ **2.** In this story the word **hung** means

    A. put   **B.** sawed   **C.** grown

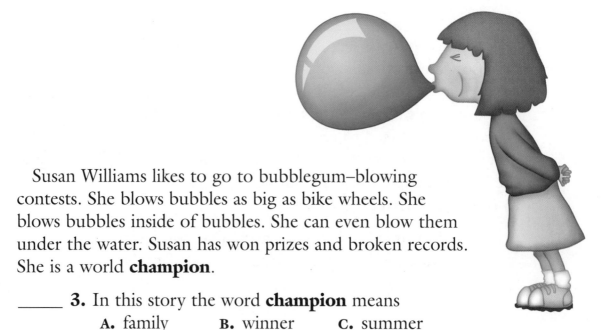

Susan Williams likes to go to bubblegum–blowing contests. She blows bubbles as big as bike wheels. She blows bubbles inside of bubbles. She can even blow them under the water. Susan has won prizes and broken records. She is a world **champion**.

_____ **3.** In this story the word **champion** means

    A. family   **B.** winner   **C.** summer

The *Mary Celeste* was a ship. It set sail more than 100 years ago. On board were the captain and a **crew** of eight sailors. One month after the *Mary Celeste* set sail, it was seen by another ship's captain. He saw that the *Mary Celeste* was going the wrong way. The captain went to find out what was wrong. He saw that no one was on board. He never found out what had happened to the people on the *Mary Celeste*.

_____ **4.** In this story the word **crew** means

        A. ladder   **B.** rock   **C.** team

A stinkbug is an insect. It can be green or brown. It can also be other colors. A stinkbug has a special trick. It uses its back legs or its stomach to make a bad smell. When the stinkbug gets scared, it can **spray** out the smelly liquid.

_____ **5.** In this story the word **spray** means

        A. splash   **B.** climb   **C.** find

The Big Dipper can be seen in the northern sky at night. It has seven stars. They form the **outline** of a pot. Three of the stars make the dipper's handle. Four of the stars make the rest of the pot. Two stars in the Big Dipper are brighter than the rest. They are called pointer stars. They can be used to find the North Star.

_____ **6.** In this story the word **outline** means

        A. shape   **B.** river   **C.** candle

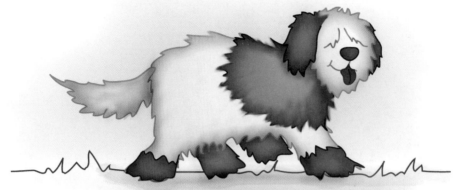

Some people think English sheepdogs make great pets. These dogs are cute and often friendly. They need much care. Their long, **shaggy** coats must be brushed every day. The dogs need lots of love and must have space in which to run.

_____ **1.** In this story the word **shaggy** means

    A. hairy   **B.** sorry   **C.** tiny

Roller coaster cars are hooked to a chain at first. A motor on the ground runs the chain. It pulls the cars to the top of the first hill. Then the cars are unhooked. When the cars roll downhill, they speed up. The cars slow down as they **coast** up the next hill. They speed up again as they go down it. Each hill is a bit lower than the last. The cars can't go up a hill that is as high as the one they just came down.

_____ **2.** In this story the word **coast** means

    A. move   **B.** park   **C.** leak

Stevie Wonder was blind from birth. This did not **prevent** him from using his talent. He found that he was good with music. He learned how to play many instruments. He wrote his own songs. At the age of 12, he sang his first hit. Since then he has made many recordings. He has even written music for movies.

_____ **3.** In this story the word **prevent** means

    A. help   **B.** take   **C.** stop

The Chicago River is in Illinois. It goes through the city of Chicago. People used to dump their **trash** into the river. This dirty water flowed to a nearby lake. Soon the lake water was dirty. Then the people found a way to keep the lake clean. They built dams on the river. The dams forced the water to flow away from the lake. Now the lake water stays clean.

_____ **4.** In this story the word **trash** means
   A. banana   **B.** garbage   **C.** sign

There's a special place in Michigan. It's a museum for children. The children come to learn about science. Some come from school. The museum sends a special truck for them. The children look at science **kits** during the ride. They look at rocks, models, and books.

_____ **5.** In this story the word **kits** means
   A. packages   **B.** organs   **C.** hills

Forest rangers watch for a fire in the woods. They try to stop a fire before it spreads. But this is not an easy job. Most fires start where the woods are thick. There aren't any roads in the middle of the woods, so firefighters can't drive to the fire. They must **parachute** from a plane to get there.

_____ **6.** In this story the word **parachute** means
   A. shoot   **B.** refuse   **C.** jump

Writing Roundup

Each of the sentences on this page is missing a word. Read the sentences. Choose a word from the word box to go in each one. Write the word on the line.

loud	feed	stood
leaves	glass	joke
wide	wear	true
afternoon	table	careful

1. It rained all _____.

2. The _____ on the trees turn red in the fall.

3. We _____ our pets every day.

4. Please pour me a _____ of milk.

5. Your funny _____ made me laugh.

6. That dog has a very _____ bark.

7. Please be _____ not to fall down.

8. It is _____ that all birds have feathers.

9. The puddle was too _____ to jump across.

10. We _____ in line to buy our tickets.

Read each story. Write a word on each line that makes sense in the story.

LaToya wanted to go outside. Snow was falling fast. "It looks (1)_____ in my front yard. Maybe I should put on my (2)_____," she said.

My dog Walter really likes to play with a (3)_____. I always hide it in the (4)_____. He uses his nose to find it. Then he brings it back to me.

The cow looked so funny! A yellow bird was sitting on its (5)_____! The cow switched its tail. Then the bird flew over to a (6)_____.

unit 4

What Is a Main Idea?

The main idea of a story tells what the whole story is about. Each story in this book has a main idea. It is usually one sentence somewhere in each story.

Why do stories have sentences other than the main idea sentence? The other sentences are *details*. They tell you more about the main idea. They also make the story more fun to read.

The example below may help you think about main ideas. All the details add up to the main idea.

detail + detail + detail = main idea

$$3 + 4 + 5 = 12$$

The *3*, *4*, and *5* are like details. They add up to the main idea. The main idea is like the *12*. It is bigger than the details. It is made up of many smaller parts.

Try It!

Read the story below. Draw a line under the main idea.

Do you sing in the bathtub? Do you sing in the car? Here's how you can become a singing star! You can go to a store. Someone will play music while you sing a song. Then the people there will make a recording of your song. You can take it home and surprise your friends!

How to Choose a Main Idea

The main idea of the story is the sentence about becoming a singing star. All the other sentences are details. They tell how you can become a star. Write the details on the lines below.

Detail 1:   You might sing in the _____

or in the _____.

Detail 2:   You can go to a _____.

Detail 3:   Someone will play _____.

Detail 4:   The people will make a _____ of your song.

Detail 5:   You can _____ your friends.

Now write the main idea on the lines below. It is the sentence that is not a detail.

Main Idea: _____

_____

- What do all the sentences add up to? Remember that the main idea is bigger than the details. It is made up of many smaller parts.

- Read each story. As you read, think about each sentence. Does it tell only a small part of the whole story? If it does, it is a detail. Does it tell what the story is about? Then it is the main idea.

LESSON 1

Read each passage. After each passage you will answer a question about the main idea of the passage. Remember, the main idea is the main point in a story.

1. There's a lot of snow in some parts of the world. Schoolchildren in these places learn to make snowshoes. Snowshoes are big and flat. They are like duck feet. You put them on over your shoes. They are hard to walk in. But they keep your feet from sinking in the deep snow.

_____ **1.** The story mainly tells
  A. why snow falls
  B. why some children make snowshoes
  C. who wears duck feet in cold places

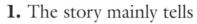

2. Newborn bats start life in a pocket. The mother bat makes her tail into a pocket. When a baby is born, the baby lives in it. The baby holds tight to its mother's fur. The mother hunts for food at night. The baby rides in its pocket. So baby bats get a free ride high in the sky each night.

_____ **2.** The story mainly tells
  A. why bats hold their mother's fur
  B. when to find bats in caves
  C. where baby bats live

3. What can you do if you're camping and you're caught in the rain without a tent? Rather than get wet, you can make a lean-to. First find two tree branches that are shaped like a *Y*. The branches should be tall and strong. Then put the two Y-shaped branches in the ground about eight feet apart. Next place a long, light stick across the two branches. Finally find many straight branches. Lean them against the cross stick on both sides. You will have a lean-to for sleeping and staying dry.

_____ **3.** The story mainly tells
  A. how to make a lean-to
  B. who needs a tent
  C. what to do if it rains

4. Have you seen any old trains? Most old trains were run by steam engine. The steam from the engine moved the train's wheels. The steam engine gave off puffs of smoke. The puffs came out of the train's smokestack. When the train ran fast, it gave off many puffs of smoke. A train going 50 miles per hour gave off 800 smoke puffs in a minute.

_____ **4.** The story mainly tells
  A. how trains stop
  B. about trains run by steam
  C. about train wheels

1. There's an old saying: "Sleep tight and don't let the bedbugs bite." But it's no joke. Bedbugs are real. They are small insects that eat blood. They bite animals and people, too. Their bites often hurt the skin. Bedbugs can be found hiding in beds and walls. If a bedbug does bite, a person probably won't sleep tight.

_____ **1.** The story mainly tells
    A. what bedbugs are like
    B. who gets bedbugs
    C. where bedbugs sleep

2. Read the story just before this one again. Try your best to remember it. Don't peek! How many sentences can you remember? Two? Three? None? Long ago, people told many stories. These people didn't know how to read or write, so they had to remember each story. Some stories were thousands of sentences long. How did they do it? They didn't try to remember every word. They just remembered how the story went. They told the story a little differently each time, too.

_____ **2.** The story mainly tells
    A. how many sentences you can remember
    B. who couldn't read or write
    C. how people long ago remembered stories

3. In the fall of each year, the days grow shorter and shorter. We finally reach a time when the days and nights last about the same number of hours and minutes. During these days the full moon is called a harvest moon. It rises soon after the Sun goes down. It is often a deep orange color. Since the Moon is so bright, farmers have more time to harvest their crops. That's why it's called a harvest moon.

_____ **3.** The story mainly tells
  A. what color the harvest moon is
  B. how the harvest moon got its name
  C. when the days grow shorter

---

4. The Statue of Liberty is one very big woman! Her hand is 16 feet long. One of her fingers is 8 feet long. Her head is 17 feet high. Her eyes are 2 feet wide. Even her fingernails are huge. They are more than 12 inches across.

_____ **4.** The story mainly tells
  A. how long some people's fingernails are
  B. how big the Statue of Liberty is
  C. who the tallest woman in the world is

1. Penguins are birds. But they cannot fly. They use their wings in other ways. They use them for swimming. Their wings are like flippers. In the summer they stay cool by holding their wings away from their bodies. Their wings are put to good use even if they cannot fly.

_____ **1.** The story mainly tells
- **A.** where penguins live
- **B.** how penguins use their wings
- **C.** how penguins stay warm

2. The Eiffel Tower is a very big tower. It is found in Paris, France. A man named Gustave Eiffel designed it for a fair. It is made of steel. It is more than 980 feet high. It weighs more than 7,000 tons. There are 1,652 steps to the top of the tower.

_____ **2.** The story mainly tells
- **A.** how big the Eiffel Tower is
- **B.** how many towers there are in France
- **C.** how the Eiffel Tower is used

3. A junk is a kind of boat. Junks sail on the seas of China and Southeast Asia. The sails of a junk have four sides. They are stretched over pieces of wood. Junks are used for fishing. Hong Kong is a very crowded city, so some people even live on their junks. A junk is sometimes a home for more than one family.

_____ **3.** The story mainly tells
    A. where most people in Hong Kong live
    B. about a boat called a junk
    C. what junks are made of

4. Emma Lazarus was a poet. She believed that America was the "land of the free." She knew that Jewish people were not treated fairly in many countries. She wanted to help them, so she wrote a poem. It is found on the Statue of Liberty. The statue and her famous poem greet the people who come to America.

_____ **4.** The story mainly tells
    A. that Lazarus built the Statue of Liberty
    B. that Lazarus didn't want to help people
    C. that Lazarus wrote about freedom

1. The white settlers thought bison were a kind of ox. Bison were hunted for their hides. The hides kept people warm. Bison meat made good food, too. The bison tongue was a special treat. Soon the big herds became small herds. Few bison were left. They were put on special land. Today bison live in protected herds.

_____ **1.** The story mainly tells
  A. about bison
  B. how bad bison tongue tasted
  C. that bison hides were not any good

2. Willie Mays loved baseball, but he couldn't play in the major leagues. African Americans couldn't play with white players. Mays played in the Negro Leagues. Then the New York Giants hired Mays. Mays played very well. He became a big star. He hit 660 home runs. Mays played with the Giants and the Mets. Today he is in the Baseball Hall of Fame.

_____ **2.** The story mainly tells
  A. how long Mays played baseball
  B. that Mays played for the Mets
  C. that Mays was a great baseball player

3. The fruit of the squirting cucumber looks like a little pickle. Its skin stretches as it grows. Pressure builds inside the fruit. When the fruit is ripe, it falls off the stem. This opens a hole at one end. The seeds squirt out from the hole. They can fly as far as 25 feet!

_____ **3.** The story mainly tells

    A. about a fruit that squirts its seeds

    B. about a kind of pickle

    C. where cucumber seeds come from

---

4. Fred Morrison invented the Frisbee. He wanted to make a pie tin into a toy. His first metal toy was too heavy. It didn't fly well, so he tried plastic. It sailed through the air. He sold the toy to a company that named it Pluto Platter. Later people played a game called Frisbie-ing. They threw pie tins from the Frisbie Pie Company. The toy company liked the game. It changed the spelling and called the toy a Frisbee.

_____ **4.** The story mainly tells

    A. how to spell Frisbee

    B. that Frisbee was fun to play

    C. how the Frisbee was invented

1. The first person went up into space in 1961. His name was Yuri Gagarin. He was Russian. His spacecraft was the *Vostok 1*. It circled Earth just one time. Gagarin was in space for less than two hours.

_____ **1.** The story mainly tells
  A. about the first manned spaceflight
  B. that *Vostok 1* was a planet
  C. which American was first in space

2. How are a toad and a frog different? A toad spends more time out of water than a frog does. A toad's skin is duller, rougher, and drier. The legs of a toad are shorter, too. A toad cannot jump as far as a frog can. A frog lays its eggs in a jelly-like mass. A toad lays its eggs in strings. It wraps the eggs around the stems of water plants.

_____ **2.** The story mainly tells
  A. where a frog lays its eggs
  B. how a frog and a toad are different
  C. how far a toad can jump

3. Sitting Bull was a Sioux leader. He didn't want his people to lose their land. He told the tribes to join against the white settlers. That way they might keep their homeland. In 1876, some tribes camped near the Little Bighorn River. General Custer and his troops charged the group. Sitting Bull's men destroyed the troops. It was a great win for Native Americans.

_____ **3.** The story mainly tells
  A. how Custer won the Battle of the Little Bighorn
  B. that Sitting Bull was a peaceful man
  C. how Sitting Bull's words helped the Sioux

---

4. The kiwi is a strange bird. It lives in New Zealand. The kiwi has tiny wings, but it cannot fly. It is covered with feathers that look like hair. Its bill is 6 inches long. Its nostrils are found at the end of its bill. It uses its bill to smell worms in the soil. The kiwi comes out only at night. It lives in holes near the roots of trees.

_____ **4.** The story mainly tells
  A. about the kiwi bird
  B. that a kiwi does not have feathers
  C. how far a kiwi can fly

1. Did you know that the world's largest bird can't fly? Can you name the bird? It's an ostrich. Why can't it fly? It's too big. An ostrich can be more than 8 feet tall. It can weigh more than 330 pounds. It lives in the grasslands of Africa.

_____ **1.** The story mainly tells
    A. which zoos have ostriches
    B. about the largest bird in the world
    C. how well ostriches hunt

2. How fast does the human heart beat? In most people, the heart beats 70 times per minute. A heart rate of 50 beats per minute is normal. So is a heart rate of 100. A healthy heart beats between 50 and 100 times a minute. A heart beats about three billion times in a lifetime!

_____ **2.** The story mainly tells
    A. about normal heart rates for humans
    B. how to measure your heartbeat
    C. about the heart rate during a heart attack

3. There are eight notes on a musical scale. Each scale starts and ends with the same letter. One scale is *C, D, E, F, G, A, B, C*. From one *C* to the next *C* is called an octave. *Octave* comes from the Greek word *okto* meaning "eight."

_____ **3.** The story mainly tells
   A. what a *C* note is
   B. how many scales there are
   C. what an octave is

4. Many babies were born at home in 1893. Esther Cleveland was born at home in that year. Her home was famous. It was the White House. Her father was President Grover Cleveland. Until that time, no other child of a president had been born in the White House.

_____ **4.** The story mainly tells
   A. how Cleveland was elected
   B. when Esther Cleveland was born
   C. about a baby born in the White House

1. Peeling an onion can make your eyes water. People try many things to keep from crying. Some people hold an onion under running water. Others try wearing goggles. Goggles make the cook look silly!

_____ **1.** The story mainly tells
   A. why onions make people cry
   B. ways to peel an onion without crying
   C. ways to use goggles

2. The thigh bone is the biggest bone in the body. It connects the hip bone to the knee bone. Why does it need to be big and strong? It has to support the weight of the body. It must hold up the leg muscles, too. It needs to be long so that the legs can take wide steps.

_____ **2.** The story mainly tells
   A. that the biggest bone is found in the arm
   B. why the thigh bone is so big
   C. how bones help a person walk

3. Many years ago, a company made a new tape. It was called Scotch tape. It was meant for use with clear wrapping. But some found other uses for the tape. They used it to mend old toys and torn clothing. They used it for many things. Later many companies made the same type of clear tape. They gave it new names. People bought these new tapes, but the first name given to the clear tape stuck. So now when people use clear tape, they call it Scotch tape.

_____ **3.** The story mainly tells

A. how clear tape works

B. why old toys are taped

C. why clear tapes are called Scotch tape

4. Do you like yo-yos? Where do you think they started? Some people think that the yo-yo began in the United States, but the first yo-yo came to the United States in 1929. It came from the Philippines. The word *yo-yo* means "come come" in the Filipino language.

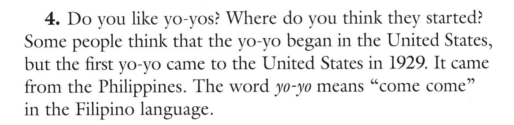

_____ **4.** The story mainly tells

A. where the yo-yo started

B. that the yo-yo was invented in 1939

C. how to say *come* in the Filipino language

1. Sometimes people can't remember their dreams, but everyone dreams while sleeping. Most people dream two hours every night. In that time they have four or five dreams. Each dream is longer than the dream before. You can tell when someone is dreaming. Their eyeballs move back and forth under their closed eyelids.

_____ **1.** The story mainly tells

    A. how much sleep people need

    B. how often people dream

    C. what dreams mean

---

2. In 1904, New York opened its subway for train travel in the city. The fast trains took 28 minutes. They went from one end of the city to the other. Some trains made more stops. They took 46 minutes. It cost 5¢ to ride the train. People loved the ride and the price.

_____ **2.** The story mainly tells

    A. how to travel in New York

    B. about the 1904 New York subway

    C. when the subway made stops

3. Do you like bananas? Have you ever seen them growing outside? Bananas grow in bunches. A bunch of bananas is called a hand. Bananas grow in big hands. Each banana is called a finger. Each finger grows upward.

_____ **3.** The story mainly tells
  A. how bananas grow
  B. how to eat bananas with your fingers
  C. how the banana got its name

4. A snake doesn't open its mouth to stick out its tongue. The snake's jaw has a notch that lets the tongue move in and out. The tongue is not poisonous. A snake uses its tongue to smell. The tongue picks up air and carries it back into the mouth. There are two small holes on the roof of the mouth. It is these holes that smell the air.

_____ **4.** The story mainly tells
  A. how a snake uses its tongue to smell
  B. that a snake's tongue is poisonous
  C. that a snake has three holes on its tongue

Writing Roundup

Read each story. Think about the main idea. Write the main idea in your own words.

1. In 1987, an 18-month-old girl fell into a well in her yard. Her name was Jessica McClure. She was trapped there. People worked to save her. It took more than two days, but she was pulled free. Jessica was lucky to be alive!

What is the main idea of this story?

_____

_____

2. We think of the White House as the home of the president, but this was not always true. George Washington did not live in the White House. He lived in New York.

What is the main idea of this story?

_____

_____

3. Gail Devers won a gold medal in the 1992 Olympic Games. She was one of the fastest women in the world. She had come a long way. Her high school had no track team or coach. So Gail had to train herself.

What is the main idea of this story?

_____

_____

Prewriting

Think of a main idea that you would like to write about, such as a family member, a hero, or a place to go. Fill in the chart below.

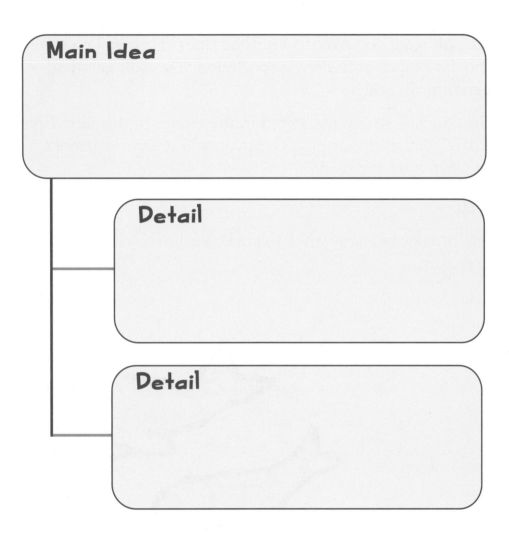

Main Idea

Detail

Detail

On Your Own

Now use another sheet of paper to write your story. Underline the sentence that tells the main idea.

unit 5

What Is a Conclusion?

A conclusion is a decision you make after thinking about all the clues. A writer does not always tell you his or her conclusions. When you read, you have to hunt for clues. Then you must put all the clues together to draw a conclusion. This will help you understand the story.

The conclusions are not stated in the stories of this unit. You will have to read the stories. Then you will draw conclusions from what you have read.

Try It!

Read this story about whales. Think about the clues it gives you.

A mother whale helps her baby take its first breath. She pushes the new baby up for air. The mother whale stays by her baby for about a year. She keeps the baby safe. She feeds it milk.

How to Draw a Conclusion

Look at the story about whales again. Look at the clues in the story. They will help you draw a conclusion about mother whales. Write the clues about mother whales on the lines. The first one has been done for you.

Clue 1: A mother whale ___helps her baby take its first breath.___ .

Clue 2: A mother whale _____

_____ .

Clue 3: A mother whale _____

_____ .

Now try to draw a conclusion about whales. Do you think that whales take care of their babies?

Conclusion: Whales take _____

_____ .

- Look at all the clues in the story. The first clue about the mother whale is that she helps her baby take its first breath. A second clue is that she keeps her baby safe. A third clue is that she feeds her baby milk.

- Look at all the clues together. If it helps, write the clues in your own words. Then make a decision about the story. Your decision will come from the clues. From the story about whales, you might decide that mother whales care for their babies. How do you know that? Mother whales help their babies breathe. They also give them safety and food.

Read each passage. After each passage you will answer a question that will require you to draw a conclusion about the story. Remember, a conclusion is a decision you make after putting together all the clues you are given.

1. When the whistle blows, everyone gets off the ice. The ice is bumpy and rough. Sharp skates have made cuts in it. A noisy machine moves around the rink like a fat duck. The machine makes the ice as smooth as glass. The machine was first built in California in 1942. Before 1942, it took two hours to smooth the ice. Three people did the job with shovels.

_____ **1.** From this story you can tell
  A. the machine makes a hard job much easier
  B. four people can work as fast as the machine
  C. three people push the machine on the ice

2. In Israel hundreds of people live together on a *kibbutz*. A kibbutz is a very large farm. Most of the people are farmers. Some are doctors, soldiers, or teachers. They all share the work. Everyone decides which crops to grow. The children live together in a special house. They see their parents only at night or on weekends.

_____ **2.** From this story you can tell
  A. people grow apples on the farms
  B. the children never play with other children
  C. a kibbutz is a special kind of farm

3. Without the sun nothing could live on Earth. It would be too cold. But the sun won't last forever. Millions of years from now, the sun will stop shining. It will run out of gases to burn. When this happens, the sun will become very big. It will burn brightly for a short time. Then it will cool and become very small.

_____ **3.** From this story you can tell
- **A.** when the sun cools, it will become big
- **B.** after the sun dies, Earth will die
- **C.** someday the sun will turn bright blue

4. George Goodale loved plants. He wanted to have some plants in his museum, but he didn't want just any old plants. Dried plants wouldn't look very nice. Wax plants would melt. Live plants would need too much care. So he used glass plants. Today, people can look at them in his museum. The berries look good enough to eat. The cactus plants have spines that look real. Each glass spine was made by hand.

_____ **4.** From this story you can tell
- **A.** glass plants look nicer than dried plants
- **B.** glass plants change colors in the sun
- **C.** wax plants look as nice as glass plants

1. There are bugs that live under the ground for 17 years. As young bugs they spend their time eating roots. Finally in their seventeenth summer, they crawl up into the open air. They climb the trees and live for just a few weeks. Then they die. Everybody knows when these bugs come out. The males sing to their mates all day long. Sometimes their sound can even drown out airplane noise.

_____ **1.** From this story you can tell
    A. these bugs bite people
    B. the males sing only at night
    C. the bugs' sound is very loud

2. Did you know that your eyes bend light? When light enters the eyes, it's bent into a narrow band. This band of light lands on the back part of the eyes. The band must be bent just the right amount. If it isn't bent enough, things look fuzzy. If the world looks fuzzy, you may need eyeglasses. Eyeglasses can help your eyes see things more clearly.

_____ **2.** From this story you can tell
    A. things always look fuzzy when it's dark
    B. eyeglasses help people's eyes bend light
    C. eyeglasses come in many different colors

3. "Cooking is easy," Lisa said. "Who needs lessons? I know what to do." Lisa turned the stove on high. She put the ham over the hot flame. Jenny put some salt into the tea. Then she added water and let it boil. The girls also decided to make some bread. "What about all the lumps?" Lisa asked. Jenny said, "Just hope that nobody notices, I guess." By now the ham had burned. The tea tasted awful, too. So Lisa and Jenny had peanut butter sandwiches for dinner!

_____ **3.** From this story you can tell
  A. the girls really need cooking lessons
  B. the girls have cooked for many years
  C. the girls tried to bake a cake

4. Tara had to walk through a strange part of the city. She hid her necklace inside her shirt so that it wouldn't show. Her money was in her bag. She held the bag close to her body. She had a whistle in her hand. Tara held her head high and walked fast.

_____ **4.** From this story you can tell
  A. Tara worked for a big company in the city
  B. Tara was afraid of being robbed or hurt
  C. Tara had many necklaces

1. There is a man who makes music by playing glasses of water. He buys plain glasses at the store. Then he puts them on a table and fills them with water. He fills some glasses full. He fills others halfway. He pours just a little water in the rest of the glasses. Then he plays music by running his wet finger around the tops of the glasses. He changes the sounds by adding water or pouring water out of the glasses.

_____ **1.** From this story you can tell
  A. this man really likes to play the harp
  B. the amount of water changes the sound
  C. the man uses 15 glasses to play a song

2. Who began the idea of birthday parties? About 800 years ago, the Germans had the first birthday party. It was held on a child's birthday. The party began when the child awakened. There were candles on the birthday cake. The candles were kept lit all day long. There was also a big dinner. After the meal the child blew out the candles. Then everyone ate some birthday cake.

_____ **2.** From this story you can tell
  A. the cake was eaten in the morning
  B. the candles were blown out in the evening
  C. the candles were lit after the big meal

3. People have eaten popcorn for thousands of years. Native Americans were among the first to eat this snack. Not all corn will pop. A kernel of corn must have water in it to pop. When the water in the corn is heated, it turns to steam. The steam makes the kernels pop into puffs.

_____ **3.** From this story you can tell
   A. popcorn is a very old snack
   B. all corn is used as popcorn
   C. popcorn was first eaten at a movie

4. Two-thirds of Earth is covered with water. There are many oceans and seas. The Pacific Ocean is the biggest one. It covers more than 60 million square miles. This is about one-third of Earth's surface. This ocean holds half the world's water. Some parts of the Pacific are more than six miles deep.

_____ **4.** From this story you can tell
   A. the Pacific Ocean is bigger than Earth
   B. Earth's surface has more water than land
   C. the Pacific Ocean is not very deep

1. Have you ever looked at a map of the United States? Many states have strange shapes. The bottom part of Michigan looks like a mitten. Maine looks like the head of a buffalo. Tennessee is shaped like a sled. Also, California looks like an arm. Try to remember these strange shapes. They will help you remember the states.

_____ **1.** From this story you can tell
   A. many states have different shapes
   B. Maine has the shape of a mitten
   C. the shapes will help you forget the states

2. In Europe most people eat with the fork held in the left hand. Most Americans hold it in their right hand. Why is it different? In the pioneer days, there was not always enough food to eat. So people ate very fast. They could eat even faster by holding the fork in their right hand.

_____ **2.** From this story you can tell
   A. pioneers liked to eat slowly
   B. everyone holds the fork in his or her left hand
   C. Americans and Europeans eat differently

3. An old fairy tale tells of Goldilocks and the three bears. At first, it was not about a young girl. Instead, it was about an old woman with gray hair. Her name was Silver Hair. The story was told through the years. Some people changed the old woman to a young girl. They called her "Golden Hair." Later she was called "Goldilocks."

_____ **3.** From this story you can tell
      A. the story of Goldilocks has changed
      B. an old woman wrote the story of Goldilocks
      C. Goldilocks is an old German tale

4. In 1991, Richard Branson and Per Lindstrand did a brave thing. They flew across the Pacific Ocean. They did not fly in a jet. They crossed the ocean in a hot-air balloon! They were the first people to do this. They floated from Japan to Canada. Their trip covered more than 6,000 miles.

_____ **4.** From this story you can tell
      A. the balloon trip was not very long
      B. the men traveled very far
      C. the balloon trip ended in Japan

1. Today you can find buttons on many clothes, but buttons have not always been used to fasten clothes. Long ago only belts and pins were used to join parts of clothes. For hundreds of years, buttons were used as jewels. They were put on clothes just for their beauty. Finally in the 1200s, buttons were used as fasteners on clothes.

_____ **1.** From this story you can tell
    A. buttons are still used only for beauty
    B. pins and belts are better than buttons
    C. buttons, belts, and pins are used as fasteners

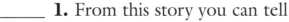

2. Marco Polo was a famous traveler. His home was in Venice, Italy. In 1271, he made a trip to the Far East. In China he became friends with the ruler. His name was Kublai Khan. Polo became his helper. He stayed in China for 20 years. Then he went back home. There he wrote a book. The book told all about the Far East.

_____ **2.** From this story you can tell
    A. Polo got lost on his trip
    B. Venice is west of China
    C. Polo did not stay long in China

3. Have you ever seen someone turn a thumbs up? Today a thumbs up means good luck. The early Egyptians used a thumbs up to mean hope. They also used it to mean winning. To them a thumbs down meant losing or bad luck.

_____ **3.** From this story you can tell
  A. a thumbs up means bad luck
  B. a thumbs down means winning
  C. a thumbs up means good things

4. The biggest cave room in the world is called the Big Room. It is found at Carlsbad Caverns in New Mexico. The edge of the Big Room is almost 2 miles around. Its floor covers 14 acres. This is bigger than 12 football fields put together. Its roof is more than 300 feet tall. A building with 30 floors could fit into the Big Room!

_____ **4.** From this story you can tell
  A. this cave room has the right name
  B. Carlsbad Caverns is a hotel
  C. the Big Room is found in New Jersey

1. Alan Shepard Jr. became famous on May 5, 1961. He was strapped to his seat inside a spaceship. The spaceship was named *Freedom 7.* All of a sudden, the ship started to shake. Its great engines roared. Then Shepard raced through the sky. Soon he reached space. His trip took only 15 minutes. He was the first American to fly in space.

_____ **1.** From this story you can tell
    A. Shepard flew to Mars
    B. Shepard's trip into space was short
    C. Shepard rode a balloon into space

2. The man who first made chewing gum was named Thomas Adams. He was really trying to make rubber, not gum. He used something called chicle. Chicle is the sticky sap from a Mexican tree. Adams was not able to make rubber from chicle. He got his money back and he sold the chicle as chewing gum!

_____ **2.** From this story you can tell
    A. chewing gum comes from trees
    B. chicle is a kind of small chicken
    C. chewing gum is now made from rubber

3. Have you ever read *Roll of Thunder, Hear My Cry?* It is a book by Mildred D. Taylor. It is told through the eyes of Cassie Logan. Cassie is a smart girl. She is nine years old. Cassie learns of the pride her family has in its roots. In this book and in others, Taylor tells wonderful stories of earlier African American life.

_____ **3.** From this story you can tell
  A. Cassie Logan is afraid of thunder
  B. Mildred D. Taylor is an African American
  C. Cassie learns about her family's roots

G. Washington   T. Jefferson   J. Madison   J. Monroe   W. H. Harrison   J. Tyler   Z. Taylor   W. Wilson

4. Virginia is part of the United States. It is known as the Mother of Presidents. Eight presidents were born in this state. More presidents have come from Virginia than from any other state. George Washington was the first president born there. Thomas Jefferson was another. James Madison, James Monroe, and William Henry Harrison were next. Then came John Tyler and Zachary Taylor. Woodrow Wilson was the last president from Virginia.

_____ **4.** From this story you can tell
  A. Virginia is really eight states put together
  B. many presidents have been born in Virginia
  C. Washington's mother was born in Virginia

1. Some towns in the United States have strange names. Many of these names are not English. Take Baton Rouge as an example. It's the capital of Louisiana. Its name comes from French words. *Baton rouge* means "red stick." Long ago, Native Americans used red sticks to mark off their hunting grounds. The French settlers named the town after these red sticks.

_____ **1.** From this story you can tell

    A. the names of towns are not always English

    B. Baton Rouge is a French settler's name

    C. Louisiana is part of England

2. There are different ways to tell how hot or cold it is outside. Do you know a fun way to measure the heat? First you must listen for the cricket chirps. Then you need to count the chirps for 15 seconds. Then add 40 to the number of chirps. Your answer should be close to the real temperature.

_____ **2.** From this story you can tell

    A. crickets chirp louder when it is cold

    B. only crickets are used to measure the heat

    C. crickets chirp faster as the heat rises

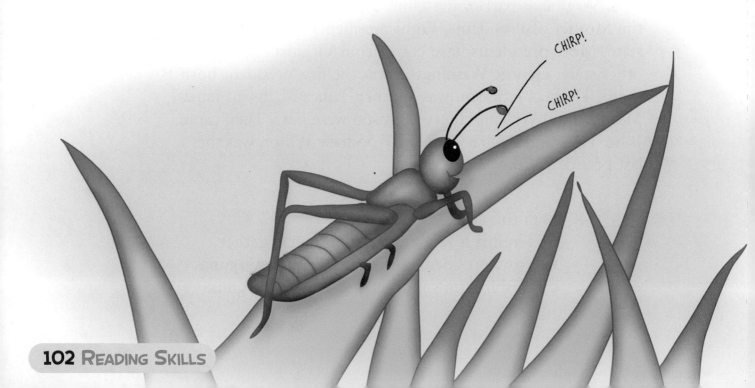

CHIRP!

CHIRP!

3. Charles Blondin was a brave man.
In 1859, he crossed Niagara Falls on a tightrope.
Then he put on a blindfold and crossed the rushing water
again. But that wasn't all he did. He walked the rope with stilts.
As his last trick, he walked halfway across the tightrope. There he
stopped for breakfast! He cooked some eggs and ate them. Then
he made his way to the other side.

_____ **3.** From this story you can tell
     A. Blondin was a poor swimmer
     B. Blondin was comfortable on the tightrope
     C. Blondin was not afraid of water

---

4. Many states have nicknames. Alaska is the Great Land.
Texas is called the Lone Star State. Maine is known as the Pine
Tree State. Why do they have these nicknames? There are stories
behind them. One example is Wyoming. It's called the Equality
State. Wyoming became a state in 1890. Its laws gave women the
right to vote. It was the first state to do this for women.

_____ **4.** From this story you can tell
     A. Alaska has many pine trees
     B. Texas became a state in 1890
     C. Wyoming gave equal rights to women

1. An astronaut is someone who works in space. Ellen Ochoa is the first Hispanic woman astronaut. She does experiments in space. Some of the experiments help us know how the Sun works. This helps us see how the Sun affects Earth. In her spare time, she likes to play the flute. She rides her bike and plays volleyball, too.

_____ **1.** From this story you can tell
  A. Ellen Ochoa plays flute in a band
  B. Ellen Ochoa wins bike races
  C. Ellen Ochoa works in space

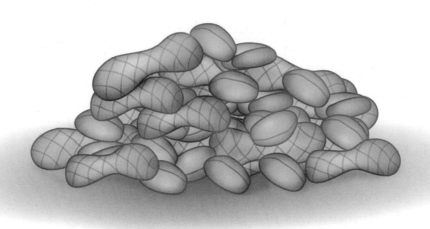

2. Do you like peanuts? Many people do. In fact, March is known as Peanut Month. People in the United States eat many peanuts. They eat more than 1 billion pounds of peanuts per year. Half of this is eaten as peanut butter.

_____ **2.** From this story you can tell
  A. peanuts are a favorite American snack
  B. May is Peanut Month
  C. peanut butter is made from walnuts

3. The year was 1960. Chubby Checker was only 19 years old. Checker liked to dance, but he was tired of the same old dances. He wanted a new dance. So he made up a few new steps. The dance was called the Twist. He even wrote a song to go along with his new dance. Soon young people everywhere were doing the Twist.

_____ **3.** From this story you can tell
  A. people did not like Checker's new song
  B. Checker never learned to dance
  C. the Twist became a well-known dance

---

4. The 1939 World's Fair was held in New York. One of the fun parts of the fair was called Futurama. It tried to show what the future might be like. It showed how people would one day use air conditioners. This idea became true. It also showed people living in houses that could be thrown away. This idea has yet to become real.

_____ **4.** From this story you can tell
  A. the World's Fair took place in New Jersey
  B. Futurama showed things from the past
  C. it's hard to tell about the future

Writing Roundup

Read each story. Think about a conclusion you can draw. Write your conclusion in a complete sentence.

1. Dorothy Kelly became famous in 1977. The plane she was on crashed into another plane. She helped to save many lives during the accident. She thought she was only doing her job. The airline thought she did more than she had to do.

What conclusion can you draw?

_____

_____

2. In basketball, you get points when you make a basket. Some baskets give you more points than others. These baskets are not easy to make. They are a big risk. That is why they are not tried as often as other basketball shots.

What conclusion can you draw?

_____

_____

_____

3. Mrs. Paz opened the classroom. Then she pulled up the blinds. Next she watered the plants. She put the new books on the desks. The room was ready. The girls and boys would be there soon. Mrs. Paz liked all of them.

What conclusion can you draw?

_____

_____

_____

Read the story below. What conclusions can you draw? Use the clues in the story to answer the questions in complete sentences.

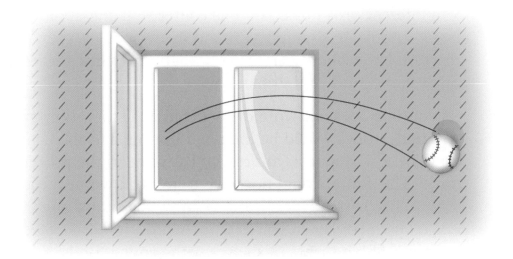

The living room window was open. Cody was not happy to see the open window. He had asked his little brother Tom to keep the window closed. Tom said that he needed more fresh air. All of a sudden, a baseball came sailing through the open window. It landed on the couch. Cody smiled at his little brother and Tom smiled back at him.

1. Who opened the window? How do you know?

_____

_____

2. Where was Cody? How do you know?

_____

_____

3. Was it good that the window was open? How do you know?

_____

_____

What Is an Inference?

An inference is a guess you make after thinking about what you already know. For example, a friend invites you to a party. From what you know about parties, you might infer that there will be games, gifts, food, and drinks.

An author does not write every detail in a story. If every detail were told, stories would be long and boring, and the main point would be lost. Suppose you read, "Pat went to the grocery store." The writer would not have to tell you what a grocery store is. The writer expects you to know that it is a place where people buy food. When you hear the words "grocery store," you may think of long rows of shelves with canned foods. You may think of cases filled with cheese and milk. By filling in these missing details, you could infer that Pat went to the store to buy food. The writer expects you to infer the missing details from what you know.

Try It!

Read this story about Sam. Think about the facts in the story.

Sam's Morning

Sam walked down the hall at school. He pushed back his straight, red hair with one hand. He hadn't combed it. He rubbed his eyes with a fist. He hadn't washed his face. His shirt was wrinkled. One shoelace was untied. It dragged along the floor as he walked.

How to Make an Inference

Look at the story about Sam again. Look at the facts in the story. They will help you make an inference about Sam. Write the facts on the lines. The first one has been done for you.

Fact 1: Sam had forgotten _to comb his hair_ .

Fact 2: He hadn't _____ .

Fact 3: His shirt _____ .

Fact 4: One shoelace _____ .

Now try to make an inference about Sam. Do you think Sam cares about how he looks?

Inference: Sam _____ .

- Look at all the facts in the story. Sam hadn't combed his hair. He hadn't washed his face. His shirt was wrinkled. One shoelace was not tied.

- Now go beyond what you've read. What can you guess about Sam? Your inference will come from what you read and what you already know. Did you guess that Sam doesn't care about how he looks? You can infer that because Sam hadn't combed his hair or washed his face. Also, his shirt was wrinkled, and his shoelace was not tied.

Read each passage. After you read each passage you will be asked to make an inference about the story. Remember, an inference is a guess you make by putting together what you know and what you read or see in the stories.

1. Manx cats come from an English island. It is the Isle of Man in the Irish Sea. Manx cats have short hair. Rumpy Manx cats have no tail at all. Stumpy Manx cats have short tails. Longie Manx cats have long tails. They all have short front legs and long back legs. They have short, round heads, faces, and bodies. Sometimes they hop. For that reason, people once thought they were part rabbit.

_____ **1.** Which of these sentences is probably true?
    A. Manx cats are part rabbit.
    B. Only cats live on the Isle of Man.
    C. Manx cats were named after the island.

---

2. The Blues moved the ball down the field. One player kicked it to another. The Reds could not take the ball away. The Blues got closer to the net. The Reds' goalie caught one of the balls that was kicked into the net. She did not catch the next one. The Blues scored still another point.

_____ **2.** Which of these sentences is probably true?
    A. The Blues were winning the game.
    B. The Reds needed more players.
    C. The Blues were sore losers.

3. The whooping crane is one of two kinds of cranes that live in North America. It is a large bird with a long neck and long legs. Long ago these cranes lived on the grasslands. Then people moved to these places. The people took the land where these cranes had made homes. The cranes began to disappear. At one point there were just 21 cranes left. Then people started to help these cranes. They gave them space to build nests. They helped keep the cranes safe.

_____ **3.** Which of these sentences is probably true?
    A. People found that the cranes needed help.
    B. People used whooping cranes for food.
    C. No whooping cranes are left today.

---

4. The Smithsonian is a big museum. The bones of animals that lived long ago are kept there. You can also see clothes, tools, and cars that people have used in the past. The first U.S. rocket is there, too.

_____ **4.** Which of these sentences is probably true?
    A. The Smithsonian sells cars.
    B. You can learn about the past at the Smithsonian.
    C. The Smithsonian has live animals.

1. Yin-May was driving on the road. She saw an airplane over her car. It was a warm day, and her windows were rolled down. Yin-May heard the plane's engine go off and then on. This happened many times. The plane turned and came in low over the road. The plane turned again. Yin-May pulled off the road.

_____ **1.** Which of these sentences is probably true?
   A. Yin-May was waiting for her mother.
   B. The plane had problems and needed to land.
   C. The pilot was counting the cars on the road.

2. Siamese cats come from Thailand. Thailand is in Asia. It was once called Siam. Some people say that the king of Siam kept cats to guard his palace. Their meows would wake him up if someone tried to break in. Another story is that they would walk on the tops of the walls at night and jump on the backs of strangers. Siamese cats have short hair. They have blue eyes. They are light colored with dark faces, ears, paws, and tails.

_____ **2.** Which of these sentences is probably true?
   A. Siamese cats have blue faces.
   B. Siamese cats are afraid of the king.
   C. Siamese cats are loud.

3. The Tennessee River runs through high hills. For years the river flooded. Water ran over the banks of the river. The water ruined fields and houses. People built a high dam. Water collected behind the dam. This made a lake. When it rained, the floodwater went into the lake.

_____ **3.** Which of these sentences is probably true?
  A. The Tennessee River dried up.
  B. Dams help stop flooding.
  C. River water is not safe to drink.

4. Maria uses her new tools to build a bluebird house. She draws the shape of each side on a piece of cedar. She cuts the board with her hand saw. She nails each side to the floor. Then she nails on the roof. She uses a large drill to make a door for the birds. Her friend Suki helps her find a good place to hang the birdhouse. Now they wait for the bluebirds to move in and raise a family.

_____ **4.** Which of these sentences is probably true?
  A. Maria likes bluebirds.
  B. All birdhouses are made of cedar.
  C. Suki has new tools.

1. Oil is a resource. Coal and gas are also resources. They are all fuels. We burn these fuels to make heat and power. We use gas and oil to run our cars. All three of these resources come from the ground. They were formed long before people lived on Earth.

_____ **1.** Which of these sentences is probably true?
  A. No one uses resources.
  B. Oil, gas, and coal are not resources.
  C. Oil, coal, and gas help people to meet needs.

2. In the 1800s, a man from France wanted people all over the world to know that America stood for freedom. He asked an artist friend to help him. First the artist drew a picture of a woman wearing a long robe. He showed the woman holding a torch and wearing a crown. The statue was finished in 1886. Now it stands on Liberty Island. It has greeted many people who have come to America.

_____ **2.** Which of these sentences is probably true?
  A. The man's statue was never finished.
  B. The statue is the Statue of Liberty.
  C. The statue stands for all artists.

3. Even though she didn't speak, I knew Mom was mad. Her face was red. Her arms were crossed. She was standing in the doorway, tapping her foot. I was late again. I tried to run up to my room fast.

_____ **3.** Which of these sentences is probably true?
   A. Mom was pleased with me.
   B. People can say things without using words.
   C. Mom shouted, and I knew she was mad.

---

4. The two children lay on their backs in the grass. They were looking up at the sky. "I see a whale. See him spout!" said one. "That doesn't look like a whale," said the other. "It looks like an elephant." Neither could agree on the shapes they saw.

_____ **4.** Which of these sentences is probably true?
   A. The children were watching cartoons outside.
   B. An elephant was riding a whale.
   C. The children were seeing shapes in the clouds.

1. How is the air heated in a hot-air balloon? Pilots use a gas flame to heat the air. If a pilot wants to go up, he or she shoots the flame up into the balloon. This makes the air hot. The pilot must cool the air to go down. Once the balloon is up, the wind guides the balloon. If there is no wind, the balloon stays in one place.

_____ **1.** Which of these sentences is probably true?
   A. Hot air makes the balloon rise.
   B. Balloons get you places fast.
   C. Hot-air balloons fly with wings.

2. Some insects have built-in ways to hide from their enemies. One insect looks just like a stick. Its body is long, thin, and brown. Its legs are very thin. When birds see it, they think it is a twig, so they don't eat it. Another insect looks like a leaf. It is green and flat, and it hangs on a plant. Birds think it is part of the plant.

_____ **2.** Which of these sentences is probably true?
   A. Birds are not very smart.
   B. Some insects are shaped like parts of plants.
   C. Insects love to play tricks.

3. We put all the books away in boxes. The teacher took our little bits of crayon and threw them away. She put our big ones in a box. Some children took the pictures off the walls. I washed the chalkboard. The janitor came in to lock the windows. The teacher put her plants in a box to take home.

_____ **3.** Which of these sentences is probably true?
    A. It is the first day of school.
    B. It is the last day of school.
    C. There has been a fire at school.

4. Some words sound just alike. Sometimes this can cause trouble. Suppose someone asks you to pick up rocks with a crane. What should you do? Do you use a bird with a long neck? Or do you use a machine? How will you know which crane to use?

_____ **4.** Which of these sentences is probably true?
    A. Words can sound alike but have different meanings.
    B. _Crane_ and _crane_ do not sound the same.
    C. All words have the same meaning.

1. Jan counted out five pairs of socks. She put one extra pair in the pile. She found the T-shirt she liked to sleep in. She chose some shorts and shirts. "Don't forget your teddy bear," her dad called.

_____ **1.** Which of these sentences is probably true?

    A. Jan wants to see how many socks she has.

    B. Jan doesn't like nightgowns.

    C. Jan is getting ready for a trip.

2. Your skin is made of a thick layer of tiny, living parts called cells. Your skin helps keep you alive. It holds in the moisture that your body must have. Sometimes skin from one part of the body can be put onto another part. This is called a skin graft. Skin grafts can help someone who has had a bad burn.

_____ **2.** Which of these sentences is probably true?

    A. Skin grafts don't work.

    B. Skin grows on only one part of the body.

    C. A skin graft can save a person's life.

3. A cave is a hole under the ground. Most caves are formed in rock called limestone. Caves are made by water. Water eats away part of the rock. Over many years a small hole or crack in a rock becomes very big. Then it becomes a home for bears or bats. It also becomes a place people want to explore.

_____ **3.** Which of these sentences is probably true?
   A. Water collects in limestone cracks.
   B. Animals stay away from caves.
   C. Caves are open to the sun.

---

4. Could you buy an apple today with a seashell? No, but long ago you could. People used seashells as money. In Africa, you could buy a goat for 100 seashells. You can still find these shells on the beach. They are about the size of a bean. But don't try to buy an apple with them. They're not worth a penny.

_____ **4.** Which of these sentences is probably true?
   A. Long ago it was good to have many seashells.
   B. Today people shop with seashells.
   C. Wood is made from seashells.

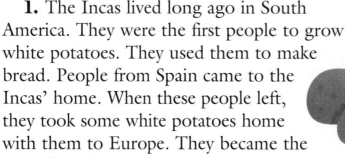

1. The Incas lived long ago in South America. They were the first people to grow white potatoes. They used them to make bread. People from Spain came to the Incas' home. When these people left, they took some white potatoes home with them to Europe. They became the main food for many people there. When the English came to North America, they brought the potatoes back across the sea.

_____ **1.** Which of these sentences is probably true?
   A. Potatoes can grow well in different places.
   B. The Spanish grew the first white potatoes.
   B. White potatoes taste like sweet potatoes.

---

2. Don and his dad walked into the bank. "Where does a bank get money?" Don asked. "The bank gets money from people like us," Dad said. "We put money into a savings account. Then the bank uses that money to cash checks or make loans to people. The bank's money comes from all the money that people put into bank accounts."

_____ **2.** Which of these sentences is probably true?
   A. The bank uses your money for many things.
   B. Banks print the money they lend.
   C. The government takes the bank's money.

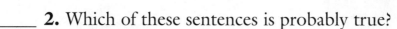

3. Long ago, people made furniture, clothes, and tools at home. Each family worked together to make a certain thing. If you wanted to buy a table, you went to a family who made tables. Back then it took a long time to make things. Now tables, dresses, and other things are made quickly in factories. Then they are shipped to a store. You don't have to wait for what you want. You can just go in and buy it.

_____ **3.** Which of these sentences is probably true?
   A. Things are made faster at home than in a factory.
   B. People come to your home to make things.
   C. Today most things are not made at home.

---

4. A large truck pulled into the driveway. Four men got out of the truck. They pushed up the back door and rolled a large, black object off the truck. It had a set of white keys on one end. Two men pushed it, and two men pulled it. When it was in the house, they screwed on three legs. The men lifted it so that it was right side up. One man sat down to play a song.

_____ **4.** Which of these sentences is probably true?
   A. Playing the piano is easy for everyone.
   B. No one wants to move a piano.
   C. It takes at least four people to move a piano.

1. Every country makes money for people to use. People use coins that are made from metals. Coins might be silver or copper. Gold is too soft for a coin. People use paper money. Paper money might have pictures of kings, queens, or buildings on it. A check is a kind of money, too. A check means you have money in a bank to pay for what you buy.

_____ **1.** Which of these sentences is probably true?
   A. Money looks different in different countries.
   B. Silver coins are the only kind of money.
   C. A check is not as good as money.

2. Beth wanted to find out where her aunt lived. She looked at a map. She found the name of the town. Then she saw a star by the town. Her teacher told her that a star meant the town was the capital of the state. Beth looked at other states on the map. Each state had one town that was marked by a star.

_____ **2.** Which of these sentences is probably true?
   A. Each state has two capitals.
   B. Each state has one capital.
   C. Some states don't have capitals.

3. Sea turtles come out of the water to lay their eggs. The female turtle comes up on the beach when it is dark and no one is there. She digs a hole in the sand. She lays the eggs in the hole and covers them with sand. Then she goes back into the water. The baby turtles hatch in a few weeks. They hurry to get into the water.

_____ **3.** Which of these sentences is probably true?
   A. The mother sea turtle never sees her babies.
   B. Mother sea turtles live on land.
   C. Sea turtles stay to watch the eggs hatch.

4. Venus is the second planet from the sun.
It is close to Earth. It is very bright. It looks like a star in our sky. Venus is almost as big as Earth. There are thick clouds in the sky. They hold the heat from the sun. It is very hot. It is hot enough to melt a car. Venus has tall mountains. They are taller than any on Earth.

_____ **4.** Which of these sentences is probably true?
   A. Venus is bigger than Earth.
   B. You cannot see stars at night on Venus.
   C. It is easy to drive on Venus.

1. Jake and his dad took turns mowing the grass. They tried to cut it once each week. They used a mower with a sharp blade. After many weeks the grass began to look uneven after it was mowed. It was high in some places and low in other places. Jake looked at the blade. It was dull and needed to be sharpened.

_____ **1.** Which of these sentences is probably true?
   A. Jake watched his dad cut the grass all year.
   B. Water made the blade get rusty.
   C. A sharp blade on a mower cuts grass evenly.

2. A dirt road changes over time. When it rains, water washes away some of the dirt. The road becomes very wet and muddy. Cars get stuck in the mud. They make big holes as they try to get out. When the road dries, it has big holes in it. When the weather is hot and dry, the dirt on the road cracks. Some of it blows away.

_____ **2.** Which of these sentences is probably true?
   A. Weather can change a dirt road.
   B. Water helps a dirt road stay smooth.
   C. Muddy roads are fun to drive on.

3. Sam built a fence in his yard. He dug eight deep holes. He put a post in each hole. The posts would hold up the boards for the fence. Sam laid a board across the top of the posts. He used a special tool to see if the posts were all the same height. The tool was called a level. Sam did not start nailing on the boards until the level showed that each post was the same height. He wanted the fence to look just right.

_____ **3.** Which of these sentences is probably true?
   A. A fence should always be painted.
   B. A level helps you see if things are even.
   C. It is easy to make a fence.

4. In the fall the leaves fall off the trees onto the roof. Often they get stuck in the gutters. A gutter on a house catches rain as it runs off the roof. The gutter takes the rain away from the house. The rain runs down a pipe to the ground. If a gutter is filled with leaves, rain does not run away from the house. The gutters fill up, and the water spills over.

_____ **4.** Which of these sentences is probably true?
   A. Gutters hold water for plants.
   B. Things on a roof get washed into the gutter.
   C. Leaves help gutters drain water.

Writing Roundup

Read each story. Then read the question that follows it. Write your answers on the lines below each question.

1. Robert looked at the menu. Every dinner on it cost more than $15, and Robert had $10 for food. Robert put down the menu. He had to get out of there. He had to find a place to eat.

Why did Robert want to leave?

_____

_____

_____

2. Carla took her math book to the library. She made copies of some pages in it. She went home. Now she has the copies, but she doesn't have the book.

Where is Carla's book?

_____

_____

3. Koji got ready to play basketball. He pressed down on the foot pump. It was working. He pumped it up and down about 20 times. Was that enough pumping? One bounce would tell him the answer.

What was Koji doing?

_____

_____

Read the paragraph below. Then answer the questions.

The moving truck was two hours late. Aisha had hoped it would be on time. The moving man didn't have any helpers. Aisha thought he needed help. She did not see how he could do all the work. She thought about talking to the man, but she did not know what to say. The man didn't seem to be very friendly, but he hadn't done anything wrong. Aisha waited. She needed to see how the man loaded her things. She just hoped that nothing would be broken.

1. Why had the moving truck come there?

_____

_____

2. Why doesn't Aisha talk to the man?

_____

_____

3. What kind of person is Aisha?

_____

_____

4. Why does Aisha seem worried?

_____

_____

Spelling
Skills

spelling strategies

What can you do when you aren't sure how to spell a word?

Say the word aloud. Make sure you say it correctly. Listen to the sounds in the word. Think about letters and patterns that might spell the sounds.

Look in the Spelling Table on page 265 to find common spellings for sounds in the word.

Think about related words. They may help you spell the word you're not sure of.

longer—long

Guess the spelling of the word and check it in a dictionary.

Write the word in different ways. Compare the spellings and choose the one that looks correct.

tyger   tieger
 (tiger) tigher

Draw the shape of the word to help you remember its spelling.

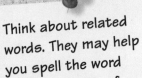 thing

Choose a rhyming helper and use it. A rhyming helper is a word that rhymes with the word and is spelled like it.

fell—bell

Create a memory clue to help you remember the spelling.

<u>Cold</u> has the word <u>old</u>.

Proofreading Marks

Mark	Meaning	Example
◯	spell correctly	I (liek) dogs.
⊙	add period	They are my favorite kind of pet ⊙
?	add question mark	What kind of pet do you have ?
☰	capitalize	My dog's name is scooter
¶	indent paragraph	¶Scooter is my best friend. He wakes me up every morning. He sleeps with me every night. He plays with me all the time.
⌄⌄ ⌄⌄	add quotation marks	"You are a good dog," I tell him.

Words with Short a

van	an	after	flat	hand	cat
and	has	am	than	add	man

Say and Listen

Say each spelling word. Listen for the vowel sound you hear in van.

cat

Think and Sort

The vowel sound in van is called short a. All of the spelling words have the short a sound. It is spelled a. Spell each word aloud.

Look at the letters in each word. Is the short a at the beginning or in the middle of the word?

1. Write the **five** spelling words that have short a at the beginning, like add.

2. Write the **seven** spelling words that have short a in the middle, like van.

1. Beginning Short a

_____   _____

_____   _____

_____

2. Middle Short a

_____   _____

_____   _____

_____

Clues

Write the spelling word for each clue.

1. pet that meows _____

2. part of an arm _____

3. what you can do with numbers _____

4. the opposite of **before** _____

5. what a boy grows up to be _____

Letter Scramble

Unscramble the letters in dark type to make a spelling word. Write the word to complete the sentence.

6. na   I ate _____ apple.

7. hant His friend is older _____ he is.

8. ahs   Rita is not here because she _____ a cold.

9. ma   You are tall, but I _____ short.

10. latf The top of a table is _____.

11. dna Sam likes blue _____ purple.

van	an	after	flat	hand	cat
and	has	am	than	add	man

Proofreading

Proofread the report below. Use these proofreading marks to correct four spelling mistakes, one capitalization mistake, and one punctuation mistake. See the chart on page 131 to learn how to use the proofreading marks.

Proofreading Marks

◯ spell correctly
≡ capitalize
⊙ add period

Science Field Trip   Monday, October 3

1. Where did you go?

we went to Lance Wildlife Park.

2. What did you see?

A mann held a baby bottle in his handd.

He fed a baby tiger We saw ane alligator swim.

3. What did you like best?

I liked the elephant best. I amm glad we went.

Language Connection

Capital Letters

Use a capital letter to begin the first word of a sentence.

| My cat climbs trees all the time. |

Choose the correct word in dark type to complete each sentence. Then write the sentence correctly. Remember to begin the sentence with a capital letter.

1. my (**cat**, **and**) is stuck in a tree.

_____

2. a (**flat**, **man**) comes to help.

_____

3. he (**hand**, **has**) a ladder.

_____

4. she jumps down (**after**, **and**) runs home.

_____

More Words with Short a

catch	fast	matter	have	land	that
back	last	thank	ask	sang	black

catch

Say and Listen

Say each spelling word. Listen for the short a sound.

Think and Sort

All of the spelling words have the short a sound. It is spelled a. Spell each word aloud.

Look at the letters in each spelling word. Is the short a at the beginning or in the middle of the word?

1. Write the **one** word that has short a at the beginning.

2. Write the **eleven** words that have short a in the middle, like back and fast. One word has an e at the end, but the e is silent. Circle the word.

1. Beginning Short **a**

_____

2. Middle Short **a**

_____   _____

_____   _____

_____   _____

_____   _____

_____

Word Groups

Write the spelling word that belongs in each group.

1. danced, acted, _____

2. sea, sky, _____

3. orange, yellow, _____

4. throw, hit, _____

5. quick, swift, _____

6. had, has, _____

Rhymes

Write the spelling word that completes each
sentence and rhymes with the underlined word.

7. Why did Dee _____ for that silly <u>mask</u>?

8. Hector wanted to _____ me for the piggy <u>bank</u>.

9. What is the _____ with the pancake <u>batter</u>?

10. Ming ran around the <u>track</u> and _____ home.

11. What is the name of _____ <u>cat</u>?

catch	fast	matter	have	land	that
back	last	thank	ask	sang	black

Proofreading

Proofread the letter below. Use proofreading marks to correct four spelling mistakes, one capitalization mistake, and one punctuation mistake.

Proofreading Marks

◯ spell correctly
≡ capitalize
⊙ add period

Sidney,

Do you know where I can cach bus

145? Thet bus will take me to my piano lesson.

I love to play. Laste week I learned a new

song. my teacher will aske me to play it

Maybe I will play it for you, too.

Max

Language Connection

Periods

Use a period at the end of a sentence that tells something.

Camels live in the desert.

Choose the word from the sun below that completes each sentence. Then write the sentence correctly. Remember to put a period at the end.

fast   **back**   **land**   **have**

1. A camel can carry people on its _____

   _____

2. Some camels _____ one hump

   _____

3. Camels can run _____

   _____

4. They run across dry _____

   _____

Words with Short e

ten	when	bed	shelf	jet	yes
said	went	kept	says	next	end

bed

Say and Listen

Say each spelling word. Listen for the vowel sound you hear in ten.

Think and Sort

The vowel sound in bed is called short e.
All of the spelling words have the short e sound.
Spell each word aloud.

Look at the letters in each word. Think about how short e is spelled.

1. Write the **ten** spelling words that have short e spelled e, like ten.

2. Write the **one** spelling word that has short e spelled ay.

3. Write the **one** spelling word that has short e spelled ai.

1. e Words

_____   _____

_____   _____

_____   _____

_____   _____

_____   _____

2. ay Word   3. ai Word

_____   _____

Word Math

Add and subtract letters and picture names. Write each spelling word.

1. b +  − sl = _____

2. sh + ___ = _____

3. w + ___ = _____

4. ___ − am + et = _____

5. ___ − p + d = _____

Word Groups

Write the spelling word that belongs in each group.

6. near, beside, _____

7. told, asked, _____

8. saved, stored, _____

9. eight, nine, _____

10. no, maybe, _____

11. tells, asks, _____

ten	when	bed	shelf	jet	yes
said	went	kept	says	next	end

Proofreading

Proofread the postcard below.
Use proofreading marks to
correct four spelling mistakes,
one capitalization mistake,
and one punctuation mistake.

Proofreading Marks

⬭ spell correctly

≡ capitalize

⊙ add period

Dear Lan,

  We wint on a train trip When the

train turned a big corner, we saw the

train car at the very ende! I slept in the

top bed. ted slept in the bottom one.

He sayd the sounds kept him awake.

I slept great. I want you to come with

us naxt time.

Love, Fern

Lan Chin

12 Ventura Dr.

Cleveland, OH

44108

Sentences

A sentence begins with a capital letter and ends with a period or other end mark. Unscramble each sentence and write it correctly.

1. ten cats my friend has

_____

2. hid they under the bed

_____

3. on a shelf they sat

_____

4. they toy played mouse with a

_____

More Words with Short e

best	well	any	seven	many	dress
desk	rest	bell	send	help	egg

bell

Say and Listen

Say each spelling word. Listen for the short e sound.

Think and Sort

Look at the letters in each word. Think about how short e is spelled. How many spellings for short e do you see?

1. Write the **ten** spelling words that have short e spelled e, like desk.

2. Write the **two** spelling words that have short e spelled a, like any.

1. e Words

_____   _____

_____   _____

_____   _____

_____   _____

_____   _____

2. a Words

_____   _____

Word Groups

Write the spelling word that belongs in each group.

1. five, six, _____

2. several, lots, _____

3. table, chair, _____

4. good, better, _____

5. one, every, _____

6. good, fine, _____

What's Missing?

Write the missing spelling word.

7. the chicken and the _____

8. ring the _____

9. _____ an e-mail

10. _____ when you're tired

11. a woman's _____

best	well	any	seven	many	dress
desk	rest	bell	send	help	egg

Proofreading

Proofread the diary page below.
Use proofreading marks to
correct four spelling mistakes,
one capitalization mistake, and
one punctuation mistake.

Proofreading
Marks

◯ spell correctly

≡ capitalize

? add question
mark

Dear Diary,

What will I do with so meny baby turtles

Grandfather can take sevan. Riley says she

does not want eny. I asked Mom if I could

keep just one. that is the bist idea. She says I

can. I will take good care of my baby turtle.

That's all for today.

Dictionary Skills

Using the Spelling Table

A spelling table can help you find a word in a dictionary. It shows different spellings for a sound. Suppose you are not sure how to spell the last sound in **pick**. Is it **c**, **k**, **ch**, or **ck**? First, find the sound and the example words in the table. Then read the first spelling for the sound and look up **pic** in a dictionary. Look for each spelling in the dictionary until you find the correct one.

Sound	Example Words	Spellings
k	can, keep, school, sick	c k ch ck

Use the Spelling Table on page 265 and a dictionary to write the missing letters in the picture names.

1.  _____ ity

2. bla _____

3.  _____ ale

4. s _____ ool

5. mou _____ e

6. sn _____ l

People Words

had	class	him	you	children	boys
our	girls	the	them	her	child

Say and Listen

Say the spelling words. Listen to the sounds in each word.

girls

Think and Sort

Look at the letters in each word. Think about how each sound in the word is spelled. Spell each word aloud.

1. Write the **six** spelling words that have three letters, like him.

2. Write the **six** spelling words that have more than three letters, like boys.

1. Three Letters

_____   _____

_____   _____

_____   _____

2. More Than Three Letters

_____   _____

_____   _____

_____   _____

Letter Scramble

Unscramble the letters in dark type to make a spelling word. Write the word to complete the sentence.

1. **hmet** The lions have their cubs with _____.

2. **reh** That is _____ new dress.

3. **hte** I saw a baby bird at _____ park.

4. **lascs** My _____ went to the zoo.

5. **cdlnerhi** Young people are called _____.

6. **lihdc** The little _____ had a toy boat.

7. **rou** Four people will fit in _____ car.

Rhymes

Write the spelling word that completes each sentence and rhymes with the underlined word.

8. Do you know what <u>Dad</u> _____?

9. Those two _____ have lots of <u>toys</u>.

10. Happy birthday <u>to</u> _____!

11. Did you see _____ <u>swim</u>?

had	class	him	you	children	boys
our	girls	the	them	her	child

Proofreading

Proofread the journal page below. Use proofreading marks to correct four spelling mistakes, one capitalization mistake, and one punctuation mistake.

Proofreading Marks

◯ spell correctly
≡ capitalize
⊙ add period

September 2

Today was my first day at Pine School. I had fun. My clas has twenty childrin. There are three new gurls, counting me

I played tag with Ellie and Adam at recess. when the bell rang, I knew I had made new friends. Owr teacher seems nice, too!

Dictionary Skills

ABC Order

Look at a dictionary. The first word begins with an **a**. The last word begins with a **z**. The words in a dictionary are in ABC order. This order is also called alphabetical order.

Write the missing letters in the alphabet.

a ___ c d ___ f ___ ___ i j k ___ m

n ___ p q ___ ___ t u v ___ x y ___

Write these words in alphabetical order.

1. _____

2. _____

3. _____

4. _____

5. _____

6. _____

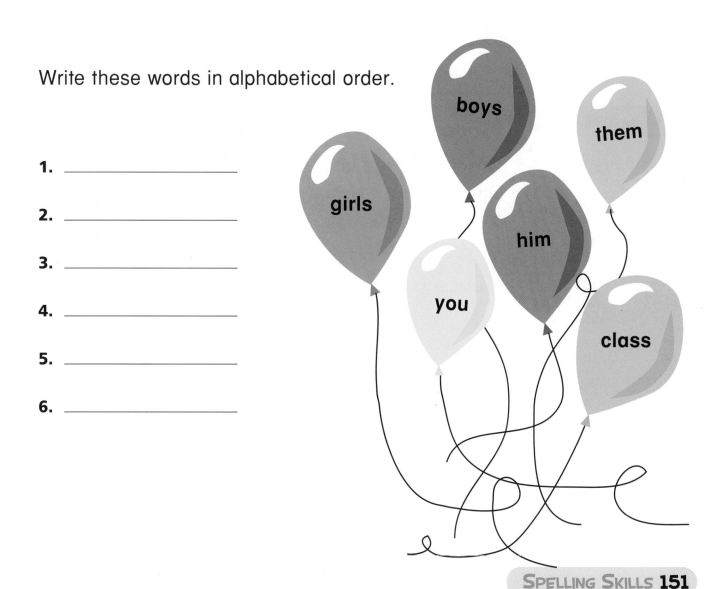

unit 1 review
Lessons 1-5

LESSON **1**

am

after

than

hand

Words with Short *a*

Write the spelling word that completes each sentence.

1. Look at the shell in my _____.

2. I _____ going
   to have strawberry jam.

3. What did they want to do

   _____ the show?

4. I ran faster _____ James did.

LESSON **2**

ask

have

catch

that

More Words with Short *a*

Unscramble the letters in dark type to make a spelling
word. Then write the word
to complete the sentence.

5. **hatt**   Is _____ your puppy?

6. **ska**   Let's _____ them to come
   with us.

7. **avhe**   Did you _____ fun
   at the pool?

8. **tchac**   I can _____ a football.

LESSON 3

kept

when

says

said

Words with Short e

Write the spelling word for each definition.

9. speaks _____

10. stored _____

11. at what time _____

12. talked _____

LESSON 4

seven

egg

many

any

More Words with Short e

Write the spelling word for each clue.

13. This is what a baby bird comes from.

_____

14. You have this when you have a lot

of things. _____

15. This is one of several. _____

16. Four and three make this. _____

LESSON 5

our

you

girls

children

People Words

Write the missing spelling word.

17. a cake for me and _____

18. games for boys and _____

19. mothers and their _____

20. your team and _____ team

Words with Short i

big	will	fill	this	pick	hid
ship	six	hill	wind	his	trick

ship

Say and Listen

Say each spelling word. Listen for the vowel sound you hear in big.

Think and Sort

The vowel sound you hear in big is called short i. All the spelling words have the short i sound. Spell each word aloud.

Look at the letters in each word. Think about how short i is spelled.

1. Write the **four** spelling words that have three letters.

2. Write the **seven** spelling words that have four letters.

3. Write the **one** spelling word that has five letters.

1. **Three Letters**

_____   _____

_____   _____

2. **Four Letters**

_____   _____

_____   _____

_____

3. **Five Letters** _____

Clues

Write the spelling word for each clue.

1. something you can climb   _____

2. a big boat   _____

3. to play a joke on someone   _____

4. the number after five   _____

5. what makes a kite fly   _____

Rhymes

Write the spelling word that completes each sentence and rhymes with the underlined word.

6. <u>Jill</u>, please _____ my glass

   with water.

7. Luis said that _____ hat <u>is</u> lost.

8. That <u>wig</u> is too _____ for my head.

9. <u>Mick</u> will _____ an apple from that tree.

10. I will <u>miss</u> riding _____ pony.

11. Marco _____ <u>still</u> be here tomorrow.

big	will	fill	this	pick	hid
ship	six	hill	wind	his	trick

Proofreading

Proofread the letter below. Use proofreading marks to correct four spelling mistakes, one capitalization mistake, and one punctuation mistake.

Proofreading Marks

◯ spell correctly
≡ capitalize
⊙ add period

Hi, Jason!

   I just got a new model ship. Now I have sixe

If I had to pik my favorite one, it would be the

sailing ship. it is very big. The sails really work, too.

When the winde hits them, they fil with air. The

ship looks great sailing on the water! What is

your favorite kind of ship?

                              Ryan

Question Marks

Use a question mark at the end of
a sentence that asks a question.

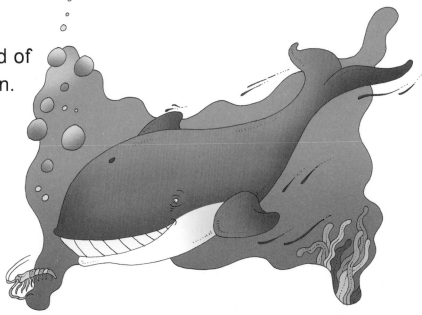

> What is the biggest
> animal in the world**?**
> Where is it found**?**

Choose the correct word in dark type to complete each question.
Then write the question correctly. Remember to end it with a
question mark.

1. How (**big**, **pick**) is a blue whale

_____

2. Is it as large as a (**ship**, **six**)

_____

3. What does (**this**, **trick**) animal eat

_____

4. Can you see (**hid**, **his**) tail

_____

More Words with Short i

ring	fish	thing	spring	live	swim
give	think	wish	with	sister	bring

Say and Listen

Say each spelling word. Listen for the short i sound.

fish

Think and Sort

All of the spelling words have the short i sound. Spell each word aloud.

Look at the letters in each word. Think about how short i is spelled.

1. Write the **seven** spelling words that have four letters. Two of the words with four letters have an e at the end, but the e is silent. Circle these words.

2. Write the **three** spelling words that have five letters.

3. Write the **two** spelling words that have six letters.

1. Four Letters

2. Five Letters

3. Six Letters

Rhymes

Write the spelling word that completes each
sentence and rhymes with the underlined word.

1. Birds <u>sing</u> in the _____.

2. The fried _____ was on the <u>dish</u>.

3. The <u>king</u> wore a shiny gold _____.

4. I _____ Ben is at the skating <u>rink</u>.

5. Please _____ us some <u>string</u> for the kite.

Word Meaning

Write the spelling word for each meaning. Use a dictionary
if you need to.

6. to hope for something _____

7. to hand something over _____

8. a girl with the same parents as another child _____

9. an object _____

10. to move through water _____

11. having _____

ring	fish	thing	spring	live	swim
give	think	wish	with	sister	bring

Proofreading

Proofread this paragraph from a newspaper article. Use proofreading marks to correct four spelling mistakes, one capitalization mistake, and one punctuation mistake.

Proofreading Marks

◯ spell correctly

≡ capitalize

? add question mark

It is time to plant gardens! First, thnk about what you want to plant. Do you want to grow flowers or vegetables Then head out to your yard. Brang your shovel witt you. it is the best thinge for getting the soil ready for seeds.

Vegetables Finest Quality Seeds

Flowers Finest Quality Seeds

Dictionary Skills

ABC Order

When two words begin with the same letter, use the second letter to put the words in alphabetical order. Look at the words in the box. **Bell** comes before **big** because **e** comes before **i** in the alphabet.

Bell	Big

Read each pair of words. Write the word that comes first in ABC order.

1. swim, sister _____

2. got, give _____

3. ring, run _____

4. luck, live _____

5. spring, stick _____

6. thing, trick _____

7. woman, wish _____

Words with Short o

hot	dot	block	job	top	hop
what	not	was	jog	on	got

block

Say and Listen

Say each spelling word. Listen for the vowel sound you hear in hot.

Think and Sort

The vowel sound you hear in hot is called short o. All the spelling words have the short o sound. Spell each word aloud.

Look at the letters in each word. Think about how short o is spelled. How many spellings for short o do you see?

1. Write the **ten** spelling words that have short o spelled o, like dot.

2. Write the **two** spelling words that have short o spelled a, like was.

1. o Words

_____   _____

_____   _____

_____   _____

_____   _____

_____   _____

2. a Words

_____   _____

Word Groups

Write the spelling word that belongs in each group.

1. run, trot, _____

2. cold, warm, _____

3. skip, jump, _____

4. spot, mark, _____

5. work, chore, _____

6. town, street, _____

7. took, grabbed, _____

Presto Change-O

Change the order of each word in dark type
to make a spelling word. Write the spelling word
to complete the sentence.

8. no   Please turn _____ the light.

9. ton   Do _____ touch the oven!

10. thaw   Please tell me _____ this is.

11. saw   Who _____ at the door?

hot	dot	block	job	top	hop
what	not	was	jog	on	got

Proofreading

Proofread the sign below. Use proofreading marks to correct four spelling mistakes, one capitalization mistake, and one punctuation mistake.

Proofreading Marks

◯ spell correctly
≡ capitalize
⊙ add period

Jason's Pet Care

do you have a cat or a dog? I can care for it when you are nat home My name is Jason White. I live un this blok. My phone number is 555-4100. Call and tell me wat you need. I will give you a good price. I will also take great care of your pet.

Capital Letters

Use a capital letter for the word **I** and
to begin the names of people and pets.

Choose the correct word in dark type to complete
each sentence. Then write the sentence. Remember
to use capital letters.

1. corey jones wanted to go for a (**jog**, **got**).

_____

2. He and i ran around the (**block**, **dot**).

_____

3. i saw rusty (**top**, **hop**) on the porch.

_____

4. She (**not**, **got**) the paper.

_____

5. rusty (**was**, **what**) running fast.

_____

More Words with Short o

box	rock	want	clock	chop	pond
wash	spot	drop	stop	ox	shop

pond

Say and Listen

Say each spelling word. Listen for the short o sound.

Think and Sort

All of the spelling words have the short o sound. Spell each word aloud.

Look at the letters in each word. Think about how short o is spelled. How many spellings for short o do you see?

1. Write the **ten** spelling words that have short o spelled o, like shop.

2. Write the **two** spelling words that have short o spelled a, like want.

1. o Words

_____   _____

_____   _____

_____   _____

_____   _____

_____   _____

2. a Words

_____   _____

Word Groups

Write the spelling word that belongs in each group.

1. time, watch, _____

2. wish, need, _____

3. wait, quit, _____

4. cut, slice, _____

5. cow, horse, _____

6. ocean, lake, _____

7. clean, scrub, _____

More Than One Meaning

Some words have more than one meaning. Complete each pair of sentences with the correct spelling word.

8. We like to _____ at that store.

   I buy my skates at a sports _____.

9. There's a dirty _____ on my dress.

   Put the book in that _____.

10. I just felt a _____ of rain.

    That glass will break if you _____ it.

11. I found this _____ in my back yard.

    Will you _____ the baby?

box	rock	want	clock	chop	pond
wash	spot	drop	stop	ox	shop

Proofreading

Proofread the note below. Use proofreading marks to correct four spelling mistakes, one capitalization mistake, and one punctuation mistake.

Proofreading Marks

○ spell correctly

≡ capitalize

? add question mark

Mom,

Can we go shopping at the new supermarket today? We need some soap to wosh our hands. i would like a bax of cereal. Can I have the kind with nuts Maybe we can shopp for a new clok, too. Dad says he wants one with big numbers.

milk
eggs
bread
fruit
soup

Dictionary Skills

Word Meanings

The dictionary entry for a word gives its meaning.

> **ox** *plural* **oxen.** A male animal of the cattle family. *A strong ox is a useful farm animal.* ← **meaning**

Write the word from the box below that names each picture. Then find each word in a dictionary. Complete the meaning for the word.

pond   ox   spot   rock

Word		Meaning
1. _____		a male animal of the _____ family
2. _____		a small body of _____
3. _____		a _____ mark
4. _____		_____ stone

Plural Words

men	eggs	vans	hands	jets	desks
dresses	ships	cats	jobs	bells	backs

Say and Listen

Say the spelling words.
Listen to the ending sounds.

cats

Think and Sort

All of the spelling words are plural words.
Plural words name more than one thing. Spell each word aloud.

Most plural words end in s or es. Look at the letters in each word.

1. Write the **ten** words that end in s, like hands.

2. Write the **one** word that ends in es.

3. Write the **one** word that does not end in s or es.

1. Plural with **s**

_____   _____

_____   _____

_____   _____

_____   _____

_____   _____

2. Plural with **es**   3. Other Plural

_____   _____

Clues

Write the spelling word for each clue.

1. what women wear _____

2. things to ring _____

3. big boats _____

4. what chickens lay _____

Letter Scramble

Unscramble the letters in dark type to make a
spelling word. Write the word to complete the sentence.

5. **navs**   The school _____ have ten seats.

6. **bosj**   Both my brothers have _____.

7. **cabks**   These chairs have tall _____.

8. **nem**   Those _____ are my uncles.

9. **shand**   My _____ are in my pockets.

10. **tejs**   Two _____ flew across the sky.

11. **kedss**   We sit at the _____ in our classroom.

Plural Words

men	eggs	vans	hands	jets	desks
dresses	ships	cats	jobs	bells	backs

Proofreading

Proofread the letter below. Use proofreading marks to correct four spelling mistakes, one capitalization mistake, and one punctuation mistake.

Proofreading Marks

⬯ spell correctly

≡ capitalize

⊙ add period

James,

I went to the circus on its last day here. I watched the workers do their jobz. I saw mens put big cats in cages Some workers carried boxes on their backes, to put in vanz. they're going to your town next!

Sam

Dictionary Skills

Entry Words

A singular word names one thing. To find a plural word in a dictionary, look for its singular form. For example, to find **cats**, look for **cat**.

> **cat** *plural* **cats.** A small furry animal. *Why is a **cat** a good pet? (Because it is purr-fect!)*

Write these plural words in alphabetical order. Then look each one up in a dictionary. Write the entry word and its page number.

Plural	Entry Word	Page
1. _____	_____	_____
2. _____	_____	_____
3. _____	_____	_____

LESSON **6** Words with Short i

six
this
will
pick

Write the spelling word for each meaning.

1. to choose something _____

2. the number before seven _____

3. going to _____

4. the thing here _____

LESSON **7**

live
give
think
sister

More Words with Short i

Write the spelling word for each clue.

5. what you do with a present _____

6. what a girl can be _____

7. what you do with your brain _____

8. what you do in your home _____

LESSON 8

not

block

was

what

Words with Short o

Write the spelling word that completes each sentence.

9. I put a red _____ on top of the blue one.

10. Mr. Silva _____ not at school yesterday.

11. Tell me _____ you want to eat.

12. Leo is going, but I am _____ .

LESSON 9

stop

clock

want

wash

More Words with Short o

Unscramble the letters in dark type to make a spelling word. Write the word to complete the sentence.

13. natw I _____ to go home now.

14. locck The _____ has stopped ticking.

15. stpo Please _____ the car at the corner.

16. shwa I have to _____ this messy shirt.

LESSON 10

hands

desks

dresses

men

Plural Words

Write the spelling word that belongs in each group.

17. ears, _____ , feet

18. tables, chairs, _____

19. women, _____ , children

20. _____ , coats, hats

Words with Short u

sun	club	bug	mud	bus	up	of
under	run	from	summer	us	cut	but

bus

Say and Listen

Say each spelling word. Listen for the vowel sound you hear in sun.

Think and Sort

The vowel sound in sun is called short u. All of the spelling words have the short u sound. Spell each word aloud.

Look at the letters in each word. Think about how short u is spelled. How many spellings for short u do you see?

1. Write the **twelve** spelling words that have short u spelled u, like sun.

2. Write the **two** spelling words that have short u spelled o, like from.

1. u Words

_____   _____

_____   _____

_____   _____

_____   _____

_____   _____

_____   _____

2. o Words

_____   _____

Antonyms

Antonyms are words that have opposite meanings. Write the spelling word that is an antonym of each underlined word.

1. climb <u>down</u> the pole   _____

2. <u>over</u> the trees   _____

3. a letter <u>to</u> you   _____

4. gave <u>them</u> a gift   _____

5. <u>winter</u> days   _____

6. everyone <u>including</u> me   _____

7. <u>walk</u> to the store   _____

Hink Pinks

Hink pinks are funny pairs of rhyming words. Read each clue. Write the spelling word that completes each hink pink.

8. a big thing that Gus drives   Gus _____

9. what you can have on a sunny day   _____ fun

10. a place to get your hair trimmed   _____ hut

11. what a baby bear uses for golf   cub _____

12. a mat made for ants and beetles   _____ rug

13. a baby rose made of dirt and water   _____ bud

sun	club	bug	mud	bus	up	of
under	run	from	summer	us	cut	but

Proofreading

Proofread the ad below. Use proofreading marks to correct four spelling mistakes, one capitalization mistake, and one punctuation mistake.

Proofreading Marks

◯ spell correctly
≡ capitalize
⊙ add period

Come to Camp Beans!

You can hike upp a hill and catch a buge. you can sit in the sunn or read undr a tree You can even swim and fish in Beans Lake. Join us for the summer!

Call (101) 001-1010

Action Words

Some words in a sentence tell what someone does or did.
These words are called action words.

> hop   skips   talked   ran

Complete each sentence with an action word from one of the boxes.

cut   jump   shut   run   dug

1. I _____ races with my brother.

2. My mother _____ my hair.

3. How high can you _____?

4. Please _____ the door.

5. The mole _____ a hole.

More Words with Short u

just	jump	come	skunk	truck	lunch	other
brother	such	love	much	mother	one	fun

Say and Listen

Say each spelling word. Listen for the short u sound.

skunk

Think and Sort

All of the spelling words have the short u sound. Spell each word aloud.

Look at the letters in each word. Think about how short u is spelled.

1. Write the **eight** spelling words that have short u spelled u, like just.

2. Write the **six** spelling words that have short u spelled o, like come. Circle the three words that have a silent e at the end.

1. u Words

_____   _____

_____   _____

_____   _____

_____   _____

2. o Words

_____   _____

_____   _____

_____   _____

Word Meanings

Write the spelling word for each meaning.
Use a dictionary if you need to.

1. a good time _____

2. a lot _____

3. exactly _____

4. very _____

5. to like a lot _____

6. different _____

Partner Words

Complete each sentence. Write the spelling word that goes
with the underlined word.

7. The cats <u>go</u> out in the morning and _____ in at night.

8. A rabbit can <u>hop</u>. A frog can _____.

9. The girl is a <u>sister</u>. The boy is a _____.

10. A <u>father</u> is a man. A _____ is a woman.

11. We eat _____ at noon and <u>dinner</u> at six.

12. I have _____ nose and <u>two</u> eyes.

13. Will we ride in a _____ or fly in a <u>plane</u>?

just	jump	come	skunk	truck	lunch	other
brother	such	love	much	mother	one	fun

Proofreading

Proofread the letter below. Use proofreading marks to correct four spelling mistakes, one capitalization mistake, and one punctuation mistake

Proofreading Marks

◯ spell correctly

≡ capitalize

? add question mark

Ben,

We got a skunk! My muther and i put him in

our garage. He is fun to watch. Mom jist came

home in the truk. It is time for lonch. Will you

come over and see our skunk this afternoon

Theo

Exclamation Points

Use an exclamation point at the end of a sentence that shows strong feeling or surprise.

> My frog won a blue ribbon!

The words in each sentence below are out of order. Put the words in order and write the sentence correctly. Remember to put an exclamation point at the end.

1. are fun Frog contests

_____

2. at has my brother frog Look the

_____

3. can jump high very That frog

_____

4. feet It jump more can ten than

_____

Words with Long a

game	today	play	whale	name	brave	maybe
baby	came	bake	ate	say	stay	gave

Say and Listen

Say each spelling word. Listen for the vowel sound you hear in game.

whales

Think and Sort

The vowel sound in game is called long a.
All of the spelling words have the long a sound. Spell each word aloud.

Look at the letters in each word. Think about how long a is spelled.

1. Write the **eight** words with long a spelled a-consonant-e, like game.

2. Write the **five** words with long a spelled ay, like stay.

3. Write the **one** word with long a spelled a.

1. a-consonant-e Words

_____   _____

_____   _____

_____   _____

_____   _____

2. ay Words

_____   _____

_____   _____

_____

3. a Word

_____

Synonyms

Synonyms are words that have the same meaning.
Write the spelling word that is a synonym for each word below.

1. cook _____

2. fearless _____

3. speak _____

4. perhaps _____

5. wait _____

Word Meanings

Write the spelling word for each meaning.
Use a dictionary if you need to.

6. to have fun _____

7. this day _____

8. contest played with rules _____

9. handed over _____

10. what a person or thing is called _____

11. swallowed food _____

12. a young child _____

13. moved towards _____

game	today	play	whale	name	brave	maybe
baby	came	bake	ate	say	stay	gave

Proofreading

Proofread the diary page below. Use proofreading marks to correct four spelling mistakes, one capitalization mistake, and one punctuation mistake.

Proofreading Marks

◯ spell correctly

≡ capitalize

⊙ add period

December 12

Dear Diary,

Alex tate cam to my home. We ate

snacks. Then we talked about the gaem.

Alex said that the best pley was at the

end Then he gave me a football with his

name on it. I can't wait to show it to Jake.

Todae was a great day!

Dictionary Skills

ABC Order

The words in a dictionary are in ABC order. Many words begin with the same letter, so the second letter is used to put them in ABC order.

Look at the two words below. Both words begin with **b**. The second letter must be used to put the words in ABC order. The letter **a** comes before **r**, so **bag** comes before **break**.

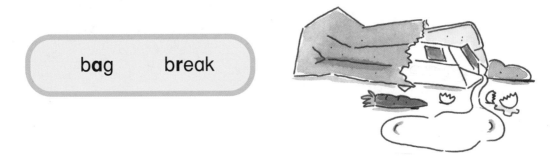

bag   break

Write the following words in alphabetical order.

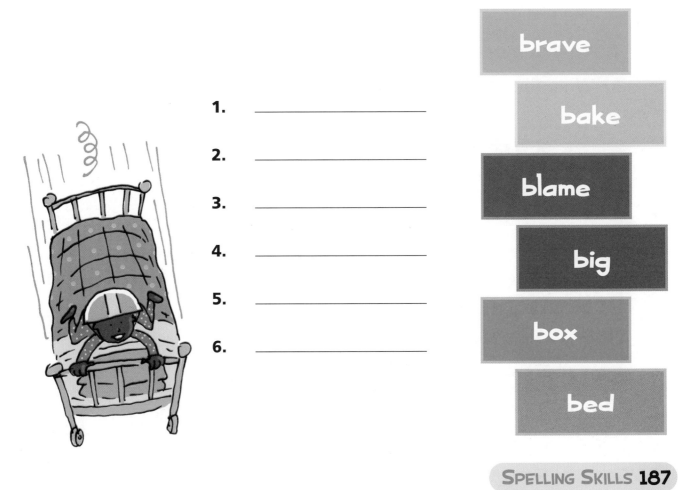

1. _____

2. _____

3. _____

4. _____

5. _____

6. _____

brave

bake

blame

big

box

bed

More Words with Long a

chain	eight	paint	pail	snail	wait	train
gain	tail	nail	they	rain	mail	sail

Say and Listen

Say each spelling word. Listen for the long a sound.

train

Think and Sort

All of the spelling words have the long a sound. Spell each word aloud.

Look at the letters in each word. Think about how long a is spelled. How many spellings for long a do you see?

1. Write the **twelve** spelling words that have long a spelled ai, like pail.

2. Write the **one** spelling word that has long a spelled ei.

3. Write the **one** spelling word that has long a spelled ey.

---

1. ai Words

_____   _____

_____   _____

_____   _____

_____   _____

_____   _____

_____   _____

2. ei Word   **3. ey Word**

_____   _____

Word Groups

Write the spelling word that belongs in each group.

1. wind, snow, _____

2. boat, plane, _____

3. hammer, saw, _____

4. grow, add, _____

5. draw, color, _____

6. turtle, worm, _____

7. he, she, _____

8. leash, rope, _____

Homophones

Homophones are words that sound the same but have different spellings and meanings. Complete each sentence by writing the spelling word that is a homophone for the underlined word.

9. The _____ for your boat is on <u>sale</u>.

10. He turned <u>pale</u> when he dropped the _____.

11. Jesse <u>ate</u> breakfast at _____.

12. I had to _____ for him to lift the <u>weight</u>.

13. The <u>tale</u> was about a cat with a long _____.

chain	eight	paint	pail	snail	wait	train
gain	tail	nail	they	rain	mail	sail

Proofreading

Proofread the letter below. Use proofreading marks to correct four spelling mistakes, one capitalization mistake, and one punctuation mistake.

Proofreading Marks

⬭ spell correctly

☰ capitalize

? add question mark

625 Oak Street

Columbus, OH 43216

June 10, 2004

Dear Andrew,

    I can't waite until you come to see me! are you

going to take the trane I am getting a pet snale

in eighte days. I will let you hold it.

Your friend,

Malik

More Than One Meaning

Some words have more than one meaning. Read the entry for **paint** in a dictionary. **Paint** has two meanings. Each meaning has a number in front of it.

> **paint 1.** *plural* **paints.** Something to color with. *We bought blue paint for the walls in my room.* **2.** To cover something with paint. *Please don't paint our front porch and steps purple!* **painted, painting**

Write **I** or **2** to tell which meaning of **paint** is used in each sentence.

1. My father will paint my room yellow. _____

2. We bought the paint for my room yesterday. _____

3. I spilled paint on the rug. _____

4. Will you help me paint the fence? _____

5. Do you want to draw or paint? _____

Words with ed or ing

helping	wishing	fishing	picking	handed	thinking	fished
tricked	ended	wished	dressing	thanked	asked	catching

Say and Listen

Say the spelling words.
Listen for the ending sounds.

fishing

Think and Sort

A **base word** is a word that can be used to make other words.

Each spelling word is made of a base word and the ending ed or ing.

Look at each word. Think about the base word and the ending.
Spell each word aloud.

1. Write the **seven** spelling words that end in ed, like fished.

2. Write the **seven** spelling words that end in ing, like fishing.

1. ed Words

_____   _____

_____   _____

_____   _____

_____

2. ing Words

_____   _____

_____   _____

_____   _____

_____

Antonyms

Antonyms are words that have opposite meanings. Write the spelling word that is an antonym of each word below.

1. answered   _____

2. began   _____

3. hurting   _____

4. throwing   _____

Clues

Write the spelling word for each clue.

5. what you did if you caught some fish   _____

6. what you did if you were polite   _____

7. what you did when you hoped   _____

8. sitting with bait at the end of a pole   _____

9. taking an apple from a tree   _____

10. putting clothes on   _____

11. what someone did to play a joke on you   _____

12. what you are doing if you are hoping   _____

13. using your brain   _____

helping	wishing	fishing	picking	handed	thinking	fished
tricked	ended	wished	dressing	thanked	asked	catching

Proofreading

Proofread the paragraph below. Use proofreading marks to correct four spelling mistakes, one capitalization mistake, and one punctuation mistake.

Proofreading Marks

◯ spell correctly

≡ capitalize

⊙ add period

The race ended, and Turtle won. He thankd Owl for the ribbon Rabbit felt triked. he wishd that he had won. Rabbit was not very smart. He should not have gone fisheng.

Present and Past Tenses

Words that end with ed tell about the past. Words that end with ing tell about now or something that keeps going on. Write the word from the gift box that completes each sentence.

1. I _____ Pam rake leaves when it started to rain.

2. I like _____ Pam, but not in the rain!

3. Yesterday I _____ for directions to Jim's party.

4. I got lost on the way, so I kept _____ for directions.

5. My brother _____ me into doing his chores.

6. Everyone was _____ me on April Fool's Day.

LESSON 11

cut
under
from
of

Words with Short u

Write the spelling word that completes each sentence and rhymes with the underlined word.

1. The <u>thunder</u> sent little Jim _____ the bed.

2. Victoria and I <u>love</u> the color _____ the sky.

3. It is hard to _____ a <u>nut</u>.

4. The <u>hum</u> came _____ my room.

LESSON 12

much
just
other
come

More Words with Short u

Unscramble the letters in dark type to make a spelling word. Write the word to complete the sentence.

5. **emoc** Will Grandmother _____ to the party?

6. **sjut** This book is _____ what I wanted.

7. **umhc** We ate too _____ popcorn at the movie.

8. **tehor** Mom liked the _____ shirt more than this one.

gave

maybe

say

baby

Words with Long *a*

Write the spelling word that goes with the underlined word or words.

9. A <u>mother</u> is big. A _____ is small.

10. We <u>sing</u> songs. We _____ words.

11. Tim <u>handed</u> me a frog. I _____ it right back.

12. Mom and Dad didn't say <u>yes</u> or <u>no</u>. They said

_____.

train

wait

eight

they

More Words with Long *a*

Write the spelling word that completes each sentence.

13. My dog had _____ puppies.

14. The _____ was an hour late.

15. I will _____ for you after school.

16. Are _____ your brothers?

asked

thanked

helping

thinking

Words with ed or ing

Write the spelling word for each meaning.

17. using the mind _____

18. questioned someone _____

19. said that you were grateful _____

20. doing something useful _____

Words with Long e

we	people	she	keep	these	street	being
see	green	he	feet	bees	week	three

Say and Listen

Say each spelling word. Listen for the vowel sound you hear in we.

bee

Think and Sort

The vowel sound in we is called long e. All of the spelling words have the long e sound. Spell each word aloud.

1. Write the **four** words with long e spelled e, like we.

2. Write the **eight** words with long e spelled ee, like keep.

3. Write the **one** word with long e spelled e-consonant-e.

4. Write the **one** word with long e spelled eo.

1. e Words
_____   _____
_____   _____

2. ee Words
_____   _____
_____   _____
_____   _____
_____   _____

3. e-consonant-e Word   **4. eo** Word
_____   _____

Word Groups

Write the spelling word that belongs in each group.

1. ants, wasps, _____

2. yellow, _____, red

3. legs, _____, toes

4. _____, him, his

5. day, _____, month

6. _____, her, hers

7. them, those, _____

8. _____, us, our

Synonyms

Synonyms are words that have the same meaning. Write the spelling word that is a synonym for each word below.

9. look _____

10. persons _____

11. road _____

12. acting _____

13. save _____

we	people	she	keep	these	street	being
see	green	he	feet	bees	week	three

Proofreading

Proofread the newspaper story below. Use proofreading marks to correct four spelling mistakes, one capitalization mistake, and one punctuation mistake.

Proofreading Marks
◯ spell correctly
☰ capitalize
⊙ add period

Sports Buzz

Redtown Runners Take a Swim

Early Friday morning the peopel of Redtown stood along the streete by the park. They waited for the runners to pass by them. soon they saw the runners jumping around and waving their hands. Some beez were chasing them! The runners jumped in the pond to kep from being stung The race was over!

Language Connection

Capital Letters

Use a capital letter to begin the names of cities and states.

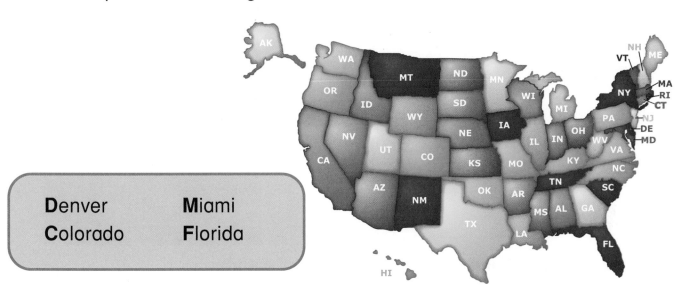

Denver	**M**iami
Colorado	**F**lorida

The sentences below have mistakes in capital letters and spelling. Write each sentence correctly.

1. I have been to ohio threa times.

_____

2. My grandfather is in dallas this weke.

_____

3. Theez trees grow all over maine.

_____

4. We went to se my aunt in seattle.

_____

More Words with Long e

happy	very	leap	peach	city	puppy	penny
clean	please	funny	eat	heat	dream	mean

Say and Listen

Say each spelling word. Listen for the long e sound.

Think and Sort

All of the spelling words have the long e sound.
Spell each word aloud.

Look at the letters in each word. Think about how long e is spelled.
How many spellings for long e do you see?

1. Write the **eight** spelling words that have long e spelled ea, like eat.

2. Write the **six** spelling words that have long e spelled y, like happy.

1. ea Words

_____   _____

_____   _____

_____   _____

_____   _____

2. y Words

_____   _____

_____   _____

_____   _____

Antonyms

Antonyms are words that have opposite meanings. Write the spelling word that is an antonym of the word in dark type.

1. The clown made us feel _____. **sad**

2. Please wear a _____ shirt. **dirty**

3. Do not be _____ to animals. **kind**

4. You can _____ this in the oven. **cool**

Clues

Write the spelling word for each clue.

5. This place has many people and buildings. _____

6. Say this to ask for something. _____

7. This fruit has a fuzzy skin. _____

8. Frogs do this to move. _____

9. Use this word instead of **silly**. _____

10. People do this to food. _____

11. Every big dog was once this. _____

12. This coin is worth one cent. _____

13. When you are asleep, you do this. _____

happy	very	leap	peach	city	puppy	penny
clean	please	funny	eat	heat	dream	mean

Proofreading

Proofread the letter below. Use proofreading marks to correct four spelling mistakes, one capitalization mistake, and one punctuation mistake.

Proofreading
Marks

◯ spell correctly

☰ capitalize

⊙ add period

233 Park Lane

peru, IL 61354

April 12, 2004

Dear John,

I found a verry old peny last week I made it

bright and cleen. I am going to take it to a coin

show in the citty. Will you go with me?

Your friend,

Anton

Dictionary Skills

Guide Words

Every dictionary page has two guide words at the top. The first guide word is the first entry word on the page. The second guide word is the last entry word on the page.

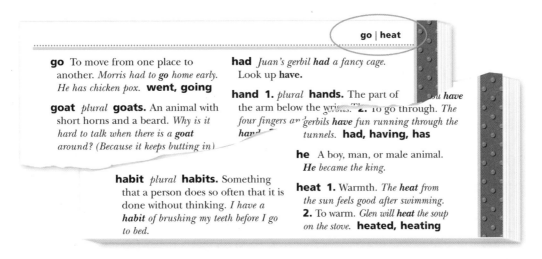

Write these entry words in alphabetical order. Then look up each one in a dictionary. Write the guide words for the page.

happy   **eat**   **leap**

Entry Word   Guide Words

1. _____   _____   _____

2. _____   _____   _____

3. _____   _____   _____

Words with Long i

like	ice	side	write	ride	eye	inside
find	bike	nine	mine	white	hide	five

Say and Listen

Say each spelling word. Listen for the vowel sound you hear in like.

bike

Think and Sort

The vowel sound in like is called long i. All of the spelling words have the long i sound. Spell each word aloud.

Look at the letters in each word. Think about how long i is spelled.

1. Write the **twelve** words with long i spelled i-consonant-e, like ride.

2. Write the **one** word with long i spelled i.

3. Write the **one** word with long i spelled eye.

1. i-consonant-**e** Words

_____   _____

_____   _____

_____   _____

_____   _____

_____   _____

_____   _____

2. i Word   **3. eye** Word

_____   _____

Word Meanings

Write the spelling word for each meaning.
Use a dictionary if you need to.

1. something with wheels to ride on _____

2. to enjoy _____

3. to sit on and be carried _____

4. the lightest color _____

5. to make words with a pencil _____

6. into _____

Rhymes

Write the spelling word that completes each sentence
and rhymes with the underlined word.

7. Let's _____ out how to wind the clock.

8. Did you try to blink your left _____?

9. Did the cat _____ under the slide?

10. We planted all _____ of the pine trees.

11. The left _____ of the road is wide.

12. I slipped twice on the snow and _____.

13. Her soup is cold, but _____ is fine.

like	ice	side	write	ride	eye	inside
find	bike	nine	mine	white	hide	five

Proofreading

Proofread the letter below. Use proofreading marks to correct four spelling mistakes, one capitalization mistake, and one punctuation mistake.

Proofreading Marks

◯ spell correctly
≡ capitalize
⊙ add period

Hi, Allie!

I really liek Alaska. Today we rode a sled over the ise. a team of wite dogs pulled us. We rode for five miles Then we went insid our cabin and lit a fire. Write and tell me how your new kitten is doing. What's her name?

Meg

Present and Past Tenses

Some words show action happening now, or in the present. Some words show action in the past. Look at the chart below. Notice the different spellings.

Present	Past
do	did
find	found
ride	rode

Choose the correct word in dark type to complete each sentence. Write the word on the line.

1. Watch my kittens (**hide**, **hid**) under my bed. _____

2. They (**hide**, **hid**) there last night, too. _____

3. Dad (**write**, **wrote**) a silly story for us. _____

4. We can (**write**, **wrote**) a poem about him. _____

5. Do you (**like**, **liked**) to ice skate? _____

6. Mom (**like**, **liked**) the present we gave her. _____

sky	tiny	lion	why	try	high	my
pie	cry	tie	by	tiger	lie	fly

Proofreading

Proofread the journal page below. Use proofreading marks to correct four spelling mistakes, one capitalization mistake, and one punctuation mistake.

Proofreading Marks

◯ spell correctly
≡ capitalize
⊙ add period

march 3

Today the skye was very blue. The clouds were

big and fluffy. I drew a tiger on some paper

and made a kite with it. I wanted the kite to

touch a cloud. It looked tinee in the air, but it

did not flie high enough I will trie again next

week. Maybe then my kite will touch a cloud.

Dictionary Skills

More Than One Meaning

Some words have more than one meaning. Study the dictionary entry below for **tie**. Then write the number of the meaning that best fits each sentence below.

> **tie 1.** *plural* **ties.** A necktie.
> *He spilled something on his tie.*
> **2.** An equal score. *The banana-eating*
> *contest ended in a tie.* **3.** To attach
> something with string or rope.
> *She tried to tie Mei's shoelaces together.*
> **tied, tying**

Meaning

1. Will you please **tie** my shoelaces for me? _____

2. The frog-jumping contest ended in a **tie**. _____

3. Dad should wear a **tie** to Robin's party. _____

4. **Tie** this rope around the tree trunk. _____

5. The man's **tie** matched his shirt. _____

More Words with ed or ing

dropping   dropped   stopping   jogged   running   hopping   dotted
cutting   spotted   hopped   jogging   shopped   stopped   shopping

Say and Listen

Say the spelling words.
Listen for the ending sounds.

running

Think and Sort

Each spelling word is made by adding ed or ing to a base word.
Each base word ends with a short vowel and consonant.

Look at the letters in each spelling word. Think about how the base
word changes when ed or ing is added. Spell each word aloud.

1. Write the **seven** spelling words that end in ed, like hopped.

2. Write the **seven** spelling words that end in ing, like hopping.

1. ed Words

_____   _____

_____   _____

_____   _____

_____

2. ing Words

_____   _____

_____   _____

_____   _____

_____

Word Meanings

Write the spelling word for each meaning.

1. moved up and down quickly _____

2. moving at a slow, steady trot _____

3. marked with a round point _____

4. ended _____

5. looked for things to buy _____

6. let something fall _____

Synonyms

Synonyms are words that have the same meaning. Write the spelling word that is a synonym for each word in dark type.

7. The apples are _____ off the tree.   **falling**

8. The woman _____ around the block.   **trotted**

9. We saw that the rain was _____.   **ending**

10. The children are _____ on one foot.   **jumping**

11. We saw a man _____ to his car.   **racing**

12. The spilled paint _____ the floor.   **marked**

13. Mom is _____ for some new shoes.   **looking**

dropping   dropped   stopping   jogged   running   hopping   dotted

cutting   spotted   hopped   jogging   shopped   stopped   shopping

Proofreading

Proofread the postcard below.
Use proofreading marks to correct
four spelling mistakes, one
capitalization mistake, and
one punctuation mistake.

Proofreading
Marks

○ spell correctly

≡ capitalize

? add question
  mark

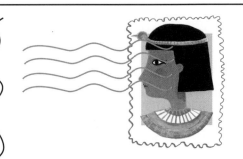

Dear Juan,

    I went joging today along the

beach. I jogd for a long time. there was

no stopin me. Everyone stopped to wave

at me as I went runnig by. What are you

doing for fun

        Your friend,

        Hector

Juan Bravo

7601 Water Road

Houston, TX 77035

Language Connection

Verb Forms

Some words show action. These words are called verbs, and they have different forms. Look at the box below. Notice the different forms of the verb.

> Dad likes to **jog** every day.
> Mom **jogged** with him last week.
> Scooter is **jogging** with him today.

Choose the correct verb in dark type to complete each sentence. Write the word on the line.

1. Maria will be (**shop**, **shopping**) in town. _____

2. I (**shop**, **shopped**) for shoes last week. _____

3. Nathan was (**hop**, **hopping**) like a rabbit. _____

4. His pet frog (**hop**, **hopped**) right out of its bowl! _____

5. Dad (**stop**, **stopped**) the car at the light. _____

6. The bus is (**stop**, **stopping**) at every corner. _____

unit 4 Review
Lessons 16-20

LESSON **16**

being
street
week
people

Words with Long e

Write the spelling word that completes each sentence.

1. I like _____ with my grandfather.
2. Our vacation starts in a _____.
3. A lot of cars were on the _____.
4. My dad invited fifty _____ to his party.

LESSON **17**

clean
please
very
funny

More Words with Long e

Write the spelling word for each meaning.

5. not dirty   _____
6. really   _____
7. silly   _____
8. be so kind as to   _____

LESSON **18**

write
white
find
eye

Words with Long i

Write the spelling word that belongs in each group.

9. read, _____, count
10. ear, nose, _____
11. see, look, _____
12. black, _____, gray

tiny

why

tie

high

More Words with Long i

Write the spelling word for each clue.

13. A man wears this around his neck.

_____

14. This word means "very small."

_____

15. Use this word to ask for a reason.

_____

16. This word is the opposite of **low**.

_____

dropped

stopped

running

hopping

More Words with ed or ing

Write the spelling word that completes
each sentence.

17. The rabbit was _____ across
our lawn.

18. The rain _____ in time for our picnic.

19. I _____ all the dishes on the floor!

20. Ling is _____ to catch up with us.

Words with Long o

go	home	grow	no	hope	snow	hole
yellow	rope	know	nose	stone	so	joke

Say and Listen

Say each spelling word. Listen for the vowel sound you hear in go.

Think and Sort

yellow

The vowel sound in all of the spelling words is called long o. Spell each word aloud.

Look at the letters in each word. Think about how long o is spelled.

1. Write the **three** spelling words with long o spelled o, like go.

2. Write the **seven** spelling words with long o spelled o-consonant-e, like hole.

3. Write the **four** spelling words with long o spelled ow, like snow.

1. o Words

_____   _____

_____

2. o-consonant-e Words

_____   _____

_____   _____

_____   _____

_____

3. ow Words

_____   _____

_____   _____

Word Groups

Write the spelling word that belongs in each group.

1. rain, _____, ice

2. red, blue, _____

3. eye, ear, _____

4. yes, _____, maybe

5. string, yarn, _____

Rhymes

Write the spelling word that completes
each sentence and rhymes with the underlined word.

6. I left my brush and <u>comb</u> at _____.

7. The tiny <u>mole</u> ran down a _____.

8. I _____ you like the fancy <u>soap</u>.

9. The dinosaur <u>bone</u> turned to _____.

10. Ned <u>woke</u> me up to tell me a _____.

11. Corn plants will _____ in each <u>row</u>.

12. The <u>bow</u> was _____ big that it hid the package.

13. I cannot _____ skating with a sore <u>toe</u>.

More Words with Long o

cold	gold	old	sold	open	roll	hold
road	goat	coat	boat	over	most	told

Say and Listen

Say each spelling word. Listen for the long o sound.

goat

Think and Sort

All of the spelling words have the long o sound. Spell each word aloud.

Look at the letters in each word. Think about how long o is spelled. How many spellings for long o do you see?

1. Write the **ten** spelling words that have long o spelled o, like cold.

2. Write the **four** spelling words that have long o spelled oa, like goat.

1. o Words

_____   _____

_____   _____

_____   _____

_____   _____

_____   _____

2. oa Words

_____   _____

_____   _____

Letter Scramble

Unscramble the letters in dark type to make a spelling word.
Write the word on the line.

1. **dols**   bought and _____

2. **roev**   under or _____

3. **atoc**   _____ and hat

4. **locd**   hot and _____

5. **enpo**   _____ or closed

Clues

Write the spelling word for each clue.

6. This travels on the water.   _____

7. This word means "did tell."   _____

8. Many rings are made of this.   _____

9. A car drives on this.   _____

10. This farm animal has horns.   _____

11. You can do this to someone's hand.   _____

12. The opposite of **new** is this.   _____

13. This word rhymes with **toast**.   _____

cold	gold	old	sold	open	roll	hold
road	goat	coat	boat	over	most	told

Proofreading

Proofread the ad below. Use proofreading marks to correct four spelling mistakes, one capitalization mistake, and one punctuation mistake.

Proofreading Marks

◯ spell correctly

≡ capitalize

⊙ add period

Goat Boat Rides!

Take a ride on a snow boat! It is the moast fun you will ever have! our brown and goeld goats will pull you in a boat.

You will fly across the snow We are open six days a week. Wear a heavy cote so that you will not get coald.

Language Connection

Synonyms and Antonyms

Synonyms are words that have the same meaning. Antonyms are words that have opposite meanings.

Synonyms	Antonyms
little, small	tall, short

Use a word from the boxes to write a synonym for each word.

1. street _____

2. said _____

3. bun _____

4. yellow _____

Use a word from the boxes to write an antonym for each word.

5. under _____

6. shut _____

7. new _____

8. hot _____

The Vowel Sound in book

book   look   pull   cook   full   cookies   foot
put   could   would   should   stood   good   took

Say and Listen

Say each spelling word. Listen for the vowel sound you hear in book.

book

Think and Sort

All of the spelling words have the vowel sound in book. Spell each word aloud.

Look at the letters in each word. Think about how the vowel sound in book is spelled.

1. Write the **eight** spelling words that have oo, like book.

2. Write the **three** spelling words that have ou, like could.

3. Write the **three** spelling words that have u, like put.

1. oo Words

_____   _____

_____   _____

_____   _____

_____

2. ou Words

_____   _____

_____

3. u Words

_____   _____

_____

Word Meanings

Write the spelling word for each meaning.

1. small, sweet cakes   _____

2. a form of the word **will**   _____

3. someone who makes food   _____

4. to set something in place _____

5. pages fastened together   _____

6. was able to do something _____

7. was upright on the feet   _____

8. to have a duty   _____

9. see   _____

Antonyms

Antonyms are words that have opposite meanings. Complete each sentence by writing the spelling word that is an antonym of the word in dark type.

10. Rita will _____ your sled up the hill. **push**

11. Mason _____ a cookie to school. **gave**

12. The cookie jar was _____. **empty**

13. This spaghetti tastes _____. **bad**

book	look	pull	cook	full	cookies	foot
put	could	would	should	stood	good	took

Proofreading

Proofread the ad below. Use proofreading marks to correct four spelling mistakes, one capitalization mistake, and one punctuation mistake.

Proofreading Marks
◯ spell correctly
≡ capitalize
⊙ add period

Woud you like a treat? Come to the

Milk and Cookies Shop at 16 oak Street.

Our shop is ful of delicious

cookies Take a good looke.

Try some. Buy some.

Our cok is the best!

Language Connection

Abbreviations

An abbreviation is a short way of writing a word. Abbreviations usually begin with a capital letter and end with a period.

> Mister = **Mr.**   Mistress = **Mrs.**
> Street = **St.**   Road = **Rd.**

The following names and addresses have mistakes.
Write each one correctly.

1. mr Roy Gray _____

2. l63l Elm rd _____

3. mrs Jean Ryan _____

4. 402 Bank st. _____

5. mr. Yoshi Ono _____

6. 6800 Burnet rd. _____

7. mrs Deana Reyna _____

8. 509 State St _____

9. Mr Jackson Palmer _____

The Vowel Sound in zoo

zoo	to	new	food	blue	tooth	moon
too	do	room	who	school	soon	two

Say and Listen

Say each spelling word. Listen for the vowel sound you hear in zoo.

Think and Sort

All of the spelling words have the vowel sound in zoo. Spell each word aloud.

Look at the letters in each spelling word. Think about how the vowel sound in zoo is spelled.

1. Write the **eight** words with oo, like zoo.

2. Write the **one** word with ue.

3. Write the **one** word with ew.

4. Write the **four** words with o, like do.

1. oo Words

_____   _____

_____   _____

_____   _____

_____   _____

2. ue Word   **3. ew** Word

_____   _____

4. o Words

_____   _____

_____   _____

Word Meanings

Write the spelling word for each meaning.

1. a body that moves around a planet   _____

2. which person   _____

3. a place where wild animals are kept   _____

4. something to eat   _____

5. in a short time   _____

6. a hard, bony growth in the mouth   _____

7. a space in a building   _____

Homophones

Homophones are words that sound the same but have different spellings and meanings. Write the spelling word that completes each sentence and is a homophone of the underlined word.

8. Our _____ umbrella <u>blew</u> away.

9. The <u>two</u> boys swam _____ the shore.

10. I <u>knew</u> that Nina had a _____ puppy.

11. How many books _____ we have <u>due</u> at the library?

12. They have _____ many things <u>to</u> do.

13. Did Chad score _____ points, <u>too</u>?

zoo	to	new	food	blue	tooth	moon
too	do	room	who	school	soon	two

Proofreading

Proofread the paragraph below. Use proofreading marks to correct four spelling mistakes, one capitalization mistake, and one punctuation mistake.

Proofreading Marks

◯ spell correctly
≡ capitalize
⊙ add period

The Strange Fish

Last summer I went fishing with my dad. I caught the strangest fish I had ever seen. dad thought it was tew strange to eat. I didn't know what to doo with it. Grandpa knew the place to call. He called the zue We soun found out that my fish was a mudfish.

Language Connection

Nouns

A noun is a word that names a person, place, or thing.

Person	Place	Thing
boy	city	toy
girl	town	dog

Find the noun in the box that completes each sentence.
Then write the sentence.

 room    zoo    tooth    moon

1. We saw lions and tigers at the ___.

_____

2. Chad lost a ___ at school.

_____

3. Which ___ should we paint next?

_____

4. The full ___ made the sky bright.

_____

More Words with ed or ing

| joking | baking | hoped | liked | lived | riding | loved |
| named | biked | living | giving | baked | writing | having |

Say and Listen

baking

Say the spelling words.
Listen for the ending sounds.

Think and Sort

Each spelling word is made by adding ed or ing to a base word. Each base word ends with e.

Look at the letters in each word. Think how the base word changes when ed or ing is added. Spell each word aloud.

1. Write the **seven** spelling words that end in ed, like liked.

2. Write the **seven** spelling words that end in ing, like joking.

1. ed Words

_____   _____
_____   _____
_____   _____
_____

2. ing Words

_____   _____
_____   _____
_____   _____
_____

Word Groups

Write the spelling word that belongs in each group.

1. hiked, skated, _____

2. reading, spelling, _____

3. frying, broiling, _____

4. laughing, teasing, _____

5. wanted, wished, _____

6. liked, cared, _____

Synonyms

Synonyms are words that have the same meaning. Complete each sentence by writing the spelling word that is a synonym for each word in dark type.

7. We _____ the dog Nicki.   **called**

8. We _____ a dozen cookies.   **cooked**

9. Mr. Reyna _____ in a house nearby.   **stayed**

10. We are _____ food to the birds.   **offering**

11. Are you _____ ice cream with your cake?   **getting**

12. I like _____ in the city.   **being**

13. Rosa will be _____ on a train.   **sitting**

| joking | baking | hoped | liked | lived | riding | loved |
| named | biked | living | giving | baked | writing | having |

Proofreading

Proofread the letter below.
Use proofreading marks to correct
four spelling mistakes, one
capitalization mistake, and
one punctuation mistake.

Proofreading Marks

◯ spell correctly
＝ capitalize
? add question mark

Franco,

Yesterday I met a man named mr. Banana.

He was a funny man. He said he bakked a

bicycle. He hopd I liked it. He wanted me

to go rideng on it. Do you think he was

just jokking Could a person really bake

a bicycle?

Peter

Dictionary Skills

Base Words

To find an **ed** or **ing** word in a dictionary, look for the base word entry. The **ed** and **ing** forms of a word are given as part of the base word entry.

Below are eight **ing** words. Write the base word for each one. Then look up each base word in a dictionary and write the page number for it.

	Base Word	Dictionary Page
1. living		
2. giving		
3. having		
4. writing		
5. loving		
6. biking		
7. naming		
8. liking		

unit 5 REVIEW
LESSONS 21-25

LESSON **21**

no

home

know

yellow

Words with Long o

Write the spelling word for each clue.

1. This means that you understand something.

_____

2. A lemon is this color. _____

3. This is the opposite of **yes**. _____

4. The place where you live is

called this. _____

LESSON **22**

cold

open

over

coat

More Words with Long o

Write the spelling word that belongs in each group.

5. sweater, jacket, _____

6. unlock, uncover, _____

7. cool, chilly, _____

8. under, beside, _____

book
could
would
pull
put

The Vowel Sound in **book**

Write the spelling word that completes each sentence.

9. I enjoyed reading this _____.

10. Dan, _____ you like some soup?

11. Don't _____ the rope too hard.

12. You need to _____ your clothes away.

13. Jay, you _____ wash the dishes.

tooth
two
blue
new

The Vowel Sound in **zoo**

Write the missing spelling word.

14. my missing _____

15. the deep _____ sea

16. one or _____ apples

17. old and _____

liked
riding
writing

More Words with **ed** or **ing**

Write the spelling word for each meaning.

18. making words with a pencil _____

19. enjoyed _____

20. sitting in and being carried _____

The Vowel Sound in out

out	town	now	flower	owl	how	cow
found	sound	mouse	round	around	house	clown

Say and Listen

Say each spelling word. Listen for the vowel sound you hear in out.

cow

Think and Sort

All of the spelling words have the vowel sound in out. Spell each word aloud.

Look at the letters in each word. Think about how the vowel sound in out is spelled.

1. Write the **seven** spelling words that have ou, like out.

2. Write the **seven** spelling words that have ow, like cow.

1. ou Words

_____ _____

_____ _____

_____ _____

_____

2. ow Words

_____ _____

_____ _____

_____ _____

_____

Letter Scramble

Unscramble each group of letters to make a spelling word.
Write the word on the line.

1. **lerfow** _____

2. **undor** _____

3. **droanu** _____

4. **tou** _____

5. **nudof** _____

Clues

Write the spelling word for each clue.

6. You see this person at the circus. _____

7. This is another word for **noise**. _____

8. This has a roof and a door. _____

9. Use this word to ask a question. _____

10. This bird is often called wise. _____

11. This is a small city. _____

12. A cat likes to chase this animal. _____

13. This word is the opposite of **then**. _____

out	town	now	flower	owl	how	cow
found	sound	mouse	round	around	house	clown

Proofreading

Proofread the postcard below.
Use proofreading marks to correct four spelling mistakes, one capitalization mistake, and one punctuation mistake.

Proofreading Marks

◯ spell correctly
≡ capitalize
? add question mark

Dear Bailey,

I am drawing pictures of my toun. First I walked arownd to get ideas. I saw a mouse by a tree. then I fownd a big green hows. Do you like to draw Draw me a picture of your town.

Eric

Bailey Oakes

986 Tell Ave.

Ventura, IA

50482

Language Connection

Was and Were

The words **was** and **were** tell about the past. **Was** tells about one person or thing. **Were** tells about two or more persons or things.

I **was**	Jed **was**	the cat **was**
we **were**	Jed and Ted **were**	the cats **were**

Choose the correct word in dark type to complete each sentence. Then find the spelling mistake. Write the sentence correctly.

1. The dog (**was**, **were**) afraid of the sownd.

_____

2. The boys (**was**, **were**) glad to see the oul.

_____

3. The child (**was**, **were**) picking a flouer.

_____

4. How many stores (**was**, **were**) in that toun?

_____

5. A mous (**was**, **were**) hiding in my shoe.

_____

The Vowel Sound in saw

saw	talk	call	off	draw	lost	walk
song	dog	frog	ball	all	small	long

Say and Listen

Say each spelling word. Listen for the vowel sound you hear in saw.

frogs

Think and Sort

All of the spelling words have the vowel sound in saw. Spell each word aloud.

Look at the letters in each word.
Think about how the vowel sound in saw is spelled.

1. Write the **two** spelling words that have aw, like saw.

2. Write the **six** spelling words that have a, like ball.

3. Write the **six** spelling words that have o, like dog.

1. aw Words

_____   _____

2. a Words

_____   _____

_____   _____

_____   _____

3. o Words

_____   _____

_____   _____

Word Groups

Write the spelling word that belongs in each group.

1. pup, hound, _____

2. yell, shout, _____

3. tadpole, toad, _____

4. run, jog, _____

5. speak, say, _____

6. paint, sketch, _____

7. looked, watched, _____

8. music, tune, _____

Antonyms

Antonyms are words that have opposite meanings. Complete each sentence by writing the spelling word that is an antonym of the word in dark type.

9. The room was very _____. **large**

10. Have you _____ your red hat? **found**

11. Last year her hair was _____. **short**

12. Please turn _____ the light. **on**

13. We found _____ of the missing screws. **none**

saw	talk	call	off	draw	lost	walk
song	dog	frog	ball	all	small	long

Proofreading

Proofread the letter below. Use proofreading marks to correct four spelling mistakes, one capitalization mistake, and one punctuation mistake.

Proofreading Marks

⟡ spell correctly

≡ capitalize

⊙ add period

Dear Amy,

    I have a smal dog named Chip. he has longe black hair He always comes when I cal him. Chip loves to chase a baul. Sometimes he doesn't want to give it back to me! Would you like to come play catch with us?

                Daniel

Dictionary Skills

Using the Spelling Table

A spelling table can help you find words in a dictionary. A spelling table shows the different spellings for sounds. Suppose you are not sure how to spell the long **e** sound in **freeze**. First, find **long e** in the spelling table. Then read the first spelling for the sound and look up **frez** in a dictionary. Look for each spelling in the dictionary until you find the correct one.

Sound	Example Words	Spellings
long e	he, eat, tree, very, people, belief	e ea ee y eo ie

Complete each picture name by writing the correct letter or letters. Use the Spelling Table on page 265 and a dictionary to decide on the correct letters.

1.  l_____bster

2.  athl_____

3.  cl_____ver

4.  r_____ng

5.  sp_____n

6.  _____ite

The Vowel Sound in for

for	door	story	snore	horse	four	floor
corn	or	short	more	storm	orange	store

Say and Listen

Say each spelling word. Listen for the vowel sound you hear in for.

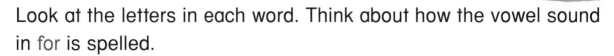

storm

Think and Sort

All of the spelling words have the vowel sound in for. Spell each word aloud.

Look at the letters in each word. Think about how the vowel sound in for is spelled.

1. Write the **eleven** spelling words that have o or o-consonant-e, like for and more.

2. Write the **two** spelling words that have oo, like door.

3. Write the **one** spelling word that has ou.

1. o or **o-consonant-e** Words

_____   _____

_____   _____

_____   _____

_____   _____

_____   _____

_____

2. oo Words

_____   _____

3. ou Word

_____

Word Meanings

Write the spelling word for each meaning. Use a
dictionary if you need to.

1. a yellow grain   _____

2. very bad weather   _____

3. a place where goods are sold   _____

4. not tall   _____

5. the number after three   _____

6. a large four-legged animal with hooves _____

Clues

Write the spelling word for each clue.

7. You want this if you want extra.   _____

8. This word is used on a gift card.   _____

9. This word can join two others.   _____

10. You can drink this juice for breakfast.   _____

11. Some people do this when they sleep.   _____

12. You go in and out through this.   _____

13. People walk on this.   _____

for	door	story	snore	horse	four	floor
corn	or	short	more	storm	orange	store

Proofreading

Proofread the ad below. Use proofreading marks to correct four spelling mistakes, one capitalization mistake, and one punctuation mistake.

Proofreading Marks

◯ spell correctly

≡ capitalize

⊙ add period

Fur and Feathers Pet Store

Feeding birds in your backyard can be fun. Our stoore has everything you need. We have cracked corne, sunflower seeds, and fruit. we also have special feeding dishes. Cut up an oringe and put it on a feeding dish In a shart time, you will have lots of feathered visitors!

Language Connection

End Marks

Put a period (.) at the end of a sentence that tells something. Put a question mark (**?**) at the end of a question. Put an exclamation point (**!**) at the end of a sentence that shows strong feeling or surprise.

It was a nice day. When did it get cold?
Now we have three feet of snow!

Choose the correctly spelled word in dark type to complete each sentence. Then write the sentence, adding the correct end mark.

1. Snow has fallen for (**fower**, **four**) days and nights

_____

2. Watch out for the snow above that (**door**, **dore**)

_____

3. Do you think we will get (**more**, **mor**) snow

_____

jar	party	arm	mark	star	dark	far
car	barn	father	farmer	are	farm	art

Proofreading

Proofread the book jacket below. Use proofreading marks to correct four spelling mistakes, one capitalization mistake, and one punctuation mistake.

Proofreading Marks

◯ spell correctly
≡ capitalize
? add question mark

every summer night the Clark children have a pardy when it gets daark. They chase fireflies around the barne. One night a firefly lands on a child's arem. The firefly blinks a message. What is it trying to say Read The Firefly Farm to find out.

Dictionary Skills

More Than One Meaning

Some words have more than one meaning. The dictionary entries for these words give the different meanings. Study the entries below.

star *plural* **stars. 1.** The sun and other bright heavenly bodies. *The **star** we see best at night is the North Star.* **2.** A leading actor or actress, athlete, or musician. *My brother is a super drummer. I think he will be a rock **star**!*

mark *plural* **marks. 1.** A spot on something. *A wet glass will leave a **mark** on a table.* **2.** A grade given in school. *I got good **marks** on my report card.*

Use the correct word above to complete each sentence.
Then write the number of the meaning used in the sentence.

1. Everyone cheered for the _____ of the show. _____

2. Dad couldn't get the _____ off the car. _____

3. One _____ shone brighter than the others. _____

4. Kim got a high _____ on her art project. _____

5. Our sun is really a _____. _____

6. The pen left a _____ on the table. _____

Words with er

colder	helper	braver	writer	longer	flatter	painter
bigger	shopper	runner	older	jumper	faster	baker

Say and Listen

Say each spelling word. Listen for the ending sounds.

painter

Think and Sort

Each spelling word is made by adding er to a base word. In which spelling words does the spelling of the base word change?

1. Write the **seven** spelling words with no change in the base word, like colder.

2. Write the **four** spelling words in which the final consonant of the base word is doubled, like flatter.

3. Write the **three** spelling words in which the final e of the base word is dropped, like braver.

---

1. No Change in Base Word

_____   _____

_____   _____

_____   _____

_____

2. Final Consonant Doubled

_____   _____

_____   _____

3. Final **e** Dropped

_____   _____

_____

Word Meanings

Write the spelling word for each meaning.

1. someone who shops   _____

2. someone who helps   _____

3. someone who writes stories   _____

4. more able to face danger   _____

5. someone who runs   _____

6. more flat   _____

7. someone who jumps   _____

8. one who colors things   _____

Antonyms

Antonyms are words that have opposite meanings. Complete each sentence by writing the spelling word that is an antonym of the word in dark type.

9. Kay is _____ than her sister.   **younger**

10. The turtle was _____ than the rabbit.   **slower**

11. My legs are _____ than yours.   **shorter**

12. Jesse's feet are _____ than mine.   **smaller**

13. The night was _____ than the day.   **hotter**

colder	helper	braver	writer	longer	flatter	painter
bigger	shopper	runner	older	jumper	faster	baker

Proofreading

Proofread the questions below. Use proofreading marks to correct four spelling mistakes, one capitalization mistake, and one punctuation mistake.

Proofreading Marks

◯ spell correctly

≡ capitalize

? add question mark

What I Want to Know

1. Does a newspaper writter have to be a good speller?

2. What does a teacher's hepler do

3. Does a firefighter have to run fastur than most other people?

4. how early does a bakker have to get up?

Dictionary Skills

ABC Order

Some of the **er** words in this lesson are describing words. To find an **er** describing word in a dictionary, look for the base word. For example, to find the word **bigger**, look for **big**.

Write these words in ABC order. Then find each word in a dictionary. Write its page number.

Word	Page Number
1. _____	_____
2. _____	_____
3. _____	_____
4. _____	_____
5. _____	_____
6. _____	_____
7. _____	_____

unit 6 review
lessons 26-30

Lesson 26 — The Vowel Sound in out

out
around
town
flower

Write the spelling word for each meaning.

1. the part of a plant that blooms _____

2. not in _____

3. a large village _____

4. in a circle _____

Lesson 27 — The Vowel Sound in saw

saw
talk
small
off

Write the spelling word that completes each sentence.

5. You must _____ softly in a library.

6. Please turn _____ the stove.

7. These shoes are too _____ for me.

8. We _____ two beavers in the pond.

Lesson 28 — The Vowel Sound in for

orange
store
floor
four

Write the spelling word that belongs in each group.

9. two, three, _____

10. wall, ceiling, _____

11. red, yellow, _____

12. shop, market, _____

LESSON 29 — The Vowel Sound in **jar**

father
dark
party
are

Write the spelling word for each clue.

13. This man has a child. _____

14. This word goes with **am** and **is**. _____

15. If it is not light outside, it is this. _____

16. You have this on your birthday. _____

LESSON 30 — Words with **er**

longer
older
bigger
writer

Write the spelling word that completes each sentence and rhymes with the underlined word.

17. A snake is _____ and <u>stronger</u> than a worm.

18. A _____ needs light that is <u>brighter</u> than candle light.

19. Please hand me the _____ <u>folder</u>.

20. The _____ <u>digger</u> found the gold.

commonly misspelled words

about	family	name	their
above	favorite	nice	then
across	friend	now	there
again	friends	once	they
a lot	get	one	though
am	getting	our	time
and	girl	out	today
another	goes	outside	too
are	guess	party	two
because	have	people	upon
been	hear	play	very
before	her	please	want
beginning	here	pretty	was
bought	him	read	went
boy	his	really	were
buy	house	right	when
can	in	said	where
came	into	saw	white
children	know	scared	with
color	like	school	would
come	little	sent	write
didn't	made	some	writing
does	make	store	wrote
don't	me	swimming	your
every	my	teacher	you're

spelling table

Consonants

Sound	Example Words	Spellings
b	big	b
ch	child, catch	ch tch
d	day, add	d dd
f	fast, off	f ff
g	get, egg	g gg
h	hand, who	h wh
j	jog, sponge	j g
k	can, keep, school, sick	c k ch ck
ks	six	x
kw	quit	qu
l	look, all	l ll
m	made, swimming, numb	m mm mb
n	not, running, knock	n nn kn
ng	thank, ring	n ng
p	pet, dropped	p pp
r	run, writer	wr
s	sat, dress, city	s ss c
sh	she	sh
t	ten, matter	t tt
th	that, thing	th
v	have, of	v f
w	went, whale, one	w wh o
y	you	y
z	zoo, blizzard, says	z zz s

Vowels

Sound	Example Words	Spellings
short a	cat, have	a a_e
long a	baby, take, play, nail, eight, they	a a_e ay ai eigh ey
ah	father, star	a
short e	red, tread, many, said, says	e ea a ai ay
long e	he, eat, tree, people, belief, very	e ea ee eo ie y
short i	is, give	i i_e
long i	find, ride, pie, high my, eye	i i_e ie igh y eye
short o	on, want	o a
long o	so, nose, road, boulder, snow	o o_e oa ou ow
oi	boy	oy
aw	off, call, haul, saw	o a au aw
o	corn, store, door, four	o o_e oo ou
long oo	zoo, blue, new, do, you	oo ue ew o ou
short oo	good, could, pull	oo ou u
ow	out, owl	ou ow
short u	run, brother	u o

Math
Skills

unit 1
counting and place value

Counting to 50

Draw lines to match numbers and groups.

27

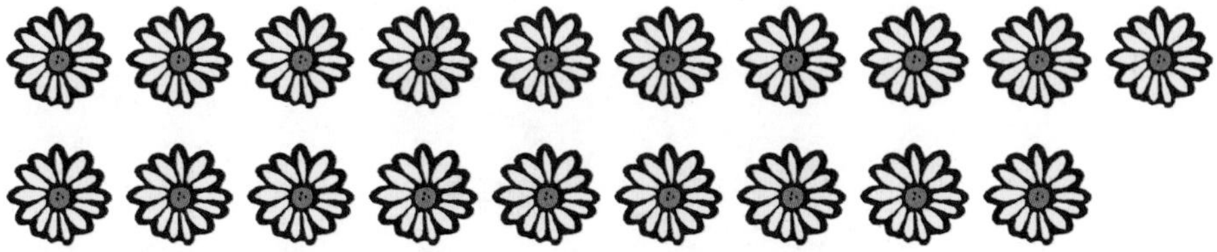

44

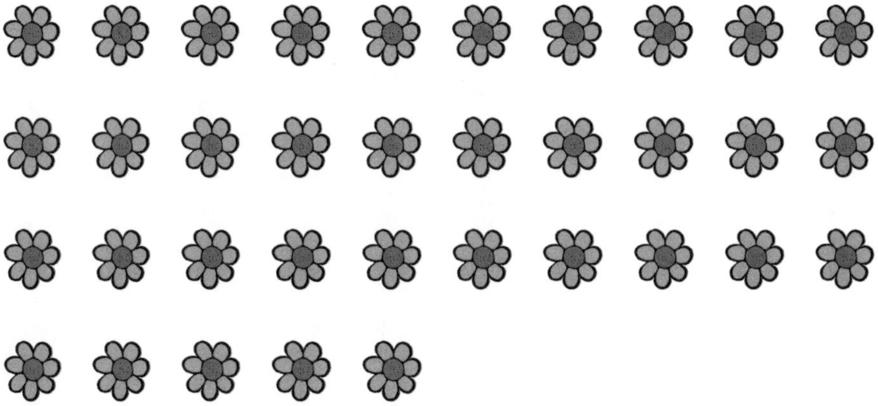

19

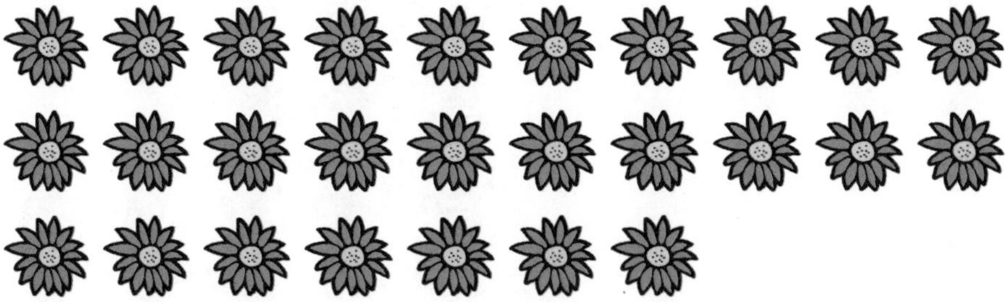

35

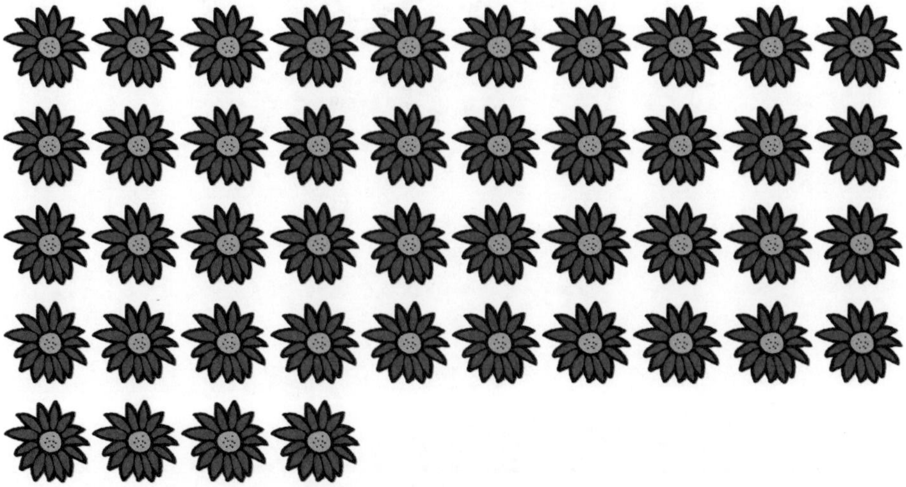

Counting to 50
Write the missing numbers.

1	2	3						9	10

11					16		18		

		23				27			

	32			35					

		44						50

Counting to 100

Write the missing numbers.

1	2	3							
11				15					
21									
	32						38		
				45					
	52								60
			64						
						76			80
							87		
		93							100

Counting to 100
Write the missing numbers in each row.

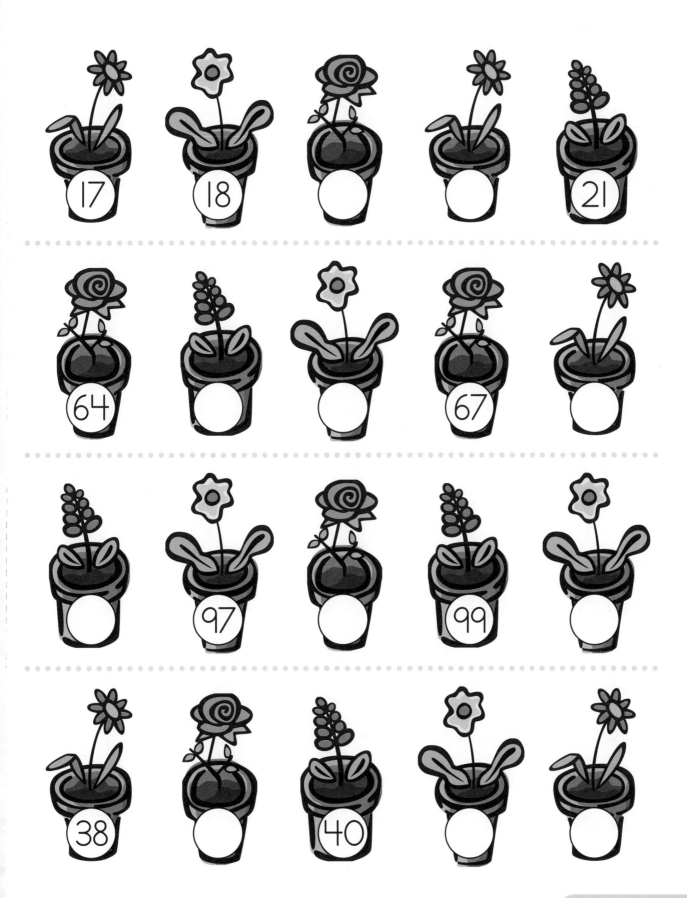

Tens and Ones

Circle groups of ten. Write how many tens and ones.

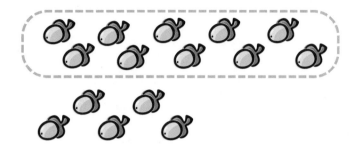

Tens	Ones
1	5

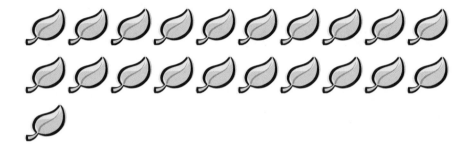

Tens	Ones

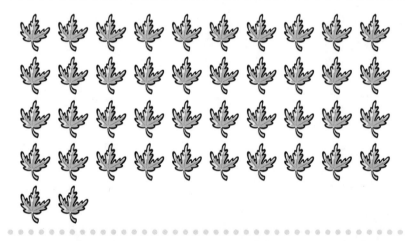

Tens	Ones

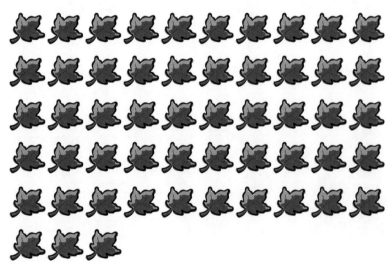

Tens	Ones

Tens and Ones

Write how many tens and ones. Then write the numbers.

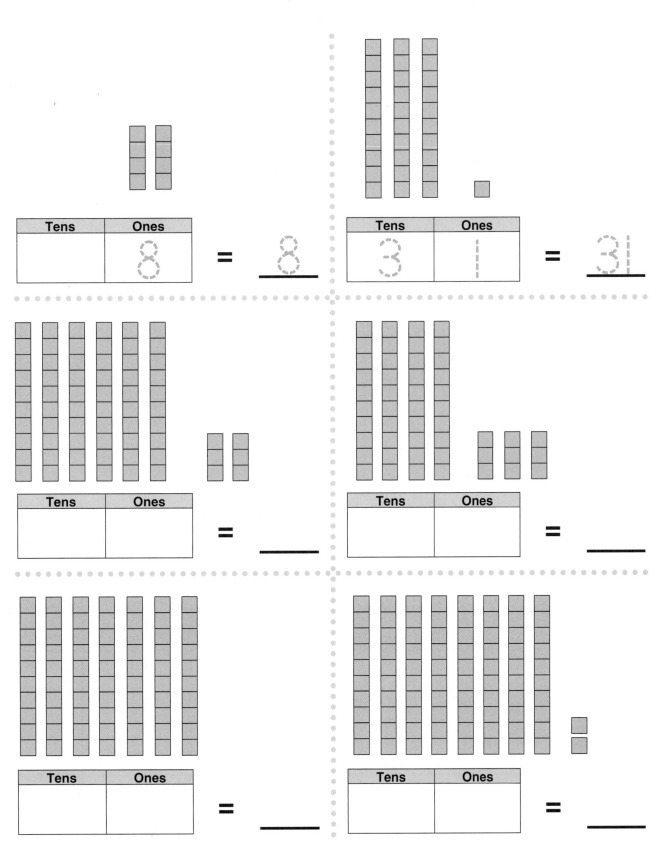

Tens	Ones
	8

= 8

Tens	Ones
3	1

= 31

Tens	Ones

= ___

Tens	Ones

= ___

Tens	Ones

= ___

Tens	Ones

= ___

Hundreds, Tens, and Ones

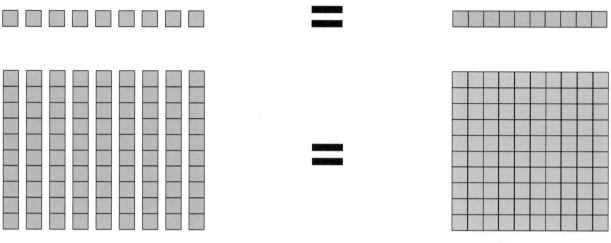

Write how many hundreds, tens, and ones.	Hundreds	Tens	Ones
	2	3	6

Hundreds, Tens, and Ones

Write how many hundreds, tens, and ones. Then write the numbers.

Hundreds	Tens	Ones
3	5	9

= 359

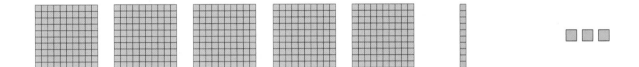

Hundreds	Tens	Ones

= _____

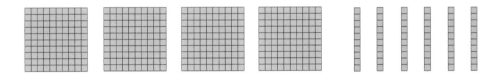

Hundreds	Tens	Ones

= _____

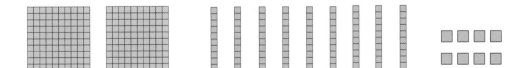

Hundreds	Tens	Ones

= _____

Counting to 150

Write the missing numbers in each row.

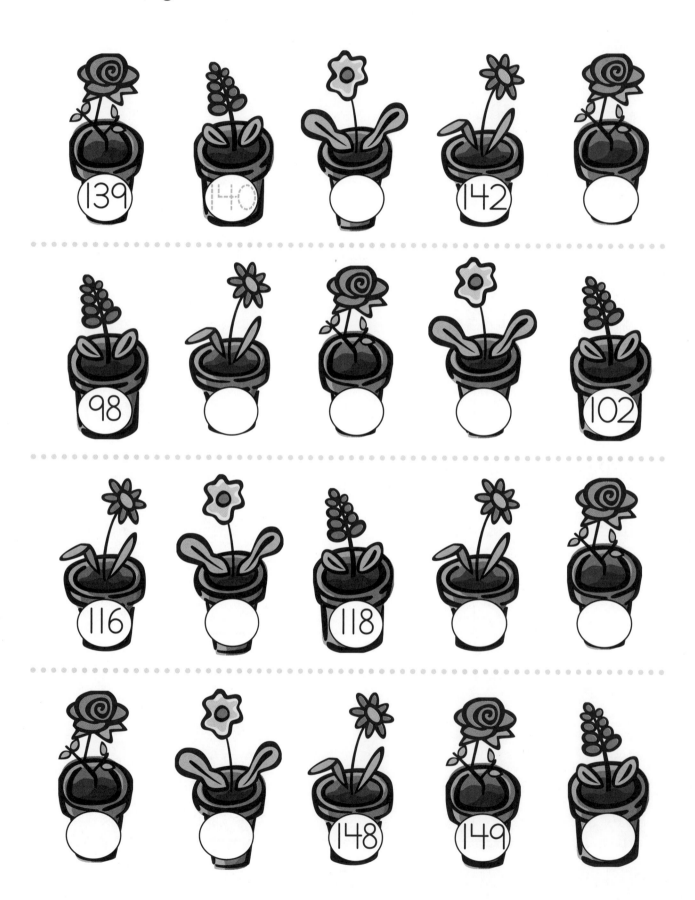

139 140 ___ 142 ___

98 ___ ___ ___ 102

116 ___ 118 ___ ___

___ ___ 148 149 ___

Counting to 200

Write the missing numbers.

101	102	103							
				115				119	
		123				127			
			134				138		
141									150
	152							159	
			164		166				
						177	178		
		183		185					
	192								200

Ordering Numbers

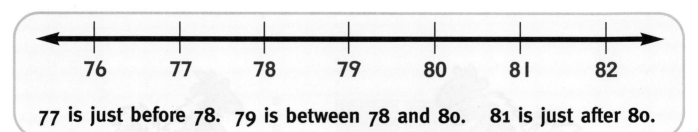

76   77   78   79   80   81   82

77 is just before **78**.   **79** is between **78** and **80**.   **81** is just after **80**.

Write the number that is just before, just after, or between.

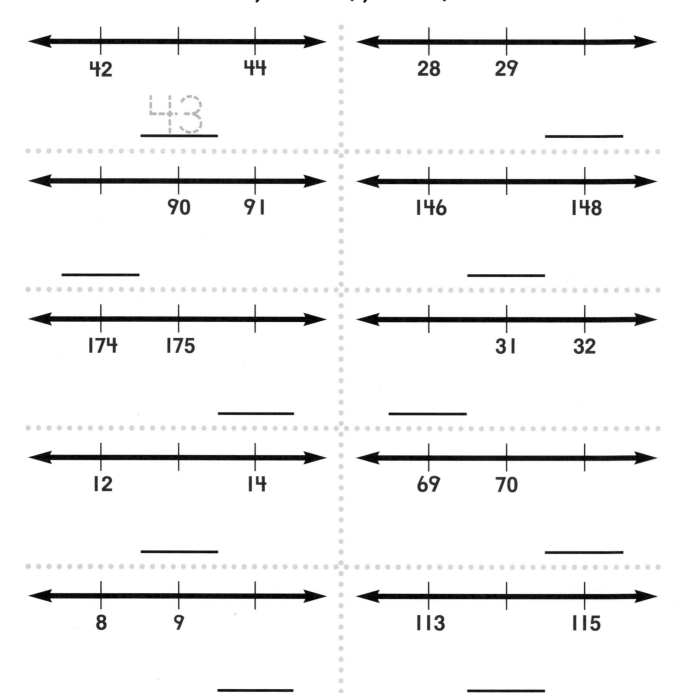

42   44

43

28   29

_____

90   91

146   148

_____

174   175

31   32

_____

12   14

69   70

_____

8   9

113   115

Ordinal Numbers to Tenth

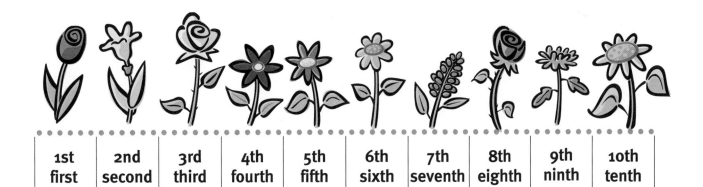

1st	2nd	3rd	4th	5th	6th	7th	8th	9th	10th
first	second	third	fourth	fifth	sixth	seventh	eighth	ninth	tenth

Write the position of each flower.

seventh
7th

fourth
4th

Ordinal Numbers to Twentieth

11th	12th	13th	14th	15th	16th	17th	18th	19th	20th
eleventh	twelfth	thirteenth	fourteenth	fifteenth	sixteenth	seventeenth	eighteenth	nineteenth	twentieth

Write the position of each flower.

thirteenth

13th

Skip Counting by Fives and Tens

Skip count by fives or tens. Write the numbers.

5   10   15

  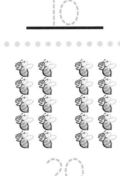 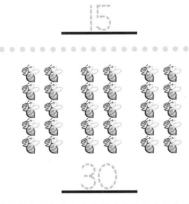

10   20   30

5¢   ¢   ¢   ¢   ¢   ¢

10¢   ¢   ¢   ¢   ¢   ¢

35   40   ___   ___   ___   ___

50   60   ___   ___   ___   ___

Skip Counting by Twos

Skip count by twos. Write the numbers.

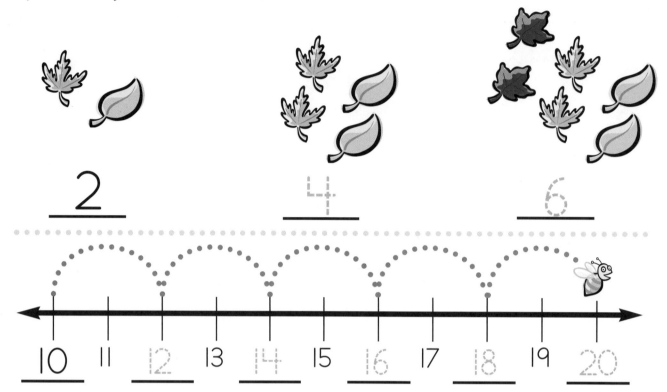

2 _____ 4 _____ 6 _____

10 | 11 | 12 | 13 | 14 | 15 | 16 | 17 | 18 | 19 | 20

8 _____ _____ _____ _____ _____

66 _____ _____ _____ _____ _____

34 _____ _____ _____ _____ _____

100 _____ _____ _____ _____ _____

20 _____ _____ _____ _____ _____

Even and Odd Numbers

Circle groups of 2. Then circle *even* or *odd*.

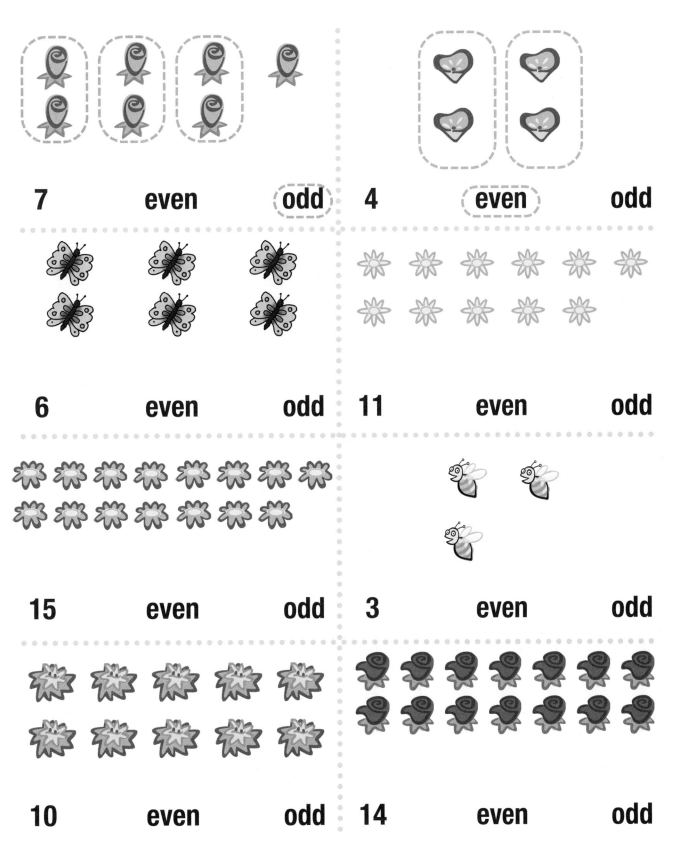

7   even   (odd)   **4**   (even)   odd

6   even   odd   **11**   even   odd

15   even   odd   **3**   even   odd

10   even   odd   **14**   even   odd

Find a Pattern

Skip count by twos. Circle those numbers.

Skip count by fives. Color those boxes blue.

1	2	3	4	5	6	7	8	9	10
11	12	13	14	15	16	17	18	19	20
21	22	23	24	25	26	27	28	29	30
31	32	33	34	35	36	37	38	39	40
41	42	43	44	45	46	47	48	49	50
51	52	53	54	55	56	57	58	59	60
61	62	63	64	65	66	67	68	69	70
71	72	73	74	75	76	77	78	79	80
81	82	83	84	85	86	87	88	89	90
91	92	93	94	95	96	97	98	99	100

Find a Pattern

Write the missing numbers in each row.

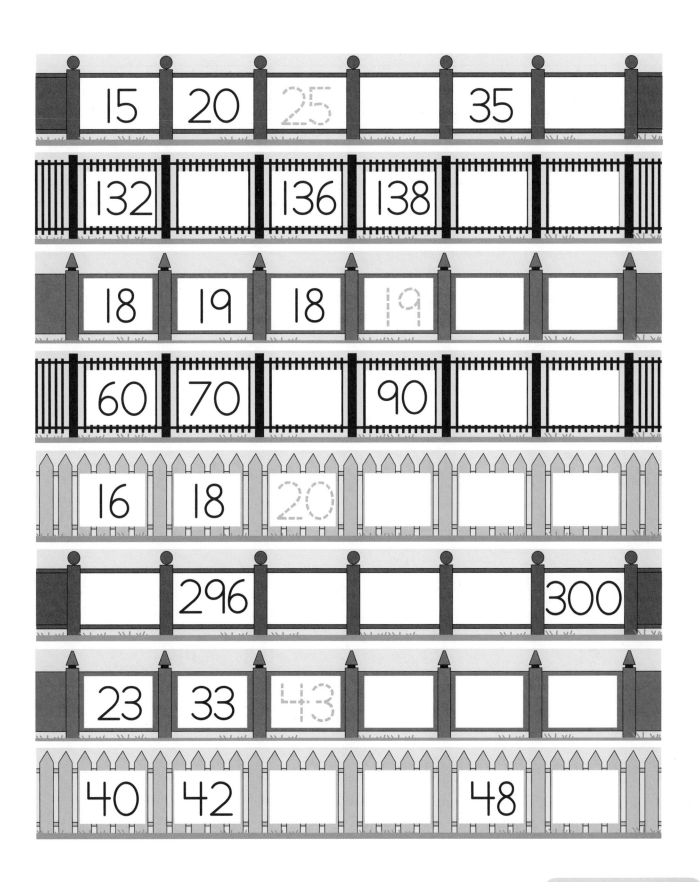

| 15 | 20 | 25 | | 35 | |

| 132 | | 136 | 138 | | |

| 18 | 19 | 18 | 19 | | |

| 60 | 70 | | 90 | | |

| 16 | 18 | 20 | | | |

| | 296 | | | 300 |

| 23 | 33 | 43 | | | |

| 40 | 42 | | | 48 | |

Write the missing numbers in each row.

36			39				
71					76		
113				117			
185							192

Count and compare. Write ‹ or › in each box.

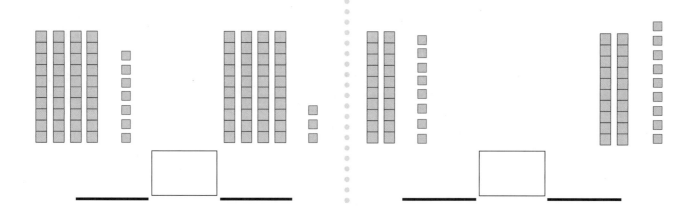

Write the number that is just after or between.

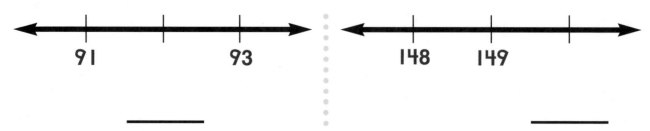

91   93   _____

148   149   _____

Circle *even* or *odd* for each number.

9   **even**   **odd**   **16**   **even**   **odd**

Unit 1 Review

Draw lines to match.

65

123

48

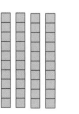

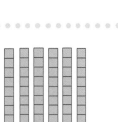

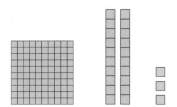

Write the missing numbers in each row.

6	8			14	

25	30		40		

60	70				

116	118				

Sums to 10

Add.

6   +   3   =   9

2   +   5   =   ___

4   +   1   =   ___

 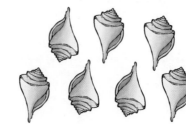

3   +   7   =   ___

Sums to 10

Write the numbers that match the pictures. Then add.

$$\begin{array}{r} 4 \\ + 5 \\ \hline 9 \end{array}$$

$$+ \\ \hline$$

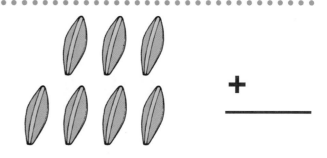

$$+ \\ \hline$$

$$+ \\ \hline$$

$$+ \\ \hline$$

Sums to 18

Add.

 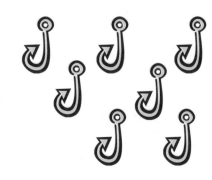

6   +   7   =   13

5   +   6   =   ____

7   +   8   =   ____

9   +   9   =   ____

Sums to 18

Write the numbers that match the pictures. Then add.

$$
\begin{array}{r}
9 \\
+\ 8 \\
\hline
17
\end{array}
$$

+ ____

+ ____

+ ____

+ ____

Adding Zero

Write the numbers that match the pictures. Then add.

$+\ 0$
___

0
$+$
___

$+\ 0$
___

0
$+$
___

$+\ 0$
___

0
$+$
___

$7\ +\ 0\ =\ 7$

$0\ +\ \rule{1cm}{0.4pt}\ =\ \rule{1cm}{0.4pt}$

$\rule{1cm}{0.4pt}\ +\ 0\ =\ \rule{1cm}{0.4pt}$

$\rule{1cm}{0.4pt}\ +\ 0\ =\ \rule{1cm}{0.4pt}$

Doubles

Write the numbers that match the fish. Then add.

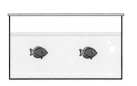 

$$\begin{array}{r} 2 \\ +\ 2 \\ \hline 4 \end{array}$$

 +  = 4

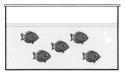

____ + ____ = ____

$$\begin{array}{r} \\ + \\ \hline \end{array}$$

____ + ____ = ____

$$\begin{array}{r} \\ + \\ \hline \end{array}$$

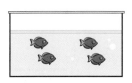

____ + ____ = ____

$$\begin{array}{r} \\ + \\ \hline \end{array}$$

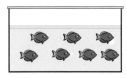 

____ + ____ = ____

$$\begin{array}{r} \\ + \\ \hline \end{array}$$

Order Property

Write the sums that match the cubes.

5 + 4 = <u>9</u>   4 + 5 = <u>9</u>

. . . .

2 + 8 = ___   8 + 2 = ___

. . . .

4 + 3 = ___   3 + 4 = ___

. . . .

1 + 7 = ___   7 + 1 = ___

Use a Graph

Find the number of each object on the graph. Then write the sums.

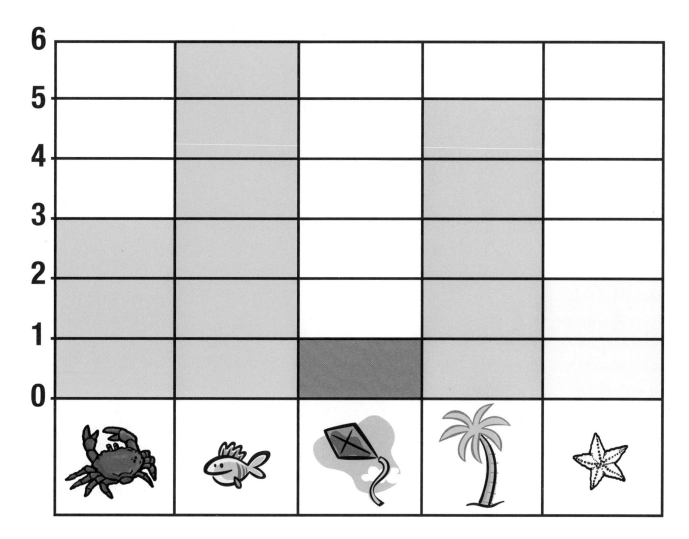

 $\underline{3} + 6 = \underline{9}$  $\underline{} + 0 = \underline{}$

 $\underline{} + 9 = \underline{}$ $\underline{} + 5 = \underline{}$

 $\underline{} + 4 = \underline{}$ $\underline{} + 2 = \underline{}$

Two-digit Addition

Combine the blocks. Then write the sums.

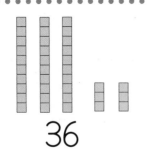

24 + 3 = *27*

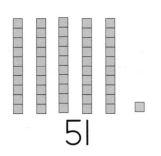

36 + 2 = ___

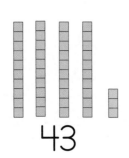

51 + 8 = ___

---

43 + 5 = ___

Two-digit Addition
Combine the blocks. Then write the sums.

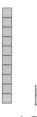

25   +   12   =   *37*

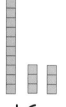 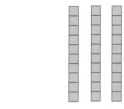

16   +   43   =   ___

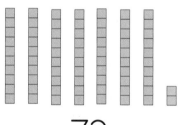 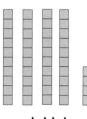

72   +   20   =   ___

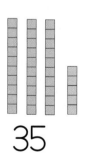

35   +   44   =   ___

Two-digit Addition

Use these steps to add two-digit numbers.

Find: 86 + 1

Step 1	Step 2
Add the ones.	Add the tens.
(6 + 1 = 7)	(8 + 0 = 8)

Step 1:
```
  T │ O
  8 │ 6
+   │ 1
────┼───
    │ 7
```

Step 2:
```
  T │ O
  8 │ 6
+   │ 1
────┼───
  8 │ 7
```

Find: 26 + 53

Step 1	Step 2
Add the ones.	Add the tens.
(6 + 3 = 9)	(2 + 5 = 7)

Step 1:
```
  T │ O
  2 │ 6
+ 5 │ 3
────┼───
    │ 9
```

Step 2:
```
  T │ O
  2 │ 6
+ 5 │ 3
────┼───
  7 │ 9
```

Add.

```
  T │ O        T │ O        T │ O        T │ O
  8 │ 6        2 │ 6        1 │ 0        5 │ 2
+   │ 1      + 5 │ 3      + 1 │ 3      +   │ 5
────┼───      ────┼───      ────┼───      ────┼───
  8 │ 7        7 │ 9
```

```
  T │ O        T │ O        T │ O        T │ O
  4 │ 3        7 │ 5        9 │ 7        1 │ 2
+ 1 │ 3      + 1 │ 0      +   │ 2      + 4 │ 2
────┼───      ────┼───      ────┼───      ────┼───
```

```
  T │ O        T │ O        T │ O        T │ O
  8 │ 0        2 │ 3        3 │ 2        6 │ 3
+ 1 │ 2      + 7 │ 0      +   │ 6      + 3 │ 1
────┼───      ────┼───      ────┼───      ────┼───
```

```
  T │ O        T │ O        T │ O        T │ O
  6 │ 8        7 │ 3        3 │ 6        4 │ 5
+ 2 │ 1      +   │ 6      + 1 │ 2      + 4 │ 4
────┼───      ────┼───      ────┼───      ────┼───
```

Add.

3 2 + 7 **3 9**	4 6 + 2 1	1 2 + 4 2	1 3 + 5 4

5 9 + 1 0	7 5 + 3	6 3 + 3 1	1 4 + 8 2

4 0 + 1 7	2 1 + 7	3 5 + 3 1	5 0 + 2 8

6 4 + 5	3 8 + 2 0	1 4 + 1 4	8 0 + 9

7 5 + 2 3	1 9 + 4 0	8 2 + 7	5 4 + 2 2

1 6 + 3	4 8 + 3 0	7 4 + 1 1	5 0 + 2 9

Two-digit Addition

Shade each area with a sum of 89.

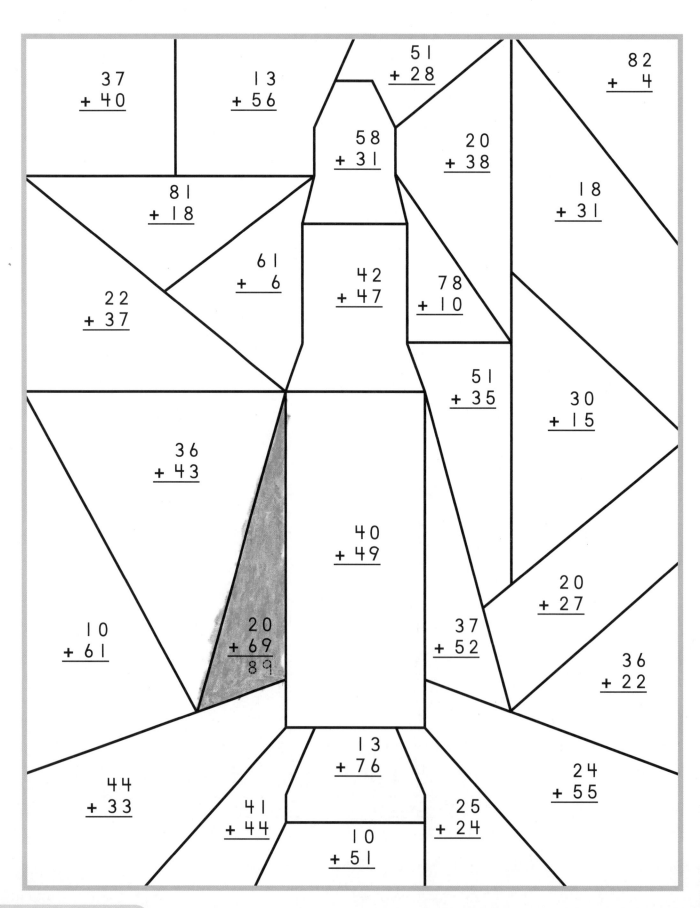

Three-digit Addition

Combine the blocks. Then write the sums.

235 + 121 = 356

143 + 136 = ___

227 + 201 = ___

 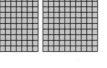

432 + 165 = ___

Three-digit Addition

Use these steps to add three-digit numbers.

Find: 301 + 375

Step 1	Step 2	Step 3
Add the ones.	Add the tens.	Add the hundreds.
(1 + 5 = 6)	(0 + 7 = 7)	(3 + 3 = 6)

	H	T	O			H	T	O			H	T	O
	3	0	1			3	0	1			3	0	1
+	3	7	5		+	3	7	5		+	3	7	5
			6				7	6			6	7	6

Add.

	H	T	O
	2	4	3
+	3	2	5
	5	6	8

	H	T	O
	4	1	0
+	4	4	6

	H	T	O
	3	3	2
+	4	2	7

	H	T	O
	2	0	6
+	7	5	1

	H	T	O
	6	2	1
+	3	5	0

	H	T	O
	1	7	6
+	3	0	2

	H	T	O
	2	4	0
+	1	2	3

	H	T	O
	1	5	2
+	8	4	7

	H	T	O
	7	0	1
+	1	1	1

	H	T	O
	5	4	2
+	3	1	0

	H	T	O
	7	1	2
+	2	0	3

	H	T	O
	2	0	2
+	4	1	4

Regroup 10 ones as 1 ten. Then write the regrouped numbers.

 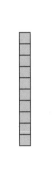

_0_ tens _12_ ones = _1_ ten _2_ ones = _12_

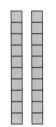 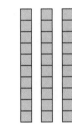

_2_ tens _14_ ones = _3_ tens _4_ ones = ___

  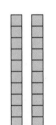 

___ tens ___ ones = ___ tens ___ ones = ___

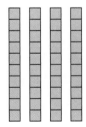 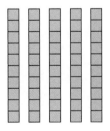

___ tens ___ ones = ___ tens ___ ones = ___

Two-digit Addition, Regrouping Ones

Regroup the ones. Write the sums.

15 + 8

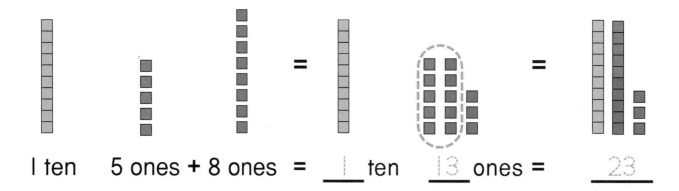

1 ten   5 ones + 8 ones = ___ ten ___ ones = _23_

26 + 5

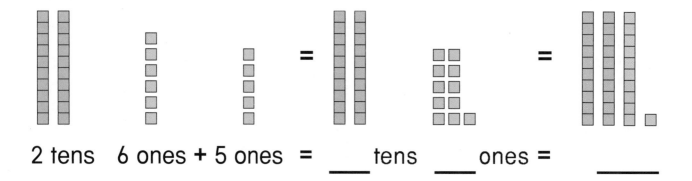

2 tens   6 ones + 5 ones = ___ tens ___ ones = _____

43 + 7

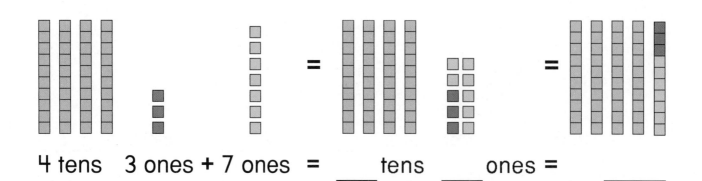

4 tens   3 ones + 7 ones = ___ tens ___ ones = _____

Two-digit Addition, Regrouping Ones

Use these steps to add two digits, regrouping ones.

Find: 34 + 38

Step 1	**Step 2**
Add the ones.	Add the tens.
(4 + 8 = 12)	(1 + 3 + 3 = 7)
Regroup as 1 ten and 2 ones.	

Step 1:
```
  [1]
  T O
  3 4
+ 3 8
─────
    2
```

Step 2:
```
  [1]
  T O
  3 4
+ 3 8
─────
  7 2
```

Add.

```
  [1]            [ ]            [ ]            [ ]
  T O            T O            T O            T O
  3 7            1 2            6 5            5 4
+ 2 8          + 3 8          + 1 7          + 2 6
─────          ─────          ─────          ─────
  6 5
```

```
  [ ]            [ ]            [ ]            [ ]
  T O            T O            T O            T O
  1 2            4 6            3 3            1 5
+ 2 9          + 4 5          + 1 7          + 1 8
─────          ─────          ─────          ─────
```

```
  [ ]            [ ]            [ ]            [ ]
  T O            T O            T O            T O
  5 7            4 3            1 7            6 9
+ 2 3          + 2 9          + 7 4          + 2 9
─────          ─────          ─────          ─────
```

Two-digit Addition, Regrouping Ones

Add.

```
  [1]
  T | O
  5 | 7
+   | 6
-------
  6 | 3
```

```
  [ ]
  T | O
  2 | 9
+ 3 | 7
-------
```

```
  [ ]
  T | O
  3 | 6
+ 4 | 4
-------
```

```
  [ ]
  T | O
  2 | 4
+ 1 | 8
-------
```

```
  [ ]
  T | O
  5 | 9
+ 1 | 2
-------
```

```
  [ ]
  T | O
  5 | 7
+   | 8
-------
```

```
  [ ]
  T | O
  1 | 9
+ 3 | 1
-------
```

```
  [ ]
  T | O
  2 | 9
+ 4 | 6
-------
```

```
  [ ]
  T | O
  2 | 9
+ 5 | 5
-------
```

```
  [ ]
  T | O
  1 | 8
+ 5 | 2
-------
```

```
  [ ]
  T | O
  4 | 6
+ 4 | 4
-------
```

```
  [ ]
  T | O
  1 | 9
+   | 6
-------
```

```
  [ ]
  T | O
  1 | 8
+ 6 | 3
-------
```

```
  [ ]
  T | O
  2 | 9
+   | 2
-------
```

```
  [ ]
  T | O
  4 | 8
+ 1 | 4
-------
```

```
  [ ]
  T | O
  1 | 9
+ 1 | 1
-------
```

Two-digit Addition, Regrouping Ones

Match the problems to their sums.

□	□	□	□	□
1 6	3 6	1 4	2 7	1 7
+ 6 7	+ 3 6	+ 6	+ 4 6	+ 4 7

8 3

72   83   73   20   64

□	□	□	□	□
3 7	1 4	1 6	5 5	2 7
+ 2 9	+ 7 7	+ 3 8	+ 5	+ 3 8

66   54   91   65   60

□	□	□	□	□
3 5	2 7	7 5	2 2	6 6
+ 1 7	+ 3	+ 1 9	+ 6 8	+ 9

30   52   94   75   90

□	□	□	□	□
1 2	6 4	7 7	2 7	6 1
+ 5 9	+ 1 8	+ 6	+ 1 4	+ 2 9

82   71   41   83   90

Two-digit Addition, Regrouping Ones

Shade each box that has a sum of 72.

☐ 52 + 19 _71_	☐ 34 + 48	☐ 34 + 17	☐ 62 + 18	☐ 47 + 26
☐ 68 + 4 72	☐ 76 + 6	☐ 39 + 33	☐ 24 + 29	☐ 16 + 56
☐ 37 + 35	☐ 23 + 18	☐ 34 + 38	☐ 13 + 29	☐ 54 + 8
☐ 27 + 45	☐ 13 + 59	☐ 54 + 18	☐ 34 + 9	☐ 19 + 53
☐ 44 + 28	☐ 54 + 7	☐ 47 + 25	☐ 44 + 37	☐ 23 + 49
☐ 59 + 13	☐ 25 + 57	☐ 28 + 44	☐ 64 + 18	☐ 26 + 46

Use Estimation

Change each number to the closest ten.
Then circle the best estimate for the sum.

13 + 29

↓ ↓

10 + 30

30   (40)   50

---

61 + 19

↓ ↓

___ + ___

60   70   80

---

37 + 8

↓ ↓

___ + ___

50   60   70

---

11 + 48

↓ ↓

___ + ___

50   60   70

---

22 + 31

↓ ↓

___ + ___

40   50   60

---

47 + 29

↓ ↓

___ + ___

70   80   90

---

12 + 12

↓ ↓

___ + ___

10   20   30

Unit 2 Review

Add.

6 + 2 = _____   4 + 5 = _____

9 + 7 = _____   8 + 6 = _____

0 + 10 = _____   9 + 9 = _____

8 + 8 = _____   3 + 9 = _____

```
   1 6          2 5          3 2          1 8
 +   3        + 4 1        + 6 2        + 5 1
```

```
   3 0          4 7          3 5          8 3
 +   9        + 1 1        + 2 3        + 1 4
```

```
 4 0 3        5 2 1        6 3 2        2 8 5
+1 6 3       +1 4 0       +3 0 5       +2 1 4
```

```
   □            □            □            □
   1 5          3 8          2 9          3 7
 +   6        + 3 5        + 1 8        + 2 4
```

```
   □            □            □            □
   5 8          2 9          8 8          4 5
 + 1 7        + 2 9        +   6        + 3 8
```

Unit 2 Review

Find the number of each object on the graph.
Then write the sums.

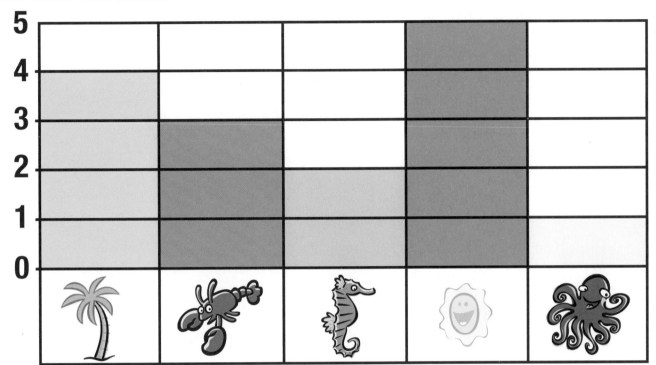

$\_\_\_ + 19 = \_\_\_$ $\_\_\_ + 23 = \_\_\_$

$\_\_\_ + 48 = \_\_\_$ $\_\_\_ + 71 = \_\_\_$

Circle the best estimate for each sum.

$43 + 18$

$\_\_\_ + \_\_\_$

50   60   70

$29 + 54$

$\_\_\_ + \_\_\_$

60   70   80

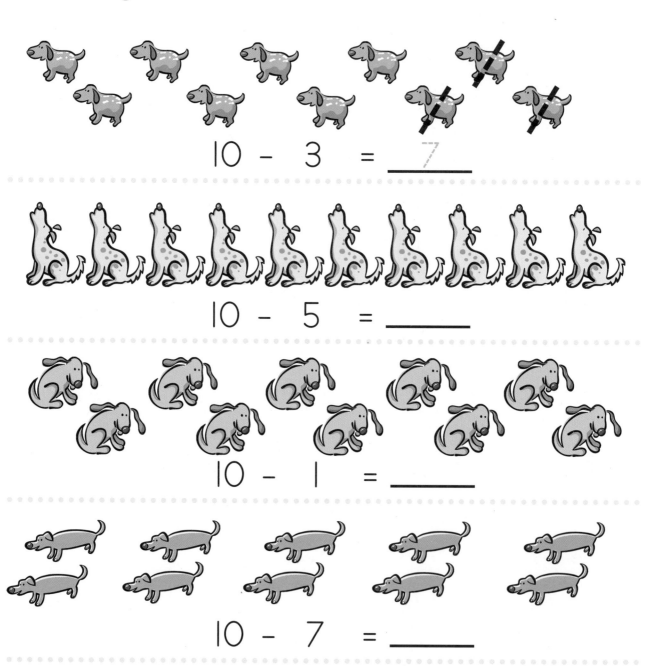

unit 3
subtraction

Differences from 10

Cross out the dogs to subtract. Then write the differences.

10 − 3 = __7__

10 − 5 = ____

10 − 1 = ____

10 − 7 = ____

10 − 2 = ____

Differences from 10

Cross out the cats to subtract. Then write the differences.

$$\begin{array}{r} 10 \\ -\ 6 \\ \hline \end{array}$$

$$\begin{array}{r} 10 \\ -\ 9 \\ \hline \end{array}$$

$$\begin{array}{r} 10 \\ -\ 4 \\ \hline \end{array}$$

$$\begin{array}{r} 10 \\ -\ 8 \\ \hline \end{array}$$

Differences from 18

Cross out the rabbits to subtract. Then write the differences.

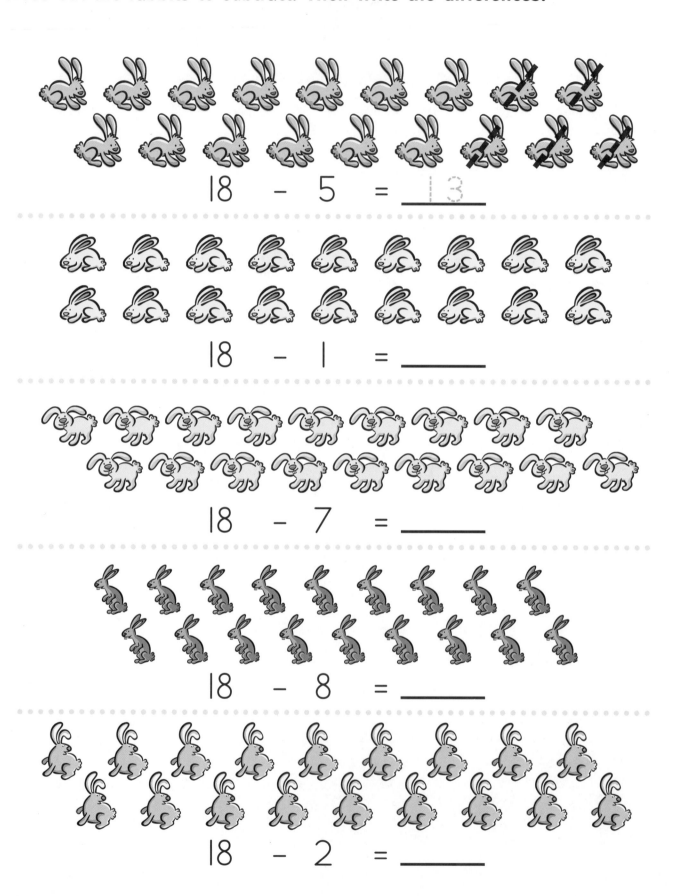

18   –   5   =   13

18   –   1   = _____

18   –   7   = _____

18   –   8   = _____

18   –   2   = _____

Differences from 18

Cross out the animals to subtract. Then write the differences.

$$
\begin{array}{r}
18 \\
- 6 \\
\hline
12
\end{array}
$$

$$
\begin{array}{r}
18 \\
- 9 \\
\hline
\end{array}
$$

$$
\begin{array}{r}
18 \\
- 4 \\
\hline
\end{array}
$$

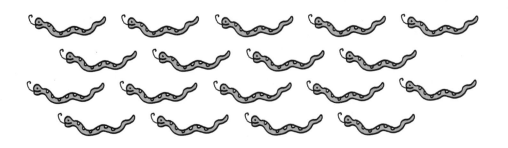

$$
\begin{array}{r}
18 \\
- 7 \\
\hline
\end{array}
$$

$$
\begin{array}{r}
18 \\
- 3 \\
\hline
\end{array}
$$

Subtracting All

Write how many animals. Then subtract.

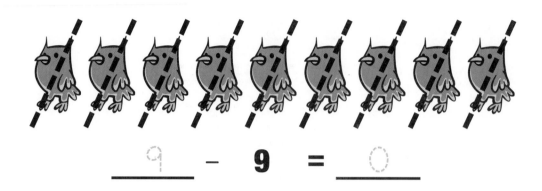

_____9_____ – **9** = _____0_____

. . . .

_____ – **12** = _____

. . . .

_____ – **5** = _____

. . . .

_____ – **17** = _____

. . . .

_____ – **10** = _____

Subtracting Zero

Write how many animals. Then subtract.

$$- \quad 0$$

$$- \quad 0$$

$$- \quad 0$$

$$- \quad 0$$

$$- \quad 0$$

Order Property

Write the numbers to match the cubes.

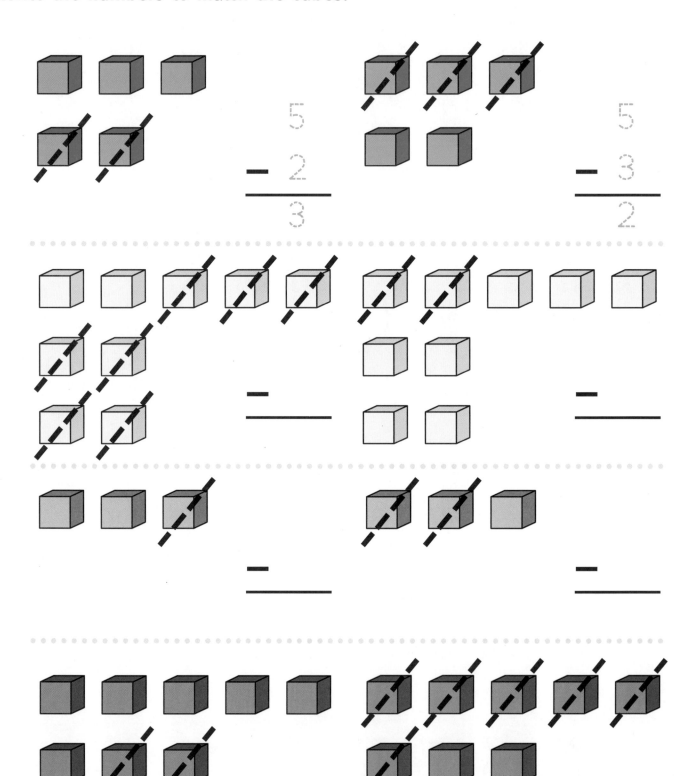

Fact Families

Write the fact family for each set of numbers.

8

_6_ + _2_ = _8_

_2_ + _6_ = _8_

_8_ - _6_ = _2_

_8_ - _2_ = _6_

8

___ + ___ = ___

___ + ___ = ___

___ - ___ = ___

___ - ___ = ___

9

___ + ___ = ___

___ + ___ = ___

___ - ___ = ___

___ - ___ = ___

9

___ + ___ = ___

___ + ___ = ___

___ - ___ = ___

___ - ___ = ___

Write a Number Sentence
Write the number sentences to match the pictures.

___9___ – ___2___ = ___7___

_____ + _____ = _____

_____ – _____ = _____

_____ – _____ = _____

_____ + _____ = _____

Write a Number Sentence

Write the number sentences to match the pictures.

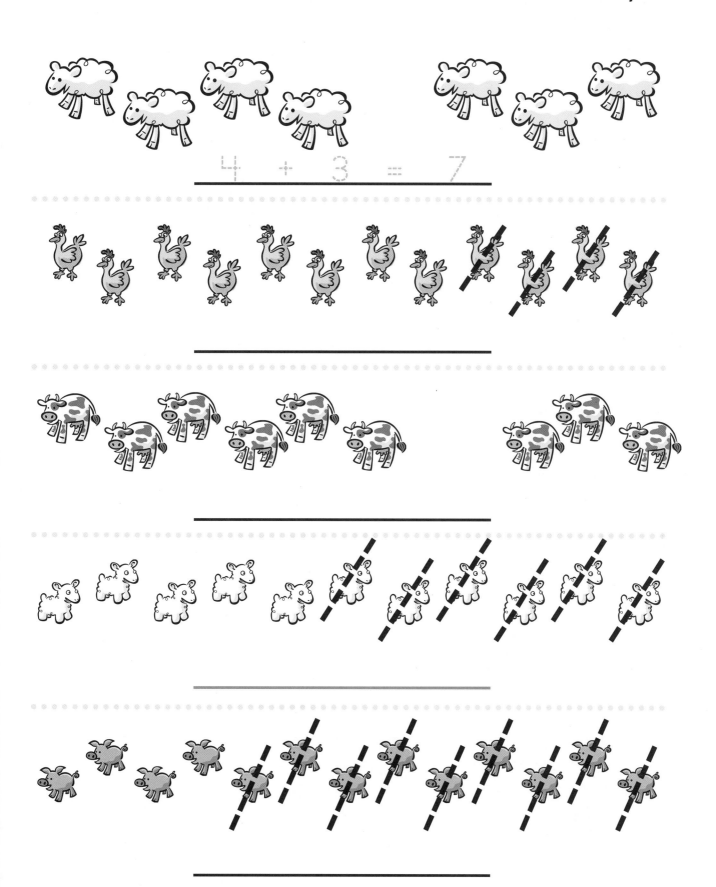

4 + 3 = 7

_____

_____

_____

_____

_____

Two-digit Subtraction

Cross out ones to subtract.

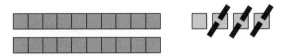

$$24 \quad - \quad 3 \quad = \quad \underline{21}$$

$$36 \quad - \quad 2 \quad = \quad \underline{\hspace{2cm}}$$

$$59 \quad - \quad 8 \quad = \quad \underline{\hspace{2cm}}$$

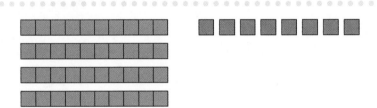

$$48 \quad - \quad 5 \quad = \quad \underline{\hspace{2cm}}$$

$$87 \quad - \quad 4 \quad = \quad \underline{\hspace{2cm}}$$

Two-digit Subtraction

Cross out tens to subtract.

$$25 - 10 = \underline{15}$$

$$42 - 20 = \underline{\hspace{1cm}}$$

$$63 - 40 = \underline{\hspace{1cm}}$$

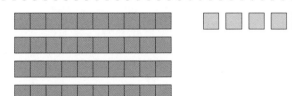

$$47 - 30 = \underline{\hspace{1cm}}$$

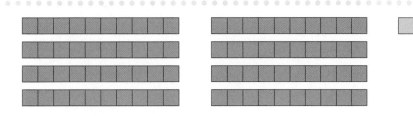

$$81 - 60 = \underline{\hspace{1cm}}$$

Two-digit Subtraction

Cross out tens and ones to subtract.

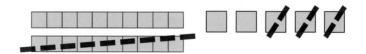

$$25 - 13 = \underline{12}$$

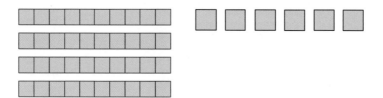

$$46 - 24 = \underline{}$$

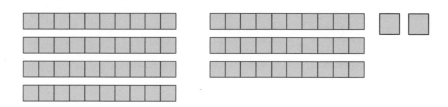

$$72 - 31 = \underline{}$$

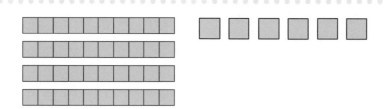

$$46 - 15 = \underline{}$$

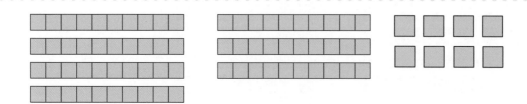

$$78 - 56 = \underline{}$$

Two-digit Subtraction

Use these steps to subtract two-digit numbers.

Find: 65 - 2

Step 1	Step 2
Subtract the ones. $(5 - 2 = 3)$	Subtract the tens. $(6 - 0 = 6)$

```
  T | O              T | O
  6 | 5              6 | 5
-   | 2            -   | 2
------              ------
    | 3              6 | 3
```

Find: 84 - 63

Step 1	Step 2
Subtract the ones. $(4 - 3 = 1)$	Subtract the tens. $(8 - 6 = 2)$

```
  T | O              T | O
  8 | 4              8 | 4
- 6 | 3            - 6 | 3
------              ------
    | 1              2 | 1
```

Subtract.

```
  T | O          T | O          T | O          T | O
  7 | 6          2 | 9          3 | 6          4 | 4
-   | 5        - 1 | 4        -   | 4        - 4 | 3
------          ------          ------          ------
  7 | 1          1 | 5
```

```
  T | O          T | O          T | O          T | O
  7 | 8          5 | 8          7 | 0          4 | 6
- 2 | 5        - 4 | 1        - 5 | 0        -   | 2
------          ------          ------          ------
```

```
  T | O          T | O          T | O          T | O
  3 | 3          4 | 2          4 | 4          7 | 9
- 1 | 0        - 3 | 1        -   | 1        - 6 | 9
------          ------          ------          ------
```

```
  T | O          T | O          T | O          T | O
  7 | 3          5 | 6          9 | 9          6 | 3
- 4 | 2        - 2 | 3        -   | 0        - 5 | 1
------          ------          ------          ------
```

Two-digit Subtraction

Subtract.

```
   8 6        2 7        7 2        1 6
 - 5 4      - 2 3      - 7 2      - 1 3
   3 2
```

```
   5 9        7 5        6 3        9 4
 - 1 0      -   3      - 3 1      - 8 2
```

```
   8 6        5 1        4 5        8 9
 - 2 2      - 5 0      - 1 5      - 6 0
```

```
   6 9        3 8        1 4        8 9
 -   5      - 2 0      - 1 4      -   9
```

```
   7 5        6 9        8 8        5 4
 - 2 3      - 4 0      -   7      - 2 2
```

```
   1 6        4 8        7 4        5 0
 -   3      - 3 0      - 1 1      - 2 0
```

Two-digit Subtraction

Shade all the areas that have a difference of 21.

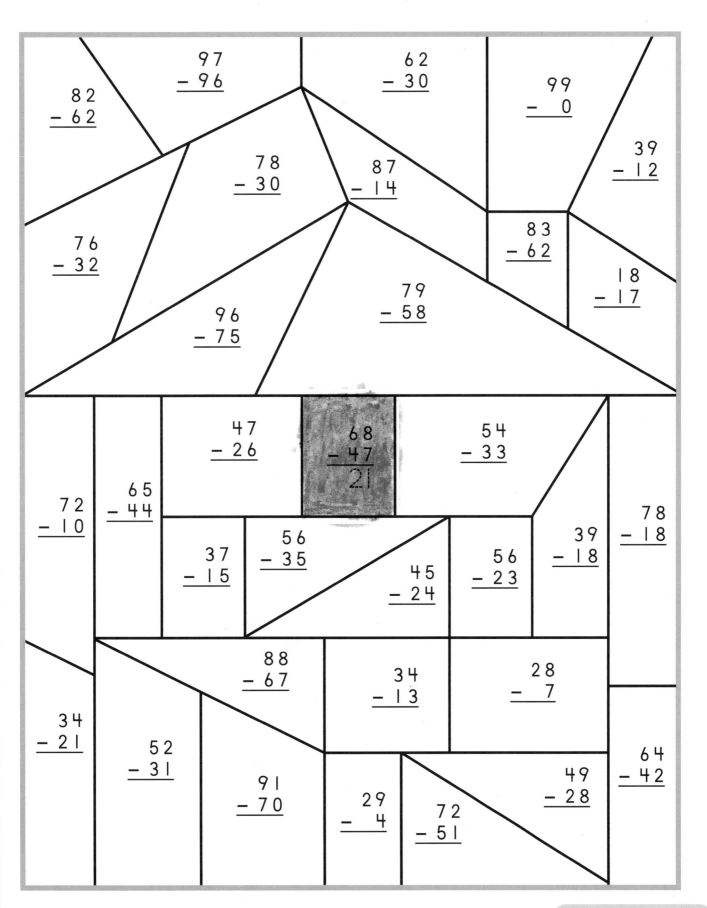

Three-digit Subtraction

Use these steps to subtract three-digit numbers.

Find: 874 - 671

Step 1	Step 2	Step 3
Subtract the ones.	Subtract the tens.	Subtract the hundreds.
$(4 - 1 = 3)$	$(7 - 7 = 0)$	$(8 - 6 = 2)$

Step 1

H	T	O
8	7	4
− 6	7	1
		3

Step 2

H	T	O
8	7	4
− 6	7	1
	0	3

Step 3

H	T	O
8	7	4
− 6	7	1
2	0	3

Subtract.

H	T	O
5	3	8
− 1	2	6
4	1	2

H	T	O
7	3	9
− 5	3	0

H	T	O
8	7	3
− 2	3	2

H	T	O
5	2	3
−	1	3

H	T	O
7	6	4
−	5	0

H	T	O
2	8	8
− 1	0	8

H	T	O
9	9	9
−		0

H	T	O
4	2	8
− 2	0	5

H	T	O
9	4	5
− 4	3	5

H	T	O
5	9	5
− 2	0	3

H	T	O
6	9	7
− 3	5	0

H	T	O
6	3	8
− 1	2	8

H	T	O
9	5	4
−	2	1

H	T	O
8	8	6
−		0

H	T	O
4	8	9
−	5	2

H	T	O
2	3	4
− 1	0	2

Two-digit Subtraction with Regrouping

Regroup the tens. Cross out ones to subtract.

2 tens   3 ones = ____ ten ____ ones

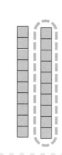

  =

---

4 tens   1 one = ____ tens ____ ones

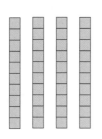

  =

---

3 tens   6 ones = ____ tens ____ ones

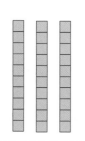

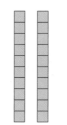 =

---

5 tens   0 ones = ____ tens ____ ones

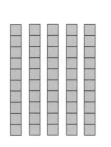

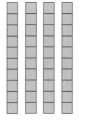 =

Two-digit Subtraction with Regrouping

Regroup the tens. Cross out tens and ones to subtract.

3 tens   5 ones   = ___2___ tens ___15___ ones

$$\begin{array}{r} 35 \\ -\ 17 \\ \hline 18 \end{array}$$

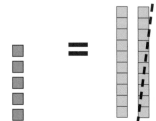 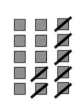

2 tens   1 one   = _____ ten _____ ones

$$\begin{array}{r} 21 \\ -\ 14 \\ \hline \end{array}$$

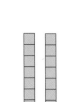 

4 tens   3 ones   = _____ tens _____ ones

$$\begin{array}{r} 43 \\ -\ 29 \\ \hline \end{array}$$

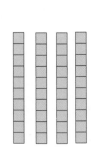

6 tens   0 ones   = _____ tens _____ ones

$$\begin{array}{r} 60 \\ -\ 37 \\ \hline \end{array}$$

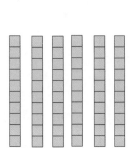 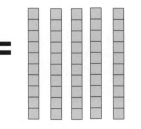

Two-digit Subtraction with Regrouping

Use these steps to subtract two-digit numbers with regrouping.

Find: 52- 13

Step 1	Step 2	Step 3	Step 4
Subtract ones. More ones are needed. $(2 - 3 = ?)$	Regroup. Show I less ten and 10 more ones.	Subtract the ones. $(12 - 3 = 9)$	Subtract the tens. $(4 - 1 = 3)$

Step 1:
```
  T | O
  5 | 2
- 1 | 3
  --+--
    | ?
```

Step 2:
```
  4 |12
  T | O
  5̷ | 2̷
- 1 | 3
  --+--
```

Step 3:
```
  4 |12
  T | O
  5̷ | 2̷
- 1 | 3
  --+--
    | 9
```

Step 4:
```
  4 |12
  T | O
  5̷ | 2̷
- 1 | 3
  --+--
  3 | 9
```

Subtract.

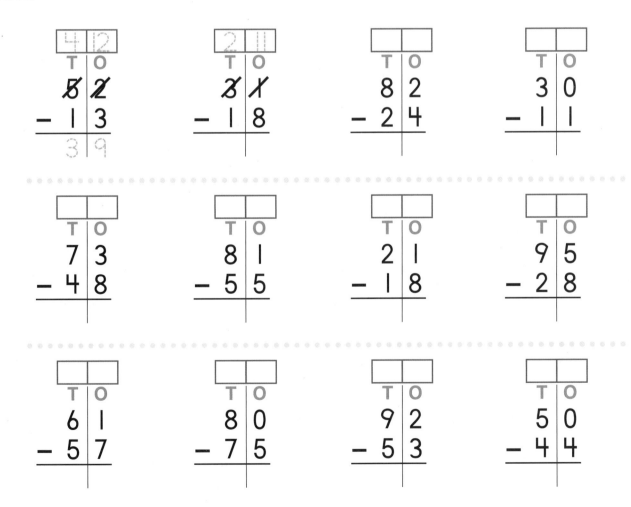

```
  4 |12
  T | O
  5̷ | 2̷
- 1 | 3
  --+--
  3 | 9
```

```
  2 |11
  T | O
  3̷ | 1̷
- 1 | 8
  --+--
```

```
  T | O
  8 | 2
- 2 | 4
  --+--
```

```
  T | O
  3 | 0
- 1 | 1
  --+--
```

```
  T | O
  7 | 3
- 4 | 8
  --+--
```

```
  T | O
  8 | 1
- 5 | 5
  --+--
```

```
  T | O
  2 | 1
- 1 | 8
  --+--
```

```
  T | O
  9 | 5
- 2 | 8
  --+--
```

```
  T | O
  6 | 1
- 5 | 7
  --+--
```

```
  T | O
  8 | 0
- 7 | 5
  --+--
```

```
  T | O
  9 | 2
- 5 | 3
  --+--
```

```
  T | O
  5 | 0
- 4 | 4
  --+--
```

Two-digit Subtraction with Regrouping

Subtract.

	T	O
☐4	☐3
	8̸	3̸
−	2	7
	2	6

	T	O
☐7	☐5
	8̸	5̸
−	6	7
	1	8

	T	O
	5	0
−	1	3

	T	O
	9	1
−	6	6

	T	O
	7	0
−	2	6

	T	O
	6	2
−	1	5

	T	O
	9	1
−	4	4

	T	O
	8	3
−	3	5

	T	O
	8	3
−	4	6

	T	O
	8	6
−	4	8

	T	O
	3	3
−	1	8

	T	O
	8	2
−	1	4

	T	O
	6	3
−	4	6

	T	O
	3	2
−		6

	T	O
	4	1
−	3	7

	T	O
	9	5
−	5	6

	T	O
	8	8
−	3	9

	T	O
	9	0
−	8	5

	T	O
	4	1
−		3

	T	O
	7	2
−	5	7

Two-digit Subtraction with Regrouping

Match the equal differences.

```
  7 10
  8 0          9 3          5 2          9 0
- 6 8        - 3 9        -   9        - 4 7
  1 2
```

```
  3 4          7 6          7 0          2 2
- 2 6        - 6 8        - 1 9        -   5
```

```
                8 11
  6 2          9 1          4 0          8 0
-   8        - 7 9        - 2 3        - 2 9
               1 2
```

```
  8 1          4 1          5 2          8 4
- 1 6        - 2 2        - 4 8        - 6 8
```

```
  9 3          9 3          7 3          1 1
- 7 4        - 2 8        -   7        -   7
```

```
  4 4          7 6          7 0          8 5
- 3 7        - 6 9        - 5 4        - 1 9
```

Two-digit Subtraction with Regrouping

Subtract.

$$
\begin{array}{r}
{\scriptstyle 5\ \ 11} \\
6\,1 \\
-\ 3\,2 \\
\hline
2\,9
\end{array}
\qquad
\begin{array}{r}
9\,4 \\
-\ 1\,9 \\
\hline
\end{array}
\qquad
\begin{array}{r}
5\,0 \\
-\ 3\,2 \\
\hline
\end{array}
\qquad
\begin{array}{r}
3\,1 \\
-\ \ \,2 \\
\hline
\end{array}
$$

$$
\begin{array}{r}
9\,4 \\
-\ \ \,8 \\
\hline
\end{array}
\qquad
\begin{array}{r}
3\,2 \\
-\ 2\,9 \\
\hline
\end{array}
\qquad
\begin{array}{r}
8\,0 \\
-\ 7\,8 \\
\hline
\end{array}
\qquad
\begin{array}{r}
7\,1 \\
-\ 2\,8 \\
\hline
\end{array}
$$

$$
\begin{array}{r}
6\,1 \\
-\ 2\,3 \\
\hline
\end{array}
\qquad
\begin{array}{r}
6\,2 \\
-\ 2\,5 \\
\hline
\end{array}
\qquad
\begin{array}{r}
9\,3 \\
-\ 8\,4 \\
\hline
\end{array}
\qquad
\begin{array}{r}
7\,0 \\
-\ 5\,7 \\
\hline
\end{array}
$$

$$
\begin{array}{r}
7\,0 \\
-\ 6\,1 \\
\hline
\end{array}
\qquad
\begin{array}{r}
8\,3 \\
-\ \ \,5 \\
\hline
\end{array}
\qquad
\begin{array}{r}
7\,0 \\
-\ 3\,9 \\
\hline
\end{array}
\qquad
\begin{array}{r}
6\,7 \\
-\ 4\,8 \\
\hline
\end{array}
$$

$$
\begin{array}{r}
6\,8 \\
-\ 4\,9 \\
\hline
\end{array}
\qquad
\begin{array}{r}
2\,3 \\
-\ 1\,7 \\
\hline
\end{array}
\qquad
\begin{array}{r}
4\,4 \\
-\ 3\,6 \\
\hline
\end{array}
\qquad
\begin{array}{r}
8\,7 \\
-\ 2\,8 \\
\hline
\end{array}
$$

$$
\begin{array}{r}
3\,6 \\
-\ 1\,9 \\
\hline
\end{array}
\qquad
\begin{array}{r}
2\,3 \\
-\ \ \,4 \\
\hline
\end{array}
\qquad
\begin{array}{r}
4\,1 \\
-\ 2\,8 \\
\hline
\end{array}
\qquad
\begin{array}{r}
8\,2 \\
-\ 7\,3 \\
\hline
\end{array}
$$

Choose an Operation

Look at the pictures. Write + or –. Then write the sum or difference.

8 $\boxed{+}$ 4 = ___12___

10 $\boxed{}$ 3 = _____

6 $\boxed{}$ 4 = _____

9 $\boxed{}$ 2 = _____

12 $\boxed{}$ 9 = _____

Subtract.

6 − 6 = ____

13 − 7 = ___

14 − 5 = ____

8 − 0 = ___

Complete the fact families.

_5_ + _4_ = _9_

___ + ___ = ___

___ − ___ = ___

___ − ___ = ___

_7_ + _3_ = _10_

___ + ___ = ___

___ − ___ = ___

___ − ___ = ___

Subtract.

```
   1 8        4 5        6 4        7 8
 −   3      − 2 3      − 5 1      − 5 1
```

```
   4 9 3      5 7 1      6 3 9      2 8 5
 − 1 6 3    − 1 4 0    − 3 0 5    − 2 1 4
```

```
   1 5        3 1        2 6        4 4
 −   6      − 2 5      − 1 8      − 3 9
```

```
   8 5        7 2
 − 5 6      − 3 8
```

Unit 3 Review

Write the number sentences to match the pictures.

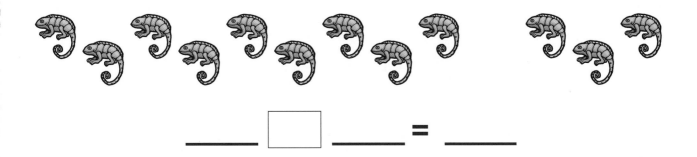

____ □ ____ = ____

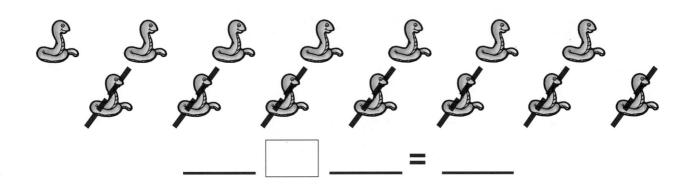

____ □ ____ = ____

____ □ ____ = ____

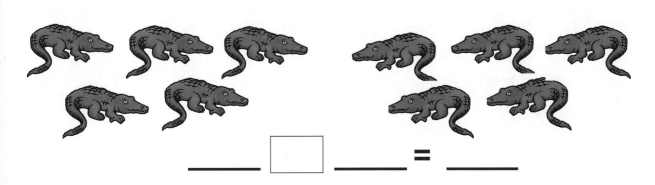

____ □ ____ = ____

unit 4
money

Pennies

= 1 cent = 1¢

Count the money. Write the total amount on each bag.

Pennies and Nickels

 = 5 cents = 5¢

Count the money. Write the total amount on each bag.

             8¢

           ¢

              ¢

            ¢

              ¢

Pennies, Nickels, Dimes, and Quarters

 = 25 cents = 25¢

Count the money. Write the total amount on each bag.

Pennies, Nickels, Dimes, and Quarters

Match each item with the money that can buy it.

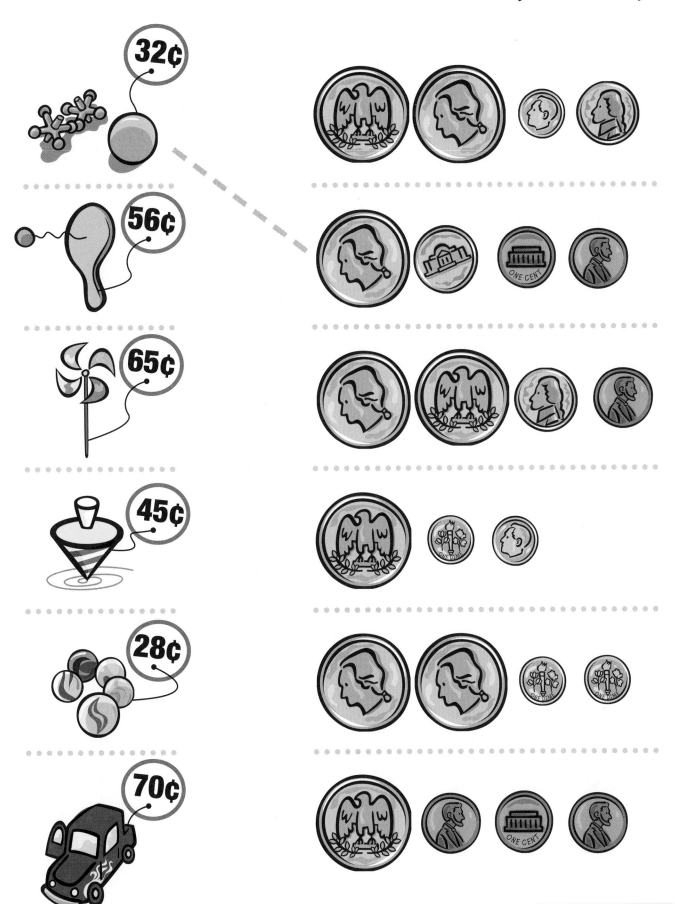

Use Logic

Write two different ways to buy each item.

	(quarter)	(dime)	(nickel)	(penny)
19¢		1	1	4
			3	4
28¢				
62¢				
97¢				

Money Equivalents

Match equal amounts of money.

Money Equivalents

Write how many of each coin you need to make the amount shown.

5¢ = ___1___ or ___5___

10¢ = _____ or _____ or _____

25¢ = _____ or _____ or _____

50¢ = _____ or _____ or _____

100¢ = _____ or _____ or _____

Show How Much

Circle the coins you need to buy each item.

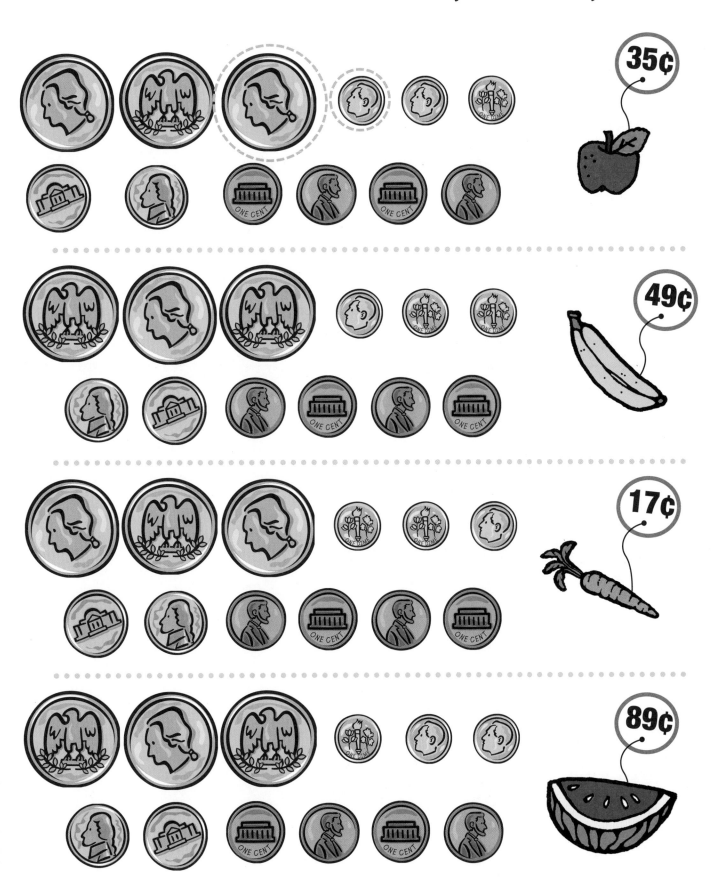

35¢

49¢

17¢

89¢

Use the Fewest Coins

Write how much money. Then draw the same amount with the fewest coins.

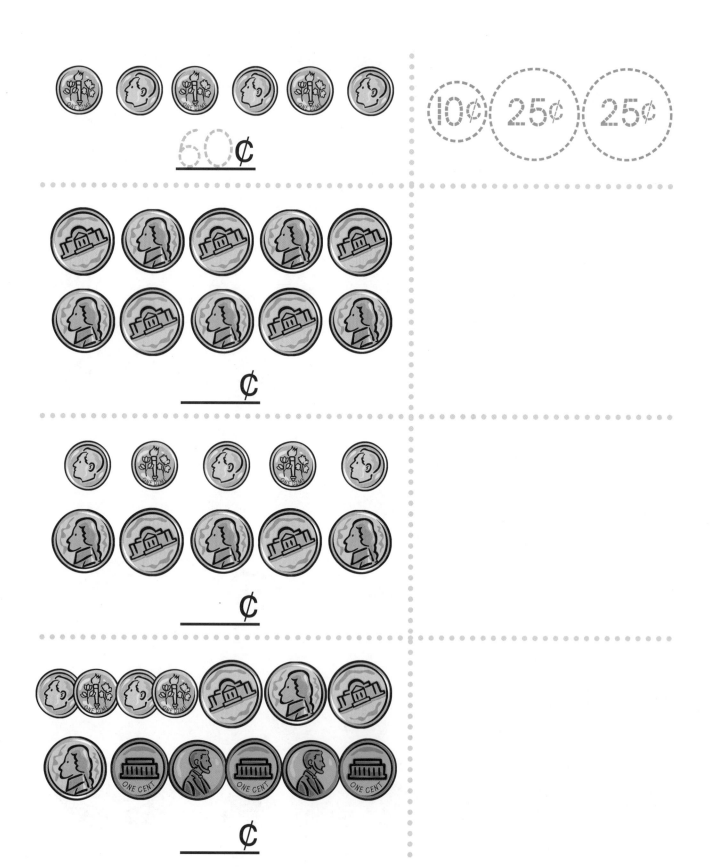

60 ¢

10¢ 25¢ 25¢

_____ ¢

_____ ¢

_____ ¢

Making Change

Write how much change you get back.

Price	You Pay	Your Change

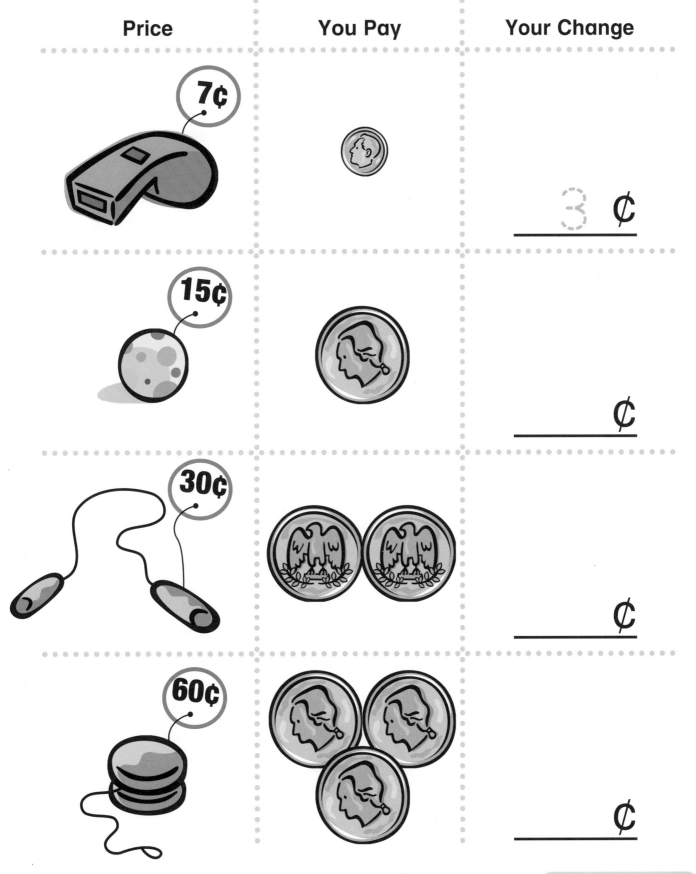

3 ¢

_____ ¢

_____ ¢

_____ ¢

Making Change

Write how much change you get back.

Price	You Pay	Your Change

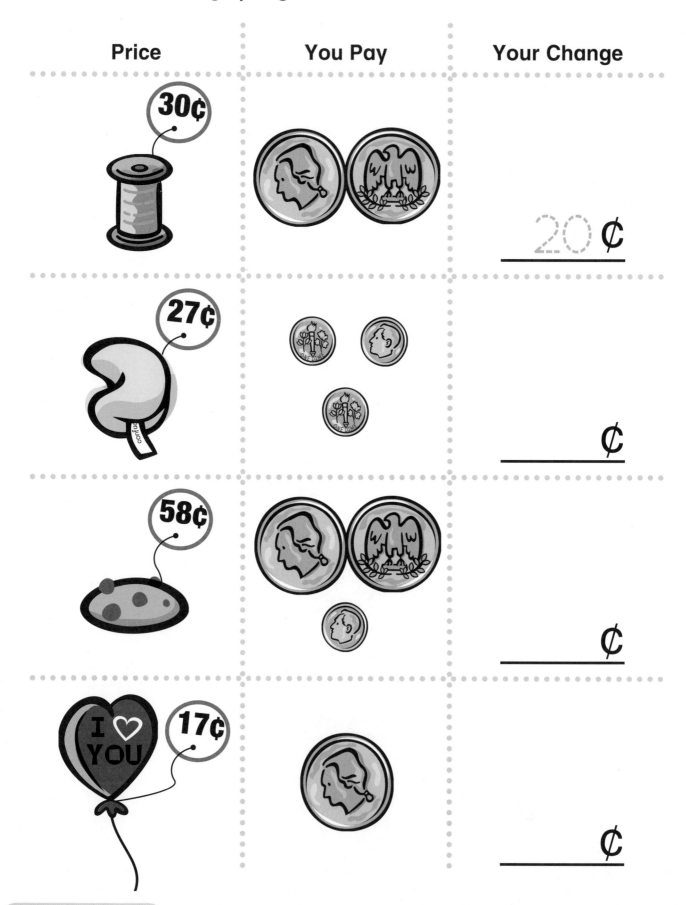

20 ¢

_____ ¢

_____ ¢

_____ ¢

Use a Picture

You pay 25¢ for each item. Write your change.

Apples 3¢ each

Pears 10¢ each

Pineapples 15¢ each

Peaches 5¢ each

Oranges 4¢ each

Bananas 20¢ each

You Pay: 25¢

22 ¢

You Pay: 25¢

___ ¢

You Pay: 25¢

___ ¢

You Pay: 25¢

___ ¢

You Pay: 25¢

___ ¢

You Pay: 25¢

___ ¢

Write how much money.

_____ ¢

_____ ¢

Write how many of each coin you need to make the amount shown.

5¢ = _____ or _____

10¢ = _____ or _____ or _____

Write how much money. Then draw the same amount with the fewest coins.

_____ ¢

Write two different ways to buy each item.

16¢				
65¢				

Write your change.

Price	You Pay	Your Change
6¢		_____ ¢
17¢ I ♥ YOU		_____ ¢

unit 5
Time

Telling Time: Hours

Write the time shown on each clock in two ways.

4:00

__4__ o'clock

___:___
_____ o'clock

___:___
_____ o'clock

___:___
_____ o'clock

___:___
_____ o'clock

___:___
_____ o'clock

___:___
_____ o'clock

___:___
_____ o'clock

___:___
_____ o'clock

Telling Time: Half Hours

Write the time shown on each clock.

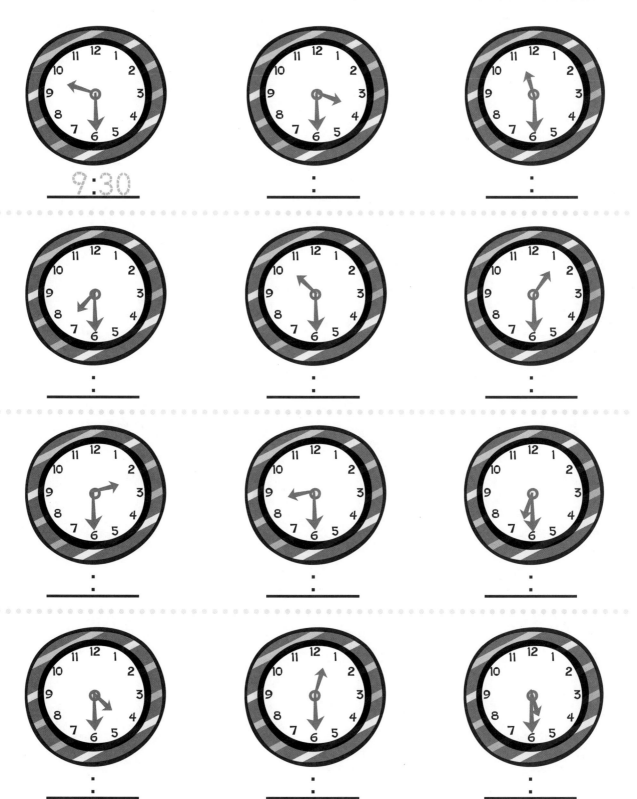

9:30

__ : __

__ : __

__ : __

__ : __

__ : __

__ : __

__ : __

__ : __

__ : __

__ : __

__ : __

Telling Time: Quarter Hours

Write the time shown on each clock.

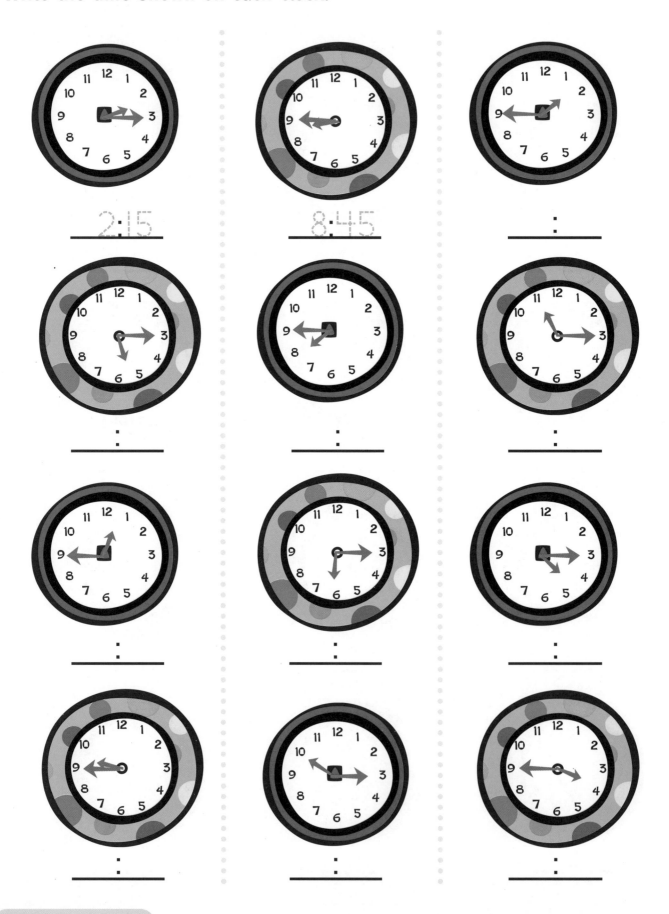

2:15

8:45

___:___

___:___

___:___

___:___

___:___

___:___

___:___

___:___

___:___

___:___

Telling Time: Quarter Hours

Write the times that are a quarter hour later.

Complete a Pattern

Draw the next clock in each pattern.

Telling Time: Five Minutes

Write the time shown on each clock in two ways.

10:05

__5__ minutes after __10__

10:15

__15__ minutes after __10__

__ : __

____ minutes after ____

__ : __

____ minutes after ____

__ : __

____ minutes after ____

__ : __

____ minutes after ____

Telling Time: Five Minutes

Write the times 5 minutes later.

Practice Telling Time
Match the clocks that show the same time.

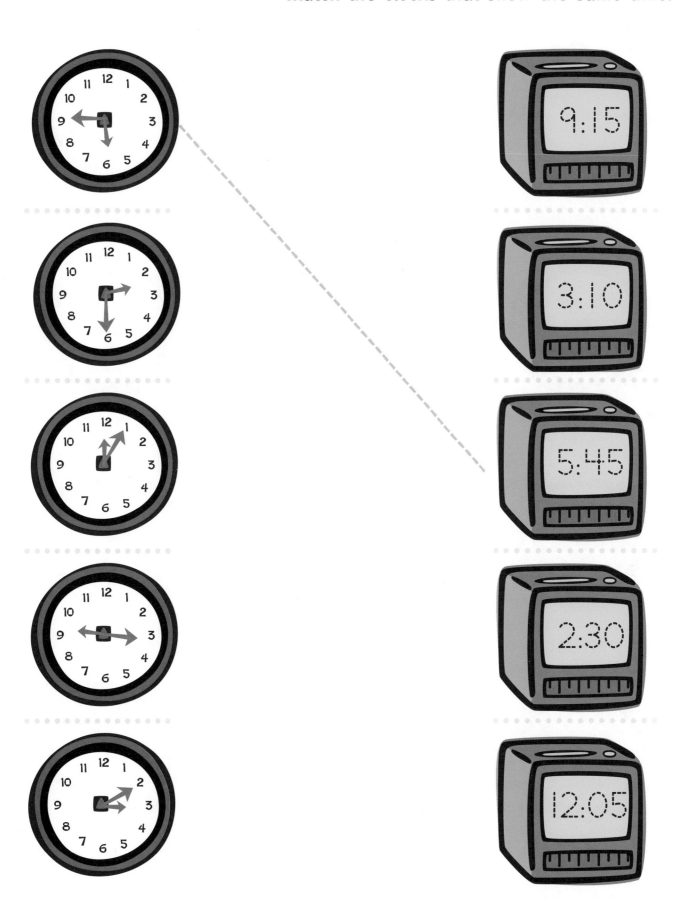

Practice Telling Time

Draw the hands on the clocks.

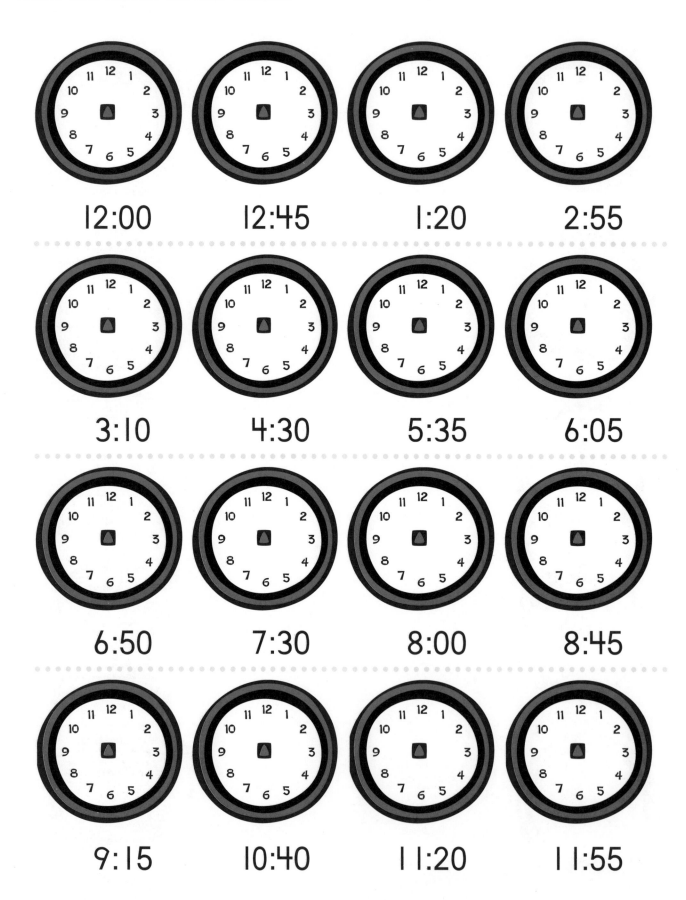

12:00	12:45	1:20	2:55
3:10	4:30	5:35	6:05
6:50	7:30	8:00	8:45
9:15	10:40	11:20	11:55

2nd   1st   3rd

_____   _____   _____

_____   _____   _____

_____   _____   _____

Solid Figures

Circle the solids that are the same as the first figure in each row.

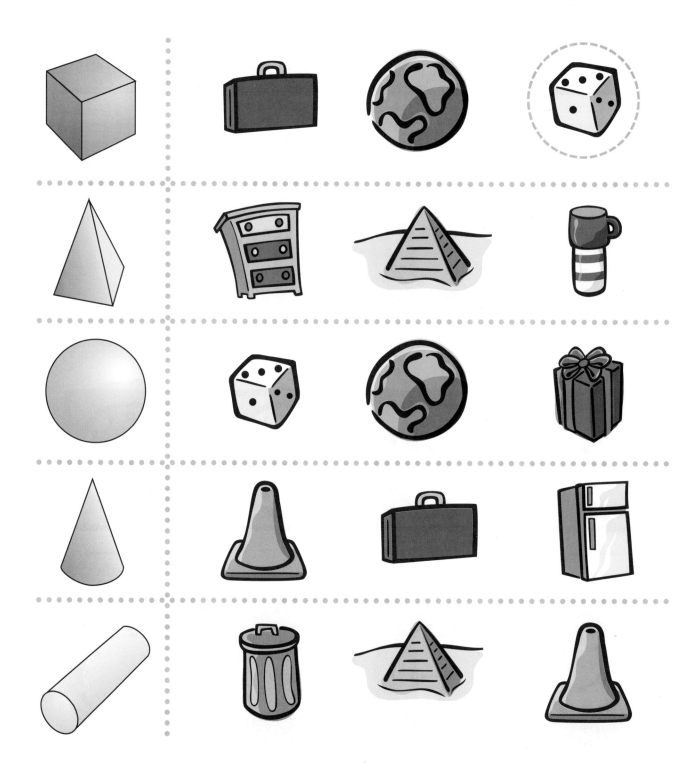

Plane Figures

Circle the figures that are the same as the first figure in each row.

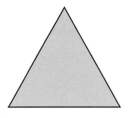   

Plane Figures

Name the figure. Then count its straight sides.

Shape	Name	Sides
Side → ☐ ← Side (Side above, Side below)	square	4
△		
▬		
●		
▮		
◣		
◆		

Congruence

Draw a figure to match each one shown.

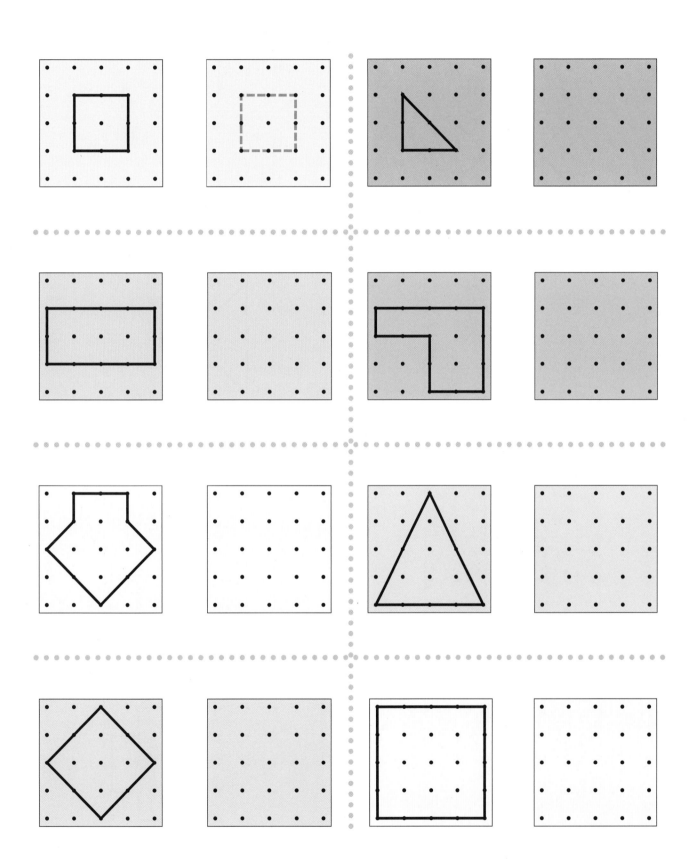

Symmetry

Draw the other half of each figure.

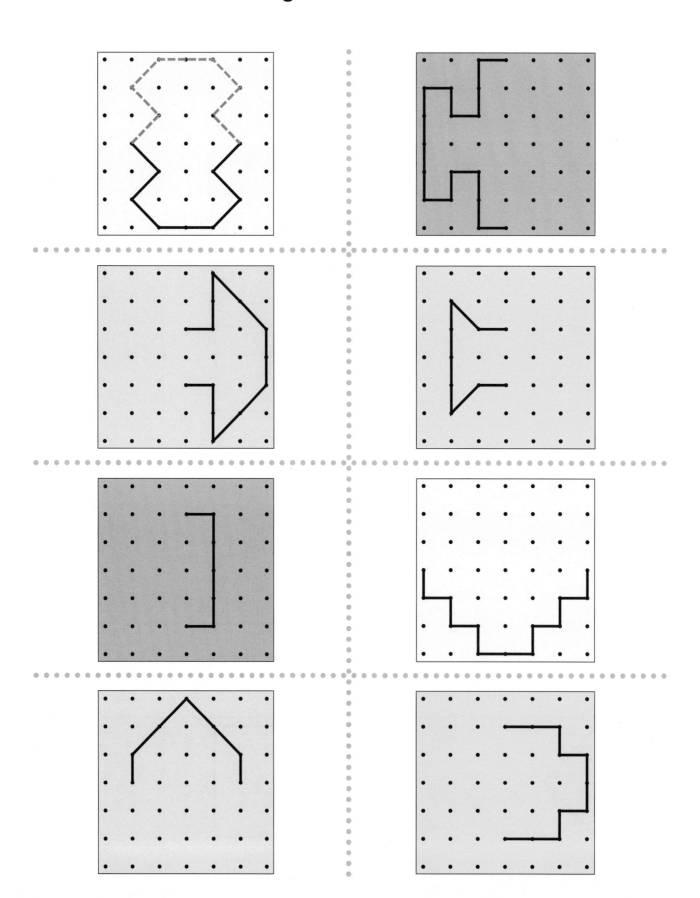

Exploring Perimeter

Count the number of units around each figure.

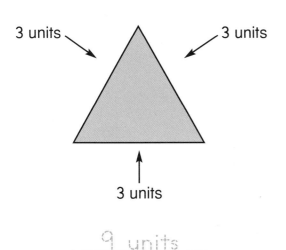

3 units   3 units

3 units

9 units

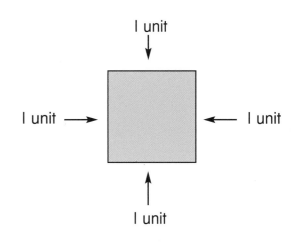

I unit

I unit   I unit

I unit

_____

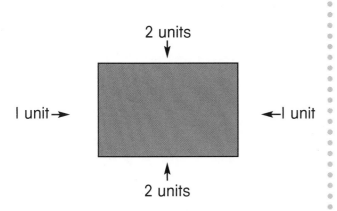

2 units

I unit→   ←I unit

2 units

_____

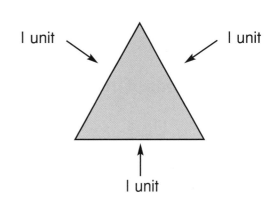

I unit   I unit

I unit

_____

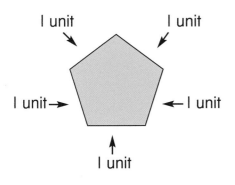

I unit   I unit

I unit→   ←I unit

I unit

_____

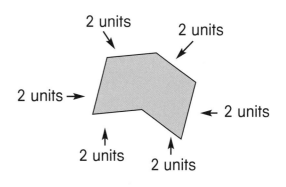

2 units   2 units

2 units →   ← 2 units

2 units   2 units

_____

Use a Picture

To find places on a grid,
always start at 0.
Count across ⟶ .
Then count up↑.

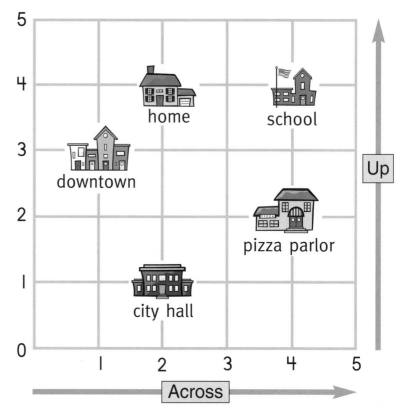

Up

Across

Follow the directions. Circle the place where you land.

Across ⟶	Up ↑			
4	2			
2	1			
1	3			
2	4			
4	4			

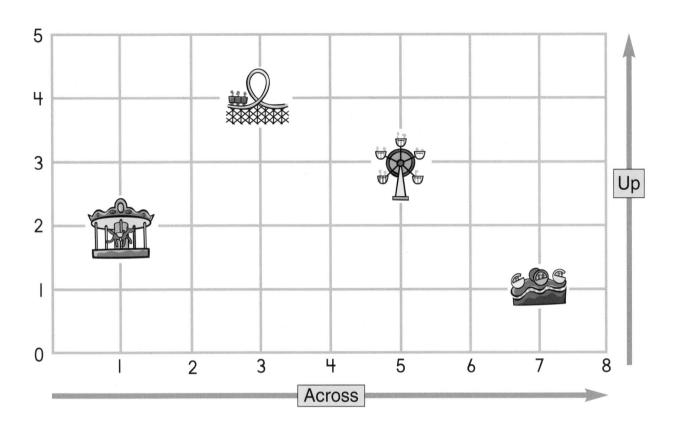

Write the directions to each place.

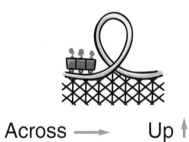

Across ⟶   Up ↑

5   3
___   ___

Across ⟶   Up ↑

___   ___

Across ⟶   Up ↑

Across ⟶   Up ↑

___   ___

Across ⟶   Up ↑

___   ___

Unit 6 Review

Circle the shapes that are the same in each row.

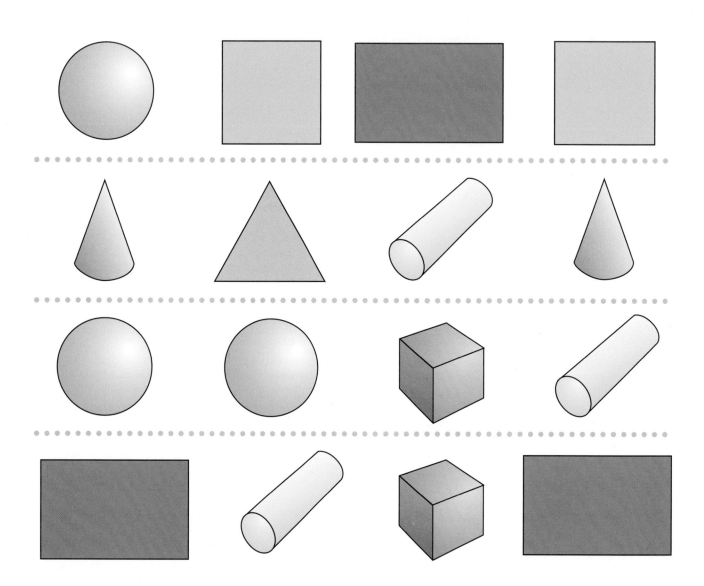

Count the units around each figure.

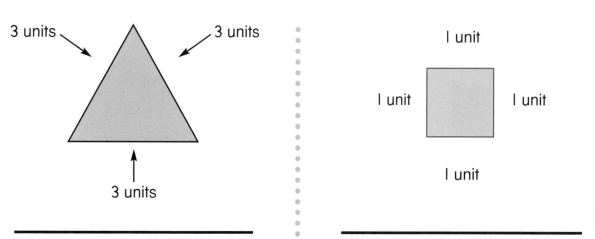

3 units   3 units

3 units

1 unit

1 unit   1 unit

1 unit

_____

Unit 6 Review

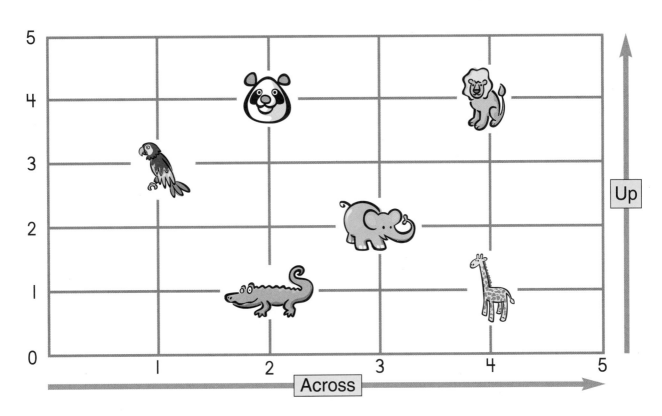

Follow the directions. Circle the animal you find.

Across → 1   Up ↑ 3

Across → 3   Up ↑ 2

Across → 4   Up ↑ 4

Across → 4   Up ↑ 1

Across → 2   Up ↑ 4

Measuring Inches
Write the length of each object.

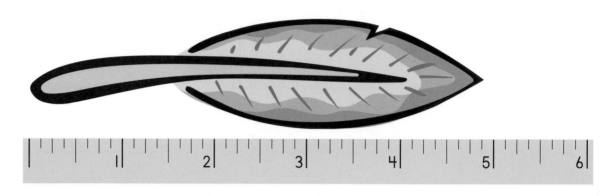

about _____5_____ inches

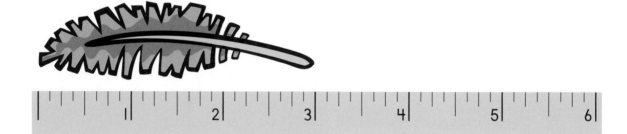

about _____ inches

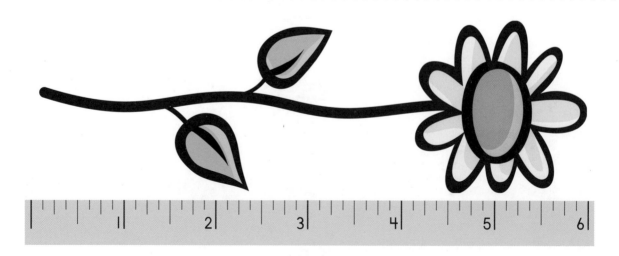

about _____ inches

Measuring Inches
Use an inch ruler to measure.

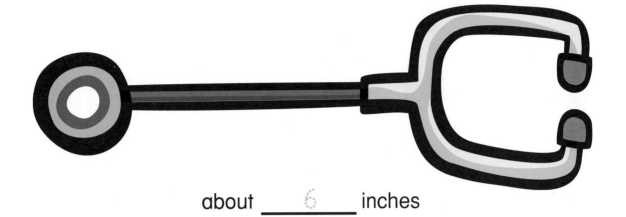

about _____6_____ inches

....

about _____ inches

....

about _____ inches

....

about _____ inches

Measuring Centimeters

Write the length of each object.

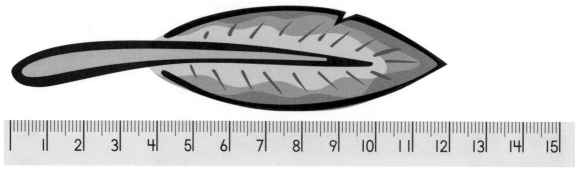

about ___12___ centimeters

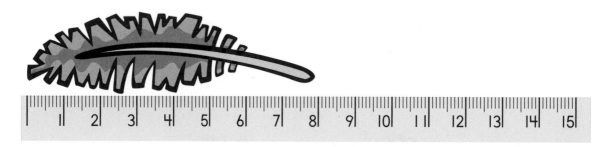

about _____ centimeters

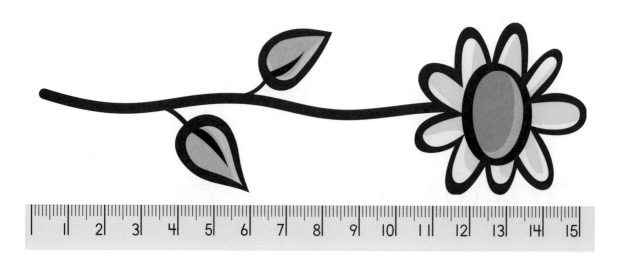

_____

Measuring Centimeters

Use a centimeter ruler to measure.

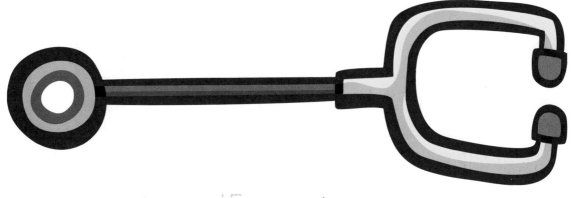

about _____15_____ centimeters

about _____ centimeters

about _____ centimeters

about _____ centimeters

Guess and Check

Guess the length. Then measure to check.

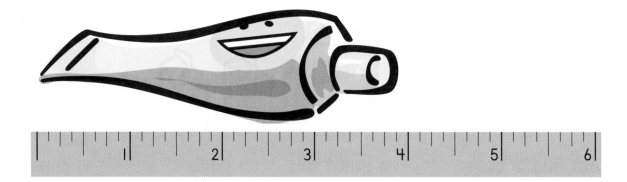

guess: about __4__ inches   check: about __4__ inches

guess: about ____ inches   check: about ____ inches

guess: about ____ inches   check: about ____ inches

guess: about ____ inches   check: about ____ inches

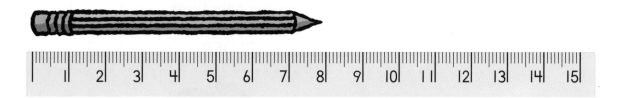

guess: about __8__ centimeters   check: about __8__ centimeters

guess: about ____ centimeters   check: about ____ centimeters

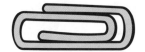

guess: about ____ centimeters   check: about ____ centimeters

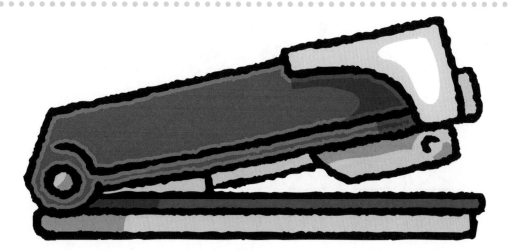

guess: about ____ centimeters   check: about ____ centimeters

Measure the lengths.

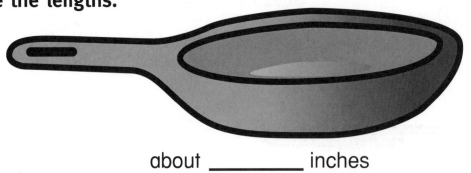

about _____ inches

about _____ centimeters

Circle the containers you can fill with the first group in each row.

Guess the length. Then measure to check.

guess: about _____ inches   check: about _____ inches

guess: about _____ inches   check: about _____ inches

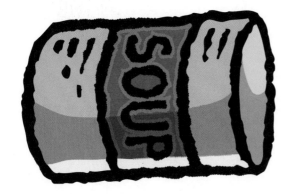

guess: about _____ centimeters   check: about _____ centimeters

Language
Arts

Nouns

A **noun** is a word that names a person, place, or thing.
The words <u>a</u>, <u>an</u>, and <u>the</u> are clues that show a noun is near.
Examples:
a <u>man</u>, an <u>elephant</u>, the <u>yard</u>

DIRECTIONS ▶ Find the nouns, or naming words, below. Write the nouns on the lines.

apple	car	eat	hear	rug	bird	chair
girl	hot	tree	boy	desk	gone	over
truck	came	dirty	grass	pen	up	tiny

1. _____
2. _____
3. _____
4. _____

5. _____
6. _____
7. _____
8. _____

9. _____
10. _____
11. _____
12. _____

DIRECTIONS ▶ Circle the two nouns in each sentence.

13. The girl eats an apple.

14. A bird flies to the tree.

15. A chair is by the desk.

16. A boy sits in the chair.

17. The girl plays with a truck.

Practice with Nouns

Remember, a word that names a person or an animal is called a noun. A word that names a place or a thing is also called a noun.
Examples:

The <u>girl</u> and her <u>dog</u> sat on a <u>bench</u> in the <u>park</u>.

DIRECTIONS Circle the noun or nouns in each sentence. You should find eleven nouns in all.

1. My sister plays in the park.

2. She rides in a car with our mother.

3. Sometimes our dog goes, too.

4. A boy feeds birds under the trees.

5. Let's go to the playground!

6. I see a cat under the slide.

DIRECTIONS Look at the nouns you circled. Decide if each noun names a person, a place, a thing, or an animal. Write the noun in the correct space in the chart below.

Person	Place	Thing	Animal

Proper Nouns

A noun is a word that names a person, place, or thing. A **proper noun** is a word that names a special person, place, or thing. A proper noun begins with a capital letter.

Examples:

Noun	Proper Noun
girl	Kayla Stone
park	Yellowstone Park
bread	Tasty Bread

DIRECTIONS ➤ Find the proper nouns in the box. Write the proper nouns on the lines.

baseball	Bob's Bikes	Bridge Road	children
China	Elf Corn	Gabriel	Lindsey
man	New York City	Oregon	Pat Green
prince	robin	State Street	town

1. _____   6. _____

2. _____   7. _____

3. _____   8. _____

4. _____   9. _____

5. _____   10. _____

DIRECTIONS ➤ Circle the proper noun in each sentence.

11. I bought apples at Hill's Store.

12. The store is on Baker Street.

13. It is near Stone Library.

14. I gave an apple to Emily Fuller.

Practice with Proper Nouns

Remember, a proper noun is a word that names a special person, place, or thing. A proper noun begins with a capital letter.

DIRECTIONS Draw a line between each noun and its matching proper noun.

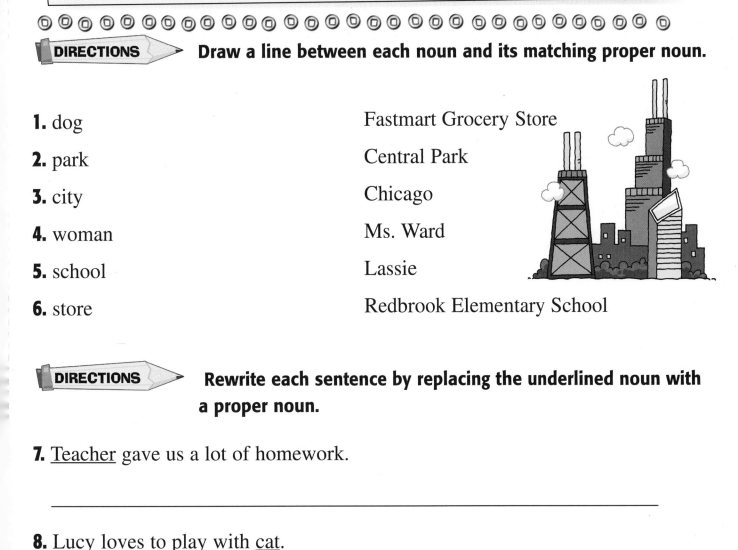

1. dog

2. park

3. city

4. woman

5. school

6. store

Fastmart Grocery Store

Central Park

Chicago

Ms. Ward

Lassie

Redbrook Elementary School

DIRECTIONS Rewrite each sentence by replacing the underlined noun with a proper noun.

7. <u>Teacher</u> gave us a lot of homework.

_____

8. Lucy loves to play with <u>cat</u>.

_____

9. Brady's best friend is <u>boy</u>.

_____

Names and Titles of People and Animals

The names of people and animals are proper nouns. The first and last names of a person or animal begin with a capital letter.

The titles of people begin with a capital letter. Most titles end with a period. These are titles of people:

    Mr.   Mrs.   Ms.   Miss   Dr.

Examples:

    <u>Jack Sprat</u> went to the airport.

    <u>Mrs. Sprat</u> is looking for her dog <u>Fluffy</u>.

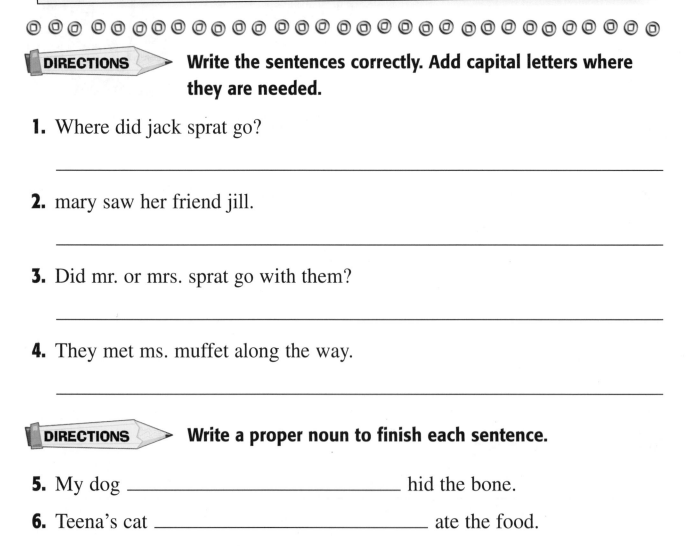

DIRECTIONS ▷ **Write the sentences correctly. Add capital letters where they are needed.**

1. Where did jack sprat go?

_____

2. mary saw her friend jill.

_____

3. Did mr. or mrs. sprat go with them?

_____

4. They met ms. muffet along the way.

_____

DIRECTIONS ▷ **Write a proper noun to finish each sentence.**

5. My dog _____ hid the bone.

6. Teena's cat _____ ate the food.

Practice with Names and Titles

Remember, the first and last names of people and animals are proper nouns. A proper noun begins with a capital letter. The titles of people also begin with a capital letter. These are titles of people:

    Mr.   Mrs.   Ms.   Miss   Dr.

DIRECTIONS **Underline the proper nouns in each sentence.**

1. Meg and Tim walked to school.

2. They were going to help Ms. Lee before class.

3. On the way, they saw Holly Green.

4. Holly's dog Lucy followed them.

5. At school, Mr. Roberts laughed.

6. No dogs at school, Lucy!

DIRECTIONS **Write two sentences about what Lucy will do next.**

7. _____

_____

8. _____

_____

Names of Special Places

The names of special places are proper nouns. Cities, states, and the names of streets begin with a capital letter. The names of countries also begin with a capital letter.
Examples:
> Jack saw his friends in <u>Miami</u>, <u>Florida</u>.
> Their house is at 212 <u>Coconut Drive</u>.
> I live in the <u>United States of America</u>.

DIRECTIONS ▸ **Write the sentences correctly. Add capital letters where they are needed.**

1. They walked along main street.

_____

2. My uncle drove through indiana and ohio.

_____

3. We went on a trip to mexico.

_____

DIRECTIONS ▸ **Write a proper noun to finish each sentence.**

4. The name of my state is _____.

5. The name of my town is _____.

6. The name of my street is _____.

7. The name of my school is _____.

8. _____ is a pretty place to see in our town.

Days of the Week, Months, and Holidays

The names of the days of the week are proper nouns. They begin with capital letters.

The names of the months are also proper nouns. They begin with capital letters.

The names of holidays are proper nouns, too. Each important word in the name of the holiday begins with a capital letter.

Examples:

The man flew in a spaceship on <u>Saturday</u>.

In <u>December,</u> he drives in the snow.

He had a picnic on the <u>Fourth of July</u>.

DIRECTIONS ➤ **Complete each sentence. Use the words from the box. Find the day, month, or holiday that begins with the same letter as the underlined word.**

Wednesday	Thanksgiving	Saturday	February	July

1. Francis Foley did not <u>walk</u> on _____.

2. He <u>flew</u> in _____.

3. Sometimes he <u>sails</u> on _____.

4. He <u>thinks</u> he will be home for _____.

DIRECTIONS ➤ **Write a proper noun to complete each sentence.**

5. My birthday is in _____.

6. My favorite day is _____.

7. My favorite holiday is _____.

Singular and Plural Nouns

A noun is a word that names a person, place, or thing.
A noun can tell about more than one person, place, or thing. Add <u>s</u> to most nouns to make them **plural nouns**, or "more than one."
Examples:

One <u>girl</u> wears a black hat.
Many <u>boys</u> wear funny masks.

DIRECTIONS   **Circle the correct noun to complete each sentence.**

1. Two (boy, boys) went out on Halloween.

2. A (girl, girls) walked with them.

3. She wore a black (robe, robes).

4. There were two red (star, stars) on it.

5. It also had one orange (moon, moons).

6. The children walked up to a (house, houses).

7. Then, they knocked on the (door, doors).

8. Will they ask for some (treat, treats)?

9. Then, the children saw two (cat, cats).

10. Two (dog, dogs) ran down the street.

11. An (owl, owls) hooted in the darkness.

12. Many (star, stars) were in the sky.

13. The wind blew through all the (tree, trees).

14. The children clapped their (hand, hands).

15. Then, they sang a (song, songs).

Plural Nouns

Remember, add <u>s</u> to most nouns to make them name more than one.

Example:

    one <u>book</u>, four <u>books</u>

DIRECTIONS   **Rewrite these nouns to make them name more than one.**

1. cap _____

2. chair _____

3. girl _____

4. tree _____

5. flag _____

6. boy _____

DIRECTIONS   **Make the noun in ( ) mean more than one. Write the plural noun to complete the sentence.**

7. I plant _____ in my garden.
                (seed)

8. I want to grow _____.
                    (carrot)

9. I plant some _____, too.
                  (pea)

10. My _____ help me.
             (friend)

11. They want to plant _____ , too.
                    (garden)

More Plural Nouns

Add <u>es</u> to nouns that end with <u>x</u>, <u>ss</u>, <u>ch</u>, or <u>sh</u> to make them name more than one.

Examples:

    one <u>fox</u>, two <u>foxes</u>

    one <u>class</u>, ten <u>classes</u>

    one <u>branch</u>, five <u>branches</u>

    one <u>bush</u>, six <u>bushes</u>

DIRECTIONS ▸ Rewrite these nouns to make them name more than one.

1. lunch _____

2. dress _____

3. glass _____

4. dish _____

5. box _____

6. watch _____

DIRECTIONS ▸ Make the noun in ( ) mean more than one. Write the plural noun to complete the sentence.

7. Two _____ walk to the park.
        (fox)

8. They sit on two _____.
               (bench)

9. Their seats are only _____ apart.
                 (inch)

10. Then, they take out paints and _____.
                        (brush)

11. They paint pictures of trucks and _____.
                         (bus)

12. They hope to paint the _____ near the park.
                  (church)

Irregular Plural Nouns

Some nouns change spelling to name more than one.
Examples:

     man—men
     woman—women
     child—children
     foot—feet
     tooth—teeth

DIRECTIONS ▷ **Circle the correct noun in ( ) to complete each sentence.**

1. One (woman, women) is working.

2. Many (men, man) are on horses.

3. A (child, children) is wading in the stream.

4. He has no shoes on his (feet, foot).

5. The cold water makes his (teeth, tooth) chatter.

DIRECTIONS ▷ **Make the noun in ( ) mean more than one. Write the plural noun to complete the sentence.**

6. The _____ pet the dogs.
           (child)

7. The little dog has big _____.
                   (foot)

8. The big dog has little _____.
                  (tooth)

9. Those _____ feed the dogs.
         (man)

10. Those _____ walk the dogs.
         (woman)

Other Irregular Plural Nouns

Nouns that end in <u>f</u> or <u>fe</u> often change spelling to name more than one.
Examples:

calf—calves	hoof—hooves
elf—elves	knife—knives
shelf—shelves	wife—wives
wolf—wolves	

DIRECTIONS ▸ **Circle the correct noun in ( ) to complete each sentence.**

1. I keep my books on a tall (shelf, shelves).

2. One book is about a king with seven (wife, wives).

3. Another book tells about a magic (elf, elves).

4. My favorite story is about a boy who lives with (wolf, wolves).

DIRECTIONS ▸ **Write a sentence with each irregular plural.**

5. calves _____

_____

6. knives _____

_____

7. hooves _____

_____

Pronouns

A **pronoun** is a word that takes the place of one or more nouns.
Example:

The mouse and the lion are friends.
They are friends.

The pronouns I, we, he, she, it, and they are used in the naming part of a sentence.
Example:

The mouse helped the lion.
She helped the lion.

DIRECTIONS → **Read the sentences. Think of a pronoun for the underlined words. Write the pronoun on the line.**

1. The mouse and I live in the woods. _____

2. The mouse fell into the spring. _____

3. The lion saw the mouse fall. _____

4. The leaf landed in the water. _____

5. A hunter spread a net. _____

6. The net was for the lion. _____

7. The mouse and the lion helped each other. _____

8. The mouse and I will always be friends. _____

9. The mouse and the lion are happy. _____

10. The mouse and I will watch out for the hunter. _____

Practice with Pronouns

Remember, a pronoun is a word that takes the place of one or more nouns. The pronouns <u>I</u>, <u>we</u>, <u>he</u>, <u>she</u>, <u>it</u>, and <u>they</u> are used in the naming part of the sentence.

DIRECTIONS — Finish the story. Use the pronouns from the box.

We	She	They	He	I	It

My family is very big. _____ live in a house with three bedrooms. My sister Ava is five years old. _____ is the youngest. Ava shares her room with Lily. _____ sing and make music all day in their room. My brothers Todd and Ted are twins. _____ share a room with Bill. _____ says that Todd and Ted snore. _____ am glad that I have my own room! _____ is small but very quiet.

Using I or Me

The word I is always used in the naming part of a sentence.
I is always written with a capital letter.
Example:

I go to school.

When you speak of or write about another person and yourself, always name yourself last.
Example:

Tina and I are in the same class.

The word me follows a verb, or action word.
Examples:

Tina makes me laugh.

The teacher tells Tina and me to be quiet.

 **DIRECTIONS** ▷ **Write I or me to complete each sentence correctly.**

1. _____ am taking a test.

2. The teacher tells _____ to stop laughing.

3. Mother takes _____ home.

4. _____ have fun with Tina.

DIRECTIONS ▷ **Read the sentences. Circle the correct words in ( ) to complete each sentence.**

5. (Susan and I, I and Susan) are friends.

6. The teacher tells (Tina and me, me and Tina) to hush.

7. (I and Tina, Tina and I) eat lunch together.

8. Mr. Smith asks (Susan and me, Susan and I) to pass out the papers.

Practice with Action Verbs

Remember, an action verb shows action. Verbs tell what a person, place, or thing does.
Examples:
        We <u>play</u> checkers.
        Ethan <u>wins</u> every time!

DIRECTIONS **Choose an action verb from the box to complete each sentence.**

| laugh | lives | walk | makes | tells | waves |

1. Jacob _____ in the house next door.

2. We _____ to school together.

3. Jacob _____ me stories about his class.

4. He _____ his arms.

5. He _____ funny faces.

6. I _____ at his stories.

DIRECTIONS **Write an action verb to complete each sentence.**

7. At recess, I _____ hopscotch.

8. When I get tired, I _____ in the shade.

9. Sometimes I _____ with my friends.

10. Sometimes I _____ alone.

Singular Verbs

Add <u>s</u> to an action verb that tells about one person or thing.
Examples:

    The pirate <u>walks</u> quickly.

    He <u>sees</u> his friends.

 **DIRECTIONS** **Read the sentences. Circle the correct verb in ( ) to complete each sentence.**

1. The cat (skip, skips) down the steps.

2. Two cats (play, plays) on the stairs.

3. The children (hug, hugs) the cat.

4. The cat (purr, purrs) happily.

5. A puppy (bark, barks) at the cat.

6. The boys (hide, hides) from the girls.

7. An ape (wave, waves) to them.

8. The wind (blow, blows) the trees.

9. My shadow (follow, follows) me.

10. A girl (see, sees) a shadow.

11. Mary (hear, hears) the tree speak.

12. The branches (move, moves) in the wind.

13. An owl (hoot, hoots) in the tree.

14. The children (take, takes) their treats home.

15. They (eat, eats) some fruit.

Practice with Singular Verbs

Remember to add <u>s</u> to an action verb that tells about one person or thing.

Examples:

      The boy <u>wants</u> an apple.

      My sister <u>loves</u> her kitten.

 **DIRECTIONS**   **Circle the singular verbs in the story.**

1.   It is a rainy day. We stay inside. Margo reads a book in the den. Dad takes a nap in his room. Mom rests on the couch. The baby sleeps in her crib. The dog snores in its bed. I guess I can't practice the piano right now.

 **DIRECTIONS**   **Circle the correct verb in ( ) to complete each sentence.**

2. Ella (skate, skates) every Saturday at the skating rink.

3. She (wear, wears) pink ice skates.

4. Her coach (teach, teaches) her new moves.

5. The other students (learn, learns), too.

6. They all (practice, practices) together.

7. Sometimes Ella's mom (come, comes) to watch her skate.

8. She always (clap, claps) after Ella (perform, performs).

Helping Verbs

A **helping verb** works with the main verb to show action.
Use <u>has</u>, <u>have</u>, and <u>had</u> with other verbs to show action that happened in the past.
Examples:
> Chen <u>has</u> worked hard.
> Brit and Katie <u>have</u> helped.
> They <u>had</u> stopped earlier for a snack.

 **DIRECTIONS** ▷ **Circle the helping verb in each sentence.**

1. Now we have arrived at the camp.

2. Tom and Bill have unloaded the car.

3. Mr. Green had shopped for food the day before.

4. Bob has gathered firewood.

5. Something strange has happened.

6. A spaceship has landed nearby!

DIRECTIONS ▷ **Circle the correct helping verb in ( ) to complete each sentence.**

7. We (has, have) built a new playground.

8. Mom and Dad (had, has) sawed the boards before.

9. Donna (has, have) sanded the wood.

10. They (has, have) painted the fence.

11. My brother and I (has, have) raked the leaves.

12. But my mother (had, have) forgotten the leaf bags.

Verbs That Do Not Show Action

Some verbs do not show action. They tell about being.
Examples:

A snake <u>is</u> a reptile.

The snake <u>was</u> hungry.

Use <u>am</u> or <u>was</u> with the word <u>I</u>.
Examples:

I <u>am</u> in the tree.

I <u>was</u> under the tree.

Use <u>is</u> or <u>was</u> with one person or thing. Use <u>are</u> or <u>were</u> with more than one person or thing.
Examples:

A lizard <u>is</u> in my garden.

Two turtles <u>were</u> in a box.

 **DIRECTIONS** **Read the sentences. Circle the correct verb in ( ) to complete each sentence.**

1. Reptiles (are, is) cold-blooded animals.

2. Some snakes (are, is) dangerous.

3. Many kinds of lizards (were, was) at the zoo.

4. A draco (is, am) a lizard.

5. Crocodiles (are, is) the largest reptiles.

6. The crocodiles (were, was) very noisy.

7. One lizard (is, are) in the box.

8. I (is, am) near the turtle's box.

9. The box (was, were) near the window.

10. The turtle (is, are) sleeping.

Present-Tense Verbs

> **Present-tense verbs** tell about action that happens now.
> *Example:*
>   Max and Lisa <u>walk</u> to school.
> Add <u>s</u> to an action verb that tells about one person or thing.
> *Example:*
>   Lisa <u>walks</u> to school.

DIRECTIONS Read the sentences. Circle the correct verb in ( ) to complete each sentence.

1. Max (play, plays) baseball.

2. He (run, runs) fast.

3. The girls (dance, dances) to the music.

4. Some friends (wait, waits) for Max.

5. Lisa (leap, leaps) across the floor.

DIRECTIONS Finish the story. Add action verbs. You may use words from the box.

sits	stands	asks	takes	walks	dances

Max _____ his sister to her dancing class.
He _____ on a chair to watch. The teacher
_____ him to join the class. First, he
_____ with a girl. Then, he _____
by a wall. Last, he _____ home.

More Present-Tense Verbs

Remember, present-tense verbs tell about action that happens now.
Example:

     Sam and Olivia <u>eat</u> apples.

Add <u>s</u> to an action verb that tells about one person or thing.
Example:

     Parker <u>eats</u> a pear.

DIRECTIONS ➤ **Read the sentences. Circle the correct verb in ( ) to complete each sentence.**

1. Maddie (paint, paints) pictures.

2. She (use, uses) many colors.

3. Her parents (hang, hangs) her pictures in the living room.

4. Visitors (look, looks) at the pictures.

5. They (say, says) Maddie is talented.

DIRECTIONS ➤ **Finish each sentence using a present-tense verb.**

6. My dog _____ in the yard.

7. I _____ her because she is muddy.

8. I _____ her to stay out of the dirt.

9. As soon as I clean her, she _____ outside again!

Past-Tense Verbs

Past-tense verbs can tell about actions in the past. Form the past tense of most verbs by adding <u>ed</u>.

Example:

    Mary Jo <u>planted</u> vegetables yesterday.

DIRECTIONS ▷ Make each sentence tell about the past. Circle the correct verb in ( ) to complete each sentence.

1. Jeff (plays, played) with his sister.

2. The family (visited, visits) Grandmother often.

3. Mary Jo (looks, looked) out the window.

4. Then, she (jumped, jumps) up and down.

5. Grandmother (leans, leaned) back on the pillow.

6. Mary Jo (helps, helped) Grandmother.

7. Grandmother (laughs, laughed) at the baby chicks.

DIRECTIONS ▷ Change each sentence. Make the verb tell about the past. Write the new sentence.

8. The girls play in the park.

_____

9. They climb over rocks.

_____

10. Their fathers call to them.

_____

More Past-Tense Verbs

Remember, verbs can tell about actions in the past. Form the past tense of most verbs by adding ed.

Examples:

The girls <u>talked</u> to their mother.

The horse <u>jumped</u> over the fence.

I <u>laughed</u> at the joke.

 **DIRECTIONS** **Make each sentence tell about the past. Circle the correct verb in ( ) to complete each sentence.**

1. Jake (wants, wanted) to make his mom's birthday special.

2. He (baked, bakes) a cake with his dad's help.

3. He (walks, walked) to the store to buy a gift.

4. He (signs, signed) a big card.

5. He (picked, picks) some flowers from the garden.

6. That night, Jake (surprised, surprises) his mom.

7. His mom (looks, looked) very happy.

DIRECTIONS **Finish each sentence using a past-tense verb.**

8. Last year, I _____ every day at recess.

9. Emily and I _____ on the monkey bars.

10. We _____ with jump ropes.

11. When Mr. Hill _____ us back to class, we were tired.

Irregular Verbs

Some action verbs do not add <u>ed</u> to tell about the past.

Present	Past
go, goes	went
come, comes	came
run, runs	ran

Examples:

The boys <u>went</u> to sleep.

A dog <u>came</u> to a farm.

The raccoons <u>ran</u> into the woods.

 **DIRECTIONS** Read the sentences. Circle the correct verb in ( ) to complete each sentence.

1. Three robbers (ran, runs) out the door.

2. They (comes, came) back.

3. Four animals (goes, went) by the house.

4. The rooster and the dog (go, goes) into the kitchen.

5. The friends (run, runs) down the road.

6. A cat (goes, go) very fast.

DIRECTIONS Circle the verb in each sentence. Then, write each verb in the past tense.

7. The man goes to the mill. _____

8. A donkey comes to town. _____

9. The animals come to a big house. _____

10. They run to the window. _____

More Irregular Verbs

Here are some other action verbs that do not add <u>ed</u> to tell about the past.
Present: bring, do, does, fall, eat, fly, flies, sell, break
Past: brought, did, fell, ate, flew, sold, broke
Example:
   He got sick after he <u>ate</u> seven hamburgers.

DIRECTIONS ▷ **Read the sentences. Circle the correct past-tense verb in ( ) to complete each sentence.**

1. We (brought, bring) valentines to school last February.

2. Last week, I (fall, fell) down the stairs.

3. What (did, do) you do at school today?

4. Last summer, we (fly, flew) to Maine on an airplane.

5. My brother (breaks, broke) the dish last night.

6. Yesterday, I (sold, sell) a glass of lemonade to Mr. Green.

7. At the party, I (eat, ate) two slices of cake.

DIRECTIONS ▷ **Circle the verb in each sentence. Then, write each verb in the past tense.**

8. A bird flies through the window. _____

9. It breaks Mom's favorite vase. _____

10. How does it get in here? _____

Adding ed or ing to Verbs

To show that something happened in the past, add <u>ed</u> to most verbs.
Example:
    Don <u>visited</u> Liz yesterday.
To show that something is happening now, you can add <u>ing</u> to most verbs.
Example:
    Sue is <u>visiting</u> Liz now.

DIRECTIONS **Circle the correct verb in ( ) to complete each sentence.**

1. Terry and Joe (played, playing) basketball last week.

2. Jenna (called, calling) to them.

3. She (wanted, wanting) to play, too.

4. The boys (laughed, laughing) at her.

5. But Jenna (jumped, jumping) for the ball.

6. She (played, playing) well.

7. Terry and Joe are not (laughed, laughing) anymore.

8. Now, Jenna is (played, playing) on their team.

9. Everyone is (talked, talking) about all the games they've won.

DIRECTIONS **Add <u>ed</u> or <u>ing</u> to each verb. Then, rewrite each sentence.**

10. Carmen help _____ Grandma cook yesterday.

_____

11. Grandma is cook _____ some soup today.

_____

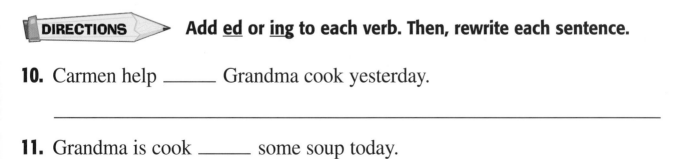

Using Is or Are

Use is and are to tell about something that is happening now.
Use is to tell about one person, place, or thing. Use are to tell about more than one person, place, or thing. Use are with the word you.

Examples:

Judy is going.

Lynne and Ed are skating.

The cats are sleeping.

You are lost. Are you scared?

DIRECTIONS → **Write is or are to complete each sentence correctly.**

1. We _____ going to the park.

2. Al _____ going, too.

3. Kate and Mario _____ running.

4. She _____ the faster runner.

5. Where _____ the twins?

6. They _____ climbing a tree.

7. You _____ going to climb, too.

8. The children _____ having fun.

DIRECTIONS → **Write one sentence about a park using is. Then, write one sentence about a park using are.**

9. (is) _____

10. (are) _____

Practice Using <u>Is</u> or <u>Are</u>

Remember, use <u>is</u> and <u>are</u> to tell about something that is happening now. Use <u>is</u> to tell about one person, place, or thing. Use <u>are</u> to tell about more than one person, place, or thing. Use <u>are</u> with the word <u>you</u>.

Examples:

We <u>are</u> taking a walk.

She <u>is</u> swimming.

Arnold <u>is</u> painting the house.

DIRECTIONS → Write <u>is</u> or <u>are</u> to complete each sentence correctly.

1. Dad _____ building us a tree house.

2. We _____ helping him.

3. Emma and Anna _____ sanding the wood.

4. They _____ wearing gloves.

5. Mom _____ nailing the wood together.

6. She _____ very busy.

7. Matt and I _____ painting the wood.

8. We _____ excited to see the house when it is finished.

DIRECTIONS → Write one sentence about a tree house using <u>is</u>. Then, write one sentence about a tree house using <u>are</u>.

9. (is) _____

10. (are) _____

Using <u>Was</u> or <u>Were</u>

Use <u>was</u> and <u>were</u> to tell about something that happened in the past. Use <u>was</u> to tell about one person, place, or thing. Use <u>were</u> to tell about more than one person, place, or thing. Use <u>were</u> with the word <u>you</u>.

Examples:

My bat <u>was</u> on the step.
Ten people <u>were</u> there.
You <u>were</u> late. <u>Were</u> you home?

DIRECTIONS Circle the correct verb in ( ) to complete each sentence.

1. The children (was, were) indoors while it rained.

2. José (was, were) reading a book.

3. Scott and Jay (was, were) playing checkers.

4. Ann, Roy, and Jami (was, were) playing cards.

5. Sara and Tara (was, were) talking.

6. Nick (was, were) beating a drum.

7. I (was, were) drawing pictures.

8. You (was, were) dancing.

DIRECTIONS Write one sentence about a rainy day using <u>was</u>. Then, write one sentence about a rainy day using <u>were</u>.

9. (was) _____

10. (were) _____

Practice Using <u>Was</u> or <u>Were</u>

Remember, use <u>was</u> or <u>were</u> to tell about something that happened in the past. Use <u>was</u> to tell about one person, place, or thing. Use <u>were</u> to tell about more than one person, place, or thing.

DIRECTIONS Circle the correct verb in ( ) to complete each sentence in the story.

Dad and Lila (were, was) at the baseball field. Alex and I (were, was) watching a movie. My mom (were, was) watching it with us. We (was, were) eating popcorn. Alex (was, were) a little scared. I (were, was) scared, too. Alex, Mom, and I (were, was) watching the movie very carefully. We didn't hear Dad and Lila come home. They (were, was) standing right behind us. When we saw them, we (was, were) so surprised that we screamed. We spilled popcorn everywhere! Dad and Lila (were, was) laughing at our surprise. Soon, we (was, were) all laughing!

DIRECTIONS Write a sentence to tell what happens next in the story.

_____

_____

Using See, Sees, or Saw

Use <u>see</u> or <u>sees</u> to tell what is happening now. Use <u>see</u> with the words <u>you</u> and <u>I</u>. Use <u>saw</u> to tell what happened in the past.
Examples:
One boy <u>sees</u> a dog. Two boys <u>see</u> a dog.
I <u>see</u> a dog. Do you <u>see</u> a dog?
Justin <u>saw</u> Natalie last week.

DIRECTIONS Write <u>see</u>, <u>sees</u>, or <u>saw</u> to complete each sentence correctly.

1. Today Mike _____ his friend Lori.

2. He _____ her last Monday.

3. Lori _____ Mike paint now.

4. My dad _____ Mike paint now, too.

5. Mike _____ a beautiful sky last night.

6. He _____ pink in the sky on Sunday.

7. Grandpa and I _____ some trains now.

8. We _____ many trains on my last birthday.

9. We _____ old and new trains last winter.

10. Today I can _____ the train show.

DIRECTIONS Write <u>see</u>, <u>sees</u>, or <u>saw</u>. Then, rewrite each sentence.

11. Last week we _____ Lee.

_____

12. Lee _____ my painting now.

_____

Using <u>Run</u>, <u>Runs</u>, or <u>Ran</u>

Use <u>run</u> or <u>runs</u> to tell what is happening now. Use <u>run</u> with the words <u>you</u> and <u>I</u>. Use <u>ran</u> to tell what happened in the past.
Examples:

One horse <u>runs</u>. Two horses <u>run</u>.
I <u>run</u> in the park. Do you <u>run</u>?
Yesterday we <u>ran</u> to the park.

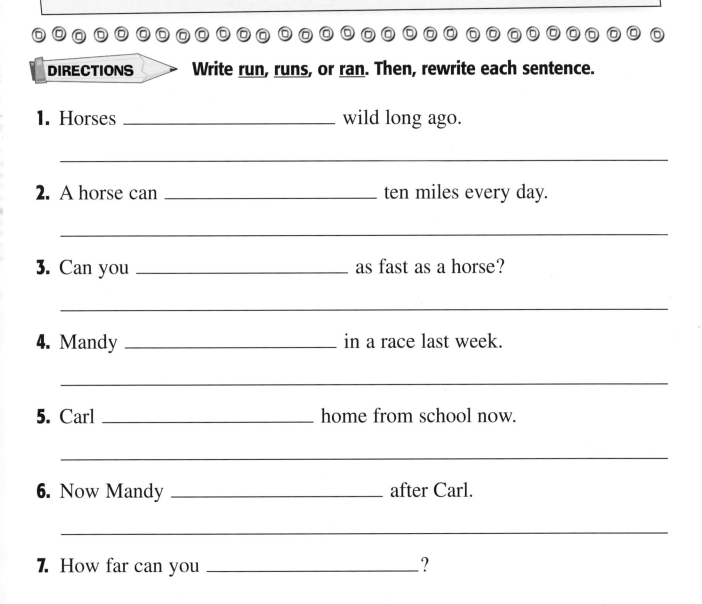

DIRECTIONS ➤ Write <u>run</u>, <u>runs</u>, or <u>ran</u>. Then, rewrite each sentence.

1. Horses _____ wild long ago.

_____

2. A horse can _____ ten miles every day.

_____

3. Can you _____ as fast as a horse?

_____

4. Mandy _____ in a race last week.

_____

5. Carl _____ home from school now.

_____

6. Now Mandy _____ after Carl.

_____

7. How far can you _____?

_____

Using <u>Give</u>, <u>Gives</u>, or <u>Gave</u>

Use <u>give</u> or <u>gives</u> to tell what is happening now. Use <u>give</u> with the words <u>you</u> and <u>I</u>. Use <u>gave</u> to tell what happened in the past.
Examples:

    One student <u>gives</u> a gift. Two students <u>give</u> a gift.

    I <u>give</u> a gift. Do you <u>give</u> one?

    Jenna <u>gave</u> me a present yesterday.

> **DIRECTIONS**   Read the sentences. Circle the correct verb in ( ) to complete each sentence.

1. Can you (give, gives, gave) the animals some food?

2. Sandi (give, gives, gave) them water yesterday.

3. Juan (give, gives, gave) the chickens corn now.

4. Chickens (give, gives, gave) us eggs to eat yesterday.

5. We (give, gives, gave) the kittens some milk last night.

6. Who (give, gives, gave) hay to the cow then?

7. Our cow (give, gives, gave) us milk yesterday.

8. I (give, gives, gave) food to the pigs last Monday.

> **DIRECTIONS**   Write three sentences about gifts using <u>give</u>, <u>gives</u>, and <u>gave</u>.

9. (give) _____

10. (gives) _____

11. (gave) _____

Using Do or Does

Use <u>does</u> to tell about one person, place, or thing.
Use <u>do</u> to tell about more than one person, place, or thing. Also use <u>do</u> with the words <u>you</u> and <u>I</u>.
Examples:

William <u>does</u> the work.

They <u>do</u> the work.

I <u>do</u> the work. You <u>do</u> the work.

DIRECTIONS Write <u>do</u> or <u>does</u> to complete each sentence correctly.

1. We _____ a lot of work in the house.

2. My dad _____ all the dishes.

3. My mom _____ the windows.

4. My sister _____ the sweeping.

5. My grandma _____ the sewing.

6. I _____ the floor.

7. My little brother _____ the dusting.

8. I _____ not cook dinner.

9. My little sister _____ put away toys.

10. We all _____ some work in our house.

DIRECTIONS Write one sentence about yourself using <u>do</u>. Then, write one sentence about a friend using <u>does</u>.

11. _____

12. _____

Using Has, Have, or Had

Use <u>has</u> to tell about one person, place, or thing. Use <u>have</u> to tell about more than one person, place, or thing. Use <u>have</u> with the words <u>you</u> and <u>I</u>. Use <u>had</u> to tell about the past.

Examples:

Jesse <u>has</u> a bird.

Cars <u>have</u> tires.

You <u>have</u> new shoes. I <u>have</u> fun.

My dogs <u>had</u> fleas. Bill <u>had</u> a cat last year.

DIRECTIONS ➤ **Circle the correct verb in ( ) to complete each sentence.**

1. My brother (has, have, had) a pet fish last year.

2. Now Dan (has, have, had) a pet mouse.

3. The pets (has, have, had) good homes now.

4. I (has, have, had) a football now.

5. Now Dana (has, have, had) a pair of roller skates, too.

6. Yesterday Dawn (has, have, had) a full balloon.

7. Now the balloon (has, have, had) a hole in it.

8. She (has, have, had) the money to buy another balloon today.

DIRECTIONS ➤ **Write <u>has</u>, <u>have</u>, or <u>had</u> to complete each sentence correctly.**

9. You _____ many friends now.

10. Your friends _____ fun together last Saturday.

11. Last week I _____ supper with Eric.

12. Now he _____ supper with me.

Practice Using <u>Has</u>, <u>Have</u>, or <u>Had</u>

Remember, use <u>has</u> to tell about one person, place, or thing.
Use <u>have</u> to tell about more than one person, place, or thing.
Also use <u>have</u> with the words <u>you</u> and <u>I</u>.
Use <u>had</u> to tell about the past.
Examples:
> Maria <u>has</u> a book.
> We <u>have</u> pizza for dinner.
> You <u>have</u> red hair. I <u>have</u> brown hair.
> I <u>had</u> a green crayon.

 **DIRECTIONS** **Circle the correct word in ( ) to complete each sentence in the story.**

My baby brother, Brady, is seven months old. He (has, had, have) two teeth. He also (has, had, have) a problem. He chews on everything! Last week, my mom (has, had, have) a cookie in her hand. Brady tried to bite it. Yesterday, my sister (has, had, have) a book in her backpack. Brady tried to eat it. This morning, my dad (has, had, have) keys in his hand. Brady tried to munch them. Now I have a big balloon. Maybe I should hide it. Brady will try to swallow it. Sometimes, it is hard to (has, had, have) a baby brother!

Adjectives

An **adjective** is a describing word. A describing word describes a noun.
Example:
> The <u>old</u> woman walked home.

Describing words can tell about color or size.
Example:
> <u>Red</u> flowers grow in the <u>small</u> garden.

Describing words can tell about shape.
Example:
> The house has a <u>square</u> window.

Describing words can tell how something feels, tastes, sounds, or smells.
Example:
> The flowers have a <u>sweet</u> smell.

DIRECTIONS ➤ **Finish the sentences. Add describing words from the box.**

round	long	brown	tiny	pink	juicy

1. The woman puts on a _____ bonnet.

2. She walks down a _____ road.

3. Some _____ squirrels run by.

4. A man gives her a _____ orange.

5. The orange is _____.

6. Do you see a _____ bone in the yard?

Practice with Adjectives

Remember, adjectives are describing words.
Describing words can describe feelings.

Examples:

The woman was <u>surprised</u>.

She was <u>happy</u>.

Describing words can also tell how many.

Example:

She picked <u>four</u> flowers.

Some describing words that tell how many do not tell exact numbers.

Examples:

There are <u>many</u> roses in the garden.

<u>Some</u> grass grows here.

DIRECTIONS ▶ **Finish the sentences. Add describing words from the box.**

happy	some	hungry	tired	three	sleepy	one	many

1. The woman was _____ from walking so far.

2. She was _____ to be home.

3. First, she put _____ flowers in a vase.

4. Next, she put _____ bone in a pot.

5. She was _____ and wanted to eat.

6. Then, she ate _____ soup.

7. She also had _____ crackers.

8. The woman was _____ and went to bed.

Adjectives That Compare

Add <u>er</u> to most describing words when they are used to compare two things.

Example:

    This tree is <u>taller</u> than that one.

Add <u>est</u> to most describing words when they are used to compare more than two things.

Example:

    The sequoia tree is the <u>tallest</u> tree of all.

DIRECTIONS ➤ **Read the chart. Fill in the missing describing words.**

1.	long	longer	longest
2.	bright		brightest
3.	tall	taller	
4.		faster	fastest

DIRECTIONS ➤ **Circle the correct describing word in ( ) to complete each sentence.**

5. That tree trunk is (thick, thicker) than this one.

6. The giant sequoia is the (bigger, biggest) living plant of all.

7. The stump of a giant sequoia is (wider, widest) than my room.

8. These trees are the (older, oldest) of all.

More Adjectives That Compare

Usually, <u>er</u> is added to a describing word when it is used to compare two things. When more than two things are being compared, <u>est</u> is usually added to the describing word.

However, not all words follow this rule. <u>Good</u> is one word that changes spelling when it is used to compare things. <u>Good</u> becomes <u>better</u> when it is used to compare two things. It become <u>best</u> when used to compare more than two things.

Examples:

That diner makes <u>good</u> hamburgers.

I think that they have <u>better</u> burgers at Sam's Place.

My dad makes the <u>best</u> burgers in the world.

<u>Bad</u> is another word that changes spelling when it is used to compare things. <u>Bad</u> becomes <u>worse</u> when it is used to compare two things. It becomes <u>worst</u> when used to compare more than two things.

Examples:

Monday was <u>bad</u>.

Tuesday was <u>worse</u> than Monday.

Today is the <u>worst</u> day ever!

DIRECTIONS **Circle the correct word in ( ) to complete each sentence.**

1. I liked the first movie, but the second movie was much (good, better, best).

2. An F is the (bad, worse, worst) grade you can get.

3. Mia is the (good, better, best) soccer player at our school.

4. Dad said the traffic is (bad, worse, worst) today than it was yesterday.

5. She is a good dancer, but if she practices, she can become even (good, better, best).

6. This is the (good, better, best) book I have ever read!

Using A or An

A and an are called **articles**. They are special adjectives.
Use an before words that begin with a vowel sound. The vowels
are a, e, i, o, and u.
Use a before words that begin with a consonant sound.
Examples:

     an apple, an egg

     a car, a skate

DIRECTIONS ➤ Choose the correct article. Write a or an before each word.

1. _____ arm

2. _____ dog

3. _____ hat

4. _____ ant

5. _____ cat

6. _____ elf

7. _____ ear

8. _____ office

9. _____ fire

10. _____ cow

11. _____ uncle

12. _____ tree

13. _____ inch

14. _____ ax

15. _____ top

16. _____ boat

17. _____ duck

18. _____ eagle

DIRECTIONS ➤ Write a or an to complete each sentence correctly.

19. Randy put _____ apple in my box.

20. Victor has _____ old bike.

21. Linda has two balls and _____ bat.

22. I have _____ sweet apple.

Practice Using <u>A</u> or <u>An</u>

Remember to use <u>an</u> before words that begin with a vowel sound.
The vowels are <u>a</u>, <u>e</u>, <u>i</u>, <u>o</u>, and <u>u</u>.
Use <u>a</u> before words that begin with a consonant sound.

DIRECTIONS **Fill out the graph below using the animal names from the box. Write each name under the correct adjective.**

dog	ape	butterfly	lizard	turtle	snake
owl	eel	bear	iguana	otter	ant

a	an

Sentences

A **sentence** is a group of words that tells or asks something. It gives a complete thought. Every sentence begins with a capital letter. Every sentence ends with a punctuation mark.

Examples:

Friends play.

Cars go fast.

DIRECTIONS Write <u>yes</u> if the group of words is a sentence. Write <u>no</u> if the group of words is not a sentence.

_____ **1.** A long time ago.

_____ **2.** The class went to the park.

_____ **3.** Near the tree.

_____ **4.** Ten children played.

_____ **5.** Mark hit the ball.

_____ **6.** A dog chased the ball.

_____ **7.** Bill and Tom.

_____ **8.** Ran and played all day.

_____ **9.** Everyone had fun.

_____ **10.** Jan lost a new red shoe.

_____ **11.** We ate lunch.

_____ **12.** Too hot for us.

_____ **13.** The boys and girls talked.

_____ **14.** Some people.

_____ **15.** Then, we went home.

Practice with Sentences

Remember, a sentence tells a complete thought.
Examples:

Mari caught the ball.

Chad read a book.

DIRECTIONS > Draw lines between the groups of words to make sentences. Then, read the sentences.

1.	Mrs. Brown	live in our building.
2.	Our building	is made of wood.
3.	Four families	lives on my street.

4.	Our class	was climbing the tree.
5.	Jennifer	went on a picnic.
6.	The sun	shone all day.

7.	Corn and beans	fed the baby goat.
8.	The wagon	has a broken wheel.
9.	The mother goat	grow on a farm.

10.	The boat	sailed in strong winds.
11.	The fisherman	were sold in the store.
12.	Some of the fish	caught seven fish.

13.	Our team	hit the ball a lot.
14.	Our batters	won ten games.
15.	The ballpark	was full of fans.

DIRECTIONS > Write a sentence about your birthday.

16. _____

_____

Sentence Parts

Every sentence has two parts. The **naming part** tells who or what the sentence is about. The naming part is called the subject.

The **action part** tells something about the naming part. The action part is called the predicate.

A naming part and an action part make a complete thought.

Example:

Naming Part	**Action Part**
Sara	plants some seeds.

 **DIRECTIONS** Each group of words needs a naming part or an action part. Add words to make each group of words a complete sentence.

1. John _____ .

2. Sara _____ .

3. _____ need sunshine and rain.

4. The flower seeds _____ .

5. John and Sara _____ .

6. _____ looks at the flower.

7. _____ grow in the garden.

8. The flowers _____ .

9. _____ bloom in the spring.

10. _____ are my favorite flowers.

11. The butterflies _____ .

12. _____ makes the flowers grow.

Naming Part of Sentences

Remember, the naming part of a sentence tells who or what the sentence is about.

Examples:

<u>Three mice</u> run away.

<u>The cat</u> plays with a ball.

◎◎◎◎◎◎◎◎◎◎◎◎◎◎◎◎◎◎◎◎◎◎◎◎◎◎◎◎◎◎◎◎◎

DIRECTIONS ▷ **Circle the naming part of each sentence.**

1. My family and I live on a busy street.

2. Sami Harper found a bird.

3. Miss Jenkins drives very slowly.

4. Mr. Chang walks his dog.

5. Henry throws a ball.

6. Mr. Byrne cuts his grass.

7. Mrs. Lee picks up her children.

8. Mr. and Mrs. Diaz shop for food.

9. Jeanine plays in the park.

10. Mr. Wolf brings the mail.

11. Amy Taft brings the paper.

12. Mr. Dowd cooks dinner.

13. Mrs. Clark washes her windows.

14. Carolyn and Alberto plant flower seeds.

15. Julie waters the garden.

Action Part of Sentences

Remember, the action part of a sentence tells what someone or something does.
Examples:
Three mice <u>run away</u>.
The cat <u>plays with a ball</u>.

ⓞ ⓞ

DIRECTIONS ➤ **Choose an action part from the box to complete each sentence. Write it on the line.**

| barks | buzz | fly | hops | moo | cluck | quack | roar |

1. Robins and blackbirds _____.

2. Yellow bees _____.

3. My little dog _____.

4. Mother Duck and her babies _____.

5. A rabbit with big feet _____.

6. Angry lions _____.

7. All the cows on the farm _____.

8. Chickens _____.

DIRECTIONS ➤ **Write a sentence about an animal that you like. Circle the naming part. Underline the action part.**

9. _____

_____

Word Order in Sentences

Words in a sentence must be in an order that makes sense.
Examples:

Grandpa plays baseball.
My sister writes stories.

DIRECTIONS ▷ **Write each group of words in an order that makes sense. Be sure to put a period at the end of each sentence.**

1. brother My apples eats

_____

2. drinks Elizabeth milk

_____

3. butter peanut Kim likes

_____

4. Justin bread wants

_____

5. corn plants Chris

_____

6. a fish Chang caught

_____

7. breakfast cooks Dad

_____

8. his shares Shawn lunch

_____

9. the Rosa grew carrot

_____

Telling Sentences and Asking Sentences

A **telling sentence** is a group of words that tells something. A telling sentence is also called a statement.

Examples:

> I fed my pony.
>
> Ponies like to run and play.

An **asking sentence** is a group of words that asks a question. You can answer an asking sentence. An asking sentence is also called a question.

Examples:

> How old are you?
>
> Where do you live?

◎◎◎◎◎◎◎◎◎◎◎◎◎◎◎◎◎◎◎◎◎◎◎◎◎◎◎◎◎◎◎

DIRECTIONS Write <u>telling</u> on the line before the group of words if it is a telling sentence. Write <u>asking</u> on the line before the group of words if it is an asking sentence. Leave the line blank if the group of words is not a sentence.

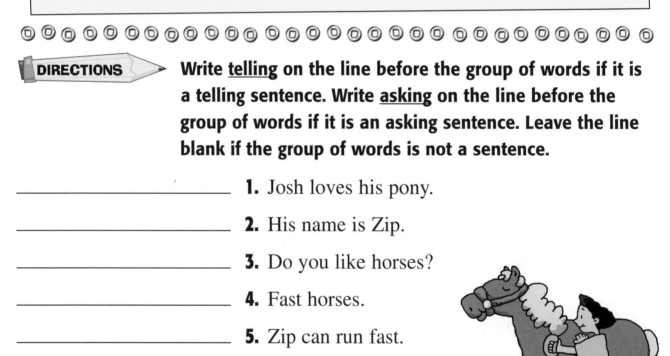

_____ **1.** Josh loves his pony.

_____ **2.** His name is Zip.

_____ **3.** Do you like horses?

_____ **4.** Fast horses.

_____ **5.** Zip can run fast.

_____ **6.** Over the hill.

_____ **7.** He eats apples.

_____ **8.** Do you eat apples?

_____ **9.** Zip has soft hair.

Kinds of Sentences

A **statement** is a sentence that tells something. It begins with a capital letter. It ends with a period (**.**).

Example:

John gives some seeds to Sara.

A **question** is a sentence that asks something. It begins with a capital letter. It ends with a question mark (**?**).

Example:

Will Sara plant seeds?

An **exclamation** is a sentence that shows strong feeling. It begins with a capital letter. It ends with an exclamation point (**!**).

Example:

What a fine garden John has!

DIRECTIONS ▸ **Read the sentences. Write <u>statement</u> for a telling sentence. Write <u>question</u> for an asking sentence. Write <u>exclamation</u> for a sentence that shows strong feeling.**

_____ **1.** John was in his garden.

_____ **2.** Who came walking by?

_____ **3.** Sara stopped to look at the garden.

_____ **4.** What did Sara do?

_____ **5.** Sara read a story to her seeds.

_____ **6.** Did Sara do anything else?

_____ **7.** Poor Sara fell asleep in her garden!

_____ **8.** The seeds started to grow.

_____ **9.** What makes seeds grow?

_____ **10.** Sara works so hard!

Practice with Kinds of Sentences

Remember, a statement tells something. End a statement with a period (.).

A question asks something. End a question with a question mark (?).

An exclamation shows strong feeling. End an exclamation with an exclamation point (!).

DIRECTIONS ➤ **Finish each sentence to make a statement. Be sure to use the correct end mark.**

1. My favorite animal is _____

2. My favorite food is _____

3. My favorite color is _____

DIRECTIONS ➤ **Finish each sentence to make a question. Be sure to use the correct end mark.**

4. What is _____

5. Where _____

6. Why _____

DIRECTIONS ➤ **Finish each sentence to make an exclamation. Be sure to use the correct end mark.**

7. I love _____

8. It's so _____

Joining Sentences

A good writer can join two short sentences. This makes the sentences more interesting to read. The word <u>and</u> is used to join the sentences.

Sometimes the naming parts of two sentences are the same. The action parts can be joined.

Example:

John planted seeds. John worked in his garden.

John planted seeds <u>and</u> worked in his garden.

How to Join Sentences

1. Look for sentences that have the same naming part.
2. Write the naming part.
3. Look for different action parts. Use the word <u>and</u> to join them.
4. Write the new sentence.

 **DIRECTIONS** ▷ **Use the word <u>and</u> to join each pair of sentences. Write the new sentences.**

1. John gave seeds to Sara. John told her to plant them.

_____

2. Sara planted the seeds. Sara looked at the ground.

_____

3. Sara sang songs to her seeds. Sara read stories to them.

_____

4. The rain fell on the seeds. The rain helped them grow.

_____

Practice with Joining Sentences

Remember, a good writer can join two short sentences. This makes the sentences more interesting to read. The word <u>and</u> is used to join the sentences.

Sometimes the action parts of two sentences are the same. Then, the naming parts can be joined.

Example:

The hunter stopped at the house. The bear stopped at the house.
The hunter <u>and</u> the bear stopped at the house.

How to Join Sentences
1. Look for sentences that have the same action part.
2. Join the naming parts. Use the word <u>and</u>.
3. Add the action part.

 **DIRECTIONS** **Use the word <u>and</u> to join each pair of sentences. Write the new sentences.**

1. The farmer stood in the doorway. His family stood in the doorway.

_____

2. The hunter stayed with the family. The bear stayed with the family.

_____

3. The mice ran out the door. The children ran out the door.

_____

4. The hunter went home. The bear went home.

_____

Adding Describing Words to Sentences

A good writer adds describing words to sentences to give a clear picture.

Example:

The moth sat on top of a clover.

The <u>black</u> moth sat on top of a <u>green</u> clover.

How to Add Describing Words to Sentences

1. Look for sentences that do not give your reader a clear picture.
2. Think of describing words that tell more about what things look like.
3. Add the describing words to the sentences.

 **DIRECTIONS** **Add describing words to these sentences. Write the new sentences.**

1. The clown wears a hat.

_____

2. A lion jumps through a hoop.

_____

3. A monkey rides on an elephant.

_____

4. A butterfly flew into the tent.

_____

Practice with Describing Words

Remember, a good writer adds describing words to sentences to give a clear picture.

Example:

      He wore a jacket to school.

      He wore a <u>red</u> jacket to school.

You can add one or more describing words to a sentence to make it more interesting.

How to Add Describing Words to Sentences

1. Look for sentences that do not give your reader a clear picture.
2. Think of describing words that tell more about what things look like.
3. Add the describing words to the sentences.

 **DIRECTIONS** ➤ **Add describing words in the blanks to make the story more interesting.**

Anna was excited about the _____ party. She chose a _____ gift. She wrapped it in _____ paper. She put on a _____ dress and _____ shoes. She put a _____ bow in her hair. She walked to Jenny's house. There were lots of _____ balloons tied to the mailbox. Inside, there were many _____ children. There was a _____ cake and _____ presents. The children played _____ games. Anna won a _____ prize. After the party, she told her _____ friend about the _____ day.

Beginning Sentences in Different Ways

A good writer should not begin every sentence with the same noun. Sometimes the words <u>he</u>, <u>she</u>, <u>I</u>, <u>we</u>, and <u>they</u> are used in place of nouns.

Example:

Ant climbed down a branch. Ant was thirsty. <u>She</u> tried to get a drink.

How to Begin Sentences in Different Ways

1. Look for sentences that begin with the same noun.
2. Use the word <u>he</u>, <u>she</u>, <u>I</u>, <u>we</u>, or <u>they</u> in place of the noun.
3. Write the new sentence.

 **DIRECTIONS** **Change the way some of these sentences begin. Begin some of them with <u>He</u>, <u>She</u>, <u>I</u>, <u>We</u>, or <u>They</u>. Write the new sentences.**

1. The ant climbed down a blade of grass. The ant fell into the spring.

_____

2. The bird pulled off a leaf. The bird let the leaf fall into the water.

_____

3. The hunter saw a lion. The hunter spread his net.

_____

4. The lion and I live in the woods. The lion and I are friends.

_____

Practice with Beginning Sentences

Remember, you can use the words <u>he</u>, <u>she</u>, <u>I</u>, <u>we</u>, and <u>they</u> in place of nouns. This will help make your sentences and stories more interesting.

DIRECTIONS ▷ **Read each set of sentences. Rewrite the second sentence so that it begins in a different way. Use <u>He</u>, <u>She</u>, <u>We</u>, or <u>They</u>.**

1. Clare and I were partners for the science fair. Clare and I were doing a project on volcanoes.

_____

2. Robert and Adam were partners, too. Robert and Adam were doing a project on bees.

_____

3. Mrs. Baldwin said that she was proud of how hard everyone was working on the science projects. Mrs. Baldwin is a nice teacher.

_____

4. Clare, Robert, Adam, and I were so excited on the day of the fair. Clare, Robert, Adam, and I all wanted to win.

_____

5. The judges took a lot of time looking at our projects. The judges were writing notes.

_____

6. Mrs. Baldwin made a speech. Mrs. Baldwin told everyone that Robert and Adam had won first prize.

_____

Writing Clear Sentences

A good writer uses exact verbs. These are verbs that give a clear picture of an action.

Example:

Spaceships <u>go</u> to the Moon.
Spaceships <u>zoom</u> to the Moon.

How to Use Exact Verbs in Sentences

1. Picture the action. Think about what a person or thing is doing.
2. Choose an action verb that tells exactly what the person or thing is doing.
3. Use the action verb in a sentence.

 **DIRECTIONS** **Think of a more exact verb for each underlined verb. Write the new word on the line.**

1. People <u>walk</u> to work. _____

2. Trains <u>move</u> along the tracks. _____

3. We <u>ride</u> our bicycles. _____

4. Fast cars <u>go</u> up the road. _____

5. The airplane <u>flies</u> in the sky. _____

6. A man <u>runs</u> around the park. _____

7. The children <u>walk</u> to school. _____

8. A bus <u>goes</u> down the highway. _____

9. The boat <u>moves</u> along the shore. _____

Writing Names of People

Each word of a person's name begins with a capital letter.

Examples:

Mary Ann Miller

Michael Jordan

Grandma Moses

DIRECTIONS ▷ **Rewrite the names. Use capital letters where they are needed.**

1. mark twain _____

2. beverly cleary _____

3. diane dillon _____

4. alicia acker _____

5. ezra jack keats _____

DIRECTIONS ▷ **Circle the letters that should be capital letters.**

6. Today mother called grandma.

7. We will see grandma and grandpa at the party.

8. Will uncle carlos and aunt kathy be there, too?

DIRECTIONS ▷ **Rewrite the sentences. Use capital letters where they are needed.**

9. mario martinez told me a story.

_____

10. ichiro and I played ball.

_____

Writing Initials

An **initial** stands for a person's name. It is a capital letter with a period **(.)** after it.
Examples:

Steven Bell Mathis = Steven **B.** Mathis or **S. B.** Mathis or **S. B. M.**

DIRECTIONS ➤ **Write the initials of each name.**

1. Clara Delrio _____

2. Carrie Anne Collier _____

3. Marcus Brown _____

4. Michael Tond _____

5. Keiko Senda _____

6. Terri Lynn Turner _____

7. Isaiah Bradley _____

8. Cata Lil Walker _____

DIRECTIONS ➤ **Rewrite the names. Use initials for the names that are underlined.**

9. Joan Walsh Anglund

_____

10. Lee Bennett Hopkins

_____

11. Arturo Martinez

_____

12. Patricia Ann Rosen

_____

DIRECTIONS ➤ **Rewrite the sentences. Be sure to write the initials correctly.**

13. The box was for m s mills.

_____

14. d e ellis sent it to her.

_____

15. t j lee brought the box to the house.

_____

Writing Titles of Respect

Begin a title of respect with a capital letter.

End <u>Mr.</u>, <u>Mrs.</u>, <u>Ms.</u>, and <u>Dr.</u> with a period. They are short forms, or abbreviations, of longer words.

Do not end <u>Miss</u> with a period.

Examples:

    Mr. George Selden

    Dr. Martin Luther King

    Miss Jane Pittman

DIRECTIONS   **Rewrite the names correctly. Place periods and capital letters where they are needed.**

1. mrs ruth scott   _____

2. mr kurt wiese   _____

3. miss e garcia   _____

4. dr seuss   _____

5. ms carol baylor   _____

6. mr and mrs h cox   _____

7. miss k e jones   _____

8. dr s tomas rios   _____

DIRECTIONS   **Rewrite the sentences correctly. Place periods and capital letters where they are needed.**

9. mrs h stone is here to see dr brooks.

_____

10. mr f green and ms miller are not here.

_____

Writing Names of Places

The names of cities, states, and countries begin with a capital letter. The names of streets, parks, lakes, rivers, and schools begin with a capital letter.
The abbreviations of the words <u>street</u>, <u>road</u>, and <u>drive</u> in a place name begin with a capital letter and end with a period.

Examples:

Reno, Nevada

Canada

First Street

Central Park

Red River

Road = Rd.   Dove Rd.

DIRECTIONS ➤ **Rewrite the sentences. Use capital letters where they are needed.**

1. James lives in dayton, ohio.

_____

2. His house is on market st.

_____

3. I think thomas park is in this town.

_____

4. We went to mathis lake for a picnic.

_____

5. Is perry school far away?

_____

Practice with Place Names

Remember, the names of cities, states, and countries begin with a capital letter. The names of streets, parks, lakes, rivers, and schools begin with a capital letter. The abbreviations of the words <u>street</u>, <u>road</u>, and <u>drive</u> in a place name begin with a capital letter and end with a period.

DIRECTIONS ➤ **Answer each question with a sentence that includes a place name. Remember to use capital letters for all place names.**

1. What is the name of your state? _____

2. What is the name of your city or town? _____

3. What is the name of the street where you live?

_____

4. What is the name of your school? _____

5. What is the name of a park, river, or lake near your house?

_____

6. What is the name of a city or town you have visited?

_____

Writing Names of Days and Months

The names of days of the week begin with a capital letter.
The names of the months begin with a capital letter.
Examples:

Monday, Friday   April, October

The abbreviations of the days of the week begin with a capital letter.
They end with a period.
The abbreviations of the months begin with a capital letter. They end
with a period. The names of May, June, and July are not usually
abbreviated.
Examples:

Sun., Mon., Tues., Wed., Thurs., Fri., Sat.

Jan., Feb., Mar., Apr., Aug., Sept., Oct., Nov., Dec.

DIRECTIONS ➤ **Write the name of a day or month to complete each sentence.**

1. The day after Sunday is _____.

2. The day before Saturday is _____.

3. Valentine's Day is in _____.

4. A month in the summer is _____.

5. Thanksgiving Day is in _____.

DIRECTIONS ➤ **Write the correct abbreviation for each day or month. Be sure to end the abbreviation with a period.**

6. Tuesday _____   **9.** Saturday _____

7. Thursday _____   **10.** January _____

8. December _____   **11.** September _____

Writing Names of Holidays

Each important word in the name of a holiday begins with a capital letter.

Examples:

Valentine's Day

Memorial Day

Fourth of July

DIRECTIONS > **Write the holiday names correctly.**

1. new year's day _____

2. mother's day _____

3. independence day _____

4. labor day _____

5. cinco de mayo _____

6. thanksgiving day _____

7. veterans day _____

DIRECTIONS > **Rewrite each sentence correctly.**

8. earth day is in April.

_____

9. boxing day is a British holiday.

_____

10. father's day is in June.

_____

Writing Titles of Books, Stories, and Poems

Begin the first word and last word in the title of a book with a capital letter. All other words begin with a capital letter except unimportant words. Some unimportant words are <u>a</u>, <u>an</u>, <u>the</u>, <u>of</u>, <u>with</u>, <u>for</u>, <u>at</u>, <u>in</u>, and <u>on</u>. Draw a line under the title of a book.

Examples:

    <u>The Snowy Day</u>

    <u>Storm at Sea</u>

Begin the first word, last word, and all important words in the title of a story or poem with a capital letter. Put quotation marks (" ") around the title of a story or poem.

Examples:

    "Jonas and the Monster" (story)

    "Something Is Out There" (poem)

DIRECTIONS   **Write these book titles correctly. Be sure to underline the title of a book.**

1. best friends

_____

2. the biggest bear

_____

3. rabbits on roller skates

_____

4. down on the sunny farm

_____

 **DIRECTIONS**   **Read the sentences. Circle the letters that should be capital letters.**

5. My favorite poem is called "we bees."

6. I read a story called "the dancing pony" last week.

7. Robert Louis Stevenson wrote a poem called "my shadow."

8. Lori wrote a story named "my summer on the farm."

Practice with Titles

Remember to use a capital letter for all of the words in a book title except for unimportant words like <u>a</u>, <u>an</u>, <u>of</u>, <u>the</u>, <u>with</u>, <u>for</u>, <u>at</u>, <u>in</u>, and <u>on</u>. Draw a line under the title of a book.

Example:

<u>The Wind in the Willows</u>

Also, capitalize all the important words in the title of a story or poem. Put quotation marks (" ") around the title of a story or poem.

Example:

"The Cat is Fat"

DIRECTIONS Rewrite each sentence correctly.

1. My mom's favorite book is called gone with the wind.

_____

2. Alison wrote a poem named hay is for horses.

_____

3. At the library, I checked out a book called learn to draw.

_____

4. I read a story about boats called sail away.

_____

5. Mrs. Gibbs read us a poem named a plan for stan.

_____

6. Sara wrote a story called what I did on vacation.

_____

7. Her favorite book is called ramona the great.

_____

Beginning Sentences

Begin the first word of a sentence with a capital letter.
Examples:
> The garden is very pretty.
> Flowers grow there.
> What kind of flowers do you see?

DIRECTIONS ▷ **Rewrite these sentences. Begin each sentence with a capital letter.**

1. there are many kinds of gardens.

_____

2. vegetables grow in some gardens.

_____

3. you can find gardens in parks.

_____

4. i like to work in the garden.

_____

5. deb likes to play ball.

_____

6. her ball is red.

_____

7. jet wants to play.

_____

8. deb throws the ball.

_____

9. the ball goes far.

_____

Ending Sentences

Put a period (.) at the end of a sentence that tells something.
Examples:
     Patty is my friend.
     We play together.
Put a question mark (?) at the end of a sentence that asks something.
Examples:
     Is he your brother?
     Do you have a sister?

DIRECTIONS   **Rewrite these telling sentences. Use capital letters and periods where they are needed.**

1. patty played on the baseball team

_____

2. patty hit two home runs

_____

3. she caught the ball, too

_____

DIRECTIONS   **Rewrite these asking sentences. Use capital letters and question marks where they are needed.**

4. what time is it

_____

5. is it time for lunch

_____

6. are you ready to eat

_____

Periods

Use a **period (.)** at the end of a statement.
Example:
> I like to read books about frogs.

Put a period at the end of most titles of people.
Example:
> Mr. Arnold Lobel wrote the book.

These are titles of people.
> Mr.   Mrs.   Ms.   Dr.   Miss

DIRECTIONS → **Correct the sentences. Add periods where they are needed.**

1. John has a nice garden

2. The flowers are pretty

3. John gave Sara some seeds

4. Sara will plant them in the ground

5. Little green plants will grow

6. Ms Sara thought the seeds were afraid.

7. Mr John told Sara not to worry.

8. Mrs Jones told Sara to wait a few days.

9. Sara showed her garden to Dr Dewey.

10. Ms Babbitt thinks Sara has a nice garden.

Question Marks, Exclamation Points, and Apostrophes

Use a **question mark (?)** at the end of a question.

Example:

Who are you?

Use an **exclamation point (!)** at the end of an exclamation.

Example:

Leave me alone!

Use an **apostrophe (')** to show that one or more letters have been left out in a contraction.

Example:

His parents didn't take Stewart anywhere.

 **DIRECTIONS** Finish the sentences correctly. Add question marks and exclamation points where they are needed.

1. Stewart just does not care

2. Does Stewart care about anything

3. Does Stewart care about his grades

4. Yes, indeed he cares

 **DIRECTIONS** Circle the correct contraction in ( ) to complete each sentence.

5. Stewart said, "I (dont, don't) know what to do!"

6. "(Ill, I'll) help you," said the teacher.

7. Stewart (didn't, didnt) want to get bad grades.

Practice with Question Marks, Exclamation Points, and Apostrophes

Remember, use a question mark **(?)** at the end of a question.
Use an exclamation point **(!)** at the end of an exclamation.
Use an apostrophe **(')** to show that one or more letters have been left out of a contraction.

 **DIRECTIONS** Finish the sentences correctly. Add question marks and exclamation points where they are needed.

1. Have you ever been camping

2. Do you like to sleep under the stars

3. It is so beautiful

4. Would you like to try it

 **DIRECTIONS** Rewrite each sentence using an apostrophe in the contraction.

5. One thing I dont like is setting up the tent.

_____

6. I cant seem to get it right!

_____

7. Ill ask my mom for help next time.

_____

Using Apostrophes in Contractions

A **contraction** is a word made by joining two words. An **apostrophe** (') shows where a letter or letters are left out.

Examples:

is not = isn't
cannot = can't
do not = don't
are not = aren't

DIRECTIONS ▷ **Draw a line from the two words to the contraction.**

1. were not   hasn't
2. was not   haven't
3. has not   wasn't
4. have not   weren't
5. did not   aren't
6. are not   didn't

DIRECTIONS ▷ **Write each contraction as two words.**

7. isn't _____ _____
8. don't _____ _____
9. wasn't _____ _____
10. can't _____ _____

11. didn't _____ _____
12. hadn't _____ _____
13. doesn't _____ _____
14. aren't _____ _____

DIRECTIONS ▷ **Write a contraction for the two words.**

15. Today (is not) _____ a good day.

16. I (do not) _____ have my lunch.

17. I (did not) _____ finish my work.

Practice with Contractions

> Remember, a contraction is a word made by joining two words. An apostrophe shows where a letter or letters are left out.
> *Examples:*
>
> does not = doesn't
> were not = weren't
> did not = didn't
> had not = hadn't

DIRECTIONS ▷ **Write a contraction for the two words.**

1. Please (do not) _____ come into my room.

2. I (can not) _____ play because I have to do my homework.

3. I (have not) _____ finished it yet.

4. Mom (does not) _____ like it when I do my homework so late.

5. She says it (is not) _____ a good habit.

DIRECTIONS ▷ **Write a sentence for each contraction.**

6. can't

_____

7. don't

_____

8. weren't

_____

Commas

Use a **comma (,)** between the name of a city and a state.
Examples:
Toledo, Ohio
Albany, New York
Use a comma between the day and the year in a date.
Examples:
July 4, 1776
November 1, 2003
Use a comma after the greeting and after the closing in a letter.
Examples:
Dear Mom and Dad,
Your friend,

 **DIRECTIONS** **Read Mary Jane's letter to Grandmother. Put commas where they are needed.**

June 8 2005

Dear Grandmother

I hope you are feeling better. Yesterday Mom and I went shopping. We found a pretty new jacket for you. The tag says it comes from Chicago Illinois. I hope you like the jacket. Please write to me soon.

Love

Mary Jane

Using Commas in Place Names

Put a comma between the name of a city and its state. Names of cities and states begin with a capital letter.

Examples:

Denver, Colorado

Dover, Delaware

DIRECTIONS → Write the names of the cities and states correctly. Put commas where they are needed.

1. akron ohio _____

2. hilo hawaii _____

3. macon georgia _____

4. nome alaska _____

5. provo utah _____

DIRECTIONS

Rewrite the sentences. Use capital letters and commas where they are needed.

6. Nancy lives in barnet vermont.

_____

7. Mr. Hill went to houston texas.

_____

8. Did Bruce like bend oregon?

_____

9. Will Amy visit newark ohio?

_____

10. How far away is salem massachusetts?

_____

Using Commas in Dates

Put a comma between the day of the month and the year.
Examples:

March 2, 1836

January 1, 2003

DIRECTIONS → **Write these dates correctly. Use capital letters, periods, and commas where they are needed.**

1. dec 12 1948 _____

2. mar 27 1965 _____

3. sept 8 1994 _____

4. nov 1 2000 _____

5. jan 5 1995 _____

DIRECTIONS → **Complete the sentences. Write the date correctly on the line.**

6. Jim was born on _____. (august 10 1967)

7. Jen's birthday is _____. (Oct 17 1983)

8. Maria visited on _____. (february 8 1991)

9. Dad's party was on _____. (july 29 1989)

10. Carrie started school on _____. (sept 3 2001)

11. Luis lost his first tooth on _____. (oct 20 1998)

12. I was born on _____.

Rhyming Words

Words that end with the same sounds are **rhyming words**. Here are some rhyming words.

Examples:

        car—star   boat—goat

A **rhyme** is two or more lines that end with rhyming words. Many rhymes are silly or funny.

Example:

        The cat took a rocket trip to the <u>moon</u>.
        It left in July and came back in <u>June</u>.

How to Write a Rhyme

1. Write two lines.
2. End each line with a rhyming word.

 **DIRECTIONS**   **Choose a word from the box to finish each rhyme.**

cow	dog	bee	hat

1. Did you ever see a cat

   Wear a funny _____?

2. The cat climbed up a tree

   And sang a song with a _____.

3. The bee said, "Meow,"

   And flew away to visit the _____.

4. The cow watched a frog

   Hop over a _____.

More Rhyming Words

Remember, words that end with the same sounds are rhyming words.

Examples:

     bat—cat

     bug—rug

A rhyme is two or more lines that end with rhyming words.

Example:

     I think that there's a tiny bug

     Sleeping on my bedroom rug!

DIRECTIONS ➤ **Draw a line between rhyming words.**

1. dog   hat

2. tall   hog

3. mouse   house

4. flat   ball

5. blue   clue

DIRECTIONS ➤ **Now use one of the rhyme pairs you made above to write a rhyme.**

6. _____

_____

_____

_____

_____

Synonyms

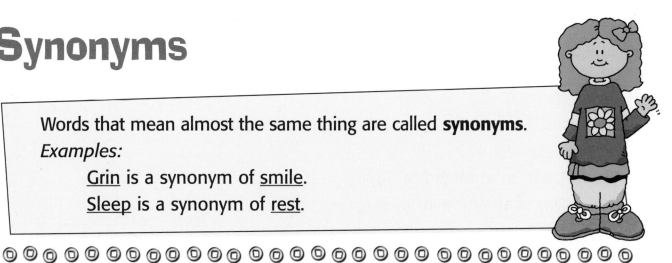

Words that mean almost the same thing are called **synonyms**.
Examples:

Grin is a synonym of smile.

Sleep is a synonym of rest.

DIRECTIONS ➤ **Read each sentence. Find a synonym in the box for each underlined word. Write it on the line.**

dog	dad	gift	large	great	home
road	sad	sick	sleep	small	yell

1. I walked across the <u>street</u>. _____

2. I went into my <u>house</u>. _____

3. I was so <u>unhappy</u>. _____

4. I almost felt <u>ill</u>. _____

5. It was my birthday. No one gave me a <u>present</u>. _____

6. Then I saw something <u>little</u>. _____

7. It had <u>big</u> eyes. _____

8. It was a little <u>puppy</u>. _____

9. I began to <u>shout</u>. _____

10. "What a <u>wonderful</u> present!" _____

11. My <u>father</u> did remember my birthday. _____

12. I don't think I will <u>rest</u> tonight. _____

Antonyms

Words that mean the opposite are called **antonyms**.
Examples:

Up is an antonym of down.

Day is an antonym of night.

DIRECTIONS ▷ **Draw a line to the antonym for each underlined word.**

1. a hard bed   dark

2. a short story   happy

3. a light color   long

4. off the table   low

5. a sad movie   on

6. a high bridge   soft

DIRECTIONS ▷ **Write the antonym for the underlined word.**

7. When you are not wet, you are _____.
(happy, dry)

8. I like to run fast, not _____.
(slow, far)

9. When food isn't good, it tastes _____.
(hot, bad)

10. Summer is hot, and winter is _____.
(cold, snow)

11. A traffic light turns red for stop and green for _____.
(high, go)

12. Some questions are easy. Others are _____.
(not, hard)

More Synonyms and Antonyms

Remember, words that mean almost the same thing are called synonyms.

Example:

Happy is a synonym of glad.

Words that mean the opposite are called antonyms.

Example:

Huge is an antonym of tiny.

DIRECTIONS ▷ Read each pair of words. If they mean almost the same thing, circle synonym. If they are opposites, circle antonym.

1.   long/short

synonym   antonym

2.   tired/sleepy

synonym   antonym

3.   mad/angry

synonym   antonym

4.   funny/boring

synonym   antonym

5.   loud/quiet

synonym   antonym

6.   pretty/cute

synonym   antonym

7.   angry/calm

synonym   antonym

8.   poor/rich

synonym   antonym

Homographs

Homographs are words that are spelled alike but have different meanings. Some homographs are pronounced differently.
Examples:

<u>felt</u>: a soft kind of cloth
<u>felt</u>: sensed on the skin

<u>wind</u>: moving air
<u>wind</u>: to turn a knob

 **DIRECTIONS** Look at each pair of pictures. Read each sentence. Then, write the letter of the correct meaning on the line.

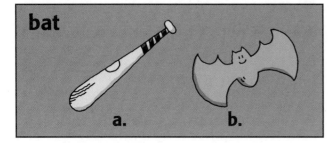

bat

a.   b.

_____ **1.** Tony has a wooden bat.

_____ **2.** The bat sleeps during the day.

_____ **3.** The bat broke when Alberto hit the ball.

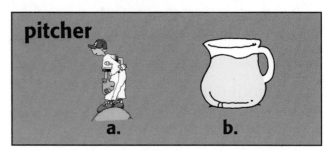

pitcher

a.   b.

_____ **7.** I put some juice in the pitcher.

_____ **8.** The pitcher threw the ball too low.

_____ **9.** The milk pitcher was empty.

plant

a.   b.

_____ **4.** Kendra wants to plant a tree.

_____ **5.** The farmer will plant his crops in the fall.

_____ **6.** Jody grew a plant at school.

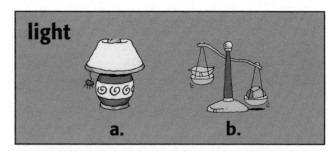

light

a.   b.

_____ **10.** I will turn on the light.

_____ **11.** The feather is light.

_____ **12.** There is only one light in my room.

Homophones

Homophones are words that sound the same but are spelled differently.

Use <u>hear</u> to mean "to listen to."

Example:

   We <u>hear</u> the bell ringing.

Use <u>here</u> to mean "to this place" or "at this place."

Example:

   Bring the ticket <u>here</u>.

Use <u>your</u> when you mean "belonging to you."

Example:

   Do you have <u>your</u> homework?

Use <u>you're</u> when you mean "you are."

Example:

   <u>You're</u> in trouble now.

DIRECTIONS ▸ Write <u>hear</u> or <u>here</u> to complete each sentence correctly.

1. Did you _____ that the circus is coming?

2. Is it coming _____ soon?

3. Yes, it will be _____ today.

4. I think I _____ the music now.

DIRECTIONS ▸ Write <u>your</u> or <u>you're</u> to complete each sentence correctly.

5. _____ a good skater, Eric.

6. Pull _____ laces tight.

7. Now, _____ ready to skate safely.

8. Were _____ legs this wobbly when you started?

More Homophones

Remember, homophones are words that sound the same but are spelled differently.

Use <u>write</u> to mean "to put words on paper."

Example:

   Please <u>write</u> your name on your paper.

Use <u>right</u> to mean "correct."

Example:

   Your answer is <u>right</u>.

Use <u>right</u> to mean "the opposite of left."

Example:

   Turn <u>right</u> to get to my school.

DIRECTIONS **Write <u>right</u> or <u>write</u> to complete each sentence correctly.**

1. Chris likes to _____ on the board.

2. Everything was _____ on Martha's math paper.

3. We turn _____ to go to the lunchroom.

4. Our class is learning to _____ stories.

5. Kim drew the picture on the _____ side.

6. Luis can _____ in Spanish.

7. The teacher marked the _____ answers.

8. Be sure you do the _____ page.

9. Jenna will _____ about her birthday party.

10. James colors with his _____ hand.

Troublesome Words

Use <u>two</u> to mean "the number 2."

Example:

    <u>Two</u> children worked together.

Use <u>too</u> to mean "more than enough."

Example:

    There are <u>too</u> many people on the bus.

Use <u>too</u> to mean "also."

Example:

    May I help, <u>too</u>?

Use <u>to</u> to mean "toward" or "to do something."

Example:

    Let's go <u>to</u> the library <u>to</u> find Kim.

DIRECTIONS   **Write <u>two</u>, <u>too</u>, or <u>to</u> to complete each sentence.**

1. The children were working _____ make a class library.

2. Andy had _____ books in his hand.

3. He gave them _____ Ms. Diaz.

4. Ms. Diaz was happy _____ get the books.

5. "We can never have _____ many books," she said.

6. Rosa said she would bring _____ or three books.

7. James wanted to bring some, _____.

8. Joann found a book that was _____ old.

9. Pages started _____ fall out when she picked it up.

10. Soon, everyone would have new books _____ read.

11. We can take out _____ of these books at a time.

More Troublesome Words

Use <u>there</u> when you mean "in that place."
Example:
      The dinosaur is over <u>there</u>.
Use <u>their</u> when you mean "belonging to them."
Example:
      This is <u>their</u> swamp.
<u>They're</u> is a contraction for <u>they are</u>. Use <u>they're</u> when you mean "they are."
Example:
      <u>They're</u> eating leaves from the trees.

DIRECTIONS   Circle the correct word in ( ) to complete each sentence.

1. Is this (their, they're) food?

2. (There, They're) huge animals.

3. A big one is over (there, their).

4. Once it was (there, their) land.

5. Dinosaurs lived (they're, there) for a while.

6. (They're, There) everywhere!

7. (They're, There) the two biggest dinosaurs.

8. The faster dinosaur is resting (their, there).

9. Small dinosaurs lived (they're, there) long ago.

10. (Their, There) land was different then.

11. I see some more dinosaurs over (they're, there).

12. (They're, There) in the lake.

Compound Words

Sometimes two words can be put together to make a new word.
The new word is called a **compound word**.

Examples:

lunch + room = lunchroom

every + day = everyday

DIRECTIONS Write compound words. Pick words from Box 1 and Box 2. Write the new word in Box 3.

	Box 1	Box 2	Box 3
1.	sun	noon	_____
2.	after	glasses	_____
3.	play	side	_____
4.	birth	ground	_____
5.	out	book	_____
6.	scrap	day	_____

DIRECTIONS Write a compound word to finish each sentence. You may use the compound words you made above.

7. Dana was wearing _____ in class.

8. In the _____, Dana was sent to the principal's office.

9. Brad put a picture of the school in his _____.

10. Brad will be eight years old on his next _____.

11. We can't go _____ if it rains.

12. The _____ will be too wet.

More Compound Words

Remember, sometimes two words can be put together to make a compound word.
Example:

      sun + flower = sunflower

DIRECTIONS Draw a line between two words that make a compound word.

1.	snow	rope
2.	rail	ball
3.	rain	bow
4.	sail	road
5.	jump	boat
6.	ear	plane
7.	air	ring

DIRECTIONS Write three sentences using three of the words you made.

8. _____

_____

9. _____

_____

10. _____

_____

Prefixes

A **prefix** is a group of letters added to the beginning of a word.
Adding a prefix to a word changes its meaning.
Example:

> The old woman was <u>happy</u>.
> The old woman was <u>unhappy</u>.

Prefix	Meaning	Example
un	not	<u>un</u>clear
re	again	<u>re</u>write

 **DIRECTIONS** → **Read each sentence. Underline the word that has a prefix. Tell the meaning of the word.**

1. The old man was unable to find something to wear.

   _____

2. The old woman reopened the drawer.

   _____

3. She told the old man they were unlucky.

   _____

4. The old man felt this was unfair.

   _____

5. He was very unhappy.

   _____

6. The woman asked the man to rewind the yarn.

   _____

7. The old woman rewashed the socks.

   _____

8. Could the socks be uneven?

   _____

9. The old man refilled his wife's glass.

   _____

10. The farmer's wife reknitted the sweater.

   _____

Suffixes

A **suffix** is a group of letters added to the end of a word. Adding a suffix to a word changes its meaning.

Example:

Josef's parents were <u>helpless</u>.

The doctor was <u>helpful</u>.

Suffix	Meaning	Example
ful	full of	hope<u>ful</u>
less	without	use<u>less</u>
able	able to be	break<u>able</u>

 **DIRECTIONS** Read each sentence. Underline the word that has a suffix. Tell the meaning of the word.

1. Is Josef careful? _____

2. Josef thought the game was harmless. _____

3. The chair Josef was on was breakable. _____

 **DIRECTIONS** Complete each sentence with a word from the box. Tell the meaning of the word you chose.

hopeful	dreadful	thankful

4. Josef's parents had a _____ shock!

_____

5. They were _____ the chair would not break.

_____

6. When Josef came out of the hospital, he was very _____ .

_____

Writing Sentences

Remember, sentences have a naming part and an action part.
Example:

Naming Part	Action Part
Sara	won the race.

 **DIRECTIONS** Draw a line from a naming part to an action part to make sentences.

Naming Part	Action Part
1. Grandma	baked
2. Aunt Sue	sings
3. My friend	skates
4. Earl's dad	reads
5. Kiko's mom	cooks
6. Jon's sister	played

DIRECTIONS Write sentences with the naming parts and action parts you put together. Add some words of your own.

7. _____

8. _____

9. _____

10. _____

11. _____

12. _____

Practice with Writing Sentences

Remember, sentences have a naming part and an action part.

DIRECTIONS ➤ Read each sentence. Circle the naming part. Underline the action part.

1. My sister sings.
2. My brother dances.
3. They perform.
4. People clap.

DIRECTIONS ➤ Rewrite each sentence, adding some words of your own.

5. My sister sings.

_____

6. My brother dances.

_____

7. They perform.

_____

8. People clap.

_____

Paragraphs

A **paragraph** is a group of sentences that tells about one main idea. The first line of a paragraph is indented. This means the first word is moved in a little from the left margin.

The first sentence in a paragraph often tells the main idea. The other sentences tell about the main idea.

Example:

A safe home keeps people from getting hurt. Shoes or toys should not be left on the stairs. Matches, medicines, and cleaners should be locked safely away. Grown-ups should get things that are on high shelves instead of letting children reach for them. Then, children will not fall and get hurt.

How to Write a Paragraph

1. Write a sentence that tells the main idea.
2. Indent the first line.
3. Write sentences that tell more about the main idea.

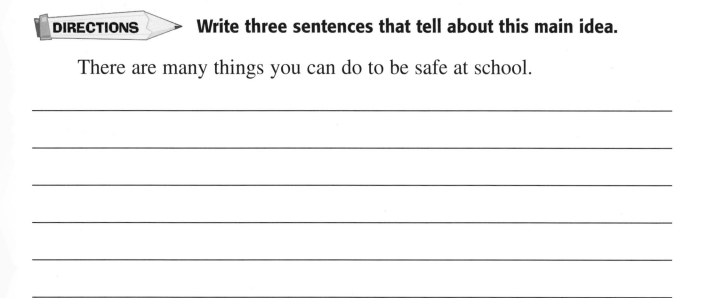

DIRECTIONS ▷ **Write three sentences that tell about this main idea.**

There are many things you can do to be safe at school.

_____

_____

_____

_____

_____

Main Idea

The **main idea** of a paragraph is often in the first sentence. It tells what the paragraph is about.

Example:

      I have nice neighbors. Ms. Hill gives me flowers. Mr. Stone always smiles and waves. Miss Higgins plays ball with me.

DIRECTIONS → **Read each paragraph. Write the sentence that tells the main idea.**

Uncle Joe is a funny man. He tells jokes about elephants. He does magic tricks that don't work. He makes funny faces when he tells stories. He always makes me laugh.

1. _____

_____

Dad told us a funny story about his dog. When Dad was a little boy, he had a dog named Tiger. One day, Dad forgot his lunch. Dad said Tiger would bring it to school. A friend thought it would be a real tiger.

2. _____

_____

Firefighters are brave people. They go into burning buildings. They put out fires. They teach families how to be safe in their homes.

3. _____

_____

Practice with the Main Idea

Remember, the main idea of a paragraph is often in the first sentence. It tells what the paragraph is about.

ⓞ ⓞ

DIRECTIONS ➤ **Read each paragraph. Write the sentence that tells the main idea.**

Making pasta is easy. First, you have to boil water. Add a little salt and oil. Let the water boil. Put the pasta in the water until it gets soft. Drain the noodles through a special bowl with holes in the bottom. Put your pasta on a plate and enjoy!

1. _____

_____

My mom is a very busy person. She works at a library. She coaches our swim team. She does all of the shopping. She helps Dad cook dinner. She reads to us every night. She even exercises after we go to bed.

2. _____

_____

Having a dog is fun, but it is also a lot of work. You have to remember to feed and walk the dog. You have to train it. Sometimes you have to play with it, even if you are tired. You have to wash and brush it. You have to clean up after it. It's a good thing that dogs are cute!

3. _____

_____

Supporting Details

The other sentences in a paragraph give details about the main idea in the beginning sentence.

Example:

I have nice neighbors. **Ms. Hill gives me flowers. Mr. Stone always smiles and waves. Miss Higgins plays ball with me.**

○○○○○○○○○○○○○○○○○○○○○○○○○○○○○○○

DIRECTIONS ➤ **Read each paragraph. Circle the main idea. Underline the sentences that give details about the main idea.**

1.   Uncle Joe is a funny man. He tells jokes about elephants. He does magic tricks that don't work. He makes funny faces when he tells stories. He always makes me laugh.

2.   Dad told us a funny story about his dog. When Dad was a little boy, he had a dog named Tiger. One day Dad forgot his lunch. Dad said Tiger would bring it to school. A friend thought it would be a real tiger.

3.   Firefighters are brave people. They go into burning buildings. They put out fires. They teach families how to be safe in their homes.

Practice with Supporting Details

Remember, the main idea tells what a paragraph is about. The other sentences in a paragraph give details about the main idea.

DIRECTIONS ▷ **Read each paragraph. Circle the main idea. Underline the sentences that give details about the main idea.**

1.   Making pasta is easy. First, you have to boil water. Add a little salt and oil. Let the water boil. Put the pasta in the water until it gets soft. Drain the noodles through a special bowl with holes in the bottom. Put your pasta on a plate and enjoy!

2.   My mom is a very busy person. She works at a library. She coaches our swim team. She does all of the shopping. She helps Dad cook dinner. She reads to us every night. She even exercises after we go to bed.

3.   Having a dog is fun, but it is also a lot of work. You have to remember to feed and walk the dog. You have to train it. Sometimes you have to play with it, even if you are tired. You have to wash and brush it. You have to clean up after it. It's a good thing that dogs are cute!

Order in Paragraphs

The sentences in a paragraph tell things in the order in which they happened.

Words such as <u>first</u>, <u>second</u>, <u>third</u>, <u>next</u>, <u>then</u>, and <u>last</u> can help tell when things happened.

Examples:

    Jane got ready for bed. **First**, she took a bath. **Next**, she brushed her teeth. **Then**, she put on her pajamas. **Last**, she read a story and got into bed.

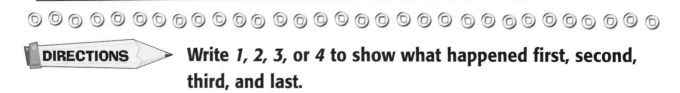

DIRECTIONS ➤ **Write *1, 2, 3,* or *4* to show what happened first, second, third, and last.**

Eva planted flowers. First, she got a shovel. Next, she dug some holes in the garden. Then, she put the flowers into the holes. Last, she put the shovel back in its place.

_____ Then, she put the flowers into the holes.

_____ Next, she dug some holes in the garden.

_____ Last, she put the shovel back in its place.

_____ First, she got a shovel.

Dan and Larry washed the car. First, they got the car wet. Next, they put soap all over it. Then, they washed all the soap off. Last, they dried the car.

_____ They put soap all over the car.

_____ They washed all the soap off.

_____ Dan and Larry dried the car.

_____ The boys got the car wet.

Practice with Order in Paragraphs

Remember, the sentences in a paragraph tell things in the order in which they happened.

Words such as <u>first</u>, <u>second</u>, <u>third</u>, <u>next</u>, <u>then</u>, and <u>last</u> can help tell when things happened.

DIRECTIONS ▷ **Write *1*, *2*, *3*, or *4* to show what happened first, second, third, and last.**

Have you ever made instant pudding? In a bowl, stir the pudding mix with 2 cups of cold milk. Next, pour the pudding into cups. Then, chill the pudding for five minutes. Finally, enjoy the yummy treat.

_____ Finally, enjoy the yummy treat.

_____ In a bowl, stir the pudding mix with 2 cups of cold milk.

_____ Then, chill the pudding for five minutes.

_____ Next, pour the pudding into cups.

Learning to swim took a long time. First, I had to get used to the water. Then, I had to learn to float. Next, my teacher taught me a swimming stroke. Finally, I was ready to try on my own.

_____ Next, my teacher taught me a swimming stroke.

_____ Then, I had to learn to float.

_____ Finally, I was ready to try on my own.

_____ First, I had to get used to the water.

Personal Narrative

A **personal narrative** is a story about the writer. In a story, a writer tells about one main idea. Every story has a beginning, a middle, and an ending.

Example:

One day my grandfather and I went to the zoo. First, we looked at lions and tigers. Next, we watched the monkeys play. Then, we went to see the bears. Last, Grandfather helped me feed the seals. My day with Grandfather was wonderful!

How to Write a Paragraph About Yourself

1. Write a sentence that tells about something that happened to you. Tell where the story took place.
2. Write sentences that tell about what happened in order. Use the words <u>first</u>, <u>next</u>, <u>then</u>, and <u>last</u>.
3. Tell how the story ended.
4. Use the words <u>I</u> and <u>me</u>.
5. Give the story a title.

 **DIRECTIONS** ▷ **Read the example paragraph above. Answer the questions.**

1. Where does the story take place?

_____

2. What happens after they look at the lions and tigers?

_____

3. What happens last?

_____

Practice with Personal Narrative

DIRECTIONS **Finish the paragraph. Add words that tell about yourself.**

I had a good day at school. First, I _____

_____. Next, I _____

_____. Then, I ate lunch with my friend

_____.

Last, I _____

_____.

DIRECTIONS **Use the chart to write a story about yourself.**

Beginning	Middle	Ending
Who is in the story? Where does the story happen?	What happens?	How do things work out?

_____

_____

_____

_____

_____

_____

_____

_____

Poem

In a **poem**, a writer paints a picture with words. Many poems have rhyming words at the end of every line or every other line.

Example:

Special Things

I like
White snow and blue bows.
I like
The sweet red rose.
I like
The crunchy sand between my toes.
I like
My puppy's wet, black nose.

How to Write a Poem
1. End some lines with rhyming words.
2. Try to paint a picture with words.
3. Give your poem a title.

 **DIRECTIONS** ➤ **Read the example poem above. Answer the questions.**

1. What is the poem about?

_____

2. Name two rhyming words in the poem.

_____

3. Name two words that describe in the poem.

_____

Practice with Poems

DIRECTIONS **Finish this poem. Think of describing words and words that rhyme. Give your poem a title.**

_____

Summer is fun.

I can _____.

I feel so free

Like a _____.

DIRECTIONS **Finish the chart. Use the chart to write a poem.**

My title
_____

Describing words I will use	Rhyming words I will use
_____	_____
_____	_____
_____	_____

_____

_____

_____

_____

_____

Describing Paragraph

In a paragraph that **describes**, a writer tells about a person, place, or thing. The sentences have describing words that help the reader see, hear, taste, smell, and feel.
Example:

> Many birds visit my backyard. Red cardinals make nests in our bushes. Tiny hummingbirds buzz around the yellow flowers in our garden. Robins chirp sweetly and wake me in the morning.

How to Write a Paragraph That Describes
1. Write a sentence that tells whom or what the paragraph is about.
2. Write sentences that tell more about the main idea.
3. Use describing words in your sentences.

 **DIRECTIONS** ⟩ Read the example describing paragraph. Answer the questions.

1. What is the topic of the paragraph?

_____

2. Which words tell what the birds are like?

_____

3. Write a describing sentence to add to the paragraph.

_____

Describing Paragraph, page 2

DIRECTIONS **Finish the paragraph. Add describing words.**

The little woman put on her ———————————— hat.
She went outside. It was a ———————————— day. The sky was
————————————. The little woman felt ————————————.

DIRECTIONS **Finish the chart. Write describing words about your topic. Use the chart to write a describing paragraph.**

My topic: ————————————————————————

Looks	Feels	Tastes	Smells	Sounds
_____	_____	_____	_____	_____
_____	_____	_____	_____	_____
_____	_____	_____	_____	_____
_____	_____	_____	_____	_____

————————————————————————————————

————————————————————————————————

————————————————————————————————

————————————————————————————————

————————————————————————————————

————————————————————————————————

————————————————————————————————

Friendly Letter

A **friendly letter** is a letter you write to someone you know.
A friendly letter has five parts. They are the heading, greeting, body, closing, and signature.
Example:

heading ⏤ October 22, 2005

greeting ⏤ Dear Grandma,

body ⏤   The sweater you knitted for my birthday is great! The fall days here have been chilly. It's nice to have a new, warm sweater to wear. It is just the right size. Thank you, Grandma.

closing ⏤ Love,

signature ⏤ Emily

How to Write a Friendly Letter
1. Choose a friend or a relative to write to.
2. Write about things you have done.
3. Be sure your letter has a heading, greeting, body, closing, and signature.
4. Use capital letters and commas correctly.

 **DIRECTIONS** > Read the example friendly letter. Answer the questions.

1. Whom did Emily write the letter to?

_____

2. Why did Emily write the letter?

_____

Friendly Letter, page 2

heading _____

greeting _____

body _____

_____

_____

_____

_____

_____

_____

_____

_____

closing _____

signature _____

Envelopes

An **envelope** is used to send a letter or a note.
Example:

Mary Jo Wood
13 West Street
Chicago, Illinois 60648 — **return address**   **stamp**

Mrs. May Williams
13 River Bend Road
Crystal Lake, Illinois 60014 — **mailing address**

How to Address an Envelope

1. In the mailing address, tell who is receiving the letter.
2. In the return address, tell who is sending the letter.
3. Put a stamp on the envelope.

DIRECTIONS ⟩ **Think of someone you want to write to. Use the organizer below to address your envelope.**

How-to Paragraph

In a **how-to paragraph**, a writer tells how to make or do something. The steps are told in order.

Example:

Here is how to make a bird feeder. You will need a pine cone, string, peanut butter, and birdseed. First, tie the string to the top of the pine cone. Next, roll the pine cone in peanut butter. Then, roll the pine cone in birdseed. Last, go outside and tie the pine cone to a tree branch.

How to Write a How-to Paragraph
1. Write a sentence that tells what the paragraph is about.
2. Write a sentence that lists things you need.
3. Tell how to do something in order.
4. Use the words <u>first</u>, <u>next</u>, <u>then</u>, and <u>last</u>.

DIRECTIONS **Read the example how-to paragraph. Answer the questions.**

1. What does the paragraph tell how to do?

_____

_____

2. What materials are needed?

_____

_____

How-to Paragraph, page 2

DIRECTIONS **Put these sentences for a how-to paragraph in order. Write 1, 2, 3, or 4 to show the order of the steps.**

_____ Next, fill the can with water.   _____ Here is how to water a plant.

_____ Last, water the plant.   _____ First, get a watering can.

DIRECTIONS **Finish the chart. Use the chart to write a how-to paragraph.**

My topic: _____

Materials needed: _____

_____

_____

Steps:

1. _____

2. _____

3. _____

4. _____

_____

_____

_____

_____

_____

Information Paragraph

In a paragraph that gives **information**, a writer gives facts and details about one topic.

Example:

      Many African American people celebrate Kwanzaa. It is a celebration of the customs and history of African American people. It is a gathering time for families, like Thanksgiving. The holiday is celebrated for seven days. It begins the day after Christmas. On each night of Kwanzaa, a candle is lit. Each candle stands for a rule to help people live their lives.

How to Write an Information Paragraph

1. Write a topic sentence. Tell who or what your paragraph is about.
2. Indent the first line.
3. Write detail sentences. Give interesting facts about the person, animal, place, or thing.

 **Read the example information paragraph. Answer the questions.**

1. What is the topic sentence of the information paragraph?

_____

_____

2. Write one detail sentence from the paragraph.

_____

_____

Information Paragraph, page 2

 Think about a topic you would like to write about. Complete the chart. Use the chart to write an information paragraph.

Topic: _____

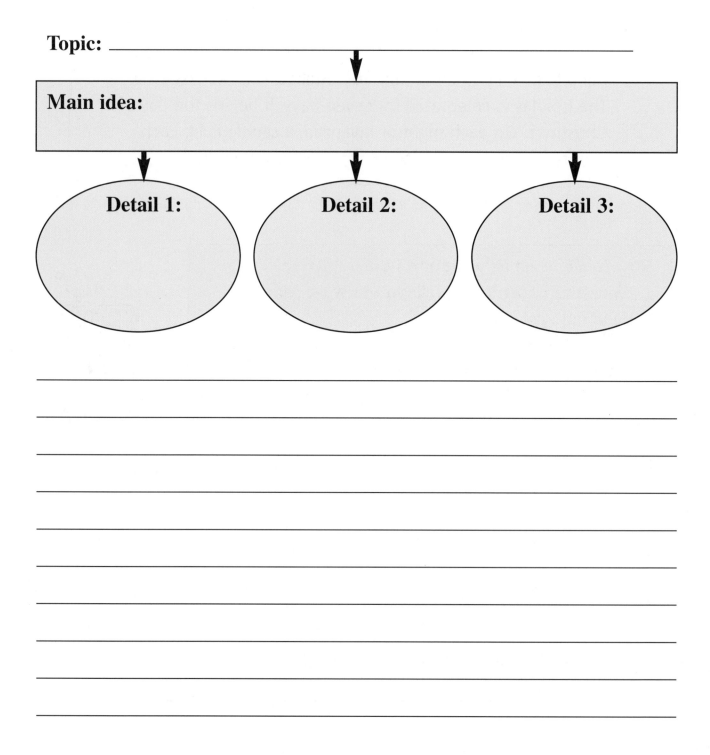

Main idea:

Detail 1:

Detail 2:

Detail 3:

_____

_____

_____

_____

_____

_____

_____

_____

Book Report

A **book report** tells about a book. It also tells what you think about the book.

Example:

Title	<u>The Koala</u>
Author	Anita Best

About the Book   This book is about koalas. It tells many facts about this animal. Here are some of them. Koalas live in Australia. They live in trees. They eat leaves.

What I Think   This is a good book. I learned many things about koalas.

How to Write a Book Report
1. Write the title of the book. Underline it.
2. Write the author's name.
3. Tell some facts about the book. Tell about important people, places, and things in the book.
4. Tell what you think about the book.

 DIRECTIONS   **Read the example book report. Answer the questions.**

1. What is the title of the book?

_____

2. Who wrote the book?

_____

3. What did the writer of the report think about the book?

_____

_____

Book Report, page 2

DIRECTIONS Think of a book you would like to tell about. Fill in the information at the top and use it to write a book report.

Title of book: _____

Author of book: _____

Facts about book: _____

_____

_____

Should others read this book? _____

DIRECTIONS Use the information above to write a book report.

_____

_____

_____

_____

_____

_____

_____

_____

_____

_____

Persuading Paragraph

A **persuading paragraph** tries to make the reader agree with the writer's opinion.

Example:

> I think that a lizard should be our class pet. A lizard is small and easy to care for. It doesn't eat much food. Lizards are interesting to watch, too. Vote for the lizard!

How to Write a Persuading Paragraph
1. Write about something you feel strongly about.
2. Tell how you feel in the first sentence.
3. Give reasons why other people should feel the same way.
4. Ask your reader to do something in the last sentence.

 **DIRECTIONS** ➤ **Read the example persuading paragraph. Answer the questions.**

1. What is the writer's opinion in the first sentence?

_____

2. What is one reason the writer gives to make the reader agree?

_____

_____

3. What does the writer want the reader to do?

_____

_____

Persuading Paragraph, page 2

DIRECTIONS Think of something you feel strongly about. Fill in the information at the top and use it to write a persuading paragraph.

Main idea: _____

Reason 1: _____

_____

Reason 2: _____

Reason 3 (your strongest reason): _____

_____

What the reader should do: _____

_____

_____

_____

_____

_____

_____

_____

_____

_____

_____

Words in ABC Order

The order of letters from <u>A</u> to <u>Z</u> is called **ABC order**, or **alphabetical order**.
When words begin with the same letter, the next letter of the word is used to put the words in ABC order: <u>c</u>ape, <u>ch</u>apel, <u>ci</u>ty.

DIRECTIONS **Number the words in ABC order. Then, write the words in the correct order.**

1. _____ bat   1. _____
_____ air   2. _____
_____ cat   3. _____

2. _____ top   1. _____
_____ sea   2. _____
_____ rock 3. _____

3. _____ egg   1. _____
_____ fish 2. _____
_____ dog   3. _____

4. _____ hat   1. _____
_____ ice   2. _____
_____ gate 3. _____

5. _____ joke 1. _____
_____ lake 2. _____
_____ king 3. _____

6. _____ neck 1. _____
_____ owl   2. _____
_____ mail 3. _____

7. _____ yes   1. _____
_____ zoo   2. _____
_____ walk 3. _____

8. _____ pan   1. _____
_____ oak   2. _____
_____ nail 3. _____

Practice with ABC Order

Remember, when words begin with the same letter, the next letter in the word is used put the words in ABC order.
Example:
    <u>ab</u>out, <u>an</u>t, <u>ap</u>ple

DIRECTIONS Number the words in ABC order. Then, write the words in the correct order. Remember to look at the second letter in each word to help you.

1. _____ hop   1. _____
     _____ hat   2. _____
     _____ hill   3. _____

2. _____ fun   1. _____
     _____ four   2. _____
     _____ far   3. _____

3. _____ ten   1. _____
     _____ train 2. _____
     _____ top   3. _____

4. _____ art   1. _____
     _____ awful 2. _____
     _____ ate   3. _____

5. _____ bug   1. _____
     _____ back   2. _____
     _____ bring 3. _____

6. _____ goat   1. _____
     _____ gate   2. _____
     _____ great 3. _____

7. _____ snake 1. _____
     _____ sad   2. _____
     _____ star   3. _____

8. _____ plane 1. _____
     _____ pig   2. _____
     _____ prince 3. _____

Using a Dictionary

A **dictionary** is a book that lists words and their meanings. The words in a dictionary are listed in ABC order.

Words can be put in ABC order. The first letters of these words were used to put them in ABC order.

f̲lower

g̲arden

h̲ome

Many words on a dictionary page begin with the same letter. When words begin with the same letter, the second letter is used to put the words in ABC order.

s̲e̲eds

s̲t̲ory

s̲u̲n

DIRECTIONS ▷ Put each group of words in ABC order. Remember to use the second letter in each word if the first letter is the same.

1. noise _____

music _____

poem _____

2. sun _____

rain _____

plant _____

3. garden _____

ground _____

frog _____

4. afraid _____

asleep _____

alone _____

Using a Dictionary, page 2

Each word listed in the dictionary is called an **entry word**. Entry words are in ABC order.

The two words at the top of a dictionary page are called **guide words**. The word on the left is the first entry word on the page. The word on the right is the last entry word on the page. All the other entry words on the page are in ABC order between the first and the last words.

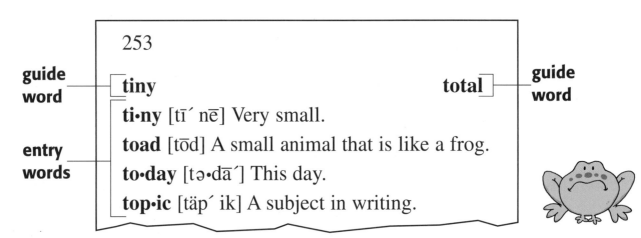

guide word ——— 253

tiny   **total**   **guide word**

entry words

ti·ny [tī´ nē] Very small.

toad [tōd] A small animal that is like a frog.

to·day [tə·dā´] This day.

top·ic [täp´ ik] A subject in writing.

> **DIRECTIONS** ▸ **Use the dictionary page above. Answer these questions.**

1. What is the first entry word on page 253? _____

2. Would you find the word <u>think</u> on this page? _____

3. What entry word tells about an animal? _____

4. What entry word means "very small"? _____

5. Could the entry word <u>together</u> be on this page? _____

Why or why not? _____

_____

Using a Dictionary, page 3

Some entry words have more than one meaning. Each meaning has a number.
The dictionary has sentences that show how to use the entry word.

bump [bump] **1** To knock against: The goblin <u>bumped</u> against the tree. **2** A part that sticks out: The goblin fell over a <u>bump</u> in the road.

burst [burst] **1** To break apart suddenly: The balloon <u>burst</u>. **2** To give way to a strong feeling: Grandfather and I <u>burst</u> into laughter.

DIRECTIONS   **Read the dictionary entries. Answer the questions.**

1. What word can mean "to break apart"? _____

2. What is the example sentence for meaning 2 of <u>burst</u>?

_____

3. Which word can mean "to knock against"?

_____

4. What is the number of the meaning of <u>bump</u> in this sentence?

The goblin fell over a <u>bump</u> in the road.

_____

5. Write your own example sentences for each meaning of <u>bump</u> and <u>burst</u>.

_____

_____

Using a Dictionary, page 4

DIRECTIONS → **Use the dictionary words to answer the questions. Write <u>yes</u> or <u>no</u>.**

always	at all times
animal	a living thing that is not a plant
bed	a place to sleep
dark	without light
green	the color of grass
hay	grass cut, dried, and used as food for cows and horses
hungry	needing food
kitten	a young cat
ladder	a set of steps used to climb up and down
library	a building where books are kept

1. Is <u>hay</u> something that alligators eat? _____

2. Is a <u>bed</u> a place for swimming? _____

3. Is grass <u>green</u>? _____

4. Is a flower an <u>animal</u>? _____

5. Can you use a <u>ladder</u> to climb to the roof? _____

6. Is a baby pig called a <u>kitten</u>? _____

7. Is a <u>library</u> a place for food? _____

8. Are you <u>hungry</u> after having lunch? _____

Using an Encyclopedia

An **encyclopedia** is a set of books that has facts on many subjects. Each book in a set is called a volume. The volumes list subjects in ABC order.

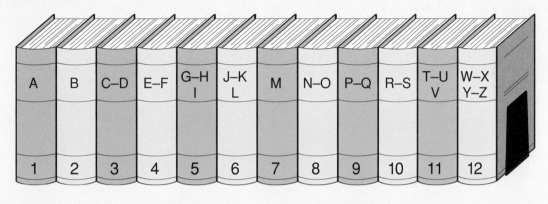

DIRECTIONS Use the model encyclopedia in the picture. Write the number of the volume in which you would find each of these subjects.

1. Ohio River _____

2. explorers _____

3. Rocky Mountains _____

4. cows _____

5. United States _____

6. farming _____

DIRECTIONS Write the word or words you would use to look up the following subjects in an encyclopedia.

7. pretty butterflies _____

8. kinds of dogs _____

9. trees in the United States _____

10. Florida history _____

Parts of a Book

The **title page** tells the title of a book. It gives the name of the author. The author is the person who wrote the book.

The **table of contents** lists the chapters or parts of the book. It tells the page where each chapter or part begins.

Some books have an **index**. It is in ABC order. It tells the pages where things can be found.

Kinds of Houses by Jack Builder	**Contents** 1. Brick Houses ....1 2. City Houses.................5 3. Country Houses.........8 4. Wood Houses..........15	Apartments, 2, 7 Basements, 25 Ceilings, 2, 9 Concrete, 4, 16 Doors, 12, 17
title page	**table of contents**	**index**

DIRECTIONS → **Look at the sample pages. Answer these questions.**

1. What is the title of the book? _____

2. Who wrote the book? _____

3. How many chapters are in this book? _____

4. On what page does chapter 4 begin? _____

5. On which pages can you find facts about ceilings? _____

Parts of a Book, page 2

Remember, the title page is in the front of a book. It tells you the title of the book. It tells you who wrote the book. It tells you who drew (illustrated) the pictures in the book. And it tells you what company published the book.

DIRECTIONS ➤ **Look at this title page from a book about cats. Then, write your answers to the questions below on the lines.**

ALL ABOUT CATS

by

Patricia L. Keller

Illustrated by

Richard H. Green

Coaster Press

New York

1. What is the title of the book? _____

2. Who wrote the book? _____

3. Who illustrated the book? _____

4. What company published the book? _____

Parts of a Book, page 3

Remember, the table of contents is near the front of a book. It tells you what each chapter of the book is about. When you want to know what a book is about, you should read the table of contents.

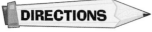 **DIRECTIONS** Look at this page from the book <u>All About Cats</u>. Then, write the correct answers to the questions on the lines below.

Table of Contents

CHAPTER	PAGE
1. Kinds of Cats	3
2. Picking the Right Cat	7
3. Taking Care of Your Cat	12
4. Playing with Your Cat	18
5. If Your Cat Gets Sick	23
6. Cats in the Wild	27

1. What chapter tells you what to do if your cat gets sick? _____

2. What chapter tells you about different kinds of cats? _____

3. What page tells you how to pick the right cat? _____

4. What is the name of the chapter on page 27?

_____

Kinds of Books

Some books are called **fiction**. They are stories about make-believe people and things. Here are some titles of books that are fiction.

> Ask Mr. Bear
>
> The Bears Go to the Hospital

Nonfiction books tell about real people or things. Here are some of the titles of books that are nonfiction.

> The Hospital Book
>
> Who Keeps Us Safe?

A library has fiction and nonfiction books. The fiction books are in one part of the library. The nonfiction books are in another part.

DIRECTIONS Read about each book. Tell if the book is <u>fiction</u> or <u>nonfiction</u>.

1. a book about a magic bear _____

2. a book that tells how to keep your home safe _____

3. a book that tells how to ride a bicycle safely _____

4. a book about a bear that can draw _____

5. a book about a house that can talk _____

6. a book about the fire department _____

7. a book about a dog that can fly _____

Kinds of Books, page 2

Remember, some books are called fiction. Fiction stories are about make-believe people or things.

Nonfiction books tell about real people or things.

A library has fiction and nonfiction books. The fiction books are in one part of the library. The nonfiction books are in another part.

DIRECTIONS **Read about each book. Tell if the book is <u>fiction</u> or <u>nonfiction</u>.**

1. a book about the first woman in space _____

2. a book about a cat that can talk _____

3. a book about types of plants _____

4. a book about a boy that can fly _____

DIRECTIONS **Go to your bookshelf and find two fiction books and two nonfiction books. Write each title below. Then write <u>fiction</u> or <u>nonfiction</u> to show what kind of book each is.**

5. _____ _____

6. _____ _____

7. _____ _____

8. _____ _____

Fact or Fantasy?

Some stories that you read tell you facts about things. They tell you what could really happen. You might read about how a kitten likes to chase a mouse. This is really true. It is a **fact**.

Some stories tell about things that could not happen. In these stories, animals may talk or act like people. People may do things that could not really happen. These stories are called **fantasy**. "Goldilocks and the Three Bears" is a fantasy. It could not really happen.

DIRECTIONS Read each sentence. Write <u>fact</u> by the sentences that are true. Write <u>fantasy</u> by the sentences that could not really happen.

_____ **1.** Some elephants live in the jungle.

_____ **2.** The elephant read three books today.

_____ **3.** The pig built a brick house.

_____ **4.** That monkey grabbed my hat!

_____ **5.** The chicken put on an apron and washed the dishes.

_____ **6.** The oven said, "The cake is done."

_____ **7.** A zookeeper takes care of animals.

_____ **8.** Annie put on her magic ring and disappeared.

Fact or Fantasy, page 2

Remember, a fact is something that is true. A story about something that really happened is a fact.

Some stories tell about things that could not happen. These stories are called fantasy.

DIRECTIONS > **Read each sentence. Write <u>fact</u> by the sentences that are true. Write <u>fantasy</u> by the sentences that could not really happen.**

_____ **1.** This morning my dog made eggs and toast for breakfast.

_____ **2.** A veterinarian takes care of sick animals.

_____ **3.** Plants need water and light to grow.

_____ **4.** We take a ride in a flying car.

_____ **5.** Learning to play the piano takes time and practice.

_____ **6.** Seals are great swimmers.

_____ **7.** My sister's hair changes colors while she sleeps.

_____ **8.** The hummingbird is a very small bird.

Writing
Skills

UNIT 1: Sentence about a Picture

HOW MUCH DO YOU KNOW?

Look at each picture. Draw a circle around the group of words that is a complete sentence.

1. The girl eats pizza.

   A slice of pizza

2. a robot and a dog

   The robot walks a dog.

Finish the sentence with the more exact word.

3. Mai eats _____ for breakfast.
   (cereal, food)

Studying a Sentence about a Picture

- A sentence tells a complete thought.
- It begins with a capital letter.
- It ends with a special mark.

Look at each picture. Draw a circle around the group of words that is a complete sentence.

1. The balloon goes up.

   man in it

2. a messy room

   The room is a mess!

3. It's a windy fall day.

   an open store

4. a good lunch

   The girls are ready to eat.

Using Details to Tell the Main Idea

- **To write a sentence about a picture, good writers look at all the details first.**
- **Then they put the details together to tell the main idea.**

Look at the pictures. Draw a line under the details you see in the pictures. Then draw a line under the sentence that tells the main idea.

1.

DETAILS

fruit bowl	2 eggs
bird cage	1 glass
bedroom	2 sinks

MAIN IDEA
One person will eat breakfast.
Fruit tastes really good!

2.

DETAILS

ticket booth	Ferris wheel
monkeys	children
roller coaster	cotton candy

MAIN IDEA
The fair is open!
I lost my ticket!

Using Exact Words

Good writers use exact words to give a reader more information.

Finish each sentence with the more exact word.

1. _____ sit in the trees.
   (Animals, Chimpanzees)

2. They are _____ for food.
   (looking, hunting)

3. _____ are the best.
   (Bananas, Fruits)

4. Can they see those big _____ bunches?
   (bright, yellow)

5. Watch the chimpanzees _____ !
   (leap, move)

Proofreading Sentences

PROOFREADING HINTS

- Be sure your sentence begins with a capital letter.
- Be sure your sentence ends with an end mark.

Read each sentence. Use the Proofreading Marks to correct the five mistakes. Write the sentences correctly.

1. bears are big animals.

2. They may weigh 1,000 pounds

3. some live in cold places

4. others like warm weather.

PROOFREADING MARKS

⬭	spell correctly
⊙	add period
?	add question mark
≡	capitalize
℘	take out
∧	add
¶	indent paragraph
ˇˇ	add quotation marks

See the chart on page 646 to learn how to use these marks.

1. _____

2. _____

3. _____

4. _____

My Favorite Food

Draw a picture of your favorite food. Think of a sentence about it. Write the sentence. Show your picture to a friend. Read your sentence aloud. Tell what makes it a complete sentence.

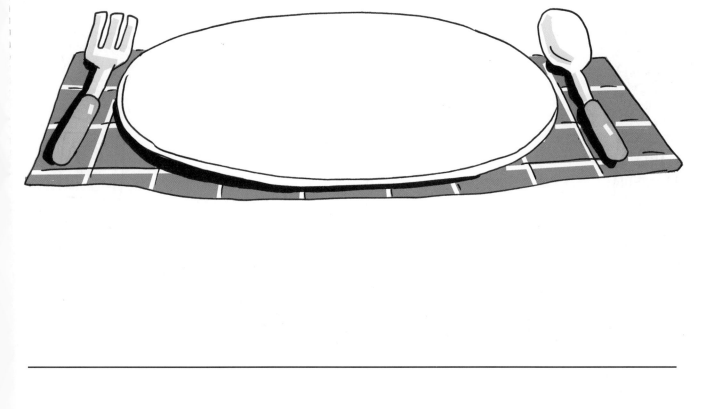

_____

_____

_____

First Place

Imagine that you just won first place in your favorite sport. What prize did you win? Draw a picture of your prize. Write a sentence to tell about your picture.

_____

_____

_____

Going on an Outing

Think of someplace you would like to go with your class.
Draw a picture of the place. Then write a sentence about it.

_____

_____

_____

A Favorite Day

The picture shows Ann's favorite day. Look at the picture.
Write a sentence about Ann's favorite day.

_____

_____

_____

Finish the Picture

Finish the picture. Draw what happens. Then write a sentence about the picture.

_____

_____

_____

Write about a Circus

Imagine that you are in a circus. What would you do? Draw a picture of yourself. Write a sentence to go with the picture.

_____

_____

_____

On a Trip

Pretend that you are on a trip. Draw a picture of something you see. Write a sentence about it.

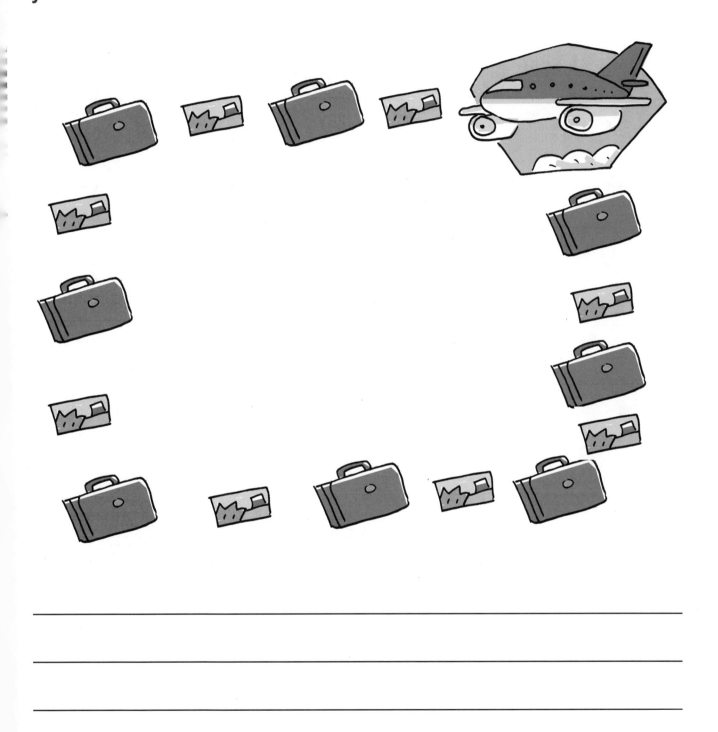

_____

_____

_____

At the Beach

Imagine you are at the beach. Draw a picture of something you might do there. Then write a sentence about it.

_____

_____

_____

On a Nature Hike

Pretend that you are on a hike through a forest. Draw a picture of something you might see on your hike. Write a sentence about it.

_____

_____

_____

Someone Special

Think about someone who is special to you. Draw a picture of that person. Then write a sentence about him or her.

_____

_____

_____

My Favorite Animal

Think about your favorite animal. Draw a picture of that animal. Write a sentence telling what you like about that animal.

_____

_____

_____

I Can Do That

Everyone has special talents, or things they can do well. Some talents might be playing an instrument, playing sports, or solving puzzles. Draw a picture of one of your special talents. Then write a sentence about it.

_____

_____

_____

Tell about It

Look at the picture. Write a sentence that explains what happened.

_____

_____

_____

UNIT 2: Personal Story

HOW MUCH DO YOU KNOW?

Read the story. Circle the words that tell the order in which things happen.

My family had fun at the summer fair yesterday. First, my brother rode a scary ride. Then, my sister and I got to pet a goat! The goat tried to bite my shirt. The goat made us laugh! Last of all, I won a prize at the fair. I can't wait for the next fair!

Write the sentence that tells what the topic is.

TOPIC SENTENCE

_____

_____

_____

Studying a Personal Story

- A personal story tells about something you have done.
- It can tell how you feel about something.
- A story tells what happened in order.
- It uses the words I, me, my, we, and our.

Read the story. Draw a line under the words that show it is a personal story. Draw a circle around the words that tell the order in which things happen.

My family and I love holidays. We think Thanksgiving is the best. All my grandparents come to our house. First, we sit at a very long table. Then, my sister brings in the food. The turkey always smells great! It tastes even better. After dinner, we sing songs. We have a good time. Last of all, we hug each other good-bye. I can't wait for the next holiday!

Write a sentence about your favorite holiday.

_____

_____

_____

Grouping Ideas by Topic

- In a personal story, good writers tell about one topic.
- Good writers use only details that tell about the topic.

Read the story about animal movies. Write the sentence that tells what the topic is. Draw a line under the details that tell about the topic.

I like many movies about animals. In one movie I saw deer, bears, and foxes in a forest. Another movie was a cartoon about mice and pigs. The best animal movie I ever saw took place in the jungle. It was about a parrot that saved a tiger's life. It was really great!

TOPIC SENTENCE

_____

_____

Write a sentence to add to the story.

_____

_____

_____

Using Synonyms

Good writers choose words to write exactly
what they mean to say.

Read each sentence. Choose the more exact word to finish
the sentence.

1. We _____ into the store before it rains.
   (go, dash)

2. There are many _____ on the shelves.
   (boxes, things)

3. My dad buys some ripe _____ .
   (fruit, apples)

4. I find some _____ peaches.
   (soft, fuzzy)

5. I feel _____ when I'm with my dad.
   (cheerful, good)

6. My dad makes me _____ .
   (laugh, giggle)

Proofreading a Personal Story

PROOFREADING HINTS

- Be sure that the word <u>I</u> is a capital letter.
- Be sure that each sentence begins with a capital letter.
- Be sure that each sentence ends with an end mark.

Read the story. Use the Proofreading Marks to correct at least eight mistakes.

PROOFREADING MARKS	
⬭	spell correctly
⊙	add period
?	add question mark
⹀	capitalize
℘	take out
∧	add
¶	indent paragraph
⌄ ⌄	add quotation marks

One day my family and I went to an apple orchard. we went to pick fresh apples. first, i got a big basket. next, I picked some ripe apples off the trees I put them in the basket After about an hour, i was too hungry to keep going. that's when i bit into a juicy, red apple The sweet, ripe apple tasted better than anything else in the world.

Write about a Pet

Do you have a pet? If not, imagine that you have one. Where does your pet sleep? What does your pet play with? Write a story about your pet.

_____

_____

_____

_____

Fun with Your Neighbors

Think of something you like to do with your neighbors. Draw a picture of you doing it. Then write a story to go with your picture. Use the words <u>men</u>, <u>women</u>, and <u>children</u> in your sentences.

I'm Late!

Think of a time when you were late. Write a story about what happened.

_____

_____

_____

_____

_____

_____

_____

_____

_____

Write about Your Feelings

Choose a feeling you sometimes have. Draw a picture of yourself with that feeling. Below the picture, write a story about a time you felt that way.

_____

_____

_____

_____

_____

Write about a Sport

Think about a game you and a friend like to play. Write a story about a time you played the game.

_____

_____

_____

_____

_____

Let's Eat!

Think of one of your favorite foods. Close your eyes and picture it in your mind. Then write words in the chart to describe the food.

FOOD: _____

_____   _____

_____   _____

_____   _____

_____   _____

Write a story about your favorite food.

_____

_____

_____

_____

_____

_____

My Favorite Holiday

Think of four things that happen on your favorite holiday. Draw four pictures to show these things. Then write a story that tells what happens. Use your pictures to help you.

FIRST	NEXT

THEN	LAST

_____

_____

_____

_____

_____

_____

A Practice Personal Story

SPELLING BEE

Last week I competed in the school spelling bee.

The contestants sat in three rows on the stage. At first, I

was not very nervous. Then, I looked up and saw that

the whole school had come to watch us take turns

spelling words aloud. Suddenly, my palms felt sweaty.

Soon, the spelling bee began. One at a time, each of us

stood at the microphone in the center of the stage. The

judge pronounced a word slowly. You had to spell it

correctly to stay in the contest. The judge began with a

list of easy words, but soon the words got harder. I had

to spell the word <u>acrobat</u>. I tried to picture it in my

mind. Then I started to spell aloud, but I said the letter <u>k</u>

instead of <u>c</u>. As soon as I said the wrong letter, I knew I had

made a mistake. But it was too late! Everyone clapped to

show they were proud of how hard I tried. I still smiled as I

left the stage. Of course, I was a little disappointed that I

did not win, but I will try again next year!

Respond to the Practice Story

After you read the story called "Spelling Bee," write your answers to the following questions.

1. What did the writer do last week?

_____

2. How did the writer show that he became nervous?

_____

3. How did the writer spell the word <u>acrobat</u> during the spelling bee?

_____

4. Did the writer win the spelling bee? How do you know?

_____

5. How did the writer feel at the end of the story?

_____

6. Using one or two sentences, summarize this story. Use these questions to help you:

   • What was the story about?
   • How does the story end?

_____

_____

_____

Writing Assignment

Think about three things you do before you leave the house each morning. Draw three pictures that show what you do first, next, and last. Then write a sentence that tells about each picture. Use this writing plan to help you write a first draft on the next page.

First Draft

TIPS FOR WRITING A PERSONAL NARRATIVE:

- Write from your point of view. Use the words I, me and my to show your readers that this is your story.
- Think about what you want to tell your reader.
- Organize your ideas into a beginning, middle, and end.
- Write an introduction that "grabs" your reader's attention.
- Write an ending for your story. Write it from your point of view.

Use your writing plan as a guide for writing a personal story. Include a catchy title.

____

____

____

____

____

____

____

(Continue on your own paper.)

Revise the Draft

Use the chart below to help you revise your draft. Check YES or NO to answer each question in the chart. If you answer NO, make notes to remind yourself how you can revise, or change, your writing to improve it.

Question	YES ✔	NO ✔	If the answer is NO, what will you do to improve your writing?
Does your story describe your morning routine?			
Does your story have a beginning?			
Do you describe events in the order they happened?			
Does your story have an ending?			
Did you add details to your story to make it interesting?			
Do you tell your story from your point of view?			
Have you corrected mistakes in spelling, grammar, and punctuation?			

Use the notes in your chart and your writing plan to revise your draft.

Writing Report Card

Read your revised draft again or ask someone else to read it. Have the person who reads your paper complete the following Report Card. Revise your paper until you have no less than a Very Good Score for each item.

Title of paper: _____

Purpose of paper: *This is a personal story. It tells about my morning routine.*

Person who scores the paper: _____

Score	Writing Goals
	Does this story have a beginning?
	Are the events described in the order they happened?
	Is there an ending?
	Are there details to make the story interesting?
	Is the story told from the writer's point of view?
	Are the story's grammar, spelling, and punctuation correct?

☺ Excellent Score   ☆ Very Good Score   + Good Score
✔ Acceptable Score   − Needs Improvement

uNIT 3: friendly Letter

HOW MUCH DO YOU KNOW?

Read the letter. Underline these parts of the letter.
Use different colors.

1. Use green to underline the heading.
2. Use blue to underline the signature.
3. Use red to underline the closing.

Then answer the question about the letter.

October 22, 2005

Dear Aunt Rosa,

   The sweater you knitted for my birthday is great! The fall days here have been chilly. It's nice to have a new warm sweater to wear. It is just the right size. Thank you, Aunt Rosa.

Love, Juan

4. Who wrote the letter?

_____

Studying a Friendly Letter

A friendly letter has five parts.

Read the letter. Draw a circle around each part of the letter. Use different colors.

1. Circle the heading with red.
2. Circle the closing with yellow.
3. Circle the greeting with blue.
4. Circle the signature with orange.
5. Circle the body with green.

July 27, 2005

Dear Chris,

    My family and I moved to a new house. I go to another school now. My new teacher is nice. I have a friend named Jimmy. He is in my class. Jimmy and I are on the same baseball team. Do you like to play baseball?

Your friend,
Richard

Picturing Events

Good writers picture events in their minds
before they write about them.

Finish the pictures. Draw what happens. Then write what happens.

1.

_____

_____

_____

2.

_____

_____

_____

Writing for Your Reader

Read the letter. Then answer the questions about it.

February 7, 2005

Dear Grandma,

   I love the flowers you brought when I was sick. Pink roses are my favorite. I feel much better now. Thank you, Grandma.

Love, Emily

1. To whom did Emily write the letter?

_____

2. Why did Emily write the letter?

_____

3. What did Emily write that Grandma might like to read?

_____

Joining Sentences

Writers often join two sentences into one.
The new sentence says the same thing in fewer words.

Read each pair of sentences. Use the word **and** to join the two sentences into one. The first one is done for you.

1. Andy talks. Andy tells jokes.

Andy talks and tells jokes.

2. He dances. He sings.

3. Andy writes plays. Andy acts them out.

4. He gets applause. He gets cheers.

Proofreading a Friendly Letter

Read the letter. Add <u>commas</u> (,) where they are needed. Correct at least six mistakes. Use the Proofreading Marks.

PROOFREADING MARKS	
◯	spell correctly
⊙	add period
?	add question mark
≡	capitalize
℘	take out
∧	add
¶	indent paragraph
⌄ ⌄	add quotation marks

February 7, 2005

dear Tanya

I had fun at your house last week! I'm so bezy at school now. I'm in the class play. I am a bear in the play My costume is brown and fuzzy. have you ever been in a play?

your friend

Brenda

Write about Summer Fun

Write a letter to a friend. Tell your friend what you like to do in the summer.

Write about a Visit

Think about a time you visited a friend or a relative. Write a letter to that friend or relative telling what you enjoyed about the visit.

_____

_____ ,

_____

_____

_____

_____

_____

_____ ,

_____

A Season Letter

Choose your favorite season. It might be fall, winter, spring, or summer. Draw a picture of your favorite season. Then write a letter to a friend telling something you would like to do during your favorite season.

My Favorite Season

A Letter to a Famous Person

Write a letter to a famous person. Tell that person something about yourself. Ask the person questions about what he or she does.

Invite a Friend

Write a letter to invite someone to do something or to go somewhere. Use these ideas or use your own ideas.

A CLASS PLAY   TO COME TO YOUR HOUSE

_____

_____ ,

_____

_____

_____

_____

_____ ,

_____

Thank You Very Much

With a friend, make a list of people at school who have helped you. Then pick someone from the list and write him or her a thank-you note.

_____   _____

_____   _____

_____   _____

THANK YOU!

_____

_____ ,

_____

_____

_____

_____

_____ ,

_____

Good News!

Think about something you did well during your school day. Write a letter to a family member to share the good news.

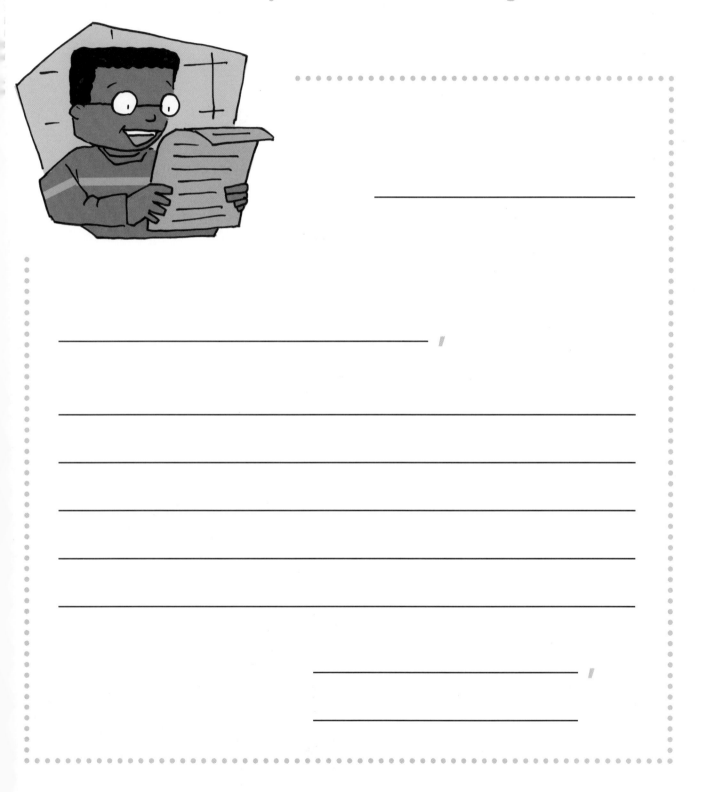

_____

_____ /

_____

_____

_____

_____

_____ /

_____

A Practice Letter

Dear Kathryn,

   We finally moved into our new house! It is a large farmhouse in the country. Our closest neighbors are two miles down the road. That is very different from our old neighborhood, but I am slowly getting used to it. Yesterday, my mom and I went on a walk down by the creek and we met a really nice girl named Shannon. She likes to go bike riding, just like you! I hope Shannon and I will be friends, but she could never replace you. I miss you so much. I hope you get to come visit soon!

                    Your best friend,

                    Anne

Respond to the Practice Letter

After you read the practice letter, write your answers to the following questions.

1. To whom is Anne writing the letter? What is her relationship to Anne?

_____

2. From the letter, what do you think is the biggest difference between Anne's old neighborhood and her new neighborhood?

_____

3. What is something that Anne and Kathryn probably used to do together?

_____

4. Whom did Anne meet by the creek?

_____

5. In one or two sentences, summarize Anne's letter. Use these questions to help you write your summary:

   • To whom is the letter written?
   • Why did Anne write the letter?
   • What is the letter about?

_____

_____

_____

_____

Writing Assignment

To write a letter, a writer must think about the purpose of the letter and the person who will receive the letter. Think of a gift that a friend or a loved one has given you. Answer the questions below. Use this writing plan to help you write a first draft on the next page.

What gift were you given?

_____

_____

Who gave you the gift?

_____

_____

Why did he or she give you the gift?

_____

_____

What do you like most about the gift?

_____

_____

First Draft

Use your writing plan as a guide to write a thank-you letter. Be sure to tell the person what you like most about the gift.

_____

_____

_____

_____

(Continue on your own paper.)

Revise the Draft

Use the chart below to help you revise your draft. Check YES or NO to answer each question in the chart. If you answer NO, make notes to remind yourself how you can revise, or change, your writing to improve it.

Question	YES ✔	NO ✔	If the answer is NO, what will you do to improve your writing?
Does your letter thank a loved one for a gift he or she has given?			
Does your letter describe what you like about the gift?			
Does your letter have a greeting?			
Does your letter have a closing?			
Do you write the letter from your point of view?			
Have you corrected mistakes in spelling, grammar, and punctuation?			

Use the notes in your chart and your writing plan to revise your draft.

Writing Report Card

Read your revised draft again or ask someone else to read it. Have the person who reads your paper complete the following Report Card. Revise your paper until you have no less than a Very Good Score for each item.

Title of paper: _____

Purpose of paper: _*This is a thank-you letter. It thanks someone for*_

*a gift I received.*

Person who scores the paper: _____

Score	Writing Goals
	Does this letter thank someone for a gift?
	Does the writer describe what he or she likes about the gift?
	Is there a greeting?
	Is there a closing?
	Is the letter written from the writer's point of view?
	Are the letter's grammar, spelling, and punctuation correct?

☺ Excellent Score ☆ Very Good Score + Good Score
✔ Acceptable Score − Needs Improvement

UNIT 4: Paragraph That Describes

HOW MUCH DO YOU KNOW?

Read the paragraph. Then answer the questions.

I just love a parade. I like to see the band march by. The uniforms shine with brass buttons and gold braid. The loud music always makes me want to clap my hands. I also like to see the floats. The floats with storybook characters are the best.

1. What is the topic of the paragraph?

_____

_____

2. Which words describe the band?

_____

_____

3. Write a sentence to add to the paragraph.

_____

_____

_____

Studying a Paragraph That Describes

- A paragraph that describes tells what someone or something is like.

- The topic sentence names the topic.

- The other sentences give details about the topic.

Read the paragraph. Then answer the questions.

Many birds visit my backyard. Red cardinals make nests in our bushes. Many tiny hummingbirds buzz around the flowers in our garden. Robins chirp sweetly to wake me in the morning.

1. What is the topic of the paragraph?

_____

_____

2. Which words tell what the birds are like?

_____

_____

3. Write a sentence to add to the paragraph.

_____

_____

_____

_____

Paying Attention to Details

Good writers use their five senses to study what they will describe. They use words to describe what they notice.

Read each topic. Close your eyes and picture it in your mind. Then write words in the chart to describe the topic.

1. TOPIC: AN ORANGE

looks

_____

_____

feels

_____

_____

tastes

_____

_____

smells

_____

_____

sounds

_____

_____

2. TOPIC: A HAMBURGER

looks

_____

_____

feels

_____

_____

tastes

_____

_____

smells

_____

_____

sounds

_____

_____

Using Colorful Words

Good writers choose colorful words to tell
what something is like.

Read the beginning of the paragraph. The topic is kitchens.
Write two more detail sentences. Use colorful words. Choose
words from the box or use your own words.

cozy
juicy
fresh
delicious
warm
yummy
sweet
shiny

    The kitchen is the best room in the house. It smells like
homemade bread and spices.

_____

_____

_____

_____

Adding Describing Words to Sentences

Writers can make a sentence clearer. They tell what someone or something is like. Find the nouns. Think of words that describe the nouns to add to each sentence. Write the new sentences.

1. The clown wears a hat.

_____

_____

2. A lion jumps through a hoop.

_____

_____

3. A monkey rides on an elephant.

_____

_____

_____

Proofreading a Paragraph That Describes

Read the paragraph. Correct at least five mistakes. Use the Proofreading Marks.

PROOFREADING MARKS

⬯	spell correctly
⊙	add period
?	add question mark
≡	capitalize
℘	take out
∧	add
¶	indent paragraph
⌄ ⌄	add quotation marks

Don't you just love a parade? I like to see the band march buy. the uniforms shine with brass buttons and gold braid. The loud musik always makes me want to clap and stamp my feet. i also like to see the floats. The floats with storybook characters are the best. the kings and queens in purple velvet are so beautiful

Write about a Zoo

Draw a picture of a zoo. Make a list of the details in your picture. Then write a sentence that tells the main idea.

_____   _____

_____   _____

_____   _____

MAIN IDEA

_____

_____

_____

Write about a Place You Like

Think of a place you like. Draw a picture of the place.
Then write three sentences to describe it.

_____

_____

_____

_____

_____

_____

_____

Describe a Movie

Talk with a friend about a movie you both like. Write the name of the movie. Choose your favorite scene. Write a paragraph that describes your favorite scene.

_____

_____

_____

_____

_____

_____

_____

_____

_____

Describe an Exciting Game

Think of an exciting game that you saw or that you have played. Write four sentences about the game.

_____

_____

_____

_____

_____

_____

_____

_____

A Day at a Lake

Work with a friend. Imagine that you and your friend are having fun at a lake. Think about how it looks, how it smells, and how it sounds. Write four sentences telling what you two do.

_____

_____

_____

_____

_____

_____

_____

_____

Write a Room Riddle

Think about a room in your house or at school. Write sentences to describe it. Do not tell the name of the room. Read your sentences to a friend. Can your friend guess the name of the room?

_____

_____

_____

_____

_____

_____

_____

_____

Write about Bugs

Write four sentences about bugs. Use describing words that tell about the shape and the color of the bugs.

_____

_____

_____

_____

_____

_____

_____

_____

Write about a Snack

Think about a snack you shared with friends. Close your eyes and picture it in your mind. Then write words in the chart to describe the snack.

looks
_____   _____

feels
_____   _____

tastes
_____   _____

smells
_____   _____

Write sentences to describe the snack.

_____

_____

_____

_____

_____

_____

Who Am I?

Draw a picture of yourself sitting at your desk. Then write sentences to go with your picture.

Tell what you can taste, smell, feel, and hear. Use describing words in your sentences.

_____

_____

_____

Write a Travel Report

Write about your city or town. Tell visitors about the special places they can see.

_____

_____

_____

_____

_____

_____

_____

Picture a Place

Think about the places in these pictures. Pick one of the places.
Write a paragraph that describes what that place is like.

on a busy street   on a beach

_____

_____

_____

_____

_____

_____

_____

_____

_____

A Practice Descriptive Story

THE RIDE HOME

I leaned forward in my seat and pressed my nose against the cool glass window. I heard the loud final whistle. Grandma and Grandpa waved good-bye to me from the platform. Slowly, the train started to pull away from the station. The car rocked slowly from side to side as it rolled along the tracks.

After a wonderful two-week visit with my grandparents, I was finally going home. I would miss Grandma's snuggly bear hugs and the sweet buttermilk taste of her pancakes. I would miss Grandpa's hearty laugh and the smell of his mint chewing gum as we talked while doing jigsaw puzzles together.

With a big smile, I sat back in the cozy seat and looked out the window. I watched as we passed through the rolling hills and fresh country air. The train headed back toward the city. My eyelids began to get heavy and I drifted off to sleep. When I woke up, Mom and Dad were there to welcome me home.

Respond to the Practice Descriptive Story

After you read "The Ride Home," write your answers to the following questions.

1. What type of transportation was the writer taking?

_____

2. Whom had the writer recently visited?

_____

3. What senses did the writer use to describe things in the story?

_____

4. What are two descriptions that the writer used to help you experience what was happening in the story?

_____

_____

5. In one or two sentences, summarize the story. Use these questions to help you write your summary:

   • What is the story about?
   • What happens first? Second?
   • How does the story end?

_____

_____

_____

Writing Assignment

To describe something, a writer tells what he or she sees, hears, feels, tastes, and smells. The writer uses interesting words. Think about the best birthday party you ever had. Then use this writing plan to help you write a first draft on the next page.

Around the circle, write words that describe what you saw, heard, felt, smelled, and tasted at your birthday party.

MY BEST
BIRTHDAY
PARTY

First Draft

TIPS FOR WRITING A DESCRIPTIVE STORY:

- Help readers see, smell, taste, feel, and hear what you are writing about.
- Use interesting words to help you describe.

Use your writing plan as a guide for writing a descriptive story. Include a catchy title.

(Continue on your own paper.)

Revise the Draft

Use the chart below to help you revise your draft. Check YES or NO to answer each question in the chart. If you answer NO, make notes to remind yourself how you can revise, or change, your writing to improve it.

Question	YES ✔	NO ✔	If the answer is NO, what will you do to improve your writing?
Does your story tell about a birthday party you have had?			
Does your story describe what happens in order?			
Do you use action words to describe what happens?			
Does your story describe what you see, hear, smell, taste, and feel?			
Have you corrected mistakes in spelling, grammar, and punctuation?			

Use the notes in your chart and your writing plan to revise your draft.

Writing Report Card

Read your revised draft again or ask someone else to read it. Have the person who reads your paper complete the following Report Card. Revise your paper until you have no less than a Very Good Score for each item.

Title of paper: _____

Purpose of paper: _*This is a descriptive story. It describes a*_ _____

*birthday party I had.* _____

Person who scores the paper: _____

Score	Writing Goals
	Does this story tell about a birthday party the writer had?
	Does it describe what happens in order?
	Are there action words to describe what happens?
	Does it describe what the writer saw, heard, smelled, tasted, and felt?
	Is the story written from the writer's point of view?
	Are the story's grammar, spelling, and punctuation correct?

☺ Excellent Score   ☆ Very Good Score   + Good Score

✔ Acceptable Score   − Needs Improvement

UNIT 5: Story

HOW MUCH DO YOU KNOW?

Read the story. Then answer the questions.

A LONG NIGHT

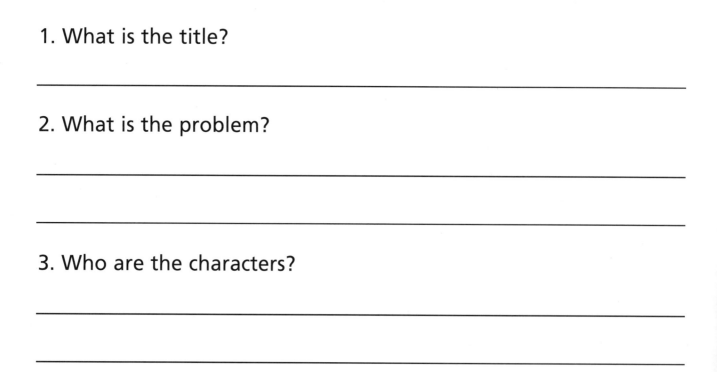

    Lateisha got into bed. She lay down, but she was too tired to sleep. She tried counting sheep. She tried reading a book. Nothing worked.

    At six o'clock in the morning, Lateisha gave up and got out of bed. She showered and dressed. When she started to eat her cereal, Mother asked why Lateisha was up so early. Mother told her it was Saturday. Without saying a word, Lateisha went back to bed.

1. What is the title?

_____

2. What is the problem?

_____

_____

3. Who are the characters?

_____

_____

Studying a Story

- A story has a beginning, a middle, and an ending.
- A story is often about solving a problem.
- A story has a title.

Read the story. Then answer the questions.

THE HOLE

One day a small boy was walking down the street. Suddenly, he fell down a hole. It was a very deep, dark hole. The small boy couldn't see. He was really scared. What did he do? He fell asleep, of course!

A few hours later, the boy was awakened by singing. The voices were high-pitched and squeaky. Then the boy saw hundreds of tiny candles.

They were being carried by hundreds of tiny mice. They led him to an underground elevator. The boy went up. He was back on the street!

1. What is the title? _____

2. Who are the characters? _____

3. What is the problem? _____

4. How is the problem solved? _____

_____

Thinking about What Might Happen

- Good writers create an interesting problem in the beginning of a story.

- Then they plan what will happen to solve the problem.

Read the beginning of the story.
Then fill in the chart.

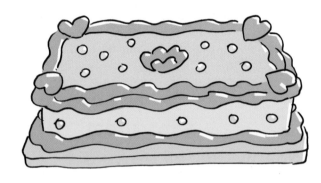

A BIRTHDAY SURPRISE

   Aunt Sally will be ninety years old tomorrow. She has lived a long time, and she is very wise. My older sister and I want to do something special for Aunt Sally's birthday. We plan to bake her the most beautiful birthday cake she has ever seen. Every time we go into the kitchen, though, Aunt Sally is there!

PROBLEM

_____

_____

HOW TO SOLVE

_____

_____

Using Enough Details

Good writers use enough details to help readers picture what happens in a story.

Read the paragraph. Then write it again. Add details to tell what John sees.

    John could feel the plane taking off. He looked out the window.

_____

_____

_____

_____

_____

_____

_____

Proofreading a Story

PROOFREADING MARKS	
◯	spell correctly
⊙	add period
?	add question mark
≡	capitalize
℘	take out
∧	add
¶	indent paragraph
ⱽ ⱽ	add quotation marks

Read the story. Correct at least six mistakes. Use the Proofreading Marks.

WHAT A DAY!

Arnold climbed the stairs. he was very tired. School had been tuff that day. The soccer game had been tuffer.

Arnold got into bed. He lay down, but he could not fall asleep. he was thinking about he soccer game and the goal he missed

Arnold felt himself kicking the ball into the goal. Suddenly, he felt cold and heard birds chirping. he looked down and saw that he had kicked off the blanket. The sun was up and it was morning. He had fallen asleep after all!

A Story about Foxes

Read the sentences. Then tell what the foxes do next. Finish the story.

Two foxes walk to the park. They sit on a bench. They eat their lunch.

_____

_____

_____

_____

_____

_____

Write about Being a Rabbit

Read the story. Then write a story about what else could happen to Pinky, Spot, and Fluffy.

My favorite movie is on now. Real rabbits are in the movie. Their names are Pinky, Spot, and Fluffy. Once, Spot got his tail stuck in a fence. Pinky and Fluffy helped him.

_____

_____

_____

_____

_____

_____

_____

_____

Write about Waiting

Think of a time you had to wait for someone else. Write a story about what happened.

_____

_____

_____

_____

_____

_____

_____

_____

_____

_____

Finish the Story

Read the story. What do you think is in the bag? What do you think happens next? Finish the story. Tell what happens.

Last night I saw a huge monster. I saw a bag in the monster's hand. The monster gave me the bag. I saw something funny inside. I gave it to my sister.

_____

_____

_____

_____

_____

_____

_____

Write a Story Beginning

Write good beginning sentences for a story about going into outer space. Draw a picture to go with your sentences.

_____

_____

_____

_____

_____

Write Animal Facts

Draw a picture of an animal. Then use the sentences below to write about it. Write exact words in place of the underlined words.

The <u>animal</u> can <u>move</u>. The <u>animal</u> eats <u>food</u>.

_____

_____

_____

_____

Characters and Settings

Look at the pictures below. Look at the settings. Choose one character and one setting. Use them to write a story.

CHARACTERS

Sammy Seal

Shawn

Kim

SETTINGS

on a planet in the future
yesterday on a farm
at a beach in winter

_____

_____

_____

_____

_____

_____

Solving a Problem

Many stories have an interesting problem that must be solved. Read the story. With a friend, write an ending to the story.

You make friends with a dinosaur and bring it to school. The dinosaur does not know how to act in school.

_____

_____

_____

_____

_____

_____

_____

A Practice Problem-and-Solution Story

JUMP IN!

Juan knew he was going to have a great summer when he and his best friend, Danny, arrived at camp. Everywhere he looked, there were tons of boys his age, laughing together, playing tennis, or swimming at the pool. Juan and Danny quickly found their cabin and met their camp counselor. After they unpacked their suitcases, the boys decided to go for a swim. They changed into their swimsuits and walked down to the pool.

At first, Juan and Danny stayed in the shallow end. They played games and splashed in the water with a few other boys. Every now and then, Juan watched other boys jump, dive, and do flips off the diving board, but he did not feel brave enough to try it himself.

After a while, Danny said that they should take turns jumping off the diving board. Juan looked nervously at

Danny and shook his head. Danny smiled and told Juan that it was not as scary as it looked. Juan finally agreed to give it a try. Slowly, he climbed to the top of the diving board. He took a few steps to the end of the board and looked over at Danny. Danny gave him a big smile. Juan took a deep breath, closed his eyes, and jumped. He hit the water with a splash and bobbed up to the surface. He was grinning from ear to ear. Juan and Danny spent the rest of the day jumping off the diving board!

Respond to the Practice Problem-and-Solution Story

After you read "Jump In!," write your answers to the following questions.

1. Where did Juan and Danny go?

_____

2. What did they do just before they walked to the pool?

_____

3. What was the problem in the story?

_____

4. How was the problem solved?

_____

5. How did Juan feel at the end of the story?

_____

6. In one or two sentences, summarize the story. Use these questions to help you write your summary:

   • What is the story about?
   • What happens first? Second?
   • How does the story end?

_____

_____

_____

Writing Assignment

A story often reveals a problem that a character has, and then the solution. Think up a character who has a problem. Answer the questions below. Use this writing plan to help you write a first draft on the next page.

Who is the character in your story?

What is your character's problem?

How is the problem solved?

What are the events that happen in your story?
(first, next, last)

How does the character feel at the end of the story?

First Draft

TIPS FOR WRITING A PROBLEM-AND-SOLUTION STORY:

- Think about the problem that your story reveals.
- Check to see that the story shows the solution to the problem.

Use your writing plan as a guide for writing a problem-and-solution story. Include a catchy title.

_____

_____

_____

_____

_____

_____

_____

_____

(Continue on your own paper.)

Revise the Draft

Use the chart below to help you revise your draft. Check YES or NO to answer each question in the chart. If you answer NO, make notes to remind yourself how you can revise, or change, your writing to improve it.

Question	YES ✔	NO ✔	If the answer is NO, what will you do to improve your writing?
Does your story identify a problem?			
Does your story have a solution?			
Does your story have a beginning, middle, and end?			
Does your story tell the events in order?			
Have you corrected mistakes in spelling, grammar, and punctuation?			

Use the notes in your chart and your writing plan to revise your draft.

Writing Report Card

Read your revised draft again or ask someone else to read it. Have the person who reads your paper complete the following Report Card. Revise your paper until you have no less than a Very Good Score for each item.

Title of paper: _____

Purpose of paper: _*This is a problem and solution story. It shows how a*_ _*character solves a problem.*_ _____

Person who scores the paper: _____

Score	Writing Goals
	Does this story identify a problem?
	Does it have a solution?
	Are there action words to describe what happens?
	Is there a beginning, middle, and end?
	Are events told in order?
	Are the story's grammar, spelling, and punctuation correct?

☺ Excellent Score   ☆ Very Good Score   + Good Score
✔ Acceptable Score   − Needs Improvement

UNIT 6: How-to Paragraph

HOW MUCH DO YOU KNOW?

Read the paragraph. Then answer the questions.

Sewing on a button can be easy. First, get a needle and thread. You will also need the button and a piece of clothing. Choose a thread color to match the clothing. Next, thread the needle. Then, sew on the button tightly. Last, make a knot in the thread. Cut the thread.

1. What is the topic sentence?

_____

_____

2. What is the first step?

_____

_____

3. What things do you need to sew on a button?

_____

_____

Studying a How-to Paragraph

- A how-to paragraph tells how to make or do something.
- The topic sentence names the topic of the paragraph.
- The detail sentences explain the steps in order.
- The paragraph is indented.

Read the paragraph. Draw a line under the topic sentence. Then draw a circle around the words that tell the order of the steps.

This is a simple way to wrap a gift. First, get wrapping paper, scissors, and tape. Next, cut the paper to fit all the way around the gift. Then, put the paper together around the middle of the gift. Tape the paper. Last, fold the paper up and over the ends of the gift. Tape it closed.

Write the things you need to wrap a gift.

_____

_____

_____

Connecting Ideas in Sequence

In a how-to paragraph, good writers tell the steps in the correct order.

Look at the pictures. Then write the four steps.

HOW TO MAKE SOUP

1. _____

_____

2. _____

_____

3. _____

_____

4. _____

_____

Getting the Reader's Interest

Good writers use good beginning sentences
to interest their readers.

Read the story beginnings. Draw a line under the better one.

1. a. Albert waded through the swamp. The alligator was close
        behind him. Albert's heart pounded like a drum.

    b. Albert walked in the swamp. An alligator was following
        him. Albert felt scared.

2. a. The skyscraper was tall and shiny. It looked like a steel box
        against the sky. I thought it was beautiful.

    b. The building was tall and gray. It stood out against the
        sky. It was interesting to look at.

3. a. One day we walked into a garden.

    b. One day we tiptoed into a strange garden. There were
        giant red and yellow flowers everywhere.

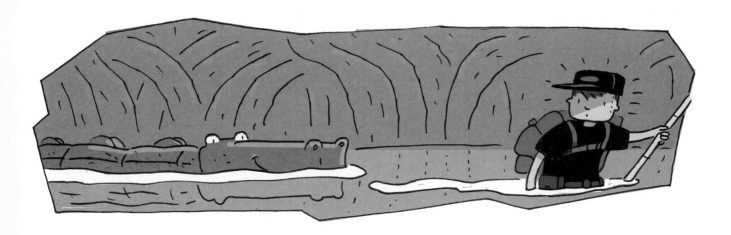

Joining Sentences

Writers often join two sentences into one.
The new sentence says the same thing in fewer words.

Read each pair of sentences. Use the word <u>and</u> to join the two sentences into one. You may need to change the verb to go with your new sentence. The first one is done for you.

1. Bob likes to sled. Jasmine likes to sled.

Bob and Jasmine like to sled.

2. Tran goes with them. Carlos goes with them.

3. Carlos packs a lunch. Bob packs a lunch.

4. Bob sleds all day. Jasmine sleds all day.

5. Bob is tired. Jasmine is tired.

Proofreading a How-to Paragraph

PROOFREADING HINTS

- Be sure you indent your paragraph.
- Be sure each sentence begins with a capital letter.
- Be sure each sentence ends with an end mark.

Read the how-to paragraph. Use the Proofreading Marks to correct at least eight mistakes.

PROOFREADING MARKS	
⬭	spell correctly
⊙	add period
?	add question mark
⁼	capitalize
⤴	take out
∧	add
¶	indent paragraph
⌄ ⌄	add quotation marks

sewing on a button can be eazy. First, get a needle and thread. you will also need the button and peece of clothing Choose a thread color to match the clothing. next, thread the needle then, sew on the button tightly. Last, make a knot in the thread. Cut the thread

Write the topic sentence correctly.

_____

_____

How to Play a Game

Work with a friend or two. Imagine that you are at a playground. You are going to play a playground game. Write a paragraph telling how to play the game.

_____

_____

_____

_____

_____

_____

_____

_____

_____

_____

_____

Write about a Job

Think of a job you have to do. Draw a picture of yourself doing that job. Write sentences telling how to do the job.

Plan a Garden

Work with a friend. Draw a picture of a garden you would both like. Write sentences that tell how you would make the garden.

_____

_____

_____

_____

_____

_____

Write about Work

Think of someone who has a job. Write sentences about what that person does at work. Tell how that person does one part of the job.

Write about School

Think of something you and your friends do at school.
Write directions for another student to follow.

_____

_____

_____

_____

_____

_____

_____

_____

_____

Write about Clown School

Imagine that you go to a school to learn to be a clown. Write sentences to tell a friend how to be a clown.

_____

_____

_____

_____

_____

_____

_____

Make a How-to Poster

Think about how you would do a chore, such as making a bed or washing the dishes. Picture the chore in four steps. Draw how to do a step in each part of this poster. Write a sentence for each step.

1.

_____

_____

2.

_____

_____

3.

_____

_____

4.

_____

_____

How to Make a Chocolate Milkshake

The pictures below show the steps to make a chocolate milkshake. In order, write what is happening in each picture. Use sequence words such as <u>first</u>, <u>next</u>, <u>then</u>, and <u>last</u> to help you.

_____

_____

_____

_____

_____

_____

_____

A Practice How-to Paragraph

Wendy is making a cake. She follows the directions on the back of the cake mix box. Here are the directions.

MAKING A CAKE

First, preheat oven to 350 degrees. Then pour the cake mix into a large bowl. Add two eggs to the bowl. Next, stir in water and vegetable oil. Mix the batter for two minutes with an electric mixer on low speed. Pour the batter into a lightly floured pan. Last, bake the cake in the oven for 30 minutes. Take the cake out of the oven and allow it to cool completely before icing.

Respond to the How-to Paragraph

After reading "Making a Cake," write your answers to the following questions.

1. At what temperature should the oven be set?

_____

2. What should you do after adding water and vegetable oil?

_____

3. For how long should the cake bake in the oven?

_____

4. What should you do before icing the cake?

_____

Writing Assignment

Think about the things you need and the steps you follow when you brush your teeth. Use this writing plan to help you write a first draft on the next page.

1. What will you need to brush your teeth?

_____

2. Write four steps you follow when you brush your teeth.

Step 1

Step 2

Step 3

Step 4

First Draft

TIPS FOR WRITING A HOW-TO PARAGRAPH:

- Choose one thing to teach someone.
- Think of all the materials you will need.
- Think of all the steps someone will follow.
- Use sequence words.

Use your writing plan as a guide for writing your first draft of a how-to paragraph. Include a catchy title.

(Continue on your own paper.)

Revise the Draft

Use the chart below to help you revise your draft. Check YES or NO to answer each question in the chart. If you answer NO, make notes to remind yourself how you can revise, or change, your writing to improve it.

Question	YES ✔	NO ✔	If the answer is NO, what will you do to improve your writing?
Does your paragraph teach the reader how to brush his or her teeth?			
Does your paragraph include the materials the person needs?			
Does your paragraph tell the steps someone must follow?			
Are the steps in order?			
Do you use sequence words, such as <u>first</u>, <u>next</u>, <u>then</u>, and <u>last</u>?			
Have you corrected mistakes in spelling, grammar, and punctuation?			

Use the notes in your chart and your writing plan to revise your draft.

Writing Report Card

Read your revised draft again or ask someone else to read it. Have the person who reads your paper complete the following Report Card. Revise your paper until you have no less than a Very Good Score for each item.

Title of paper: _____

Purpose of paper: _*This is a how-to paragraph. It tells someone how to*_____

_*brush his or her teeth.*_____

Person who scores the paper: _____

Score	Writing Goals
	Does this paragraph teach you how to brush your teeth?
	Does it tell you what materials you need?
	Does it tell you the steps you must follow?
	Are the steps in order?
	Are there sequence words, such as <u>first</u>, <u>next</u>, <u>then</u>, and <u>last</u>?
	Are the paragraph's grammar, spelling, and punctuation correct?

☺ Excellent Score   ☆ Very Good Score   + Good Score

✔ Acceptable Score   − Needs Improvement

Proofreading Marks

Use the following symbols to help make proofreading faster.

MARK	MEANING	EXAMPLE
◯	spell correctly	Today is a (specail) day. *special*
⊙	add period	It is Kevin's birthday⊙
?	add question mark	What kind of pet do you have?
≡	capitalize	My dog's name is scooter. ≡
ℒ	take out	He likes to ~~to~~ run and play.
∧	add	He even likes to get ∧ bath. *a*
¶	indent paragraph	¶ I love my dog, Scooter. He is the best pet I have ever had. Every morning he wakes me with a bark. Every night he sleeps with me.
ⱽ ⱽ	add quotation marks	ⱽYou are my best friend,ⱽ I tell him.

Test Prep

SIX READING SKILLS

SKILL 1: DETERMINING WORD MEANINGS

Suffixes are parts of some words. A <u>suffix</u> is at the end of a word. You can use suffixes to tell what the words mean.

Our class went on a trip to the zoo. We saw some monkeys climb into a tree. One monkey climbed <u>higher</u> than the others.

1 In this paragraph, the word <u>higher</u> means —

- ○ more than high.
- ○ lower.
- ○ almost as high.
- ○ on the ground.

Hint: The suffix "er" means more than.

Goldilocks walked into the three bears' home. She sat down at their table. She would not eat Papa Bear's food because it was the <u>warmest</u>.

2 In this paragraph, the word <u>warmest</u> means —

- ○ the least warm.
- ○ more than warm.
- ○ the most warm.
- ○ cool.

Hint: The suffix "est" means the most.

José walked up to the starting line for the foot race. He really wanted to win. José knew how important it was to run <u>quickly</u>. At the sound of the "bang" the race began.

3 In this paragraph, the word <u>quickly</u> describes —

- ○ how he will walk.
- ○ how he wanted to win.
- ○ how the race began.
- ○ how he will run.

Hint: When you see "ly" at the end of a word, it usually describes an action word.

GO ON ➡

Mei was getting ready for her birthday party. She invited all of her friends to come. Mei and her mother <u>baked</u> the cupcakes. They were very excited about her party.

4   **In this paragraph, the word <u>baked</u> means —**

○ the cupcakes were made already.

○ the cupcakes were not made yet.

○ they were making the cupcakes now.

○ they will not bake the cupcakes.

Hint: The suffix "ed" shows that something has already happened.

Angela's class went to the school library to take its class picture. Angela was tall, so she stood in the second row. Her friend Sulky was <u>taller</u>, so she stood in the third row.

5   **In this paragraph, the word <u>taller</u> means —**

○ more than tall.

○ the most tall.

○ not tall at all.

○ the least tall.

Hint: When you see "er" at the end of a word, what does that mean?

Kai and his mother are having fun on the playground in the park. Kai went down the slide. Then, he ran through the maze. Now he is <u>swinging</u> on the swings.

6   **In this paragraph, the word <u>swinging</u> means —**

○ it already took place.

○ it is taking place right now.

○ it did not take place yet.

○ it will never take place.

Hint: The suffix "ing" shows that something is happening now.

TEST TIP

Be sure to look for the Test Tips throughout this workbook. They will give you more test-taking strategies and specific help with certain subject areas.

STOP

SKILL 1: DETERMINING WORD MEANINGS

Sometimes you can find out the meaning of a new word by using the words around it as clues.

Martin Luther King was a great man. He did not give up when things became <u>hard</u> for him. He did not let anyone stop him from helping others.

1 **In this paragraph, the word <u>hard</u> means —**

○ simple.

○ late.

○ not easy.

○ fun.

Hint: You get a clue about the word <u>hard</u> by reading sentences 2 and 3.

There are many kinds of sharks. Some are <u>huge</u>. The whale shark grows 60 feet long. That is more than the height of most houses. Only whales are larger.

2 **In this paragraph, the word <u>huge</u> means —**

○ big.

○ small.

○ pretty.

○ fast.

Hint: You get a clue about the word <u>huge</u> by the words "60 feet long" and by reading sentences 4 and 5.

There are many ways that fire can help us. It can keep us warm. We can cook with it. But, it can also <u>harm</u> us. It can even burn down houses.

3 **In this paragraph, the word <u>harm</u> means —**

○ help us.

○ warm us.

○ fool us.

○ hurt us.

Hint: You get a clue about the word <u>harm</u> by reading the last sentence.

GO ON

We have a new cat. His name is Fluffy. I want him to learn to listen to me and do what I tell him. Fluffy should learn to <u>obey</u>.

4 **In this paragraph, the word <u>obey</u> means —**

○ run away.

○ play.

○ follow directions.

○ be quiet.

Hint: You get a clue as to what the word <u>obey</u> means from the words "listen to me" and "do what I tell him."

Lisa loved to play baseball. She knew she could <u>strike</u> the ball with the bat when it was thrown to her. She decided to join the team.

5 **In this paragraph, the word <u>strike</u> means —**

○ to hit.

○ to miss.

○ to block.

○ to catch.

Hint: You get a clue as to what the word <u>strike</u> means by looking at the words "she knew she could strike the ball with the bat..."

Amy was the new girl in the class. Mira showed her where to find things around the classroom. Mira was <u>kind</u> to Amy.

6 **In this paragraph, the word <u>kind</u> means —**

○ helpful.

○ mean.

○ quiet.

○ lazy.

Hint: You get a clue as to what the word <u>kind</u> means by looking at what Mira did for Amy.

TEST TIP

Test these answers by replacing the word in the example. For example, look at question 6. Think of the underlined word as a blank to fill in: Mira was _____ to Amy.

Which of the four answers makes the most sense in this blank?

STOP

SKILL 1: DETERMINING WORD MEANINGS

Special or technical words are used in science and social studies. You can use the information in the passage to tell what the words mean.

Andy dug a hole and put a plant in it. Next, he filled the hole with dirt. Last, Andy watered the plant. He made sure to <u>soak</u> it so that it would grow.

1 **In this paragraph, the word <u>soak</u> means —**

○ to dry out.

○ to cover with dirt.

○ to dig deep.

○ to make wet.

Hint: You get a clue as to what <u>soak</u> means by reading the sentence before the word.

Omar knew he could have a snack when he got to the <u>end</u> of his homework. He did his math. Then, he did his reading. Last, he ate.

2 **In this paragraph, the word <u>end</u> means —**

○ start.

○ finish.

○ middle.

○ test.

Hint: You get a clue as to what the word <u>end</u> means by reading the sentences after the word.

There are many kinds of dams. A dam can be hard to <u>build</u>. Some are put together with dirt while others are made from rock.

3 **In this paragraph, the word <u>build</u> means —**

○ to sell.

○ to climb.

○ to see.

○ to make.

Hint: You get a clue as to what <u>build</u> means by reading the sentence after the word.

GO ON➡

Mandy was in a bad mood. Her mother was angry with her. Toshi called her on the telephone and told her a joke. Then Mandy started to grin.

4   **In this paragraph, grin means —**

○ cry.

○ see.

○ smile.

○ frown.

Hint: You get a clue about what grin means by reading the sentence before the word.

The frog leaped into the air to chase the fly. It hopped over tall grass and rocks. The frog kept leaping until it caught the fly.

5   **In this paragraph, leaped means —**

○ walked.

○ skipped.

○ jumped.

○ crawled.

Hint: You can get a clue about what leaped means by reading the sentences after the word.

Joy was taking a spelling test. There were two words she did not know. She wanted to quit, but she didn't. Joy kept on going.

6   **In this paragraph, the word quit means —**

○ scream.

○ copy.

○ stop.

○ smile.

Hint: You get a clue about what quit means by reading sentences 3 and 4.

TEST TIP

If you have trouble with one question, skip it and go back to it later. You might find it easier when you see it again.

STOP

SKILL 2: IDENTIFYING SUPPORTING IDEAS

Facts or details are important. By finding them, you will know what the passage is about.

Long ago, ships were made from logs. The center was cut out. People sat inside. They could not go very fast. These ships were also hard to make.

Things changed 5,000 years ago. They started making better ships in Egypt. These ships had sails. People could also row them. Now, they could go much faster across the water.

1   Faster boats were first built —

○ 5,000 years ago.

○ today.

○ from logs.

○ 500 years ago.

Hint: Look at the second paragraph.

2   The first ships —

○ went very fast.

○ had sails.

○ could be rowed.

○ were hard to make.

Hint: Read the first paragraph.

3   The ships made in Egypt were better because —

○ they were made from logs.

○ they were built 5,000 years ago.

○ they went faster.

○ their centers were cut out.

Hint: Look at the last sentence.

GO ON ➤

The first airplane flew on December 17, 1903. It was built by Wilbur and Orville Wright. They were brothers who had always dreamed of flying a plane.

Wilbur and Orville played with flying toys when they were young boys. Their mother made them play with their toys outside. They even wanted to fly the toys in the house.

As they grew up, they still wanted to fly. They worked very hard to build an airplane. One day it was ready. They tried to fly it on December 14. It did not work. Three days later, they were able to take off!

4 Wilbur and Orville Wright both wanted to —

○ stay young.

○ play with toys.

○ fly an airplane.

○ listen to their mother.

Hint: Look at the last sentence of the first paragraph.

5 Wilbur and Orville were —

○ brothers.

○ cousins.

○ friends.

○ uncles.

Hint: Look at the first paragraph.

6 Wilbur and Orville's airplane —

○ flew on December 14, 1903.

○ flew indoors.

○ was just a toy.

○ flew on December 17, 1903.

Hint: Read the first sentence.

TEST TIP

Sometimes you are allowed to write on the test pages. Before a test begins, ask your teacher if you are allowed to write on the pages. You might circle important dates or facts as you read.

GO ON

SKILL 2: IDENTIFYING SUPPORTING IDEAS

It is helpful to put events in the order in which they happened. This may help you to understand a passage.

Babe Ruth was a great baseball player. He was born on February 6, 1895. He had seven brothers and sisters. His mother became sick. Babe was sent away to school.

Babe learned to play baseball. He became a very good player. When he was 19 years old, Babe got money to play baseball.

Babe started out as a pitcher. He could throw the ball very hard. He could also hit the ball very far. Many teams wanted Babe to play for them.

In 1919, Babe started to play for the New York Yankees. He was a star player for over 15 years. In 1927 he set the home run record. This record was not broken until 1961. He was the star of the 1932 World Series. Babe Ruth was one of the best baseball players ever.

1   **Which of these happened first in the story?**

○ The 1932 World Series was played.

○ Babe was sent away to school.

○ Babe Ruth was given money to play baseball.

○ The home run record was broken.

Hint: Look at the beginning of the story.

GO ON

2 **When did Babe Ruth start to play for the New York Yankees?**

○ when he first learned to play baseball

○ when his mother became sick

○ in 1919

○ in 1927

Hint: Look at the last paragraph.

3 **Which of these happened last?**

○ Babe was a star in the World Series.

○ Babe set the home run record.

○ Many teams wanted Babe to play for them.

○ Babe's home run record was broken.

Hint: Look at the last paragraph.

TEST TIP

To answer question 3, look back at the story. Notice that the story tells the events in order, from first to last. Read the answer choices and find the one that happens <u>last</u> in the story.

GO ON

SKILL 2: IDENTIFYING SUPPORTING IDEAS

Written directions tell you how to do something. Every step is important.

Did you ever make a puppet? It is a lot of fun and easy to do. There are only a few things you will need.

First, look around your house to find what you will need. Use an old sock for the body. Next, sew on buttons for the eyes. Then, glue on pieces of cloth for the mouth and ears. Last, glue yarn to the sock for hair.

1   **What should you do after you find a sock?**

   ○ glue on pieces of cloth for the mouth and ears

   ○ look around the house to find what you need

   ○ sew on buttons for the eyes

   ○ glue yarn to the sock for hair

   Hint: Read the third sentence of the second paragraph.

Gwen needed to pack for her trip. She wrote down all the things she would need. Next, she took out her suitcase. Gwen folded her clothes on the bed. Now she was ready to pack. When she was done, she closed the suitcase. Gwen was ready for her trip!

2   **To get ready for her trip, Gwen should first —**

   ○ make a list.

   ○ fold her clothes.

   ○ close her suitcase.

   ○ pack her suitcase.

   Hint: Read the passage to see what comes first.

GO ON ▶

I painted my room. I wrote down the steps that I took to get the job done.

Step 1: Go to the paint store.
Step 2: Choose a color.
Step 3: Buy the paint and brushes.
Step 4: Cover things in your room. You do not want to get paint on them.
Step 5: Paint slowly. Make sure you do a careful job.
Step 6: Clean the brushes with soap and water.
Step 7: Wait for the paint to dry.

3   Which of these would you do first?

○ Clean the brushes with soap and water.

○ Buy the paint and brushes.

○ Wait for the paint to dry.

○ Cover things in your room.

Hint: Read all the steps in order.

4   When should you start to paint?

○ Step 3

○ Step 4

○ Step 5

○ Step 7

Hint: Read all the steps in order.

5   After you finish painting, you should —

○ cover things.

○ buy more paint.

○ clean the brushes.

○ go to the paint store.

Hint: Read the last two steps.

TEST TIP

When you read directions, the order is very important. Imagine yourself following the steps in order. Questions 3, 4, and 5 all ask you about the order of events.

GO ON

The setting of a story lets you know when and where the story is taking place.

Fred Lamb had a dream to build the tallest building in the world. He wanted to put this building in New York City. Nobody had ever built such a tall building before.

All of the workers had to be very careful. They worked very hard and very long hours. They even worked at night. After six months they were done. In 1931, the Empire State Building was opened!

The Empire State Building was well built. In 1945, an airplane crashed into it. This did not knock it down.

Today, many people come to look at it. From the top, you can see for 80 miles. It is a wonderful place to visit!

1   **The story takes place in —**

○ Fred Lamb's home.

○ New York City.

○ a dream.

○ an airplane.

Hint: Read the first paragraph.

2   **The Empire State Building was built —**

○ hundreds of years ago.

○ last year.

○ in 1945.

○ in 1931.

Hint: Look at the second paragraph.

3   **The airplane crash took place —**

○ before the Empire State Building was done.

○ while Fred Lamb was dreaming.

○ after the Empire State Building was built.

○ while the people were working at night.

Hint: Look at the third paragraph.

GO ON

The first train was built in England in 1825. It did not go very fast. It could not carry many people. Sometimes it did not work at all. But it was better than riding on horses.

4 **Where was the first train built?**

- ◯ the United States
- ◯ Canada
- ◯ England
- ◯ Mexico

Hint: Read the first sentence.

5 **When was the first train built?**

- ◯ 1825
- ◯ 1852
- ◯ 1895
- ◯ 1925

Hint: Look at the first sentence.

I set up the tent in the backyard. I had my sleeping bag and my pillow. I made sure I had enough food. I took out my flashlight. It was getting dark. Before long, it was time to go to bed.

6 **When is this story taking place?**

- ◯ afternoon
- ◯ night
- ◯ morning
- ◯ lunch time

Hint: Look at the last two sentences.

TEST TIP

Always read a test story carefully. Do not skip any sentences. There could be clues anywhere in the story.

STOP

SKILL 3: SUMMARIZING MAIN IDEAS

The main idea is the meaning of a passage. Many times it is a sentence in the passage.

The Earth goes around the sun. In winter, our part of the Earth is farther away from the sun. It is very cold and it stays darker longer. In the summer, our part of the Earth is closer to the sun. Then it is very warm.

1   **What is the main idea of this story?**

   ○   The earth moves around the sun.

   ○   It is cold in the winter.

   ○   It is darker in the winter.

   ○   It is warm in the summer.

   Hint: What does the whole story talk about?

Many people play soccer. It is played in every country. Soccer has been around for almost 3,000 years. Some people played soccer in China a long time ago. Then people started to play it in other countries. Soon, it was played all around the world.

2   **What is the main idea of this passage?**

   ○   Soccer has been played for almost 3,000 years.

   ○   Soccer is played by people all over the world.

   ○   Some people played soccer in China.

   ○   People started to play soccer in other countries.

   Hint: The first two sentences and the last sentence give you the main idea.

GO ON

Hiking is a great way for you to have fun. All you need is a good pair of shoes. You can hike in many places, such as the woods or a valley. You can walk for a long or short time. Hiking is even better if you go with your friends.

3 What is the main idea of this story?

- ○ You need good hiking shoes.
- ○ You will have a good time hiking.
- ○ Hikes can be long or short.
- ○ You can hike in the woods.

Hint: What does the whole story talk about?

Mother's Day is a special day. There are many things you can do for your mother. You can make a pretty card or cook a nice meal. You can help clean the house or wash the clothes. It is a time to show your mother that you care.

4 What is the main idea of this passage?

- ○ You can cook a meal.
- ○ You can make a card.
- ○ You can help clean the house.
- ○ Mother's Day should be a special day.

Hint: Which choice is about the whole passage?

The winter in New York in 1994 was one to remember. There was a lot of snow. This made it hard for people to get around. Many schools were closed. It was also very cold. Many people were sick. People were glad when the winter was over.

5 What is the main idea of this passage?

- ○ The winter of 1994 was bad.
- ○ Many schools had to close.
- ○ People were sick.
- ○ It was hard to get around.

Hint: What does the whole story talk about?

TEST TIP

To find the main idea, ask yourself "What is this story about?" or "What is the big idea?"

GO ON ➡

A good summary contains the main idea of a passage. It is short but includes the most important points.

Bats are different from many other animals. They are the only mammal that can fly. Some bats live in trees. Most bats live in caves or in attics. They only come out at night. When they are resting they hang upside down. Bats are very interesting animals.

1   What is this mostly about?

○   Most bats live in caves or attics.

○   Bats can fly.

○   Bats only come out at night.

○   Bats are interesting animals.

Hint: Which sentence tells you about the whole passage?

Have you ever gone to Boston? It is a great city. There are all kinds of boats to see and walk around on. There are places to visit where you can learn about science. There are many places to get great food. Boston is a wonderful place with many things to see and do!

2   What is this mostly about?

○   Boston is an interesting city to visit.

○   You can eat good food in Boston.

○   Boston has all kinds of boats to see.

○   There are places to learn about science.

Hint: Which sentence tells you about the whole passage?

GO ON ▶

There is a lot to learn about owls. Owls are awake at night. They can see very well in the dark. They can hunt for their food. They can also hear things moving in the dark. Owls sleep during the day. They sleep high up in trees. This keeps them safe.

3   What is this passage mostly about?

○ There are many things to learn about owls.

○ Owls sleep during the day.

○ Owls can see in the dark.

○ Owls sleep high up in trees.

Hint: Which sentence tells you about the whole passage?

Many children enjoy bowling. To play, you need to have a few things. The bowling ball has to fit your fingers. Next, you need a special pair of shoes just for bowling. Then, you are ready to bowl. Try to throw the ball straight. With some practice, you'll do fine!

4   Which sentence tells what this story is mostly about?

○ The ball should be just right.

○ Get the right kind of shoes.

○ To bowl you need some special things.

○ Few children enjoy bowling.

Hint: Which sentence tells you about the whole passage?

Jane Addams was a famous woman. She wanted to help poor people. Jane bought an old house. She fixed it up. Then, she started a school for children. At night, grownups came to learn. Jane Addams worked hard to help more and more people.

5   What is this passage mostly about?

○ Jane Addams fixed up an old house.

○ Jane Addams helped many people.

○ Jane Addams helped teach grownups.

○ Jane Addams liked children.

Hint: Which sentence tells you about the whole passage?

TEST TIP

Find the difference between answer choices. Every answer choice in question 5 begins with "Jane Addams." The words that come next make the answers different.

STOP

SKILL 4: PERCEIVING RELATIONSHIPS AND RECOGNIZING OUTCOMES

Knowing what happened (the <u>effect</u>) and what made it happen (the <u>cause</u>) helps you to understand what you read.

Jill could not run very fast. She could never win a race. She wanted to do better. So, every day after school she practiced running. After a while she ran faster and faster. When Jill ran in the next race, she won and was very happy!

1   Why couldn't Jill win a race at first?

○   She was not happy.

○   Jill ran in too many races.

○   She was not a fast runner.

○   Jill wanted to run fast.

Hint: Look at the first sentence.

2   Why did Jill win?

○   She practiced a lot.

○   She wanted to win.

○   She was very happy.

○   She went to school.

Hint: Look at the fourth sentence.

One day, Tony saw a beautiful plant growing in his yard. He wanted it to keep growing, so each day he watered it. He also pulled up the weeds near it. After two weeks, the plant grew even bigger. Soon, it had pretty flowers. Tony felt proud.

3   What caused the plant to grow bigger?

○   It was planted in Tony's yard.

○   It had weeds near it.

○   It grew pretty flowers.

○   Tony watered it.

Hint: What did Tony do to help the plant grow bigger?

4   Why was Tony proud?

○   He cared for the plant and it grew.

○   He saw a plant growing in the yard.

○   He waited for two weeks.

○   The flowers were pretty.

Hint: Reread the passage. Why would Tony feel proud of himself?

GO ON

Long ago there lived a young woman named Margo. She lived all by herself in a house in the woods. Margo did not always like being alone. One day she found a little rabbit. The rabbit had hurt his leg. Margo felt sorry for it. She took the rabbit inside and took care of it. She gave the rabbit some lettuce to eat. The rabbit thanked Margo by licking her cheek. Margo named the rabbit Fluffy and kept it as a pet. Margo was no longer lonely.

5 Why did Margo bring the rabbit into her house?

○ She saw he was hungry.

○ She did not like to be alone.

○ She saw he was hurt.

○ She lived in the woods.

Hint: Margo brought in the rabbit. Why did she do this?

6 Why did the rabbit want to stay with Margo?

○ She took good care of him.

○ He wanted to eat more lettuce.

○ He saw Margo in the woods.

○ He did not want to be hurt.

Hint: The rabbit stayed with Margo. Why did he do this?

7 Why was Margo happy at the end of the story?

○ She did not like her house.

○ She liked to walk in the woods.

○ She wanted to find more rabbits.

○ She would not have to be alone.

Hint: Look at the last sentence. Why was Margo glad to have Fluffy?

TEST TIP

To check your answers, ask yourself, "Why did I choose this answer?"

GO ON ➡

SKILL 4: PERCEIVING RELATIONSHIPS AND RECOGNIZING OUTCOMES

Sometimes you can tell what might happen next. You must think about what would make sense if the story were to go on.

Luis came home from school. His mother told him to do his homework, but he did not want to. First, he had some milk and cookies. Then, he played with his toys. After dinner he drew some pictures. Soon, it was time to go to bed.

1   What might happen to Luis the next day?

○ He will not have his homework.

○ He will do well in school.

○ His mother will give him toys.

○ He will have milk and an apple.

Hint: What is most likely to happen the next day?

Miguel listened to the news. They said it will be very hot tomorrow. It will stay warm for the next few days. Miguel put his bathing suit on a chair. He was going to have fun.

2   What will Miguel do tomorrow?

○ sit on the chair

○ watch the news

○ go swimming

○ read a book

Hint: Read the whole paragraph.

Alicia asked to go to the bathroom. She ran down the hall. "No running in the hall," her teacher yelled. Alicia did not look where she was going. Just then, Herbie came out of his classroom. He was not looking where he was going.

3   What will happen next?

○ Alicia will return to her class.

○ Alicia and Herbie will bump into each other.

○ Alicia will say hello to Herbie.

○ Alicia's teacher will be happy.

Hint: You need to read the whole paragraph.

GO ON ➡

Chuck and Fatima wanted to put on a magic show. They practiced for a long time. They wanted to make sure they could do the tricks. When they were ready, they invited all of their friends.

4 What is probably going to happen next?

○ Fatima will decide not to do the tricks.

○ No children will come to see the show.

○ Chuck and Fatima will have a magic show.

○ Their parents will come to the show.

Hint: Think about how Chuck and Fatima got ready. What will happen next?

TEST TIP

To answer question 4, find the answer that is most <u>likely</u> to happen.

Kyle got a new dog named Lucky. Kyle was teaching him to chase after a ball. The first time Kyle threw it, Lucky did not chase it. The next time Kyle threw the ball, he put a treat near it. Lucky went to get it. Pretty soon he did not need the treat.

5 What will Lucky do the next time the ball is thrown?

○ He will go get the ball.

○ He will want a treat.

○ Lucky will run away.

○ Kyle will have to get it.

Hint: Read the last two sentences to find out what Lucky will do.

Alma loved to read. One day, her father gave her some books. There were books about sports. Some books were about science. Others had fairy tales and scary stories. She put them away in her closet. The next day her teacher gave her a book report to do.

6 What is Alma likely to do next?

○ She will clean her closet.

○ She will take out a book and read.

○ She will ask for more books.

○ She will not want the books.

Hint: What is in Alma's closet?

STOP

SKILL 5: MAKING INFERENCES AND GENERALIZATIONS

The way a character acts tells you about that person's mood.

One day, Sam's parents had some news. "We are going to move to a new town! You will be going to a new school," his father said. Sam yelled, "I don't want to go. I won't have any friends!" His mother and father talked to Sam. They told him he would meet new people. He would make new friends. Now, Sam felt a little better.

1   How did Sam feel about the news?

- ○ He was mad because he did not want to move.

- ○ He felt glad because he wanted to make new friends.

- ○ He was upset because he did not like school.

- ○ He was excited about moving.

Hint: Read what Sam said to see how he felt.

Alex lives in Florida. It is always warm there. He went to visit his cousins in Maine. It was very cold and snowy. He had never seen snow before. He could not wait to play in it. After putting on some warm clothes, Alex ran outside and jumped in it. "This is great," he yelled. He laughed and kept on playing.

2   How do you think Alex felt?

- ○ angry

- ○ excited

- ○ bored

- ○ friendly

Hint: You must read the entire passage to find out how Alex felt.

GO ON

Laura was working hard on her book report. She wrote her report using her best writing. Now she was ready to make the cover. Just then, her mom called her for dinner. When she was finished eating, she saw that her little brother had ripped the report. Now she would have to start over.

3 **How did Laura feel when she saw what her brother had done?**

○ Laura was glad.

○ Laura was angry.

○ Laura was hungry.

○ Laura was thankful.

Hint: Read the whole passage. Think about the first and last sentences.

Ari wanted to buy his mother a birthday present. He saw a necklace that he knew she would love. It cost more money than he had. Ari had a plan. Every day after school, he looked for empty soda cans. He turned them in for five cents each. Soon he had enough money to buy the necklace.

4 **How will Ari feel when he goes to buy the necklace?**

○ brave

○ mad

○ proud

○ silly

Hint: Read the whole paragraph. Think about what Ari was now able to do.

TEST TIP

The answers to these questions are not stated in the stories. You need to think about what happens to find an answer. This is called making inferences.

STOP

It is important to know the difference between fact and opinion. A <u>fact</u> is real and an <u>opinion</u> states a feeling or belief. Words that describe state opinions.

Many children are afraid of sharks. They think sharks like to eat people. Most times, this is not true. Not all sharks want to hurt people. They really want to eat tiny plants and fish. You should not be afraid of sharks.

1 **Which of these is a FACT from the passage?**

○ Sharks are the best fish.

○ Most sharks eat plants and fish.

○ Sharks are pretty fish.

○ You should be afraid of sharks.

Hint: Words like "best," "pretty," and "should" are opinion words.

Maine is a great place to visit. There are very nice beaches. You can swim in the ocean. You can also walk in the woods. Some people like to climb the mountains. They can climb to the top and see far away. There is a lot to do in Maine.

3 **Which of these is NOT a fact from the passage?**

○ Maine is a great place to visit.

○ You can walk in the woods.

○ Some people climb mountains.

○ There are beaches.

Hint: Facts are real and true. Which sentence is an opinion?

GO ON ➡

Seals are in great danger. Some people hunt them for their thick fur. They use the fur to make warm coats. Other people hunt the seals for food. In some places, laws protect seals. Seals cannot be killed for any reason. We need more laws.

3   A fact from the passage is that seals

○ live in the water.

○ are in danger.

○ like to eat meat.

○ hunt people.

Hint: A fact is real and true.

Have you ever tried to high jump? High jumping can be a lot of fun. A bar rests across two poles. You have to jump over this. You run quickly up to the bar. If you are high enough, you will go over the bar.

4   Which of these is an opinion from the passage?

○ A bar rests across two poles.

○ High jumping can be a lot of fun.

○ You run quickly up to the bar.

○ You jump over the bar.

Hint: Words that describe are opinion words.

Many things happen when we eat. We chew the food into little pieces. This is so our bodies can use it. It travels down a tube into the stomach. It goes from there to other parts of the body. We all need to eat to live.

5   Which of these is a fact from the passage?

○ Food travels from the stomach to the mouth.

○ We swallow big pieces of food.

○ Food is used in many parts of our body.

○ We should not eat too often.

Hint: A fact is real and true. What is really said in the passage?

TEST TIP

The word <u>should</u> is often found in opinions. Read these two sentences:

• We sing every day.

• We should sing every day.

The second sentence is an opinion because it includes the word <u>should</u>.

STOP

READING COMPREHENSION

Directions: Read each story carefully. Then read each question. Darken the circle for the correct answer, or write the answer on the lines.

 TRY THIS More than one answer choice may seem correct. Choose the answer that goes best with the story.

Sample A

Mr. Feld's Garden

Mr. Feld has a garden. Each day, he pulls out the weeds. He stays on his knees for a long time. Sometimes they hurt him. Today his son gave him some knee pads. Now Mr. Feld's knees won't hurt anymore.

What did Mr. Feld's son give him?

○ a watering can

○ a new rake

○ knee pads

○ some seeds

THINK IT THROUGH The correct answer is <u>knee pads</u>. The next-to-last sentence says, "Today his son gave him some knee pads."

STOP

Katie and Josephine

Katie and Josephine were waiting for the bus. They looked up at the sky. Katie put on her raincoat. Josephine pulled up her hood. The bus came. They got in fast.

1   **What were the girls doing?**

○ playing football

○ waiting for the bus

○ waiting for the train

○ riding an airplane

2   **Why did Katie and Josephine get into the bus fast?**

_____

_____

_____

_____

GO ON

The Lion and the Mouse

A big, fierce lion was sleeping under a tree. A mouse ran up on the lion's back. Then the lion woke up, and he was angry at the mouse. He caught the mouse in his paw.

"Please do not eat me," said the mouse. "If you let me go, I will help you some time."

The lion thought the mouse was funny. "How could you help me?" he laughed. But then he let the mouse go.

Later that day the lion got caught in a hunter's net. He tried and tried to get free, but he could not get out of the net. The lion was ready to give up, but then he saw the mouse.

"Please help me," the lion said. The mouse began to chew on the net. Soon the net broke apart, and the lion was able to climb out of the net. The mouse had set the lion free.

3 **How did the mouse help the lion?**

○ She brought the lion food.

○ She found the lion's friends.

○ She fixed the lion's paw.

○ She chewed the net apart.

4 **The boxes below show things that happened in the story.**

The lion caught the mouse.		The mouse set the lion free.
1	2	3

What belongs in Box 2?

○ The lion was sleeping.

○ The mouse woke up the lion.

○ The lion let the mouse go.

○ The mouse ran up the lion's back.

5 **Why was the lion angry?**

_____

_____

_____

_____

_____

_____

_____

6 **Which of these lessons best fits the story?**

○ Little friends cannot help.

○ A mouse should not walk on a lion.

○ Little friends can be good friends.

○ Laughing makes you feel better.

GO ON ➡

A Letter to Harry

Dear Harry,

I wish you lived near me. We had the best costume party last night. It would have been more fun if you had been here. I dressed up like a cat. We invited all the kids on my street. Some of my friends from school came, too.

We had the party in the garage. I helped my dad fix it up. We hung colorful banners and streamers from the ceiling. My dad dressed up like a monster. We bobbed for apples in a big pail of water. The only way I could get one was to put my whole head under the water. I pushed the apple against the bottom of the pail and finally got it.

Later my dad made some special root beer. This is how he did it:

First, he put sugar into some water, and then he added root beer *extract*. That's the flavoring that makes it taste like root beer.

To finish, my dad stirred it and added lots of dry ice. When he poured in the dry ice, it made a lot of white smoke!

Chris had one of the best costumes. He was dressed like a hot dog. At the end of the party we helped Mom make popcorn.

What have you been doing? When are you going to come and visit? My mom says you can come anytime. We're going to Texas for New Year's Day. Write me soon.

Your friend,
Tom

GO ON

7 What is Tom's letter mostly about?

○ his party

○ his class at school

○ his costume

○ his trip to Texas

8 How does Tom feel about Harry?

_____

_____

_____

_____

_____

_____

9 If you are making root beer, you should—

○ add sugar to flour.

○ stir in butter.

○ pour in milk.

○ add sugar to water.

10 What kind of party did Tom have?

○ a pizza party

○ a birthday party

○ a garden party

○ a costume party

11 In this story, Harry is the name of Tom's—

○ friend.

○ teacher.

○ uncle.

○ neighbor.

12 In this story, what does the word <u>extract</u> mean?

○ a kind of sugar

○ a kind of flavoring

○ a kind of nut

○ a kind of flour

13 When did Tom write the letter?

○ on a Monday

○ during the summer

○ the day after his party

○ on New Year's Day

14 Tom's letter does <u>not</u> tell—

○ where his friend Harry lives.

○ what costume his dad wore.

○ about bobbing for apples.

○ where he is going for New Year's Day.

GO ON ➡

Join Now!

This month is the time to join in and help others. Any second grader at Smith School can join in.

Read the list of things to do. Choose those you like best. Sign up on the sheet below by Thursday.

Ms. Salina will lead the activities. Students who do two or more things from the list this month will earn a volunteer pin.

To help others, we will:

1. Read to younger students.
2. Pick up litter at Travis Park.
3. Make greeting cards to send to a hospital.
4. Record songs on tape to send to a nursing home.

Your Name	Activity Numbers	Your Teacher's Name
Meg Klein	2, 4	Mr. Ward

15 Who will earn a pin?

- ○ all students who sign up
- ○ Ms. Salina's homeroom students
- ○ students who do at least two things from the list
- ○ students in the hospital

16 Why would students volunteer?

_____

_____

_____

_____

17 After students sign up, what will probably happen next?

- ○ Ms. Salina will speak to them.
- ○ They will sing songs.
- ○ They will get a volunteer pin.
- ○ They will go shopping.

18 Which of the following is <u>not</u> listed on the sign-up sheet?

- ○ your name
- ○ your room number
- ○ activity numbers
- ○ your teacher's name

GO ON ➡

A Great Play

Dawn had a part in the school play. She had to wear a costume. First, she put on a gray suit with a long tail. Then, she painted a pink circle on her nose. A pair of big gray ears finished the costume. It was time for her part. She walked onto the stage. A boy dressed like a cat crawled toward her. She grabbed a piece of cheese and ran. She was faster than the cat. Everyone laughed and laughed.

19 **Why did Dawn wear a costume?**

○ She was going to a party.

○ She was playing with friends.

○ She was in a school play.

○ She liked to dress up.

20 **What animal was Dawn most likely dressed as?**

○ an elephant

○ a dog

○ a cat

○ a mouse

21 **What is this story mostly about?**

○ Dawn's part in the school play

○ how to make costumes for plays

○ how to act in plays

○ animals in plays

22 **What could be another title for this story?**

_____

_____

_____

_____

_____

STOP

A sample question helps you to understand the type of question you will be asked in the test that follows.

Sample A

A Note for Ellen

Ellen's mother was going to be home late. She left a note for Ellen that said, "Please clean your room. Then you may read or watch television. I should be home about 4:00."

What should Ellen do first?

○ clean her room

○ watch television

○ read

○ call her friends

Growing Flowers

To grow flowers, do the following:

1. Put dirt in a pot.
2. Place flower seeds in the pot.
3. Cover the seeds with more dirt.
4. Put the pot in the sun.
5. Water the seeds, and wait for the flowers to grow!

1   What is the last thing you should do?

○ cover the seeds with dirt

○ put dirt in the pot

○ buy seeds

○ water the seeds

2   What is the best way to find out more about growing flowers?

○ Read a book about gardening.

○ Put cut flowers in a vase.

○ Draw pictures of flowers.

○ Sit in the sun.

3   To grow flowers you will need—

○ a shovel.

○ seeds.

○ gloves.

○ a spoon.

4   Where should you put the pot?

_____

_____

_____

_____

_____

GO ON ➡

All About Owls

Did you know that owls are good hunters? Owls sleep all day long. At night they wake up and fly around. They look for mice to eat. Owls have very big eyes. Big eyes let in more light. Owls can see better at night than we can. Owls also hear very well. They can hear a mouse running in the grass. They can fly without making any noise at all. All these things make owls good hunters.

5 This story does <u>not</u> tell—

- ○ the kind of eyes owls have.
- ○ what makes owls good hunters.
- ○ about different kinds of owls.
- ○ what owls like to eat.

6 This story was written mainly to—

- ○ ask you to join a club.
- ○ explain how important sleep is for good health.
- ○ tell about a kind of bird.
- ○ describe what animals do at night.

7 A special thing about the owl is that it can fly very—

- ○ quietly.
- ○ loudly.
- ○ quickly.
- ○ high in the air.

8 Why can owls see better at night?

_____

_____

_____

_____

_____

9 When do owls sleep?

- ○ at night
- ○ during the afternoon
- ○ through the morning
- ○ all day

GO ON ⇒

A Scary Walk

"What a great day for a walk!" John said. He could hear the birds singing. John was glad that he had made this trip to the mountains. After breakfast John took off, whistling a tune. The trail went up the mountain. He walked for a while, and then he looked for a rock to rest on. John was tired. "What a mountain man I turned out to be!" he said.

While he rested, John looked around. Suddenly he saw the opening to a cave. It was big enough to walk through. "I wonder how deep it is," he said. "I wonder if there are any cave drawings! I guess the only way to find out is to see for myself."

At first John had no trouble seeing in the cave. He went around a bend. He lit a match. "Just a little farther," he said to himself. Suddenly his match went out! He lit another one. But now things looked strange. John was lost!

When his second match went out, John got really frightened. Then he thought he heard a scratching noise. John struck his last match. In the light he saw hundreds of bats hanging on the cave walls! Their eyes glittered red. John started screaming and running as fast as he could. Luckily for John, he was running in the right direction. He ran all the way back to his camp.

GO ON

10 **What did John hear when he started his walk?**

- ○ water running
- ○ bats scratching
- ○ dogs barking
- ○ birds singing

11 **What will John probably do next?**

_____

_____

_____

_____

_____

_____

_____

12 **What is this story mostly about?**

- ○ bats hanging on cave walls
- ○ John's adventure in a cave
- ○ using matches wisely
- ○ hiking safety

13 **Why did John go into the cave?**

- ○ He liked caves.
- ○ He wanted to see what was inside the cave.
- ○ He was looking for a friend.
- ○ It started to rain.

14 **These boxes show things that happened in the story.**

John rested on a rock.		John saw hundreds of bats.
1	2	3

What belongs in Box 2?

- ○ John ran back to camp.
- ○ John walked up the mountain.
- ○ John got lost in a cave.
- ○ John ate breakfast.

15 **How did John feel when he saw the bats?**

- ○ interested
- ○ angry
- ○ frightened
- ○ sad

16 **This story is most like a—**

- ○ poem.
- ○ true story.
- ○ fairy tale.
- ○ tall tale.

17 **Another name for this story could be—**

- ○ "Mountain Man"
- ○ "Finding Cave Drawings"
- ○ "John's Surprise"
- ○ "How to Explore Caves"

STOP

UNDERSTANDING WORD MEANINGS

Directions: Darken the circle for the word or words that have the <u>same</u> or <u>almost the same</u> meaning as the underlined word.

TRY THIS	Choose your answer carefully. Some choices may seem correct. Be sure to think about the meaning of the underlined word.

Sample A

To <u>raise</u> something is to—

○ lift it   ○ fly it

○ count it   ○ open it

THINK IT THROUGH	The correct answer is <u>lift it</u>. If you raise something, you lift it up. To raise something is not to count it, fly it, or open it.

STOP

1   To <u>choose</u> is to—

○ hide   ○ color

○ check   ○ pick

2   A <u>blizzard</u> is most like a—

○ thunderstorm

○ snowstorm

○ river

○ movie

3   To <u>shout</u> is to—

○ jump

○ slip

○ yell

○ skip

4   <u>Least</u> means—

○ best   ○ smallest

○ closest   ○ fastest

5   A <u>pail</u> is most like a—

○ bucket   ○ house

○ pain   ○ hill

6   Something that is moving <u>forward</u> is going—

○ back

○ ahead

○ behind

○ over

STOP

Directions: Darken the circle beside the sentence that uses the underlined word in the same way as the sentence in the box, or write the answer on the blank lines.

TRY THIS

Read the sentence in the box. Decide what the underlined word means. Then find the sentence with the underlined word that has the same meaning.

Sample A

> Have you ever seen a two-dollar <u>bill</u>?

In which sentence does <u>bill</u> mean the same as it does in the sentence above?

○ I paid with two quarters and one dollar <u>bill</u>.

○ Uncle Carl got a <u>bill</u> for the newspaper.

○ A parrot has a big <u>bill</u>.

○ The store will <u>bill</u> us for these shoes.

THINK IT THROUGH

The correct answer is the first sentence, <u>I paid with two quarters and one dollar bill</u>. In this sentence and the sentence in the box, bill means "a type of money."

STOP

1

> The sun's <u>light</u> is bright.

In which sentence does <u>light</u> mean the same as it does in the sentence above?

○ Will you <u>light</u> the candles?

○ The <u>light</u> from the flashlight helped us to see.

○ That bag is <u>light</u>, not heavy.

○ Pink is a <u>light</u> color.

2

> It is Tia's turn to <u>ring</u> the bell.

Use <u>ring</u> in a sentence. It should have the same meaning as it does in the sentence in the box.

_____

_____

_____

_____

_____

_____

STOP

Directions: Darken the circle for the word or words that give the meaning of the underlined word, or write the answer on the blank lines.

TRY THIS	Read the first sentence carefully. Look for clue words in the sentence to help you. Then use each answer choice in place of the underlined word. Remember that the underlined word and your answer must have the same meaning.

Sample A

The magician made the rabbit <u>vanish</u> from our sight. <u>Vanish</u> means—

○ jump   ○ disappear

○ shine   ○ smile

THINK IT THROUGH	The correct answer is <u>disappear</u>. <u>Vanish</u> means to no longer be seen. All four choices are things a magician could make a rabbit do. But only <u>disappear</u> has the same meaning as vanish.

STOP

---

1 Singing, talking loudly, or whistling is <u>forbidden</u> in the library. What does <u>forbidden</u> mean?

_____

_____

_____

_____

_____

2 The artist made a quick pencil <u>sketch</u> of the village. <u>Sketch</u> means—

○ drawing   ○ song

○ story   ○ fence

3 Melissa plans to <u>save</u> money so she will be able to buy some new skates. <u>Save</u> means—

○ keep

○ bet

○ pay

○ find

4 He <u>shoved</u> the frightened actor onto the stage. <u>Shoved</u> means—

○ sang

○ returned

○ pushed

○ read

STOP

Directions: Darken the circle under the compound word.

TRY THIS Look carefully at each word. Then look for the word that is made up of two words put together.

Sample A

carrot   harbor   herself
○   ○   ○

THINK IT THROUGH **Herself** is a compound word made up of the words **her** and **self**. Each of these words can stand alone. **Harbor** and **carrot** are not made up of two words put together.

STOP

1 mailbox ○	listen ○	drawing ○

5 anyway ○	making ○	after ○

2 closet ○	airplane ○	fasten ○

6 inches ○	someone ○	teacher ○

3 football ○	looked ○	backing ○

7 fiddle ○	rather ○	bedroom ○

4 pencil ○	follow ○	outside ○

8 bottle ○	bluebird ○	hundred ○

STOP

Directions: Darken the circle under the word that shows the correct plural noun. A plural noun names more than one thing.

 TRY THIS Add –s to make many plural nouns. Add –es to make other plural nouns. Some plurals do not follow this pattern.

Sample A
more than one <u>couch</u>

 **THINK IT THROUGH** The correct answer is <u>couches</u>. Add –es to most nouns that end in <u>sh</u>, <u>ch</u>, or <u>x</u>.

couchs ○   couches ○   couch ○

STOP

---

1 more than one <u>house</u>

housees ○   housies ○   houses ○

2 more than one <u>chair</u>

chair ○   chairs ○   chaires ○

3 more than one <u>puppy</u>

puppys ○   puppes ○   puppies ○

4 more than one <u>stitch</u>

stitches ○   stitchies ○   stitchs ○

5 more than one <u>star</u>

starrs ○   stars ○   stares ○

6 more than one <u>mouse</u>

mouses ○   mousies ○   mice ○

7 more than one <u>flower</u>

flowers ○   flowes ○   floweres ○

8 more than one <u>man</u>

mans ○   manes ○   men ○

STOP

Directions: Darken the circle under the word that has the same sound or sounds as the underlined part of the first word in each row.

 TRY THIS Say the first word to yourself. Decide how the underlined part of the word sounds. Then as you say each answer choice, listen for that sound.

Sample A

n<u>o</u>se

low   night   loop
○   ○   ○

THINK IT THROUGH <u>Low</u> is the correct answer. The "o" in low makes the same sound as the "o" in <u>nose</u>.

 STOP

1   **<u>th</u>ere**
    this   think   thin
    ○   ○   ○

2   **l<u>ou</u>d**
    through   lid   cow
    ○   ○   ○

3   **but<u>t</u>er**
    mother   bunny   writing
    ○   ○   ○

4   **qui<u>lt</u>**
    mall   wilt   queen
    ○   ○   ○

5   **<u>c</u>ute**
    pulling   luck   noon
    ○   ○   ○

6   **<u>r</u>a<u>r</u>e**
    rain   fair   rough
    ○   ○   ○

7   **<u>c</u>at**
    city   kitten   hat
    ○   ○   ○

8   **<u>st</u>ep**
    desk   fast   teach
    ○   ○   ○

Directions: Darken the circle under the word that rhymes with the first word in each row.

TRY THIS Say the first word to yourself. Listen to the sounds at the end of the word. Then say each answer choice. Listen for the word that ends with the same sounds. Rhyming words end with the same vowel and consonant sounds. The spellings can be different.

Sample A

more

fear	mow	for
○	○	○

THINK IT THROUGH The correct answer is <u>for</u>. The words <u>more</u> and <u>for</u> rhyme. <u>Fear</u> ends with an <u>r</u> sound, but the vowel sound is different.

STOP

1 new

newt	now	two
○	○	○

5 moon

foot	moo	June
○	○	○

2 red

said	real	seed
○	○	○

6 rain

rake	lane	paint
○	○	○

3 mop

top	tip	tap
○	○	○

7 four

dry	fork	poor
○	○	○

4 ride

ray	cried	rice
○	○	○

8 own

now	phone	noon
○	○	○

STOP

Directions: Darken the circle for the word or words that have the same or almost the same meaning as the underlined word.

1   Hardly means—

   ○ a lot

   ○ not at all

   ○ more than

   ○ barely

2   To begin is to—

   ○ start

   ○ end

   ○ laugh

   ○ think

3   A bundle is a—

   ○ supper

   ○ mitten

   ○ bunch

   ○ bread

4   If something sparkles, it—

   ○ shines

   ○ bothers

   ○ pays

   ○ wins

Directions: Darken the circle beside the sentence that uses the underlined word in the same way as the sentence in the box, or write the answer on the blank lines.

5 | What time does the show start? |

In which sentence does time mean the same as it does in the sentence above?

   ○ I will time my brother's race.

   ○ We kept time with the music.

   ○ Everyone had a good time.

   ○ It's time for lunch.

6 | Did you feel a drop of rain? |

In which sentence does drop mean the same as it does in the sentence above?

   ○ I put the letter in the mail drop.

   ○ Please wipe up the drop of paint.

   ○ Leon's mom will drop us off.

   ○ Don't drop that glass!

GO ON➡

7

> Exercise is the <u>key</u> to good health.

In which sentence does <u>key</u> mean the same as it does in the sentence above?

- ○ A <u>key</u> on the piano is stuck.
- ○ I lost my <u>key</u> to the front door.
- ○ In what <u>key</u> are you singing?
- ○ Tim found the <u>key</u> to solving the puzzle.

8

> We planted flowers <u>last</u> spring.

Write a sentence in which <u>last</u> means the same as it does in the sentence above.

_____

_____

_____

_____

9

> Did you find the <u>iron</u> pot?

In which sentence does <u>iron</u> mean the same as it does in the sentence above?

- ○ The <u>iron</u> horseshoe is strong.
- ○ Lisa needs to <u>iron</u> her dress.
- ○ <u>Iron</u> out your differences.
- ○ Did you plug in the <u>iron</u>?

Directions: Darken the circle beside the word that gives the meaning of the underlined word.

10 We made a star <u>pattern</u> with beads. <u>Pattern</u> means—

- ○ circle
- ○ design
- ○ necklace
- ○ string

11 A family finally moved into the house that had been <u>vacant</u> for months. <u>Vacant</u> means—

- ○ white
- ○ empty
- ○ burned
- ○ filled

12 He painted <u>bold</u> colors next to soft ones. <u>Bold</u> means—

- ○ dull
- ○ bright
- ○ mixed
- ○ quiet

GO ON➡

Directions: Darken the circle under the compound word.

13   frying   mitten   raincoat
       ○   ○   ○

14   notebook   other   parent
       ○   ○   ○

15   fresher   bathtub   bottle
       ○   ○   ○

16   wisdom   upstairs   artist
       ○   ○   ○

17   finger   grassy   birthday
       ○   ○   ○

18   remain   sidewalk   happen
       ○   ○   ○

Directions: Darken the circle under the word that shows the correct plural noun.

19   **more than one <u>tree</u>**
       trees   tree   tries
       ○   ○   ○

20   **more than one <u>bone</u>**
       bons   bonies   bones
       ○   ○   ○

21   **more than one <u>wish</u>**
       wishs   wishes   wishies
       ○   ○   ○

22   **more than one <u>baby</u>**
       babys   babies   babyes
       ○   ○   ○

23   **more than one <u>child</u>**
       children   childs   childes
       ○   ○   ○

24   **more than one <u>bear</u>**
       beares   berries   bears
       ○   ○   ○

GO ON ➡

Directions: Darken the circle under the word that has the same sound or sounds as the underlined part of the first word in each row.

Directions: Darken the circle under the word that rhymes with the first word in each row.

25 rea<u>ch</u>

shore   rink   chip
  ○   ○   ○

26 <u>c</u>enter

crate   loose   inch
  ○   ○   ○

27 p<u>i</u>ne

pitch   peach   tie
  ○   ○   ○

28 <u>pi</u>e

fine   car   mop
  ○   ○   ○

29 fl<u>a</u>t

flew   apple   west
  ○   ○   ○

30 r<u>oa</u>st

grow   spoon   ripe
  ○   ○   ○

31 sip

lid   lap   lip
  ○   ○   ○

32 green

grow   grin   mean
  ○   ○   ○

33 blue

black   shoe   broom
  ○   ○   ○

34 fry

high   friend   hurry
  ○   ○   ○

35 whale

hole   hill   pail
  ○   ○   ○

36 tune

food   noon   too
  ○   ○   ○

STOP

MATH PROBLEM-SOLVING PLAN

THE PROBLEM-SOLVING PLAN

Here are the steps to solve problems:

STEP 1: WHAT IS THE QUESTION?

Read the problem. Can you see what you must find? What is the question?

STEP 2: FIND THE FACTS

Find the facts:

A. KEY FACTS are the facts you need to solve the problem.

B. FACTS YOU DON'T NEED are those facts that are not needed to solve the problem.

C. ARE MORE FACTS NEEDED? Do you need more facts to solve the problem?

STEP 3: CHOOSE A WAY TO SOLVE

Plan a way to solve the problem.

STEP 4: SOLVE

Use your plan to solve the problem.

STEP 5: DOES YOUR RESPONSE MAKE SENSE?

Write your answer in a complete sentence.

Read the problem again.

Does your answer make sense?

TEST TIP

You can use these steps to solve any math problem. These steps will help you find the best answers on tests and check your work.

Directions: Use the problem-solving plan to solve this math problem.

PROBLEM/QUESTION:

A store sells apples. The first apple costs 25¢. Each apple after that costs 20¢. If Paul buys 3 apples, how much does he pay?

STEP 1: WHAT IS THE QUESTION/GOAL?

_____

_____

_____

STEP 2: FIND THE FACTS

_____

_____

_____

STEP 3: SELECT A STRATEGY

_____

_____

_____

STEP 4: SOLVE

_____

_____

_____

STEP 5: DOES YOUR RESPONSE MAKE SENSE?

_____

_____

_____

_____

_____

Directions: Use the problem-solving plan to solve this math problem.

PROBLEM/QUESTION:

Jenny said, "I am thinking of a number. The number is less than 9 and greater than 5. It is an odd number." Name the number.

STEP 1: WHAT IS THE QUESTION/GOAL?

_____

_____

_____

STEP 2: FIND THE FACTS

_____

_____

_____

STEP 3: SELECT A STRATEGY

_____

_____

_____

STEP 4: SOLVE

_____

_____

_____

STEP 5: DOES YOUR RESPONSE MAKE SENSE?

_____

_____

_____

_____

MATH PROBLEM SOLVING

=UNDERSTANDING NUMERATION=

Directions: Darken the circle for the correct answer, or write the answer on the lines.

Sample A

Which number shows the correct way to write three hundred plus fifty?

300 + 50 | 300   3,050   350   30,050

○   ○   ○   ○

THINK IT THROUGH

Think about which numbers stand for ones, tens, and hundreds. The correct answer is <u>350</u>. This is the only number that equals 300 + 50.

STOP

---

1 Write the number that is in the hundreds place.

903   _____

---

2 Which shirt shows an even number?

    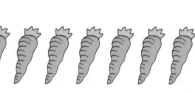

9   5   3   6

○   ○   ○   ○

---

3 Which number tells the total number of carrots?

75   57   67   58

○   ○   ○   ○

STOP

Directions: Darken the circle for the correct answer, or write the answer on the lines.

Sample A

Which shape is NOT divided into four equal pieces, or fourths?

○   ○   ○   ○

THINK IT THROUGH Look at the pictures. How many parts do you see in each picture? Find the picture that does NOT show fourths. The correct answer is the <u>third</u> shape. All the other shapes are divided into fourths.

STOP

1 Six kittens are in the basket. Two kittens are outside the basket. Which number sentence describes the total number of kittens?

○ 6 + 2 = 8   ○ 10 − 2 = 8

○ 6 − 2 = 4   ○ 8 + 2 = 10

2 Which picture shows that one of the three apples has been eaten?

○   ○   ○   ○

3 Write the number that makes this number sentence correct.

8 + □ = 8   _____

4 Which number makes this number sentence correct?

18 + □ = 21 + 18

39   21   18   3
○   ○   ○   ○

STOP

Directions: Darken the circle for the correct answer, or write the answer on the lines.

Sample A

Which number is missing in this pattern? Find the number that belongs on the door that does not have a number.

25	17	15	11
○	○	○	○

THINK IT THROUGH The correct answer is <u>15</u>. Each of the numbers is 3 greater than the one before it. 12 + 3 = 15, so this is the missing number.

STOP

1 What are the next two shapes in this pattern?

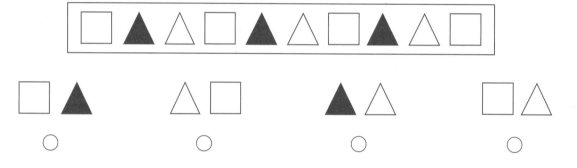

2 Write the number that is missing in this pattern.

10	15	20		30

_____

_____

_____

3 Max counted these birds. He started with 62. Which bird did Max count as number 71?

62   63   64   ○   ○   ○   ○

STOP

Directions: Darken the circle for the correct answer, or write the answer on the lines.

Sample A

Ann made this tally chart. Which picture shows the shell that Ann found six of?

Sand dollar	Conch	Whelk	Scallop

Sand dollar
○

Conch
○

Whelk
○

Scallop
○

THINK IT THROUGH The correct answer is the <u>whelk</u>. If you count the tally marks, Ann found six whelk shells.

STOP

---

1 How many points did Joe score?

Soccer Points

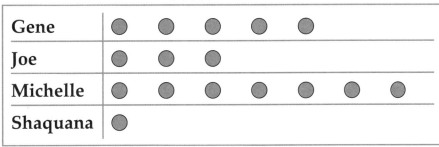

Each 🔴 = 1 point

_____

_____

_____

_____

---

2 What shape is the spinner <u>most likely</u> to land on?

○   ○   ○   ○

STOP

Directions: Darken the circle for the correct answer.

Sample A

Think about folding each shape on the dotted line. Which shape has parts that will <u>match exactly</u> when you fold on the dotted line?

○   ○   ○   ○

| THINK IT THROUGH | **The correct answer is the <u>third</u> figure. If you fold this figure on the dotted line, each side will be the same.** |

STOP

1 Which box shows two triangles?

   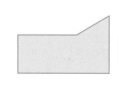   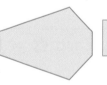   

○   ○   ○   ○

---

2 Which shape has the same number of sides as the first shape in the row?

 |

○   ○   ○   ○

---

3 Which card shows what the first card in the row looks like <u>upside down</u>?

   |

○   ○   ○   ○

STOP

Directions: Darken the circle for the correct answer, or write the answer on the lines.

Sample A

Sue has some coins. Which number shows how much money Sue will have left if she buys the banana?

    3¢   5¢   10¢   15¢

    ○   ○   ○   ○

> **THINK IT THROUGH**   The correct answer is <u>15¢</u>. Sue has 28¢. The banana costs 13¢. To find out how much Sue gets back, subtract 13¢ from 28¢. This gives you the answer, 15¢.

STOP

1 Use a centimeter ruler. How long is this key in centimeters?

_____

_____

_____

_____

2 What unit would you use to measure the weight of a dog?

    Kilometers   Pounds   Inches   Grams

      ○   ○   ○   ○

3 What day is August 13 on this calendar?

August

Sun	Mon	Tues	Wed	Thur	Fri	Sat
			1	2	3	4
5	6	7	8	9	10	11
12	13	14	15	16	17	18
19	20	21	22	23	24	25
26	27	28	29	30	31	

  ○   Monday   ○   Friday

  ○   Tuesday   ○   Saturday

STOP

Directions: Darken the circle for the correct answer, or write the answer on the lines.

Sample A

Mrs. Chong bought 12 flowers. She put 8 of the flowers in a vase. Which number sentence shows how to find the number of flowers Mrs. Chong has left?

    ○ $12 + 8 = \square$ ○ $12 + 4 = \square$

    ○ $12 - 8 = \square$ ○ $12 - \square = 6$

THINK IT THROUGH The correct answer is $\underline{12 - 8}$. The clue words, "has left," tell you to subtract. Mrs. Chong has 12 flowers and puts 8 in a vase, so $12 - 8$ is the number sentence that answers the question.

STOP

1. Nathan had three fish. He bought nine more. Which number sentence shows how to find how many fish Nathan has altogether?

    ○ $9 - 3 = \square$ ○ $3 + 9 = \square$

    ○ $12 - 9 = \square$ ○ $3 + \square = 9$

2. Sue thinks of one of these numbers. Her number is less than 35. The sum of the digits is 11. What is Sue's number?

   38   34   29   24
   ○   ○   ○   ○

3. Tia's age is between 31 and 41. The sum of the digits is 5. How old is Tia?

_____

_____

_____

_____

4. Lou thinks of one of these numbers. His number is inside the square and inside the triangle. It is even. What is Lou's number?

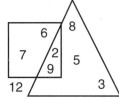

     2   5   6   8
     ○   ○   ○   ○

STOP

Directions: Darken the circle for the correct answer. If the correct answer is not given, darken the circle for NH (Not Here). If there are no choices, write the answer on the blank lines.

Sample A

It is Soon-Li's birthday. She gets nine presents from her friends. She gets five presents from her family. How many presents does she get?

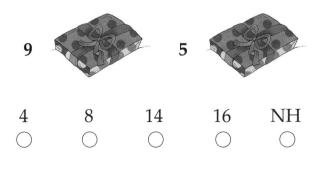

9   5

4	8	14	16	NH
○	○	○	○	○

> **THINK IT THROUGH**
> The correct answer is the third answer choice, 14.
> She gets 9 presents from her friends and 5 from her family. The word <u>altogether</u> tells you to add. So there are 14 presents altogether, because 9 + 5 = 14.

 STOP

---

1 An art gallery has 60 pictures in the first room. There are 34 pictures in the second room. How many pictures are there in all?

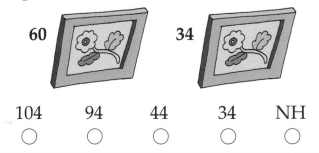

60   34

104	94	44	34	NH
○	○	○	○	○

---

2 There were five boats on the lake. Three more boats joined them. How many boats were there altogether?

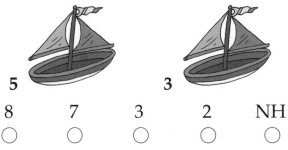

5   3

8	7	3	2	NH
○	○	○	○	○

3 The school served 56 bowls of chicken soup and 24 bowls of vegetable soup. How many bowls of soup did the school serve in all?

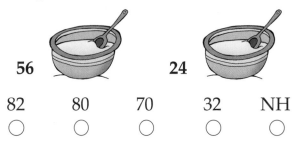

56   24

82	80	70	32	NH
○	○	○	○	○

> **TEST TIP**
>
> The words <u>in all</u>, <u>total</u>, and <u>altogether</u> are clues that you should add.

GO ON

4 A plane carries 18 large suitcases and 7 small suitcases. How many suitcases does the plane carry?

18   7

_____

_____

_____

_____

5 There were 55 cocoons at the zoo. Butterflies came out of 23 of them. How many cocoons were left?

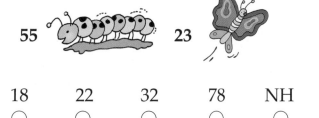

55   23

18   22   32   78   NH
○   ○   ○   ○   ○

6 A hardware store has 26 padlocks with dials and 9 locks with keys. How many more padlocks than key locks does the store have?

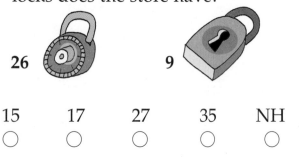

26   9

15   17   27   35   NH
○   ○   ○   ○   ○

7 There were 53 ribbons given at the county dog show. The judges gave 23 ribbons in the morning. How many ribbons did they give in the afternoon?

53   23

40   33   23   20   NH
○   ○   ○   ○   ○

8 Pat's Pizza Parlor sold 41 sausage-and-mushroom pizzas. It sold 12 plain sausage pizzas. How many more sausage-and-mushroom than plain mushroom pizzas did it sell?

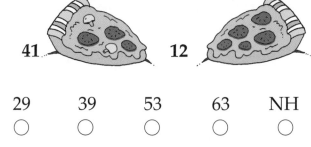

41   12

29   39   53   63   NH
○   ○   ○   ○   ○

TEST TIP

The words <u>how many more</u> are a clue that you should subtract. Subtract the smaller number from the larger number.

GO ON

9 The garden center has 123 plants. It sells 47 plants. How many plants are left?

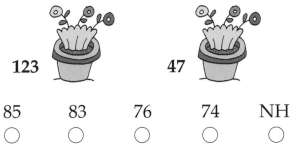

123   **47**

85	83	76	74	NH
○	○	○	○	○

10 Twelve clowns wear round hats. Nine clowns wear pointed hats. How many more clowns wear round hats?

12   **9**

21	13	11	3	NH
○	○	○	○	○

11 A fire station collects 207 toys. It gives 66 toys away. How many toys are left?

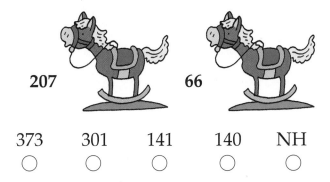

207   **66**

373	301	141	140	NH
○	○	○	○	○

12 An ice cream store sold 82 cones and 47 sundaes. How many more cones than sundaes did the store sell?

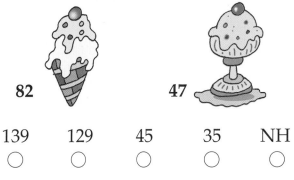

82   **47**

139	129	45	35	NH
○	○	○	○	○

13 Koji collects cars and trucks. He has 126 cars and 71 trucks. How many cars and trucks does he have altogether?

126   **71**

_____

_____

_____

_____

14 Jacob has a herd of goats. He has 30 brown goats and 16 white goats. How many more brown goats than white goats does Jacob have?

30   **16**

46	24	14	6	NH
○	○	○	○	○

STOP

Directions: Darken the circle for the correct answer. If the correct answer is not given, darken the circle for NH (Not Here). If there are no circles, write the answer on the lines.

TRY THIS	Study the problem carefully. Decide if you need to add or subtract. Then work the problem on scratch paper.

Sample A

$$17$$
$$- 9$$

  6   8   26   28   NH
  ○   ○   ○   ○   ○

THINK IT THROUGH	The correct answer is <u>8</u>. $17 - 9 = 8$. The second answer choice is correct because you can check your answer by adding the 9 and the 8, which gives you 17.

STOP

1
$$410$$
$$+ 62$$

482   472   358   348   NH
○   ○   ○   ○   ○

2 $13 - 8 = \square$

  8   7   6   5   NH
  ○   ○   ○   ○   ○

3 $5 + 2 + 9 = \square$

17   16   15   14   NH
○   ○   ○   ○   ○

4 $24 + 13 = \square$

11   21   37   47   NH
○   ○   ○   ○   ○

5 $8 + 7 = \square$

  1   14   16   25   NH
  ○   ○   ○   ○   ○

6
$$51$$
$$- 17$$

_____

_____

_____

_____

STOP

Directions: Darken the circle for the correct answer. If the correct answer is not given, darken the circle NH (Not Here). If there are no circles, write the answer on the lines.

1 There were 13 bees in a garden. Six bees flew away. How many bees were left?

13  6

6	7	9	29	NH
○	○	○	○	○

2 Mr. Lopez picks 27 apples on Monday. He picks 8 apples on Tuesday. How many apples does he pick in all?

27 8

_____

_____

_____

3 Anton went to the zoo. He saw eight giraffes in the morning and three more in the afternoon. How many giraffes did Anton see?

8 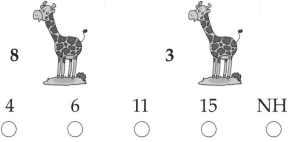 3

4	6	11	15	NH
○	○	○	○	○

4 Keesha grew 32 red roses and 16 yellow roses. How many roses did Keesha grow?

32  16

16	26	48	58	NH
○	○	○	○	○

5 What number makes this number sentence true?

$$7 + 5 = \square$$

12	11	3	2	NH
○	○	○	○	○

6 Lina works at a hot dog stand. She cooked 80 hot dogs. She sold 67 hot dogs. How many hot dogs does she have left?

80  67

147	137	27	17	NH
○	○	○	○	○

7 Bob collects comic books. He had 614 comic books. Then he bought 44 more comic books. How many comic books does he have in all?

614  44

1,054	1,008	658	638	618
○	○	○	○	○

GO ON ➡

8

$$14$$
$$-\ 8$$

22   12   7   6   NH

○   ○   ○   ○   ○

---

9 $39 + 20 = \square$

69   59   29   19   NH

○   ○   ○   ○   ○

10

$$76$$
$$+\ 8$$

68   74   78   84   NH

○   ○   ○   ○   ○

11

$$25$$
$$10$$
$$+\ 13$$

58   52   48   38   NH

○   ○   ○   ○   ○

12

$$61$$
$$-\ 35$$

26   36   86   96   NH

○   ○   ○   ○   ○

13

$$417$$
$$-\ 12$$

439   429   425   405   NH

○   ○   ○   ○   ○

---

14 $9 + \square = 12$

2   3   4   5   NH

○   ○   ○   ○   ○

15

$$45$$
$$-\ 8$$

_____

_____

_____

_____

16

$$515$$
$$+\ 46$$

561   551   461   451   NH

○   ○   ○   ○   ○

---

17 $15 - 6 = \square$

7   8   10   11   NH

○   ○   ○   ○   ○

STOP

Directions: Darken the circle for the correct answer. If the correct answer is not given, darken the circle NH (Not Here). If there are no circles, write the answer on the lines.

1 Which number is between 72 and 95?

72		95

43   71   89   96

○   ○   ○   ○

---

2 What number is in the ones place?

294   0   2   4   9

○   ○   ○   ○

---

3 Which number names the greatest amount?

156   198   220   314

○   ○   ○   ○

---

4 Which number is the same as six hundred ninety-two?

60,092   6,092   6,902   692

○   ○   ○   ○

GO ON ➤

5 Write the number that is one hundred more than five hundred thirty-eight.

538 _____
_____
_____
_____

6 Write the number that is missing in the pattern.

_____
_____
_____
_____

7 What number makes the number sentence true?

23 + 17 = ☐ + 23

| 6 | 17 | 32 | 40 |
| ○ | ○ | ○ | ○ |

8 Marta counts shirts. She begins with 13. Which shirt does Marta count as number 22?

13   14   15   ○   ○ ○   ○

GO ON ➡

9 Which fraction tells the part of the triangle that is shaded?

$\frac{1}{2}$ $\frac{1}{3}$ $\frac{1}{4}$ $\frac{2}{1}$

○   ○   ○   ○

10 Which picture shows one-quarter of the buttons shaded?

○   ○   ○   ○

11 Who is tallest?

Name	Height
Jimmy	45 in.
Ming	48 in.
Ralph	52 in.
Anna	60 in.

Jimmy   **Ming**   **Ralph**   **Anna**

○   ○   ○   ○

12 Which shape comes next in the pattern?

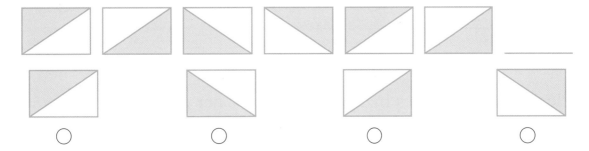

○   ○   ○   ○

GO ON ➡

Animals at Walker Park

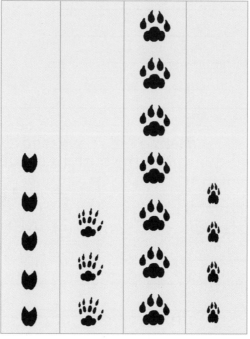

1 paw = 1 animal

Deer   Raccoon   Fox   Rabbit

13 What animal does Walker Park have only three of?

Deer   Raccoon   Fox   Rabbit
○   ○   ○   ○

14 How many foxes are there at Walker Park?

_____

_____

_____

_____

15 The clocks show the times Inga starts and ends her piano lesson. How long does her lesson last?

_____

_____

_____

_____

GO ON ▶

16 Which shape will NOT match exactly when folded on the dotted line?

○　　　　　○　　　　　○　　　　　○

17 Fred cut a shape from the card at the beginning of the row. Which shape did Fred cut out?

 |

○　　　　　○　　　　　○　　　　　○

18 Use an inch ruler. How long is this toy bus in inches?

　　7　　　　　　4　　　　　　3　　　　　　2

　　○　　　　　　○　　　　　　○　　　　　　○

19 Alice picks a card without looking. What letter is she most likely to pick?

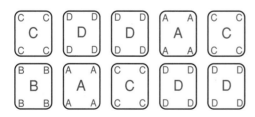

A　　　B　　　C　　　D

○　　　○　　　○　　　○

GO ON ➡

20 Which piece of chalk is the longest?

    ○   ○   ○   ○

---

21 What is the value of these coins?

30¢	15¢	11¢	6¢
○	○	○	○

---

22 Which month is this spinner least likely to land on?

_____

_____

_____

_____

---

23 What unit is best to use to measure the amount of juice in a jar?

Pounds	Teaspoons	Inches	Ounces
○	○	○	○

GO ON ➡

24 Jenna is thinking of one of these numbers. Her number is inside the square and outside the circle. Her number is odd. What is Jenna's number?

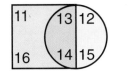

16	15	13	11
○	○	○	○

---

25 Kyle is thinking of a number between 20 and 30. The sum of the digits is 8. Which is Kyle's number?

24	26	28	29
○	○	○	○

---

26 There are 16 children on a bus. Five more children get on the bus. Which number sentence shows how to find the total number of children on the bus?

○ $16 - 5 = \square$

○ $16 - \square = 5$

○ $16 + 5 = \square$

○ $5 + \square = 16$

LANGUAGE

PREWRITING, COMPOSING, AND EDITING

Directions: Darken the circle for the correct answer, or write the answer on the blank lines.

Sample A

Max is at summer camp. He will write a letter to his family telling about his favorite camp activities. Look at the three boxes below "Letter to My Family." Which idea will Max NOT write about in his letter?

Letter to My Family		
The food at camp is good.	I like to sail in the morning.	We have fun swimming when it is hot.
○	○	○

THINK IT THROUGH You should have darkened the circle for the <u>first</u> choice. The answer is <u>The food at camp is good.</u> Adam wanted to write about activities in his letter. This is an idea.

🛑 STOP

Soccer Fun

Soccer is my favorite sport.
I like to run up and down the field.
Sometimes the ball I take away from the other team.
It is fun when I score a goal.

1 Read "Soccer Fun." Which of these sentences should be written next?

○ I play soccer after school.

○ My mother watches me play soccer.

○ Everyone cheers for me.

2 Look at the sentence in "Soccer Fun" that reads <u>Sometimes the ball I take away from the other team</u>. Is this sentence written correctly? Choose the way it should be written, or choose <u>Correct the way it is</u>.

○ The ball I take away sometimes from the other team.

○ Sometimes I take the ball away from the other team.

○ Correct the way it is.

3 Leila's teacher asked the students in the class to write a story about their favorite sport. Leila likes to play soccer. She decided to write about soccer. What should Leila do before she begins writing her story?

○ watch a soccer game

○ draw a picture of herself playing soccer

○ make a list of reasons she likes soccer

GO ON

4 Why will Leila write a story about soccer?

_____

_____

_____

_____

_____

_____

_____

TEST TIP

To answer question 4, you may need to reread the information about Leila in question 3.

GO ON ➡

Here is what Leila wrote in her story.

> The name of my team is the Panthers.
>
> We practice two times each week.
>
> To warm up, we <u>running</u> around the field.
>
>   **(1)**
>
> We also <u>kick</u> the ball to each other.
>
>   **(2)**
>
> My best friends are on my team.
>
> We have so much fun together.

5 Look at the underlined word with the number 2 under it. Did Leila use the right word? Choose the word that Leila should have used, or choose <u>Correct the way it is.</u>

kicking   kicked   Correct the way it is.
○   ○   ○

6 Look at the underlined word with the number 1 under it. Did Leila use the right word? Choose the word that Leila should have used, or choose <u>Correct the way it is.</u>

ran   run   Correct the way it is.
○   ○   ○

7 Dinah's family went on a trip. When Dinah got home, she made a book telling about the things she had seen and done on her trip. She is not sure how to spell the word <u>visit</u>. She will look it up in the dictionary. Which of these words will probably be on the same page as the word <u>visit</u>?

van   train   water
○   ○   ○

GO ON

8 Look at the three boxes below "A Book about My Trip." Dinah is deciding what to write in her book. Which idea will Dinah NOT write about in her book?

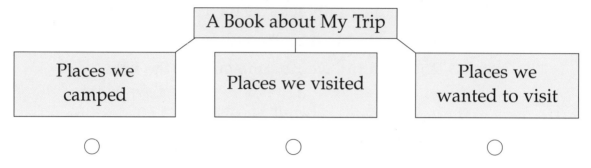

A Book about My Trip

Places we camped	Places we visited	Places we wanted to visit
○	○	○

TEST TIP

To answer question 8, you may need to remember the reason Dinah is writing her book. Look at the information about Dinah in question 7. Ask yourself, "Why is Dinah writing?" Your answer will help you find the idea that Dinah will NOT include in her book.

9 Dinah put this Table of Contents at the beginning of her book. What did Dinah write about on page 27?

Table of Contents

1. The Beach............page 5
2. The Mountains.....page 16
3. The Desert..........page 27

rocks   oceans   cactus
○   ○   ○

GO ON ➡

Here is one part of the story Dinah wrote.

> We saw a very tall cactus in the desert.
> We asked a park ranger about it.
> The park ranger's name was <u>Mr. elkhorn</u>.
> (1)
> He said, "<u>A flower</u> will bloom on the cactus after it rains."
> (2)

10 Look at the underlined words with the number 1 under them. Did Dinah capitalize these words correctly? Write your answer for the way Dinah should write the underlined words.

_____

_____

_____

_____

11 Look at the underlined words with the number 2 under them. Did Dinah capitalize these words correctly? Choose the words that show the correct capitalization, or choose <u>Correct the way it is</u>.

A Flower   a flower   Correct the way it is.
○   ○   ○

GO ON

Here is one part of Dinah's finished story.

<u>Travel Fun</u>

My family went on a trip in June.
We slept in a tent every night.
My father cooked over a campfire.
We sang songs in school.
We went to many interesting places.

12 Which sentence does not belong in this story?

○ My family went on a trip in June.

○ My father cooked over a campfire.

○ We sang songs in school.

13 Dinah wants to tell about a beach she visited. Which of these sentences would she probably write?

○ We had a picnic in the park.

○ The huge waves crashed against the white sand.

○ I bought some colorful postcards.

TEST TIP

Remember that the ideas in a story or paragraph should all tell about the main idea. To answer question 12, find the sentence that does not tell about Dinah's trip with her family.

STOP

Directions: Darken the circle for the underlined word that is NOT spelled correctly.

| TRY THIS | Look at each of the underlined words carefully and say each of these words silently to yourself. Decide which words you know are spelled correctly. Then look at the other words to make your choice. |

Sample A

The <u>magical</u> king <u>granted</u> the shoemaker three <u>wishs</u>.
    ○   ○   ○

| THINK IT THROUGH | You should have darkened the circle for the last underlined word. <u>Wishs</u> is the word that is not spelled correctly. Wishes is |

spelled w-i-s-h-e-s.

STOP

1 The car <u>started</u> <u>slideing</u> on the icy <u>highway</u>.
    ○   ○   ○

2 The <u>wave</u> <u>carryed</u> the shell onto the <u>beach</u>.
   ○   ○   ○

3 <u>Please</u> <u>sit</u> on the <u>char</u>.
  ○ ○   ○

4 Carley <u>loves</u> to <u>read</u> <u>storys</u> about pirates.
    ○   ○ ○

5 The <u>puppy</u> was sitting up and <u>beging</u> for a <u>treat</u>.
   ○   ○   ○

GO ON

6   The horse tryed to eat my carrot.
     ○   ○   ○

7   My uncle was swiming in the ocean.
     ○   ○   ○

8   The garden is filled with menny pretty flowers.
     ○   ○   ○

9   We will go two the movies on Tuesday.
       ○   ○   ○

10   I heard the loud trane whistle.
    ○   ○   ○

11   The ice finally stopped driping.
     ○   ○   ○

12   The king and the queen walked togethir.
    ○   ○   ○

13   My best frend knows lots of funny riddles.
     ○   ○   ○

14   I would like to have a milion dollars.
   ○   ○   ○

STOP

Sample A

The school newspaper was looking for stories about people who worked in the town. Heather's father is a police officer. Heather decided to write a story about her father.

Look at the three boxes below "Writing a Story." What should Heather do before writing her story?

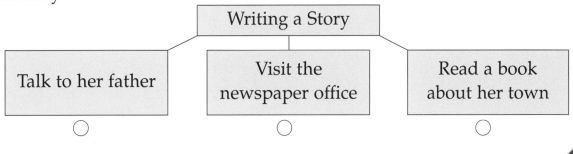

Writing a Story

Talk to her father	Visit the newspaper office	Read a book about her town
○	○	○

STOP

1 What should Heather do <u>before</u> she talks to her father?

   ○ Ride in a police car

   ○ Watch a movie about police officers

   ○ Make a list of questions to ask her father

GO ON

Here is the story Heather wrote.

> ### A Police Officer's Job
>
> My father is a police officer.
> He has an important job.
> My bike has a flat tire.
> He helps people who are hurt.
> Sometimes he directs cars.

2 Which of the sentences does NOT belong in Heather's story? Write the sentence that does NOT belong in this story.

_____

_____

_____

Randy's teacher asked the students to write a story about something they would like to do when they get older. Randy likes to read stories about traveling in space. He also likes to study the stars and the planets through his telescope.

He wants to take a trip to the moon when he is older. He wants to learn more about the moon before he writes his story. So he got a book from the library. This is the Table of Contents in the book Randy found at the library.

Table of Contents

3 When Randy looks at page 2, what will he read about?

- ○ the big holes on the moon
- ○ the miles between the Earth and moon
- ○ the first person who visited the moon

GO ON ➡

4 Which page should Randy turn to if he wants to read about people who have visited the moon?

_____

_____

_____

_____

_____

_____

_____

_____

_____

_____

TEST TIP

Remember that a Table of Contents helps you find information in a book. The chapter titles tell you what each chapter discusses. Read each chapter title carefully and think about what kind of information you would find in the chapter.

Here is one part of Randy's story.

> The big holes <u>is</u> called craters.
> **(1)**
> I would <u>like</u> to go inside a crater.
> **(2)**
> It would be like walking inside a cave.

5 Look at the word with the number 1 under it. Did Randy use the right word? Should he write <u>are</u>, <u>were</u>, or is the word correct the way it is? Write the word Randy should use.

_____

_____

6 Look at the word with the number 2 under it. Did Randy use the right word? Choose the correct word or choose <u>Correct the way it is</u>.

○ liking

○ likes

○ Correct the way it is.

GO ON ➡

Here is another part of Randy's story.

> ## Seeing the Moon
>
> The moon is very far away.
> I would like to ride in a spaceship to get there.
> A spacesuit I could wear to keep me safe.
> I would like to see what is in the moon's big holes.

7 Which of these sentences would Randy probably write at the beginning of his story?

- ○ When I get older, I want to visit the moon.
- ○ The big holes are deep.
- ○ A spaceship moves very fast.

8 Look at the sentence that reads <u>A spacesuit I could wear to keep me safe</u>. Did Randy write this sentence correctly? Choose the correct sentence or choose <u>Correct the way it is.</u>

- ○ A spacesuit to keep me safe I could wear.
- ○ I could wear a spacesuit to keep me safe.
- ○ Correct the way it is.

GO ON ⮞

Shakia is going to visit her Aunt Donna. Aunt Donna lives on a farm. Shakia decided to write a letter to let her aunt know when she would arrive. Here is the first part of Shakia's letter.

Dear Aunt Donna,

Thank you for inviting me to visit.
The farm this summer.
<u>May I stay for two weeks</u>
I want to learn how to take care of animals.

9 Which group of words in Shakia's letter does NOT make a complete sentence? Write the words here.

_____

_____

_____

_____

_____

GO ON ➡

10 Which sentence should Shakia write next in her letter?

○ I want to milk and feed the cows and chickens.

○ The cows I want to milk and the chickens I want to feed.

○ I want to milk the cows and feed the chickens.

11 Look at the underlined sentence in Shakia's letter. Which punctuation mark should Shakia place at the end of the underlined sentence? Choose the word that ends with the correct punctuation.

weeks?   weeks.   weeks!

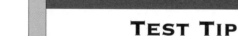

TEST TIP

To answer question 10, find the sentence that tells a clear idea. Notice that the first sentence is confusing. You cannot milk a chicken! Read the other two choices carefully. Choose the sentence that is complete and clear.

GO ON ▶

Here is the second part of Shakia's letter.

I am leaving this <u>tuesday</u>.
        (1)
<u>Will you pick me up at the bus station</u>
(2)
I can't wait to see you.
Love,
Shakia

12 Look at the underlined sentence with a number 2 under it. Which punctuation mark should Shakia place at the end of this sentence? Write the punctuation mark here.

_____

_____

_____

13 Look at the underlined word with the number 1 under it. Did Shakia capitalize this word correctly? Choose the correct way to capitalize this word, or choose <u>Correct the way it is.</u>

Tues Day   Tuesday   Correct the way it is.
   ○   ○   ○

TEST TIP

Remember some rules about capitalization. Always capitalize the first word in a sentence. Always capitalize the names of months and days of the week. Always capitalize people's names.

GO ON

Directions: Darken the circle for the underlined word that is NOT spelled correctly.

14   Wher does your family like to swim?
     ○   ○   ○

15   Go down the hall and tern to the right.
         ○   ○   ○

16   The frog was hoping along the path.
         ○   ○   ○

17   Your dog is very frendly.
     ○   ○   ○

18   Watr the plants before you leave.
     ○   ○   ○

19   We saw many interesting butterflys in the woods.
                    ○   ○   ○

20   Grandpa gave me three big pushs on the swing.
                    ○   ○   ○

21   The boxs were stacked in the corner.
         ○   ○   ○

STOP

READING COMPREHENSION

Directions: Darken the circle next to the best answer.

Sample A

Going to School

Jim lives on a farm. The farm is five miles from his school. He rides a bus to school because he lives too far to walk.

How does Jim get to school?

- ○ He walks.
- ○ His mom drives him in a car.
- ○ He rides a horse.
- ○ He rides a bus.

STOP

Curtis's Jobs

Mr. Ford asked Curtis to do some jobs. Curtis likes to help Mr. Ford. Mr. Ford always gives him a dollar for each job.

Curtis got a hose and soap. He washed the windows, the doors, and the trunk. Finally, Curtis washed the tires.

When Curtis was done, Mr. Ford looked at the car. "You worked very hard. I will give you two dollars," said Mr. Ford. "Tomorrow morning you will need a rake. I will pay you two more dollars if you do as well."

"Thank you, Mr. Ford. I will be back tomorrow," said Curtis.

1 Why did Mr. Ford give Curtis two dollars?

- ○ Curtis did a good job.
- ○ Curtis wanted to buy candy.
- ○ Curtis did two jobs.
- ○ Curtis needed a loan.

2 What did Curtis wash?

- ○ a bike
- ○ a car
- ○ a house
- ○ a dog

3 Curtis will go to Mr. Ford's—

- ○ in the middle of the night.
- ○ in the morning.
- ○ in the afternoon.
- ○ in the evening.

4 You can tell that tomorrow Curtis will—

- ○ trim trees.
- ○ mow the grass.
- ○ sweep the sidewalk.
- ○ rake leaves.

GO ON

Tia's Ride

   Tia lived in the mountains with her family and a donkey named Clyde. Tia and Clyde went everywhere together. Clyde was a good mountain climber. He never slipped or fell. Tia was not as good at climbing. She had to be careful where she walked. When the path was dangerous, Tia would ride on Clyde's back. Tia rode the donkey on the path down to the stream. There were fish swimming in the stream. Tia and the donkey splashed in the cool, clear water. Later when they returned home, Tia gave Clyde a pail of food. Then Tia went inside for dinner.

5 **The boxes show things that happened in the story.**

Tia rode the donkey down to the stream.		Tia gave Clyde a pail of food.
1	2	3

What belongs in Box 2?

- ○ Tia went inside the house for dinner.
- ○ Clyde slipped on the path to the stream.
- ○ Tia and Clyde caught some fish.
- ○ Tia and Clyde splashed in the water.

6 **What is another good name for this story?**

- ○ "Walking in the Mountains"
- ○ "A Girl and Her Donkey"
- ○ "How to Train a Donkey"
- ○ "Fishing in Mountain Streams"

7 **Where did Tia and Clyde live?**

- ○ on a farm
- ○ in the mountains
- ○ in the city
- ○ by a store

8 **Why did Tia ride the donkey to the stream?**

- ○ The donkey was tired.
- ○ The path was long.
- ○ The path was dangerous.
- ○ The donkey hurt his foot.

GO ON➡

Telling a Tree's Age

Have you ever looked closely at the top of a tree stump? You might see many rings. The rings are often narrow near the center of the tree and wider near the outside.

Each ring stands for a year of growth. As a tree grows, more and more rings are added. After the tree has been cut down, you can see the rings on the stump. The number of rings tells the tree's age. The more rings you count, the older the tree is.

9   The rings on a tree stump are all—

○   the same size.

○   narrow.

○   wide.

○   different sizes.

10   How do you find the age of a tree?

○   see if the rings are wide or narrow

○   count the leaves

○   count the rings

○   see how tall it is

11   What can you say about a tree with many rings?

○   It is old.

○   It is young.

○   It is tall.

○   It needs water.

12   What is the best way to find out more about trees?

○   Recycle paper.

○   Plant a garden.

○   Read a book about the life of a tree.

○   Read a list of things made from wood.

GO ON➡

Peanut Butter and Banana Bun

You will need:
1 hot dog bun
1 tablespoon peanut butter
1 banana

Follow these steps:

1. Spread the peanut butter on the bun.

2. Peel the banana and set it in the bun.

3. Slice the bun in half and serve one half per person.

If you like, you can add an optional topping. Sprinkle on coconut or pour on a little bit of honey. Or, think of your own special topping. "Peanut Butter and Banana Bun" is great with or without toppings.

13 **Right after you spread the peanut butter, you should—**

○ slice the bun in half.

○ serve the bun.

○ spread butter.

○ add the banana.

14 **"Peanut Butter and Banana Bun" is most like a—**

○ soup.

○ sandwich.

○ salad.

○ cookie.

15 **How many servings will each banana and bun make?**

○ four

○ three

○ two

○ one

16 **In these directions, optional means—**

○ something you may or may not do.

○ something you must do.

○ something you cook.

○ something you taste.

GO ON

Maciel Visits the Lighthouse

Maciel and her mother went to the beach in Cape May, New Jersey, last summer. One day they went to see the lighthouse.

Maciel and her mom climbed to the top of the tower. From there they could see very far. They saw miles of ocean and beach. It was a beautiful sight.

Mr. Foreman, the man who works at the lighthouse, told Maciel and her mom all about it. The Cape May Lighthouse is over 130 years old. It is all white, and it is 165 feet tall. It has a very strong light. Mr. Foreman said that the lighthouse is still very important to sailors. Sailors can see its light from 24 miles out at sea. The light helps ships come into Delaware Bay.

Mr. Foreman told Maciel and her mom how the sailors take care of the lighthouse. Their <u>tasks</u> are cleaning the light and making sure it is working. Mr. Foreman said that many people who live in Cape May also help keep the lighthouse in good shape. They want others to enjoy it for many years to come. Some people help fix parts of the lighthouse. Some clean the lighthouse. Others paint it.

Maciel can't wait to visit the lighthouse again next summer. She wants Mr. Foreman to show the lighthouse to her best friend, Josephine.

GO ON➧

17 In this story, Mr. Foreman is—

○ a sailor who cleans the light at the lighthouse.

○ the man who works at the lighthouse.

○ Maciel's father.

○ Maciel's best friend.

18 Why is it important to take care of the lighthouse?

○ so that Mr. Foreman can have a job

○ so people can look out of the tower

○ so that sailors at sea can find land

○ so that visitors have a place to go

19 How does Maciel feel at the end of the story?

○ She is tired and wants to leave.

○ She wants to live in the lighthouse.

○ She worries that sailors do not take care of the lighthouse.

○ She is excited about the visit and wants to come back.

20 What does the word <u>tasks</u> in this story mean?

○ jobs

○ friends

○ joys

○ games

21 This story was written mainly to—

○ tell about big ships.

○ ask for help in fixing the lighthouse.

○ tell about a special lighthouse.

○ tell how to build a lighthouse.

22 Which of these is another good name for this story?

○ "Maciel and Her Mom Have Fun at the Beach"

○ "A Visit to a Lighthouse"

○ "Sailing in Delaware Bay"

○ "How to Take Care of a Lighthouse"

GO ON➡

All about Ducks

Ducks are interesting birds. They can fly in the air, and they can walk on the land. Mostly, they like to swim in the water. Ponds and streams are full of good things to eat. There are little fish, big bugs, and tender plants. Ducks can swim very fast. They have big feet for pushing the water. They cannot walk as fast as they swim. On land, ducks must be careful. A fox or a wolf might catch them.

23 **What is another good name for this story?**

- ○ "Why Ducks Like Water"
- ○ "Why Ducks Fly"
- ○ "What Ducks Like to Eat"
- ○ "How to Catch a Duck"

24 **How do big feet help ducks?**

- ○ Big feet help them walk fast.
- ○ Big feet help them catch bugs.
- ○ Big feet help them push the water.
- ○ Big feet help them hide from foxes.

25 **What is something that ducks do not do?**

- ○ swim
- ○ climb
- ○ walk
- ○ fly

26 **Why might a fox want to catch a duck?**

- ○ to eat it
- ○ to play with it
- ○ to see who is faster
- ○ to learn to swim

STOP

READING VOCABULARY

Directions: Darken the circle under the compound word.

Directions: Darken the circle under the word that shows the correct plural noun.

1   sorry   circus   ladybug
    ○   ○   ○

2   open   inside   under
    ○   ○   ○

3   before   something   story
    ○   ○   ○

4   balloon   myself   making
    ○   ○   ○

5   quiet   again   cupcake
    ○   ○   ○

6   penny   wishing   suitcase
    ○   ○   ○

7   more than one <u>tent</u>
    tens   tents   tentes
    ○   ○   ○

8   more than one <u>farmer</u>
    farmeres   farmer   farmers
    ○   ○   ○

9   more than one <u>box</u>
    boxes   boxs   boxies
    ○   ○   ○

10 more than one <u>cherry</u>
    cherries   cherrys   cherryes
    ○   ○   ○

11 more than one <u>leaf</u>
    leafes   leafs   leaves
    ○   ○   ○

12 more than one <u>animal</u>
    animales   animals   animalls
    ○   ○   ○

GO ON ➡

Directions: Darken the circle under the word that has the same sound or sounds as the underlined part of the first word in each row.

13   n<u>ear</u>

  rocky   speed   knee
    ○   ○   ○

14   t<u>i</u>me

  shy   lip   feel
    ○   ○   ○

15   str<u>o</u>ng

  toe   mouth   jaw
    ○   ○   ○

16   b<u>ow</u>

  front   road   should
    ○   ○   ○

17   v<u>oi</u>ce

  lost   enjoy   who
    ○   ○   ○

18   h<u>o</u>pped

  locking   only   worn
    ○   ○   ○

Directions: Darken the circle under the word that rhymes with the first word in each row.

19   rain

  plate   play   plane
    ○   ○   ○

20   speed

  feet   knee   bead
    ○   ○   ○

21   eight

  gate   day   note
    ○   ○   ○

22   hope

  no   soap   hop
    ○   ○   ○

23   chair

  chore   cheer   pear
    ○   ○   ○

24   night

  kite   kit   cat
    ○   ○   ○

GO ON➡

Directions: Darken the circle next to the answer that best completes the sentence.

25 <u>Closer</u> means—

○ nearer

○ around

○ away

○ farther

26 To <u>whisper</u> is to—

○ talk softly

○ play a game

○ run a race

○ sing loudly

27 To <u>hunt</u> means to—

○ talk

○ sit on

○ break

○ look for

28 If something is <u>still</u>, it is not—

○ sorry

○ strong

○ moving

○ sleeping

29 A <u>carpet</u> is most like a—

○ chair

○ window

○ rug

○ truck

30 <u>Foolish</u> means—

○ next

○ silly

○ last

○ sleepy

31 A <u>subway</u> is a kind of—

○ train

○ walk

○ book

○ number

32 A <u>chuckle</u> is a kind of—

○ song

○ laugh

○ story

○ river

33 A <u>dish</u> is most like a—

○ desk

○ plate

○ pillow

○ cup

GO ON➡

34 | Is it my turn to <u>bat</u>?

In which sentence does <u>bat</u> mean the same as it does above?

○ A <u>bat</u> is an interesting animal.

○ Please hand me the other <u>bat</u>.

○ Let's <u>bat</u> some ideas around.

○ I will <u>bat</u> the ball to the fence.

35 | Can you <u>float</u> on your back in the water?

In which sentence does <u>float</u> mean the same as it does above?

○ Dad made me a root beer <u>float</u>.

○ Which <u>float</u> did you like?

○ The small boat began to <u>float</u> on the lake.

○ Carol had a <u>float</u> to play with in the pool.

36 | We watched the sun <u>dip</u> below the trees.

Write a sentence in which <u>dip</u> means the same as it does above.

_____

_____

_____

_____

_____

37 | We climbed over the steep <u>bank</u> to the lake.

In which sentence does <u>bank</u> mean the same as it does above?

○ My <u>bank</u> is in a big, gray building.

○ She has a new purple piggy <u>bank</u>.

○ Don't <u>bank</u> on his promise.

○ Flowers grow along the river <u>bank</u>.

GO ON➡

Directions: Darken the circle next to the answer that best completes the sentence or fill in the answer on the lines.

38 That painting is <u>famous</u> all over the world. <u>Famous</u> means—

○ well-known

○ cheap

○ new

○ funny

39 The bridge is closely <u>modeled</u> after one in England. <u>Modeled</u> means—

○ paid

○ painted

○ added

○ copied

40 I tried but I couldn't <u>budge</u> the heavy box. <u>Budge</u> means—

○ buy

○ pack

○ move

○ seal

41 It is dangerous to play with matches because they could <u>harm</u> someone. <u>Harm</u> means—

○ look

○ hurt

○ help

○ hear

42 He will <u>compose</u> a new song for the movie. What does <u>compose</u> mean?

_____

_____

_____

_____

43 Her truck has <u>tough</u> tires that last a long time. <u>Tough</u> means—

○ little

○ strong

○ many

○ old

44 We tried to be quiet and <u>conceal</u> the surprise. <u>Conceal</u> means—

○ hide

○ miss

○ show

○ end

STOP

PART 1: MATH PROBLEM SOLVING

Directions: Darken the circle for the correct answer, or write the answer on the lines.

1 Which brush is the fifth brush from the bucket?

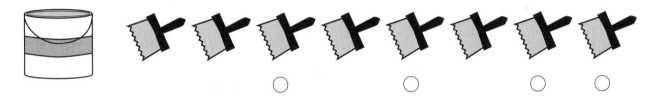

○   ○   ○   ○

---

2 Which number means two hundreds, three tens, and four ones?

    234   2,034   20,304   200,304

    ○   ○   ○   ○

---

3 Which number is between 43 and 68?

43		68

    39   41   55   71

    ○   ○   ○   ○

---

4 Which number is the same as one hundred seventy-three?

    173   1,730   1,073   10,073

    ○   ○   ○   ○

GO ON ➡

5 How many marbles are there in this picture?

_____

_____

_____

_____

6 What is another way to show four times three?

4 × 3 | 4 + 3   3 + 3 + 3 + 3   4 − 3   4 + 4 + 4

       ○   ○   ○   ○

7 Write the number that is one hundred more than eight hundred twenty-one.

| 821 |

_____

_____

_____

_____

8 Which tent has an even number on it?

    ○   ○   ○   ○

GO ON➡

9 What number makes this number sentence true?

$4 + \square = 4$

    0 ○   1 ○   4 ○   8 ○

---

10 Which number sentence can describe this picture?

○ $10 + 9 = 19$ ○ $10 - 8 = 2$

○ $9 - 1 = 8$ ○ $9 + 1 = 10$

---

11 Which picture shows three-fourths of the flags shaded?

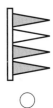 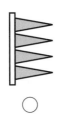 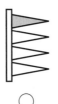 

  ○   ○   ○   ○

---

12 What number is missing in this pattern?

36	33		27	24

25 ○   30 ○   34 ○   35 ○

GO ON ➡

13 Which shape is NOT divided into fourths?

            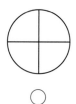

○   ○   ○   ○

---

14 Felipe is counting stamps. He begins at 73. Which stamp will Felipe count as number 83?

73   74   75   ○   ○ ○   ○

---

15 Which fraction tells what part of the circle is shaded?

$\frac{1}{4}$ $\frac{1}{5}$ $\frac{4}{5}$ $\frac{4}{1}$

○   ○   ○   ○

GO ON➡

Students Playing Musical Instruments							
Piano	🎹	🎹	🎹	🎹			
French Horn	📯	📯					
Trumpet	🎺	🎺	🎺				
Guitar	🎸	🎸	🎸	🎸	🎸	🎸	🎸 🎸
Drums	🥁	🥁	🥁	🥁	🥁		

Each instrument = 1 student

16 How many students play guitar?

    4   5   8   9
    ○   ○   ○   ○

17 How many more students play drums than trumpets?

_____

_____

_____

_____

18 Carly folded a card and cut out a shape. Which shape did Carly cut out?

    |

              ○   ○   ○   ○

GO ON ➡

19 Which player scored the fewest number of points?

Lou	Laurie	Alex	Patti
ꜱ꜠꜠ ꜱ꜠꜠	ꜱ꜠꜠	/	///

_____

_____

_____

_____

20 Which pencil is the shortest?

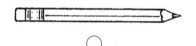  

　○　　　　　○　　　　　○　　　　　○

21 Which shape is exactly the same as the shape at the left?

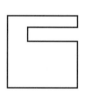 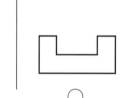 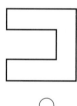

　　　　　○　　　　○　　　　○　　　　○

22 Tina puts these shapes in a box. She picks one without looking. Which shape is she most likely to pick?

　　　　　　　　○　　　　○　　　　○　　　　○

GO ON➡

23 What time is shown on this clock?

2:15 ○   3:15 ○   2:45 ○   3:45 ○

---

24 Which shape will not match exactly when it is folded on the dotted line?

   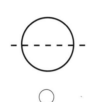   

○   ○   ○   ○

---

25 Use a centimeter ruler. How long is the pen in centimeters?

5 ○   7 ○   8 ○   9 ○

---

26 What is the value of these coins?

6¢ ○   11¢ ○   26¢ ○   30¢ ○

STOP

Sample A

$$102 - 12 = \square$$

78	80	82	90	NH
○	○	○	○	○

STOP

For questions 1–17, darken the circle for the correct answer. If the correct answer is not here, darken the circle for NH. If no choices are given, write the answer.

1

$$\begin{array}{r} 53 \\ 4 \\ + 21 \\ \hline \end{array}$$

77	78	87	88	NH
○	○	○	○	○

2

$$\begin{array}{r} 400 \\ - 50 \\ \hline \end{array}$$

150	300	350	450	NH
○	○	○	○	○

3

$$8 + \square = 16$$

5	7	9	11	NH
○	○	○	○	○

4

$$\begin{array}{r} 28 \\ + 87 \\ \hline \end{array}$$

105	115	151	155	NH
○	○	○	○	○

5

$$\begin{array}{r} 54 \\ - 8 \\ \hline \end{array}$$

42	44	46	48	NH
○	○	○	○	○

6

$$\begin{array}{r} 307 \\ - 125 \\ \hline \end{array}$$

182	187	282	432	NH
○	○	○	○	○

7

$$\begin{array}{r} 99 \\ + 98 \\ \hline \end{array}$$

_____

_____

_____

_____

8

$$\begin{array}{r} 71 \\ - 9 \\ \hline \end{array}$$

_____

_____

_____

_____

GO ON

9

$$528$$
$$+\ 82$$

446   600   610   688   NH
○   ○   ○   ○   ○

10

$$777 - 333 = \square$$

4   44   444   555   NH
○   ○   ○   ○   ○

11

$$911$$
$$-\ 903$$

7   14   80   108   NH
○   ○   ○   ○   ○

12

$$456$$
$$-\ 321$$

135   153   333   777   NH
○   ○   ○   ○   ○

13

$$45 + 4 + 12 = \square$$

49   57   61   97   NH
○   ○   ○   ○   ○

14

$$82 - \square = 75$$

_____

_____

_____

_____

---

15 There were 34 students on a school bus. At the first stop, 5 students got off the bus. How many students were still on the bus?

25   29   30   39   NH
○   ○   ○   ○   ○

---

16 Pam and Rosa ran a race. Pam ran the race in 58 seconds. Rosa ran the race in 47 seconds. How many seconds faster was Rosa?

9   10   11   12   NH
○   ○   ○   ○   ○

---

17 Bonnie works on a big puzzle. She has put 119 pieces together. There are 131 more pieces to put together. How many pieces are there in all?

200   250   300   350   NH
○   ○   ○   ○   ○

STOP

LANGUAGE

1 Ingrid was having a birthday party. She was going to write her own party invitations. This is what she first wrote.

> I <u>hope</u> to see you at my party.
> Please let me know if you can come.
>
> Your friend,
> Ingrid

Look at the underlined word. Did Ingrid use the correct word? Choose the correct word or choose <u>Correct the way it is.</u>

hoped	hoping	Correct the way it is.
○	○	○

---

2 Ingrid realized that she had to let everyone know when her party was. Here is what Ingrid added to her invitation.

> I am having a birthday party at my house.
> On Friday at two o'clock.
> We will play games.

Which group of words is NOT a complete sentence?

- ○ I am having a birthday party.
- ○ On Friday at two o'clock.
- ○ We will play games.

GO ON➡

3

Look at the three boxes below the box that reads Writing Invitations. What did Ingrid NOT write about in her invitations?

Sal's class was studying food and nutrition. The teacher asked the students to keep a diary for one week telling what kinds of foods they ate. She wanted them to find out if they ate healthy meals and snacks. Here is the first part of Sal's diary.

> **A Big Breakfast**
>
> I was hungry when I woke up.
>
> I poured a glass of milk for everyone.
>
> A glass of orange juice I also drank.
>
> Father made banana muffins.

4 Which sentence will Sal probably write next?

○ I didn't drink all of my milk.

○ I will eat an apple for a snack.

○ The muffins were so good that I ate two.

GO ON ➡

5 Look at the sentence that reads <u>A glass of orange juice I also drank</u>. Did Sal write this sentence correctly? Choose the correct sentence, or choose <u>Correct the way it is.</u>

○ I also drank a glass of orange juice.

○ I drank a glass also of orange juice.

○ Correct the way it is.

6 What did Sal do <u>before</u> he wrote in his diary?

○ ask his mother what his family will eat for dinner

○ make a list of healthy foods

○ think about the food he ate during the day

7 Why did Sal write a diary?

○ to find out if he eats good food

○ to write a food menu

○ to tell about his favorite foods

GO ON ➡

I <u>gone</u> to a friend's house for dinner.
  (1)

We ate hot dogs.

Hot dogs <u>are</u> my favorite food.
                (2)

We had salad and peas, too.

Of course, I drank another glass of milk.

8 Look at the word with the number 2 under it. Did Sal use the correct word? Choose the correct word, or choose <u>Correct the way it is.</u>

is ○   was ○   Correct the way it is. ○

9 Look at the word with the number 1 under it. Did Sal use the correct word? Choose the correct word, or choose <u>Correct the way it is.</u>

is going ○   went ○   Correct the way it is. ○

GO ON ➡

Ellen's class is learning about how people lived about 50 years ago. Her teacher asked the students to talk to a grandparent or older neighbor to get more information. Then the students are to write a story telling what they learned. Ellen talked to her grandmother.

10 Ellen is not sure how to spell the word <u>television</u>. She will look it up in the dictionary. Which word will probably be on the same page as <u>television</u>?

      hay   chicken   train

      ◯   ◯   ◯

11 Look at the three boxes under the box that says "In Grandma's Time." What will Ellen NOT write about in her story?

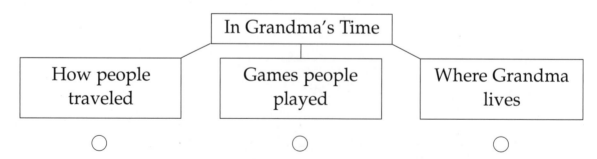

      ◯   ◯   ◯

GO ON➡

Ellen put this Table of Contents at the front of her story.

12 What did Ellen write about on page 3?

long skirts ○   milking cows ○   riding horses ○

Here is the first part of Ellen's story.

<u>When Grandma Was Young</u>

Grandma lived on a farm when she was little.

The family grew most of their own food.

They grew corn, beans, and potatoes.

Grandma shops at the store on Friday.

They had to raise cows and chickens for meat.

13 Ellen wants to tell how Grandma's family cooked food. Which sentence would she probably write next?

○ Grandma cooked food in a big black pan on a wood stove.

○ The stove made the kitchen hot in the summer.

○ Grandma helped make bread every day.

GO ON➡

14 Which of these sentences does NOT belong in Ellen's story?

○ Grandma lived on a farm when she was little.

○ They grew corn, beans, and potatoes.

○ Grandma shops at the store on Friday.

> The family could not grow everything they needed.
>
> They had to buy things like flour and sugar.
>
> "Are you ready for some fun?" Great Grandpa would ask.
> **(1)**
>
> Then the family knew it was time to go to town.
>
> They would visit mr barton's store.
> **(2)**

15 Look at the underlined words with the number 2 under them. Did Ellen capitalize these words correctly? Choose the correct words, or choose <u>Correct the way it is.</u>

mr. Barton's   Mr. Barton's   Correct the way it is.

○   ○   ○

16 Look at the underlined words with the number 1 under them. Did Ellen capitalize these words correctly? Choose the correct words, or choose <u>Correct the way it is.</u>

are you ready   Are you Ready   Correct the way it is.

○   ○   ○

GO ON➡

Kareem likes to go fishing. Every Saturday he walks to a stream near his house. One Saturday he caught a type of fish he had never seen before. Kareem went to the library to check out a book about fish. He wanted to find out what kind of fish he had caught.

17 In which part of the book should Kareem look to find out about the topics the book will discuss?

Table of contents   Title page   First chapter
       ○   ○   ○

Kareem decided to write a story about the fish he caught. Here is the first part of Kareem's story.

> A Rainbow Fish
>
> I went fishing.
>
> On Saturday morning.
>
> I caught a fish I have never seen before.

18 Kareem wanted to describe the fish he caught. Which sentence should he write?

○ Pink and blue stripes the fish had on its body.

○ On its body pink and blue stripes the fish had.

○ The fish had pink and blue stripes on its body.

GO ON

19 Which group of words does NOT make a complete sentence?

○ I went fishing.

○ On Saturday morning.

○ I caught a fish I have never seen before.

Here is the second part of Kareem's story.

I did not know what kind of fish it was.

I went to the library to look in a book.

"Where are the books about fish" I asked.
 (1)

The librarian helped me.

I found a picture of the fish.
 (2)

It was called a rainbow trout.

20 Look at the underlined word with the number 2 under it. Did Kareem use the correct word? Choose the correct word, or choose <u>Correct the way it is</u>.

finding   finds   Correct the way it is.

○   ○   ○

GO ON➡

21 Look at the underlined words with the number 1 under them. Which punctuation mark should Kareem place at the end of this sentence? Write the punctuation mark here.

_____

Directions: Darken the circle under the word that does NOT have the correct spelling.

22   Dad <u>bought</u> two new <u>leashs</u> for our <u>dog</u>.
       ○   ○   ○

23   Grover is <u>diging</u> a <u>hole</u> to bury his dog <u>bone</u>.
              ○   ○   ○

24   Angie is <u>bakeing</u> a <u>birthday</u> <u>cake</u>.
              ○   ○   ○

25   John <u>walkt</u> to the <u>store</u> to <u>buy</u> milk.
            ○   ○   ○

26   The <u>baby</u> <u>cryed</u> herself to <u>sleep</u>.
          ○   ○   ○

27   Water is <u>driping</u> off the <u>roof</u> of the <u>house</u>.
              ○   ○   ○

28   Do you <u>like</u> to eat <u>cherrys</u> for a <u>snack</u>?
            ○   ○   ○

29   We are <u>moveing</u> to <u>another</u> <u>state</u>.
              ○   ○   ○

STOP

ANSWER KEY

READING SKILLS

P. 10-11
1. B
2. C
3. B
4. B
5. A
6. B
7. B
8. A

P. 12-13
1. C
2. A
3. A
4. B
5. B
6. A
7. C
8. B

P. 14-15
1. B
2. A
3. A
4. B
5. C
6. B
7. B
8. C

P. 16-17
1. C
2. B
3. B
4. A
5. C
6. A
7. C
8. B

P. 18-19
1. C
2. C
3. C
4. B
5. A
6. C
7. B
8. A

P. 20-21
1. C
2. A
3. B
4. B
5. A
6. A
7. A
8. C

P. 22-23
1. C
2. C
3. B
4. A
5. C
6. B
7. A
8. C

P. 24-25
1. A
2. B
3. C
4. C
5. A
6. A
7. A
8. C

P. 26
Possible answers include:
1. Humans have traveled there and brought back soil to study.
2. The soil is made of rock and glass.
3. Each glass bit is about as small as a period.

P. 27
Check that you have three facts in your story.

P. 29
2, 1

P. 30-31
1. 1, 2
2. A
3. C
4. B

P. 32-33
1. 1, 2
2. B
3. A
4. B

P. 34-35
1. 2, 1
2. A
3. C
4. B

P. 36-37
1. 2, 1
2. A
3. A
4. C

P. 38-39
1. 2, 1
2. B
3. A
4. C

P. 40-41
1. 1, 2
2. C
3. A
4. B

P. 42-43
1. 2, 1
2. A
3. C
4. B

P. 44-45
1. 2, 1
2. C
3. A
4. B

P. 46
Possible answers include:
1. The frog eggs started to hatch after a week.
2. The tadpoles grew back legs in seven weeks.
3. The tadpoles grew front legs after they grew back legs.

P. 47
Check that your story is written in sequence.

Check that you have used time order words, such as first, next, and last.

P. 49
In the story on page 46, the sentences "You're really good!" and "Go ahead and try to make the big time." should be circled.

Any words that mean *to help someone* may be written on the line. Words with this meaning include *to cheer up, to support, to back,* and *to help.*

P. 50-51
1. B
2. C
3. A
4. A
5. B
6. C

P. 52-53
1. B
2. A
3. B
4. A
5. C
6. B

P. 54-55
1. B
2. C
3. C
4. B
5. C
6. B

P. 56-57
1. C
2. B
3. C
4. A
5. B
6. B

P. 58-59
1. A
2. B
3. C
4. C
5. B
6. A

P. 60-61
1. B
2. A
3. A
4. A
5. C
6. A

P. 62-63
1. B
2. A
3. B
4. C
5. A
6. A

P. 64-65
1. A
2. A
3. C
4. B
5. A
6. C

P. 66
1. afternoon
2. leaves
3. feed
4. glass
5. joke
6. loud
7. careful
8. true
9. wide
10. stood

P. 67
Possible answers include:
1. cold or snowy
2. coat or gloves
3. ball or stick
4. house or yard
5. back or tail
6. tree or bush

P. 69
Detail 1: bathtub, car
Detail 2: store
Detail 3: music while you sing a song
Detail 4: recording
Detail 5: take it home and surprise
Main Idea: Here's how you can become a singing star!

P. 70-71
1. B
2. C
3. A
4. B

P. 72-73
1. A
2. C
3. B
4. B

P. 74-75
1. B
2. A
3. B
4. C

p. 76–77
1. A
2. C
3. A
4. C

p. 78–79
1. A
2. B
3. C
4. A

p. 80–81
1. B
2. A
3. C
4. C

p. 82–83
1. B
2. B
3. C
4. A

p. 84–85
1. B
2. B
3. A
4. A

p. 86
Possible answers include:
1. Jessica McClure was lucky to be alive.
2. Not all presidents lived in the White House
3. Gail Devers trained herself to be a runner.

p. 87
Check that you underlined your main idea.
Check that you used two details.

p. 89
Clue 2: A mother whale stays by her baby for about a year.
Clue 3: A mother whale feeds her baby milk.
Conclusion: Whales take care of their babies.

p. 90–91
1. A
2. C
3. B
4. A

p 92–93
1. C
2. B
3. A
4. B

p. 94–95
1. B
2. B
3. A
4. B

p. 96–97
1. A
2. C
3. A
4. B

p. 98–99
1. C
2. B
3. C
4. A

p. 100–101
1. B
2. A
3. C
4. B

p. 102–103
1. A
2. C
3. B
4. C

p. 104–105
1. C
2. A
3. C
4. C

p. 106
Possible answers include:
1. Dorothy Kelly worked for an airline.
2. Some basketball shots are harder than others.
3. Mrs. Paz is the teacher.

p. 107
Possible answers include:
1. Tom opened the window. He said that he needed more fresh air.
2. Cody was inside his house. He watched the ball come into the house and land on the couch.
3. It was good that the window was open. If the window had been closed, the basketball might have broken it.

p. 109
Fact 2: He hadn't washed his face.
Fact 3: His shirt was wrinkled.
Fact 4: One shoelace was not tied.
Inference: Sam doesn't care about how he looks.

p. 110–111
1. C
2. A
3. A
4. B

p. 112–113
1. B
2. C
3. B
4. A

p. 114–115
1. C
2. B
3. B
4. C

p. 116–117
1. A
2. B
3. B
4. A

p. 118–119
1. C
2. C
3. A
4. A

p. 120–121
1. A
2. A
3. C
4. C

p. 122–123
1. A
2. B
3. A
4. B

p. 124–125
1. C
2. A
3. B
4. B

p. 126
Possible answers include:
1. Robert didn't have enough money to eat there.
2. Carla's book is in the copy machine at the library.
3. Koji was filling a basketball with air.

p. 127
Possible answers include:
1. Aisha was moving.
2. Aisha doesn't want to talk to the man because he doesn't seem friendly. She wants to give the man a chance. She wants to see if the man knows what he is doing.
3. Aisha is careful and shy, and she worries about things.
4. Aisha is afraid that some of her things might get broken.

SPELLING SKILLS

p. 132
1. an, after, and, am, add
2. van, flat, hand, cat, has, than, man

p. 133
1. cat
2. hand
3. add
4. after
5. man
6. an
7. than
8. has
9. am
10. flat
11. and

p. 134
Spell correctly: man, hand, an, am
Capitalize: We
Add period after: tiger

p. 135
1. My cat is stuck in a tree.
2. A man comes to help.
3. He has a ladder.
4. She jumps down and runs home.

p. 136
1. ask
2. catch, fast, matter, (have), land, that, back, last, thank, sang, black

p. 137
1. sang
2. land
3. black
4. catch
5. fast
6. have
7. ask
8. thank
9. matter
10. back
11. that

p. 138
Spell correctly: catch, That, Last, ask
Capitalize: My
Add period after: it (at the end of the fifth sentence)

p. 139
1. A camel can carry people on its back.
2. Some camels have one hump.
3. Camels can run fast.
4. They run across dry land.

p. 140
1. ten, when, bed, shelf, jet, yes, went, kept, next, end
2. says
3. said

p. 141
1. bed
2. shelf
3. when
4. jet
5. end
6. next
7. said
8. kept
9. ten
10. yes
11. says

p. 142
Spell correctly: went, end, said, next
Capitalize: Ted
Add period after: trip

p. 143
1. My friend has ten cats.
2. They hid under the bed.
3. They sat on a shelf.
4. They played with a toy mouse.

p. 144
1. best, well, seven, dress, desk, rest, bell, send, help, egg
2. any, many

p. 145
1. seven
2. many
3. desk
4. best
5. any
6. well
7. egg
8. bell
9. send
10. rest
11. dress

p. 146
Spell correctly: many, seven, any, best
Capitalize: That
Add question mark after: turtles

p. 147
1. city
2. black
3. whale
4. school
5. mouse
6. snail

p. 148
1. had, him, you, our, the, her
2. class, children, boys, girls, them, child

p. 149
1. them
2. her
3. the
4. class
5. children
6. child
7. our
8. had
9. boys
10. you
11. him

p. 150
Spell correctly: class, children, girls, Our
Capitalize: When
Add period after: me

p. 151
These missing letters should be written: b, e, g, h, l, o, r, s, w, z
1. boys
2. class
3. girls
4. him
5. them
6. you

p. 152–153
1. hand
2. am
3. after
4. than
5. that
6. ask
7. have
8. catch
9. says
10. kept
11. when
12. said
13. egg
14. many
15. any
16. seven
17. you
18. girls
19. children
20. our

p. 154
1. big, six, his, hid
2. ship, will, fill, hill, this, wind, pick
3. trick

p. 155
1. hill
2. ship
3. trick
4. six
5. wind
6. fill
7. his
8. big
9. pick
10. this
11. will

p. 156
Spell correctly: six, pick, wind, fill
Capitalize: It (the first word in the fourth sentence)
Add period after: six

p. 157
1. How big is a blue whale?
2. Is it as large as a ship?
3. What does this animal eat?
4. Can you see his tail?

p. 158
1. ring, give, fish, wish, with, live, swim
2. think, thing, bring
3. spring, sister

p. 159
1. spring
2. fish
3. ring
4. think
5. bring
6. wish
7. give
8. sister
9. thing
10. swim
11. with

p. 160
Spell correctly: think, Bring, with, thing
Capitalize: It (in the last sentence)
Add question mark after: vegetables

p. 161
1. sister
2. give
3. ring
4. live
5. spring
6. thing
7. wish

p. 162
1. hot, dot, not, block, job, jog, top, on, hop, got
2. what, was

p. 163
1. jog
2. hot
3. hop
4. dot
5. job
6. block
7. got
8. on
9. not
10. what
11. was

p. 164
Spell correctly: not, on, block, what
Capitalize: Do
Add period after: home

p. 165
1. Corey Jones wanted to go for a jog.
2. He and I ran around the block.
3. I saw Rusty hop on the porch.
4. She got the paper.
5. Rusty was running fast.

p. 166
1. box, rock, spot, drop, clock, stop, chop, ox, pond, shop
2. wash, want

p. 167
1. clock
2. want
3. stop
4. chop
5. ox
6. pond
7. wash
8. shop
9. spot
10. drop
11. rock

p. 168
Spell correctly: wash, box, shop, clock
Capitalize: I (would like a box of cereal)
Add question mark after: nuts

p. 169
1. ox; cattle
2. pond; water
3. spot; small
4. rock; solid

p. 170
1. eggs, ships, vans, cats, hands, jobs, jets, bells, desks, backs
2. dresses
3. men

p. 171
1. dresses
2. bells
3. ships
4. eggs
5. vans
6. jobs
7. backs
8. men
9. hands
10. jets
11. desks

p. 172
Spell correctly: jobs, men, backs, vans
Capitalize: They're
Add period after: cages

p. 173
1. bells; bell; page number will vary.
2. eggs; egg; page number will vary.
3. jets; jet; page number will vary.

p. 174–175
1. pick
2. six
3. will
4. this
5. give
6. sister
7. think
8. live
9. block
10. was
11. what
12. not
13. want
14. clock
15. stop
16. wash
17. hands
18. desks
19. men
20. dresses

p. 176
1. sun, under, club, run, bug, mud, summer, bus, us, up, cut, but
2. from, of

p. 177
1. up
2. under
3. from
4. us
5. summer
6. but
7. run
8. bus
9. sun
10. cut
11. club
12. bug
13. mud

p. 178
Spell correctly: up, bug, sun, under
Capitalize: You (can sit in the sun)
Add period after: tree

p. 179
1. run
2. cut
3. jump
4. shut
5. dug

p. 180
1. just, jump, such, skunk, much, truck, lunch, fun
2. brother, come, love, mother, one, other

p. 181
1. fun
2. much
3. just
4. such
5. love
6. other
7. come
8. jump
9. brother
10. mother
11. lunch
12. one
13. truck

p. 182

Spell correctly: mother, just, truck, lunch

Capitalize: I (put him in our garage)

Add question mark after: afternoon

p. 183

1. Frog contests are fun!
2. Look at the frog my brother has!
3. That frog can jump very high!
4. It can jump more than ten feet!

p. 184

1. game, came, bake, whale, ate, name, brave, gave
2. today, play, say, stay, maybe
3. baby

p. 185

1. bake
2. brave
3. say
4. maybe
5. stay
6. play
7. today
8. game
9. gave
10. name
11. ate
12. baby
13. came

p. 186

Spell correctly: came, game, play, Today

Capitalize: Tate

Add period after: end

p. 187

1. bake
2. bed
3. big
4. blame
5. box
6. brave

p. 188

1. chain, gain, tail, paint, nail, pail, snail, rain, wait, mail, train, sail
2. eight
3. they

p. 189

1. rain
2. train
3. nail
4. gain
5. paint
6. snail
7. they
8. chain
9. sail
10. pail
11. eight
12. wait
13. tail

p. 190

Spell correctly: wait, train, snail, eight

Capitalize: Are

Add question mark after: train

p. 191

1. 2
2. 1
3. 1
4. 2
5. 2

p. 192

1. tricked, ended, wished, handed, thanked, asked, fished
2. helping, wishing, fishing, dressing, picking, thinking, catching

p. 193

1. asked
2. ended
3. helping
4. catching
5. fished
6. thanked
7. wished
8. fishing
9. picking
10. dressing
11. tricked
12. wishing
13. thinking

p. 194

Spell correctly: thanked, tricked, wished, fishing

Capitalize: He (wished that he had won)

Add period after: ribbon

p. 195

1. helped
2. helping
3. asked
4. asking
5. tricked
6. tricking

p. 196–197

1. under
2. of
3. cut
4. from
5. come
6. just
7. much
8. other
9. baby
10. say
11. gave
12. maybe
13. eight
14. train
15. wait
16. they
17. thinking
18. asked
19. thanked
20. helping

p. 198

1. we, he, she, being
2. see, green, keep, feet, bees, street, week, three
3. these
4. people

p. 199

1. bees
2. green
3. feet
4. he
5. week
6. she
7. these
8. we
9. see
10. people
11. street
12. being
13. keep

p. 200

Spell correctly: people, street, bees, keep

Capitalize: Soon

Add period after: stung

p. 201

1. I have been to Ohio three times.
2. My grandfather is in Dallas this week.
3. These trees grow all over Maine.
4. We went to see my aunt in Seattle.

p. 202

1. clean, please, leap, peach, eat, heat, dream, mean
2. happy, very, funny, city, puppy, penny

p. 203

1. happy
2. clean
3. mean
4. heat
5. city
6. please
7. peach
8. leap
9. funny
10. eat
11. puppy
12. penny
13. dream

p. 204

Spell correctly: very, penny, clean, city

Capitalize: Peru

Add period after: week

p. 205

1. eat
2. happy
3. leap

Guide words will vary.

p. 206

1. like, ice, bike, side, nine, write, mine, ride, white, hide, inside, five
2. find
3. eye

p. 207

1. bike
2. like
3. ride
4. white
5. write
6. inside
7. find
8. eye
9. hide
10. nine
11. side
12. ice
13. mine

p. 208

Spell correctly: like, ice, white, inside

Capitalize: A (team of white dogs pulled us)

Add period after: miles

p. 209

1. hide
2. hid
3. wrote
4. write
5. like
6. liked

p. 210

1. lion, tiny, tiger
2. sky, cry, why, by, try, my, fly
3. pie, tie, lie
4. high

p. 211

1. high
2. cry
3. tiny
4. lie
5. my
6. pie
7. tie
8. lion
9. try
10. why
11. sky
12. tiger
13. by

p. 212

Spell correctly: sky, tiny, fly, try

Capitalize: March

Add period after: enough

p. 213

1. 3
2. 2
3. 1
4. 3
5. 1

p. 214

1. dropped, spotted, hopped, jogged, shopped, stopped, dotted
2. dropping, cutting, stopping, jogging, running, hopping, shopping

p. 215
1. hopped
2. jogging
3. dotted
4. stopped
5. shopped
6. dropped
7. dropping
8. jogged
9. stopping
10. hopping
11. running
12. spotted
13. shopping

p. 216
Spell correctly: jogging, jogged, stopping, running
Capitalize: There
Add question mark after: fun

p. 217
1. shopping
2. shopped
3. hopping
4. hopped
5. stopped
6. stopping

p. 218-219
1. being
2. week
3. street
4. people
5. clean
6. very
7. funny
8. please
9. write
10. eye
11. find
12. white
13. tie
14. tiny
15. why
16. high
17. hopping
18. stopped
19. dropped
20. running

p. 220
1. go, no, so
2. home, rope, nose, hope, stone, hole, joke
3. yellow, grow, know, snow

p. 221
1. snow
2. yellow
3. nose
4. no
5. rope
6. home
7. hole
8. hope
9. stone
10. joke
11. grow
12. so
13. go

p. 222
Spell correctly: go, rope, snow, stone
Capitalize: Last
Add question mark after: trip

p. 223
1. whole
2. hole
3. know
4. no
5. sew
6. so
7. so

p. 224
1. cold, gold, old, sold, open, over, roll, most, hold, told
2. road, goat, coat, boat

p. 225
1. sold
2. over
3. coat
4. cold
5. open
6. boat
7. told
8. gold
9. road
10. goat
11. hold
12. old
13. most

p. 226
Spell correctly: most, gold, coat, cold
Capitalize: Our
Add period after: snow

p. 227
1. road
2. told
3. roll
4. gold
5. over
6. open
7. old
8. cold

p. 228
1. book, look, cook, stood, cookies, good, foot, took
2. could, would, should
3. put, pull, full

p. 229
1. cookies
2. would
3. cook
4. put
5. book
6. could
7. stood
8. should
9. look
10. pull
11. took
12. full
13. good

p. 230
Spell correctly: Would, full, look, cook
Capitalize: Oak
Add period after: cookies

p. 231
1. Mr. Roy Gray
2. 1631 Elm Rd.
3. Mrs. Jean Ryan
4. 402 Bank St.
5. Mr. Yoshi Ono
6. 6800 Burnet Rd.
7. Mrs. Deana Reyna
8. 509 State St.
9. Mr. Jackson Palmer

p. 232
1. zoo, too, room, food, school, tooth, soon, moon
2. blue
3. new
4. to, do, who, two

p. 233
1. moon
2. who
3. zoo
4. food
5. soon
6. tooth
7. room
8. blue
9. to
10. new
11. do
12. too
13. two

p. 234
Spell correctly: too, do, zoo, soon
Capitalize: Dad
Add period after: zoo

p. 235
1. zoo
2. tooth
3. room
4. moon

p. 236
1. named, biked, hoped, liked, lived, baked, loved
2. joking, baking, living, giving, riding, writing, having

p. 237
1. biked
2. writing
3. baking
4. joking
5. hoped
6. loved
7. named
8. baked
9. lived
10. giving
11. having
12. living
13. riding

p. 238
Spell correctly: baked, hoped, riding, joking
Capitalize: Mr.
Add question mark after: joking

p. 239
1. live
2. give
3. have
4. write
5. love
6. bike
7. name
8. like
Page numbers will vary.

p. 240-241
1. know
2. yellow
3. no
4. home
5. coat
6. open
7. cold
8. over
9. book
10. would
11. pull
12. put
13. could
14. tooth
15. blue
16. two
17. new
18. writing
19. liked
20. riding

p. 242
1. out, found, sound, mouse, round, around, house
2. town, now, flower, owl, how, cow, clown

p. 243
1. flower
2. round
3. around
4. out
5. found
6. clown
7. sound
8. house
9. how
10. owl
11. town
12. mouse
13. now

p. 244
Spell correctly: town, around, found, house
Capitalize: Then
Add question mark after: draw

p. 245
1. The dog was afraid of the sound.
2. The boys were glad to see the owl.
3. The child was picking a flower.
4. How many stores were in that town?
5. A mouse was hiding in my shoe.

p. 246
1. saw, draw
2. talk, call, ball, all, small, walk
3. song, dog, frog, off, lost, long

p. 247
1. dog
2. call
3. frog
4. walk
5. talk
6. draw
7. saw
8. song
9. small
10. lost
11. long
12. off
13. all

p. 248
Spell correctly: small, long, call, ball
Capitalize: He (has long black hair).
Add period after: hair

p. 249
1. o
2. ete
3. o
4. i
5. oo
6. k

p. 250
1. for, corn, or, story, short, snore, more, horse, storm, orange, store
2. door, floor
3. four

p. 251
1. corn
2. storm
3. store
4. short
5. four
6. horse
7. more
8. for
9. or
10. orange
11. snore
12. door
13. floor

p. 252
Spell correctly: store, corn, orange, short
Capitalize: We (also have special feeding dishes)
Add period after: dish

p. 253
1. Snow has fallen for four days and nights.
2. Watch out for the snow above that door!
3. Do you think we will get more snow?

p. 254
1. father
2. jar, car, party, barn, arm, mark, farmer, star, are, dark, farm, far, art

p. 255
1. farmer
2. art
3. arm
4. jar
5. are
6. farm
7. father
8. dark
9. far
10. party
11. mark
12. star
13. barn

p. 256
Spell correctly: party, dark, barn, arm
Capitalize: Every
Add question mark after: say

p. 257
1. star; 2
2. mark; 1
3. star; 1
4. mark; 2
5. star; 1
6. mark; 1

p. 258
1. colder, helper, older, longer, jumper, faster, painter
2. bigger, shopper, runner, flatter
3. braver, writer, baker

p. 259
1. shopper
2. helper
3. writer
4. braver
5. runner
6. flatter
7. jumper
8. painter
9. older
10. faster
11. longer
12. bigger
13. colder

p. 260
Spell correctly: writer, helper, faster, baker
Capitalize: How
Add question mark after: do

p. 261
1. bigger
2. braver
3. colder
4. flatter
5. hotter
6. longer
7. rounder
Page numbers will vary.

p. 262-263
1. flower
2. out
3. town
4. around
5. talk
6. off
7. small
8. saw
9. four
10. floor
11. orange
12. store
13. father
14. are
15. dark
16. party
17. longer
18. writer
19. older
20. bigger

MATH SKILLS

p. 268
Students should draw lines between numbers and the groups of flowers.
27 matches the third set of flowers.
44 matches the fourth set of flowers.
19 matches the first set of flowers.
35 matches the second set of flowers.

p. 271

17	18	19	20	21
64	65	66	67	68
96	97	98	99	100
38	39	40	41	42

p. 272
15
21
42
53

p. 273

Tens	+	Ones		
0		8	= 8
6		6	= 66
7		0	= 70
3		1	= 31
4		9	= 49
8		2	= 82

p. 274

Hundreds	Tens	Ones
2	3	6
3	1	4
2	4	8
3	2	0
1	8	4

p. 275

Hundreds	Tens	Ones	
3	5	9	= 359
5	1	3	= 513
4	6	0	= 460
2	9	8	= 298

p. 276

139	140	141	142	143
98	99	100	101	102
116	117	118	119	120
146	147	148	149	150

p. 278
136 matches the second model.
18 matches the third model.
205 matches the fourth model.
452 matches the first model.

p. 279

14 < 16	19 > 2
33 < 57	28 > 25
40 > 39	36 > 26

p. 280

43	30
89	147
176	30
13	71
10	114

p. 281

seventh; 7th	fourth; 4th
first; 1st	ninth; 9th
third; 3rd	tenth; 10th
fifth; 5th	second; 2nd
sixth; 6th	eighth; 8th

p. 282

thirteenth; 13th	seventeenth; 17th
eleventh; 11th	twentieth; 20th
twelfth; 12th	eighteenth; 18th
sixteenth; 16th	nineteenth; 19th
fifteenth; 15th	fourteenth; 14th

p. 283

5	10	15
10	20	30

5¢	10¢	15¢	20¢	25¢	30¢
10¢	20¢	30¢	40¢	50¢	60¢
35	40	45	50	55	60
50	60	70	80	90	100

p. 284

2	4	6

10	12	14	16	18	20
8	10	12	14	16	18
66	68	70	72	74	76
34	36	38	40	42	44
100	102	104	106	108	110
20	22	24	26	28	30

p. 285

odd	even
even	odd
odd	odd
even	even

p. 286

1	②	3	④	5	⑥	7	⑧	9	10
11	⑫	13	⑭	15	16	17	18	19	20
21	㉒	23	24	25	26	27	28	29	30
31	32	33	34	35	36	37	38	39	40
41	42	43	44	45	46	47	48	49	50
51	52	53	54	55	56	57	58	59	60
61	62	63	64	65	66	67	68	69	70
71	72	73	74	75	76	77	78	79	80
81	82	83	84	85	86	87	88	89	90
91	92	93	94	95	96	97	98	99	100

p. 287

15	20	25	30	35	40
132	134	136	138	140	142
18	19	18	19	18	19
60	70	80	90	100	110
16	18	20	22	24	26
295	296	297	298	299	300
23	33	43	53	63	73
40	42	44	46	48	50

p. 288

36	37	38	39	40	41	42	43
71	72	73	74	75	76	77	78
113	114	115	116	117	118	119	120
185	186	187	188	189	190	191	192

47 > 43   28 < 29
92   150
odd   even

p. 289

65 matches the second model.
123 matches the third model.
48 matches the first model.

6	8	10	12	14	16
25	30	35	40	45	50
60	70	80	90	100	110
116	118	120	122	124	126

p. 290
9
7
5
10

p. 291
4 + 5 = 9
7 + 1 = 8
3 + 4 = 7
3 + 2 = 5
1 + 9 = 10

p. 292
13
11
15
18

p. 293
9 + 8 = 17
7 + 9 = 16
7 + 5 = 12
5 + 7 = 13
5 + 9 = 14

p. 294
1 + 0 = 1   0 + 2 = 2
3 + 0 = 3   0 + 4 = 4
5 + 0 = 5   0 + 6 = 6
7 + 0 = 7   0 + 8 = 8
9 + 0 = 9   10 + 0 = 10

p. 295
2 + 2 = 4
5 + 5 = 10
9 + 9 = 18
4 + 4 = 8
7 + 7 = 14

p. 296
9   9
10   10
7   7
8   8

p. 297
3 + 6 = 9   6 + 0 = 6
1 + 9 = 10   5 + 5 = 10
2 + 4 = 6   3 + 2 = 5

p. 298
27
38
59
48

p. 299
37
59
92
79

p. 300

87	79	23	57
56	85	99	54
92	93	38	94
89	79	48	89

p. 301

39	67	54	67
69	78	94	96
57	28	66	78
69	58	28	89
98	59	89	76
19	78	85	79

p. 302
Shading will show a rocket.

p. 303
356
279
428
597

p. 304

568	856	759	957
971	478	363	999
812	852	915	616

p. 305
0 tens 12 ones = 1 ten 2 ones = 12
2 tens 14 ones = 3 tens 4 ones = 34
1 ten 16 ones = 2 tens 6 ones = 26
4 tens 13 ones = 5 tens 3 ones = 53

p. 306
1 ten 13 ones = 23
2 tens 11 ones = 31
4 tens 10 ones = 50

p. 307

65	50	82	80
41	91	50	33
80	72	91	98

p. 308

63	66	80	42
71	65	50	75
84	70	90	25
81	31	62	30

p. 309

83	72	20	73	64
66	91	54	60	65
52	30	94	90	75
71	82	83	41	90

p. 310

71	82	51	80	73
72	82	72	53	72
72	41	72	42	62
72	72	72	43	72
72	61	72	81	72
72	82	72	82	72

Shading will show the word Hi.

p. 311
10 + 30 = 40
40 + 10 = 50
20 + 30 = 50
10 + 10 = 20
60 + 20 = 80
10 + 50 = 60
50 + 30 = 80

p. 312

8	9		
16	14		
10	18		
16	12		
19	66	94	69
39	58	58	97
566	661	937	499
21	73	47	61
75	58	94	83

p. 313
4 + 19 = 23   5 + 23 = 28
2 + 48 = 50   3 + 71 = 74
40 + 20 = 60   30 + 50 = 80

p. 314
7
5
9
3
8

p. 315
4
1
6
2

p. 316
13
17
11
10
16

p. 317
12
9
14
11
15

p. 318
9 − 9 = 0
12 − 12 = 0
5 − 5 = 0
17 − 17 = 0
10 − 10 = 0

p. 319
11 − 0 = 11
18 − 0 = 18
3 − 0 = 3
5 − 0 = 5
14 − 0 = 14

p. 320
5 − 2 = 3   5 − 3 = 2
9 − 7 = 2   9 − 2 = 7
3 − 1 = 2   3 − 2 = 1
10 − 4 = 6   10 − 6 = 4

p. 321
6 + 2 = 8   5 − 3 = 8
2 + 6 = 8   3 + 5 = 8
8 − 6 = 2   8 − 5 = 3
8 − 2 = 6   8 − 3 = 5

5 + 4 = 9   6 + 3 = 9
4 + 5 = 9   3 + 6 = 9
9 − 5 = 4   9 − 6 = 3
9 − 4 = 5   9 − 3 = 6

p. 322
9 − 2 = 7
3 + 5 = 8
14 − 10 = 4
7 − 6 = 1
2 + 8 = 10

p. 323
4 + 3 = 7
12 − 4 = 8
6 + 3 = 9
11 − 6 = 5
13 − 9 = 4

p. 324
21
34
51
43
83

p. 325
15
22
23
17
21

p. 326
12
22
41
31
22

p. 327

71	15	32	1
53	17	20	44
23	11	43	10
31	33	99	12

p. 328

32	4	0	3
49	72	32	12
64	1	30	29
64	18	0	80
52	29	81	32
13	18	63	30

p. 329
Shading will show a house.

p. 330

412	209	641	510
714	180	999	223
510	392	347	510
933	886	437	132

p. 331
2 tens 3 ones = 1 ten 13 ones; 15
4 tens 1 one = 3 tens 11 ones; 35
3 tens 6 ones = 2 tens 16 ones; 27
5 tens 0 ones = 4 tens 10 ones; 43

p. 332
3 tens 5 ones = 2 tens ones; 18
2 tens 1 one = 1 ten 11 ones; 7
4 tens 3 ones = 3 tens 13 ones; 14
6 tens 0 ones = 5 tens 10 ones; 23

p. 333

39	13	58	19
25	26	3	67
4	5	39	6

p. 334

26	18	37	25
44	47	47	48
37	38	15	68
17	26	4	39
49	5	38	15

p. 335

12	54	43	43
8	8	51	17
54	12	17	51
65	19	4	16
19	65	66	4
7	7	16	66

p. 336

29	75	18	29
86	3	2	43
38	37	9	13
9	78	31	19
19	6	8	59
17	19	13	9

p. 337
8 + 4 = 12
10 – 3 = 7
6 + 4 = 10
9 + 2 = 11
12 – 9 = 3

p. 338

0	9
6	8

5 + 4 = 9	7 + 3 = 10
4 + 5 = 9	3 + 7 = 10
9 – 5 = 4	10 – 7 = 3
9 – 4 = 5	10 – 3 = 7

15	22	13	27
330	431	334	71
9	6	8	5
29	34		

p. 339
9 + 3 = 12
14 – 7 = 7
8 – 3 = 5
5 + 5 = 10

p. 340
5¢
12¢
17¢
15¢

p. 341
8¢
10¢
13¢
15¢
17¢

p. 342
16¢
15¢
20¢
24¢
27¢

p. 343

13¢	17¢
26¢	31¢
48¢	45¢

p. 344
41¢
35¢
50¢
59¢
96¢

p. 345
32¢ matches the second set of coins.
56¢ matches the third set of coins.
65¢ matches the first set of coins.
45¢ matches the fourth set of coins.
28¢ matches the last set of coins.
70¢ matches the fifth set of coins.

p. 346
Possible answers are given.
1 dime, 1 nickel, 4 pennies or
3 nickels, 4 pennies

1 quarter, 3 pennies or 2 dimes,
1 nickel, 3 pennies

2 quarters, 1 dime, 2 pennies or
6 dimes, 2 pennies

2 quarters, 4 dimes, 1 nickel,
2 pennies or 9 dimes, 1 nickel,
2 pennies

p. 347
Students should draw lines between
equal amounts of money.
1 nickel matches 5 pennies.
1 dime matches 2 nickels.
1 quarter matches 2 dimes and
    1 nickel.
1 nickel and 2 pennies match
    7 pennies.
2 quarters match 5 dimes.
1 quarter and 1 dime match 3 dimes
    and 1 nickel.

p. 348
1 nickel or 5 pennies
1 dime or 2 nickels or 10 pennies
1 quarter or 5 nickels or 25 pennies
4 quarters or 10 dimes or 100
    pennies

p. 349
Students should circle the coins.
Possible answers are given.
35¢: Circle 1 quarter and 1 dime
49¢: Circle 1 quarter, 2 dimes, and
    4 pennies
17¢: Circle 1 dime, 1 nickel, and
    2 pennies
89¢: Circle 3 quarters, 1 dime, and
    4 pennies.

p. 350
60¢; 2 quarters, 1 dime
50¢; 2 quarters
75¢; 3 quarters
65¢; 2 quarters, 1 dime, 1 nickel

p. 351
3¢
10¢
20¢
15¢

p. 352
20¢
3¢
2¢
8¢

p. 353

22¢	15¢
5¢	21¢
10¢	20¢

p. 354
28¢
67¢
1 nickel or 5 pennies
1 dime or 2 nickels or 10 pennies
50¢; Students should draw
2 quarters.

p. 355
Possible answers are given.
1 dime, 1 nickel, 1 penny or
1 dime, 6 pennies

2 quarters, 1 dime, 1 nickel or
6 dimes, 1 nickel

4¢
8¢

p. 356

4:00; 4	10:00; 10	6:00; 6
3:00; 3	8:00; 8	5:00; 5
7:00; 7	12:00; 12	2:00; 2

p. 357

9:30	3:30	11:30
7:30	10:30	1:30
2:30	8:30	6:30
4:30	12:30	5:30

p. 358

2:15	8:45	1:45
5:15	7:45	11:15
12:45	6:15	4:15
9:45	10:15	3:45

p. 359

7:15	11:45
1:45	8:15
3:15	10:45
5:45	9:15

p. 360
Clocks should show the following
times:
7:00
9:00
6:15
8:00

p. 361
10:05; 5 minutes after 10
1:25; 25 minutes after 1
7:55; 55 minutes after 7
10:15; 15 minutes after 10
9:40; 40 minutes after 9
11:10; 10 minutes after 11

p. 362

6:30	12:40
5:15	9:05
2:20	11:50
1:35	8:00

p. 363
5:45 matches the third clock.
2:30 matches the fourth clock.
12:05 matches the last clock.
9:15 matches the first clock.
3:10 matches the second clock.

p. 365
2nd; 1st; 3rd
2nd; 3rd; 1st
2nd; 3rd; 1st
2nd; 1st; 3rd

p. 366

5:00	9:00	12:00
10:30	2:30	7:30
3:15	8:45	11:15
2:25	6:40	10:05

p. 367
10:00
2:00
1:15
7:45

p. 368
cubes—die
pyramids—ancient pyramid
spheres—Earth
cones—traffic cone
cylinders—trash can

p. 369
triangle—warning sign
circle—bullseye
square—cd case
rectangle—beware sign

p. 370
square; 4
triangle; 3
rectangle; 4
circle; 0
rectangle; 4
triangle; 3
square; 4

p. 373

9 units	4 units
6 units	3 units
5 units	12 units

p. 374
Students should circle each map
location.
pizza parlor
city hall
downtown
home
school

p. 375

Across	Up
5	3
3	4
7	1
1	2

p. 376
squares
cones
spheres
rectangles
9 units
4 units

578
in., 3 in., 6 in.

579
in., 3 in., 2 in., 5 in.

580
cm, 8 cm, 15 cm

581
cm
m
m
cm

582
re than 1 pint
s than 1 quart
than 1 cup
re than 1 quart

583
ups, 2 pints, 4 cups, 4 cups

584
esses may vary. 4 in., 2 in., 3 in.,
n.

585
esses may vary. 8 cm, 13 cm,
m, 14 cm

586
in.
cm
ups
ups
ints

587
esses may vary.
n.
n.
cm

ANGUAGE ARTS

390
der may vary.
apple
car
rug
bird
chair
girl
tree
boy
desk
. truck
. grass
. pen
. girl, apple
. bird, tree
. chair, desk
. boy, chair
. girl, truck

P. 391
1. sister, park
2. car, mother
3. dog
4. boy, birds, trees
5. playground
6. cat, slide
Chart: Person: sister, mother, boy;
Place: park, playground; Thing: car,
trees, slide; Animal: dog, birds, cat

P. 392
Order may vary.
1. Bob's Bikes
2. Bridge Road
3. China
4. Elf Corn
5. Gabriel
6. Lindsey
7. New York City
8. Oregon
9. Pat Green
10. State Street
11. Hill's Store
12. Baker Street
13. Stone Library
14. Emily Fuller

P. 393
1. dog/Lassie
2. park/Central Park
3. city/Chicago
4. woman/Ms. Ward
5. school/Redbrook Elementary
School
6. store/Fastmart Grocery Store,
7.–9. Answers will vary.

P. 394
1. Where did Jack Sprat go?
2. Mary saw her friend Jill.
3. Did Mr. or Mrs. Sprat go with
them?
4. They met Ms. Muffet along the
way.
5.–6. Proper nouns will vary.

P. 395
1. Meg, Tim
2. Ms. Lee
3. Holly Green
4. Lucy
5. Mr. Roberts
6. Lucy
7.–8. Answers will vary.

P. 396
1. They walked along Main Street.
2. My uncle drove through Indiana
and Ohio.
3. We went on a trip to Mexico.
4–8. Proper nouns will vary.

P. 397
1. Wednesday
2. February
3. Saturday
4. Thanksgiving
5.–7. Answers will vary.

P. 398
1. boys
2. girl
3. robe
4. stars
5. moon
6. house
7. door
8. treats
9. cats
10. dogs
11. owl
12. stars
13. trees
14. hands
15. song

P. 399
1. caps
2. chairs
3. girls
4. trees
5. flags
6. boys
7. seeds
8. carrots
9. peas
10. friends
11. gardens

P. 400
1. lunches
2. dresses
3. glasses
4. dishes
5. boxes
6. watches
7. foxes
8. benches
9. inches
10. brushes
11. buses
12. churches

P. 401
1. woman
2. men
3. child
4. feet
5. teeth
6. children
7. feet
8. teeth
9. men
10. women

P. 402
1. shelf
2. wives
3. elf
4. wolves
5.–7. Answers will vary.

P. 403
1. We
2. She or He
3. She or He
4. It
5. She or He
6. It
7. They
8. We
9. They
10. We

P. 404
We, She, They, They, He, I, It

P. 405
1. I
2. me
3. me
4. I
5. Susan and I
6. Tina and me
7. Tina and I
8. Susan and me

P. 406
1. We
2. us
3. We
4. us
5. us
6. We
7. us
8. We
9. us
10. we
11. We

P. 407
1. runs
2. kicks
3. breaks
4. looks
5. shakes
6. turns
7. runs
8. talks
9. sends
10. pays
11.–15. Answers may vary.
11. The boy reads.
12. The baby cries.
13. The rabbit hops.
14. The birds sing.
15. The dogs bark.

P. 408
1. lives
2. walk
3. tells
4. waves
5. makes
6. laugh
7.–10. Answers will vary.

P. 409
1. skips
2. play
3. hug
4. purrs
5. barks
6. hide
7. waves
8. blows
9. follows
10. sees
11. hears
12. move
13. hoots
14. take
15. eat

P. 410
1. The following verbs should be circled: reads, takes, rests, sleeps, snores, guess, practice
2. skates
3. wears
4. teaches
5. learn
6. practice
7. comes
8. claps, performs

P. 411
1. have
2. have
3. had
4. has
5. has
6. has
7. have
8. had
9. has
10. have
11. have
12. had

P. 412
1. are
2. are
3. were
4. is
5. are
6. were
7. is
8. am
9. was
10. is

P. 413
1. plays
2. runs
3. dance
4. wait
5. leaps
Paragraph (Answers may vary.):
takes; sits; asks; dances; stands; walks

P. 414
1. paints
2. uses
3. hang
4. look
5. say
6.–9. Answers will vary.

P. 415
1. played
2. visited
3. looked
4. jumped
5. leaned
6. helped
7. laughed
8. The girls played in the park.
9. They climbed over rocks.
10. Their fathers called to them.

P. 416
1. wanted
2. baked
3. walked
4. signed
5. picked
6. surprised
7. looked
8.–11. Answers will vary.

P. 417
1. ran
2. came
3. went
4. go
5. run
6. goes
7. goes, went
8. comes, came
9. come, came
10. run, ran

P. 418
1. brought
2. fell
3. did
4. flew
5. broke
6. sold
7. ate
8. flies, flew
9. breaks, broke
10. does, did

P. 419
1. played
2. called
3. wanted
4. laughed
5. jumped
6. played
7. laughing
8. playing
9. talking
10. Carmen helped Grandma cook yesterday.
11. Grandma is cooking some soup today.

P. 420
1. are
2. is
3. are
4. is
5. are
6. are
7. are
8. are
9.–10. Sentences will vary.

P. 421
1. is
2. are
3. are
4. are
5. is
6. is
7. are
8. are
9.–10. Sentences will vary.

P. 422
1. were
2. was
3. were
4. were
5. were
6. was
7. was
8. were
9.–10. Sentences will vary.

P. 423
1. The following verbs should be circled: were, were, was, were, was, was, were, were, were, were.
2. Answers will vary.

P. 424
1. sees
2. saw
3. sees
4. sees
5. saw
6. saw
7. see
8. saw
9. saw
10. see
11. saw; Last week we saw Lee.
12. sees; Lee sees my painting now.

P. 425
1. ran; Horses ran wild long ago.
2. run; A horse can run ten miles every day.
3. run; Can you run as fast as a horse?
4. ran; Mandy ran in a race last week.
5. runs; Carl runs home from school now.
6. runs; Now Mandy runs after Carl.
7. run; How far can you run?

P. 426
1. give
2. gave
3. gives
4. gave
5. gave
6. gave
7. gave
8. gave
9.–11. Sentences will vary.

P. 427
1. do
2. does
3. does
4. does
5. does
6. do
7. does
8. do
9. does
10. do
11.–12. Sentences will vary.

P. 428
1. had
2. has
3. have
4. have
5. has
6. had
7. has
8. has
9. have
10. had
11. had
12. has

P. 429
The following verbs should be circled: has, has, had, had, had, have.

P. 430
Answers may vary.
1. pink
2. long
3. brown
4. round
5. juicy
6. tiny

P. 431
Answers will vary.
1. tired
2. happy
3. many
4. one
5. hungry
6. some
7. three
8. sleepy

P. 432
2. brighter
3. tallest
4. fast
5. thicker
6. biggest
7. wider
8. oldest

P. 433
1. better
2. worst
3. best
4. worse
5. better
6. best

P. 434
1. an
2. a
3. a
4. an
5. a
6. an
7. an
8. an
9. a
10. a
11. an
12. a
13. an
14. an
15. a
16. a
17. a
18. an
19. an
20. an
21. a
22. a

P. 435
In the column for **an**: ape, owl, eel, iguana, otter, ant
In the column for **a**: dog, butterfly, lizard, turtle, snake, bear

P. 436
1. no
2. yes
3. no
4. yes
5. yes
6. yes
7. no
8. no
9. yes
10. yes
11. yes
12. no
13. yes
14. no
15. yes

P. 437
Answers may vary.
1. Mrs. Brown lives on my street.
2. Our building is made of wood.
3. Four families live in our building.
4. Our class went on a picnic.
5. Jennifer was climbing the tree.
6. The sun shone all day.
7. Corn and beans grow on a farm.
8. The wagon has a broken wheel.
9. The mother goat fed the baby goat.
10. The boat sailed in strong winds.
11. The fisherman caught seven fish.
12. Some of the fish were sold in the store.
13. Our team won ten games.
14. Our batters hit the ball a lot.
15. The ballpark was full of fans.
16. Sentences will vary.

P. 438
Answers will vary.

P. 439
The following parts of each sentence should be circled:
1. My family and I
2. Sami Harper
3. Miss Jenkins
4. Mr. Chang
5. Henry
6. Mr. Byrne
7. Mrs. Lee
8. Mr. and Mrs. Diaz
9. Jeanine
10. Mr. Wolf
11. Amy Taft
12. Mr. Dowd
13. Mrs. Clark
14. Carolyn and Alberto
15. Julie

P. 440
1. fly
2. buzz
3. barks
4. quack
5. hops
6. roar
7. moo
8. cluck
9. Sentences will vary.

P. 441
1. My brother eats apples.
2. Elizabeth drinks milk.
3. Kim likes peanut butter.
4. Justin wants bread.
5. Chris plants corn.
6. Chang caught a fish.
7. Dad cooks breakfast.
8. Shawn shares his lunch.
9. Rosa grew the carrot.

P. 442
1. telling
2. telling
3. asking
4. not a sentence
5. telling
6. not a sentence
7. telling
8. asking
9. telling

P. 443
1. statement
2. question
3. statement
4. question
5. statement
6. question
7. exlamation
8. statement
9. question
10. exclamation

P. 444
Sentences will vary. Be sure each sentence is the specified type of sentence.

P. 445
1. John gave seeds to Sara and told her to plant them.
2. Sara planted the seeds and looked at the ground.
3. Sara sang songs and read stories to them.
4. The rain fell on the seeds and helped them grow.

P. 446
1. The farmer and his family stood in the doorway.
2. The hunter and the bear stayed with the family.
3. The mice and the children ran out the door.
4. The hunter and the bear went home.

P. 447
Answers will vary. Be sure each new sentence contains describing words.

P. 448
Answers used to fill in the story will vary but should all be adjectives.

P. 449
1. The ant climbed down a blade of grass. He (or She) fell into the spring.
2. The bird pulled off a leaf. He (or She) let the leaf fall into the water.
3. The hunter saw a lion. He spread his net.
4. The lion and I live in the woods. We are friends.

P. 450
1. We were doing a project on volcanoes.
2. They were doing a project on bees.
3. She is a nice teacher.
4. We all wanted to win.
5. They were writing notes.
6. She told everyone that Robert and Adam had won first prize.

P. 451
Answers will vary. Possible responses:
1. stroll
2. race
3. pedal
4. speed
5. zooms
6. jogs
7. skip
8. travels
9. sails

P. 452
1. Mark Twain
2. Beverly Cleary
3. Diane Dillon
4. Alicia Acker
5. Ezra Jack Keats
The first letter of these words should be circled:
6. mother, grandma
7. grandma, grandpa
8. uncle carlos, aunt kathy
9. Mario Martinez told me a story.
10. Ichiro and I played ball

P. 453
1. C.D.
2. C.A.C.
3. M.B.
4. M.T.
5. K.S.
6. T.L.T.
7. I.B.
8. C.L.W.
9. J.W.A.
10. L.B. Hopkins
11. A. Martinez
12. Patricia A. Rosen
13. The box was for M. S. Mills.
14. D. E. Ellis sent it to her.
15. T. J. Lee brought the box to the house.

P. 454
1. Mrs. Ruth Scott
2. Mr. Kurt Wiese
3. Miss E. Garcia
4. Dr. Seuss
5. Ms. Carol Baylor
6. Mr. and Mrs. H. Cox
7. Miss K. E. Jones
8. Dr. S. Tomas Rios
9. Mrs. H. Stone is here to see Dr. Brooks.
10. Mr. F. Green and Ms. Miller are not here.

P. 455
1. James lives in Dayton, Ohio.
2. His house is on Market St.
3. I think Thomas Park is in this town.
4. We went to Mathis Lake for a picnic.
5. Is Perry School far away?

P. 456
1.–6. Answers will vary.

P. 457
1. Monday
2. Friday
3. February
4. Answers will vary.
5. November
6. Tues.
7. Thurs.
8. Dec.
9. Sat.
10. Jan.
11. Sept.

P. 458
1. New Year's Day
2. Mother's Day
3. Independence Day
4. Labor Day
5. Cinco de Mayo
6. Thanksgiving Day
7. Veterans Day
8. Earth Day is in April.
9. Boxing Day is a British holiday.
10. Father's Day is in June.

P. 459

1. <u>Best Friends</u>
2. <u>The Biggest Bear</u>
3. <u>Rabbits on Roller Skates</u>
4. <u>Down on the Sunny Farm</u>

The first letter of these words should be circled:

5. we, bees
6. the, dancing, pony
7. my, shadow
8. my, summer, farm

P. 460

1. My mom's favorite book is called <u>Gone with the Wind</u>.
2. Alison wrote a poem named "Hay Is for Horses."
3. At the library, I checked out a book called <u>Learn to Draw</u>.
4. I read a story about boats called "Sail Away."
5. Mrs. Gibbs read us a poem named "A Plan for Stan."
6. Sara wrote a story called "What I Did on Vacation."
7. Her favorite book is called <u>Ramona the Great</u>.

P. 461

The first letter in each sentence should be capitalized.

P. 462

1. Patty played on the baseball team.
2. Patty hit two home runs.
3. She caught the ball, too.
4. What time is it?
5. Is it time for lunch?
6. Are your ready to eat?

P. 463

1.–5. Each sentence should end with a period.
6. Ms.
7. Mr.
8. Mrs.
9. Dr.
10. Ms.

P. 464

1. !
2. ?
3. ?
4. !
5. don't
6. I'll
7. didn't

P. 465

1. ?
2. ?
3. !
4. ?
5. One thing I don't like is setting up the tent.
6. I can't seem to get it right!
7. I'll ask my mom for help next time.

P. 466

1. were not, weren't
2. was not, wasn't
3. has not, hasn't
4. have not, haven't
5. did not, didn't
6. are not, aren't
7. is not
8. do not
9. was not
10. can not
11. did not
12. had not
13. does not
14. are not
15. isn't
16. don't
17. didn't

P. 467

1. don't
2. can't
3. haven't
4. doesn't
5. isn't
6.–8. Answers will vary.

P. 468

June 8, 2005 / Dear Grandmother, / The tag says it comes from Chicago, Illinois. / Love,

P. 469

1. Akron, Ohio
2. Hilo, Hawaii
3. Macon, Georgia
4. Nome, Alaska
5. Provo, Utah
6. Nancy lives in Barnet, Vermont.
7. Mr. Hill went to Houston, Texas.
8. Did Bruce like Bend, Oregon?
9. Will Amy visit Newark, Ohio?
10. How far away is Salem, Massachusetts?

P. 470

1. Dec. 12, 1948
2. Mar. 27, 1965
3. Sept. 8, 1994
4. Nov. 1, 2000
5. Jan. 5, 1995
6. August 10, 1967
7. Oct. 17, 1983
8. February 8, 1991
9. July 29, 1989
10. Sept. 3, 2001
11. Oct. 20, 1988
12. Answers will vary.

P. 471

1. hat
2. bee
3. cow
4. dog

P. 472

1. dog/hog
2. tall/ball
3. mouse/house
4. flat/hat
5. blue/clue
6. Rhymes will vary.

P. 473

1. road
2. home
3. sad
4. sick
5. gift
6. small
7. large
8. dog
9. yell
10. great
11. dad
12. sleep

P. 474

1. soft
2. long
3. dark
4. on
5. happy
6. low
7. dry
8. slow
9. bad
10. cold
11. go
12. hard

P. 475

1. antonym
2. synonym
3. synonym
4. antonym
5. antonym
6. synonym
7. antonym
8. antonym

P. 476

1. a
2. b
3. a
4. a
5. a
6. b
7. b
8. a
9. b
10. a
11. b
12. a

P. 477

1. hear
2. here
3. here
4. hear
5. You're
6. your
7. you're
8. your

P. 478

1. write
2. right
3. right
4. write
5. right
6. write
7. right
8. right
9. write
10. right

P. 479

1. to
2. two
3. to
4. to
5. too
6. two
7. too
8. too
9. to
10. to
11. two

P. 480

1. their
2. They're
3. there
4. their
5. there
6. They're
7. They're
8. there
9. there
10. Their
11. there
12. They're

P. 481

1. sunglasses
2. afternoon
3. playground
4. birthday
5. outside
6. scrapbook
7. sunglasses
8. afternoon
9. scrapbook
10. birthday
11. outside
12. playground

P. 482

1. snowball
2. railroad
3. rainbow
4. sailboat
5. jumpsuit
6. earring
7. airplane
8.–10. Answers will vary.

P. 483

1. unable; not able
2. reopened; opened again
3. unlucky; not lucky
4. unfair; not fair
5. unhappy; not happy
6. rewind; wind again
7. rewashed; washed again
8. uneven; not even
9. refilled; filled again
10. reknitted; knitted again

P. 484

1. careful; full of care
2. harmless; without harm
3. breakable; able to be broken
4. dreadful; full of dread
5. hopeful; full of hope
6. thankful; full of thanks

P. 485

Answers will vary.

P. 486
1. My sister (circled) sings (underlined)
2. My brother (circled) dances (underlined)
3. They (circled) perform (underlined)
4. People (circled) clap (underlined)
5.–8. Answers will vary.

P. 487
Answers will vary. Sentences should be about school safety.

P. 488
1. Uncle Joe is a funny man.
2. Dad told us a funny story about his dog.
3. Firefighters are brave people.

P. 489
1. Making pasta is easy.
2. My mom is a very busy person.
3. Having a dog is fun, but it is also a lot of work.

P. 490
1.–3. The first sentence in each paragraph should be circled. The remaining sentences should be underlined.

P. 491
1.–3. The first sentence in each paragraph should be circled. The other sentences should be underlined.

P. 492
Top: 3, 2, 4, 1
Bottom: 2, 3, 4, 1

P. 493
Top: 4, 1, 3, 2
Bottom: 3, 2, 4, 1

P. 494
1. The story takes place at the zoo.
2. They watch the monkeys play.
3. They feed the seals.

P. 495
Answers will vary.

P. 496
1. The poem is about things the writer likes.
2. Answers will vary: bows, rose, toes, nose.
3. Answers will vary: white, blue, sweet, red, crunchy, wet, black.

P. 497
Answers will vary.

P. 498
1. birds in the writer's backyard.
2. red, tiny, sweetly, buzz
3. Sentences will vary. Be sure that the sentence supports the topic.

P. 499
Answers will vary.

P. 500
1. her grandmother
2. to thank her grandmother

P. 501
Letters will vary. Check that the parts are all correct.

P. 502
Check that the envelope is filled in correctly.

P. 503
1. how to make a bird feeder
2. a pine cone, string, peanut butter, and birdseed

P. 504
Order of steps:
1. Here is how to water a plant.
2. First, get a watering can.
3. Next, fill the can with water.
4. Last, water the plant.
Paragraphs will vary.

P. 505
1. Many African American people celebrate Kwanzaa.
2. Answers will vary but should be any sentence in the paragraph except the first.

P. 506
Answers will vary.

P. 507
1. The Koala
2. Anita Best
3. that it is a good book

P. 508
Reports will vary.

P. 509
1. that a lizard should be the class pet
2. Answers will vary. A lizard is small and easy to care for. A lizard doesn't eat much food. A lizard is interesting to watch.
3. vote for the lizard

P. 510
Reports will vary.

P. 511
1. 2, 1, 3; air, bat, cat
2. 3, 2, 1; rock, sea, top
3. 2, 3, 1; dog, egg, fish
4. 2, 3, 1; gate, hat, ice
5. 1, 3, 2; joke, king, lake
6. 2, 3, 1; mail, neck, owl
7. 2, 3, 1; walk, yes, zoo
8. 3, 2, 1; nail, oak, pan

P. 512
1. 3, 1, 2; hat, hill, hop
2. 3, 2, 1; far, four, fun
3. 1, 3, 2; ten, top, train
4. 1, 3, 2; art, ate, awful
5. 3, 1, 2; back, bring, bug
6. 2, 1, 3; gate, goat, great
7. 2, 1, 3; sad, snake, star
8. 2, 1, 3; pig, plane, prince

P. 513
1. music, noise, poem
2. plant, rain, sun
3. frog, garden, ground
4. afraid, alone, asleep

P. 514
1. tiny
2. no
3. toad
4. tiny
5. yes, because the word together falls between tiny and total in ABC order.

P. 515
1. burst
2. Grandfather and I burst into laughter.
3. bump
4. 2
5. Answers will vary; examples: I have a bump on my head., The water pipe burst.

P. 516
1. no
2. no
3. yes
4. no
5. yes
6. no
7. no
8. no

P. 517
1. 8
2. 4
3. 10
4. 3
5. 11
6. 4
7. butterflies
8. dogs
9. trees or United States
10. history, Florida

P. 518
1. Kinds of Houses.
2. Jack Builder
3. 4
4. page 15
5. 2, 9

P. 519
1. All About Cats
2. Patricia L. Keller
3. Richard H. Green
4. Coaster Press

P. 520
1. 5
2. 1
3. 7
4. "Cats in the Wild"

P. 521
1. fiction
2. nonfiction
3. nonfiction
4. fiction
5. fiction
6. nonfiction
7. fiction

P. 522
1. fiction
2. fiction
3. nonfiction
4. fiction
5.–8. Answers will vary.

P. 523
1. fact
2. fantasy
3. fantasy
4. fact
5. fantasy
6. fantasy
7. fact
8. fantasy

P. 524
1. fantasy
2. fact
3. fact
4. fantasy
5. fact
6. fact
7. fantasy
8. fact

Writing Skills

Answers to the practice paper exercises questions may vary, but examples are provided here to give you an idea of how your child may respond.

P. 526
1. The girl eats pizza.
2. The robot walks a dog.
3. cereal

P. 527
1. The balloon goes up.
2. The room is a mess!
3. It's a windy fall day.
4. The girls are ready to eat.

P. 528
1. fruit bowl, 2 eggs, 1 glass
One person will eat breakfast.
2. ticket booth, roller coast, Ferris wheel, children.
The fair is open!

P. 529
1. Chimpanzees
2. hunting
3. Bananas
4. yellow
5. leap

P. 530
1. bears are big animals.
2. They may weigh 1,000 pounds.
3. some live in cold places
4. others like warm weather.

P. 544
Circle: first, then, last of all
My family had fun at the summer fair yesterday.

P. 545
Underline: I, we, my, our
Circle: first, then, after, last of all

p. 546

Underline: In one movie I saw deer, bears, and foxes in a forest. Another movie was a cartoon about mice and pigs. The best animal movie I ever saw took place in the jungle. It was about a parrot that saved a tiger's life.
Topic sentence: I like many movies about animals.
Sentence added: Sentences will vary. Be sure that the detail supports the topic.

p. 547

1. dash
2. boxes
3. apples
4. fuzzy
5. cheerful
6. giggle

p. 548

One day my family and I went to an apple orchard. we went to pick fresh apples. first, i got a big basket. next, I picked some ripe apples off the trees○ I put them in the basket○ After about an hour, i was too hungry to keep going. that's when i bit into a juicy, red apple   The sweet, ripe apple tasted better than anything else in the world.

p. 558

1. He competed in the school spelling bee.
2. He said his palms got sweaty.
3. akrobat
4. No. The last sentence says he did not win.
5. The writer felt a little disappointed.
6. Be sure your child correctly summarizes the significant events in the story, paraphrasing as needed. Summaries should be organized in a thoughtful way, with the main ideas and important details clearly presented in order. Spelling, punctuation, capitalization, and grammar should be correct.

p. 563

1. green: October 22, 2005
2. blue: Juan
3. red: Love,
4. Juan

p. 564

1. red: July 27, 2005
2. yellow: Your friend,
3. blue: Dear Chris,
4. orange: Richard
5. green: body of letter

p. 565

Responses will vary. Be sure that pictures are complete and that sentences tell about the pictures.

p. 566

1. her grandmother
2. to thank her
3. Possible responses: The pink roses are her favorite flowers. Emily feels much better now.

p. 567

2. He dances and sings.
3. Andy writes plays and acts them out.
4. He gets applause and cheers.

p. 568

February 7, 2005

dear Tanya ∧

¶ I had fun at your house last week! I'm so (bezy) *busy* at school now. I'm in the class play. I'm a bear in the play○ My costume is brown and fuzzy.

have you ever been in a play?

your friend ∧

Brenda

p. 577

1. Kathryn, best friend
2. Her new neighborhood is in the country.
3. They probably used to ride bikes together.
4. Shannon
5. Be sure your child correctly summarizes the significant events in the story, paraphrasing as needed. Summaries should be organized in a thoughtful way, with the main ideas and important details clearly presented in order. Spelling, punctuation, capitalization, and grammar should be correct.

p. 582

1. I just love a parade.
2. uniforms shine with brass buttons and gold braid, loud music always makes me want to clap my hands
3. Sentences will vary. Be sure that the detail supports the topic.

p. 583

Possible responses:
1. Many birds visit my backyard.
2. red, tiny, buzz, sweetly
3. Sentences will vary. Be sure that the sentence supports the topic.

p. 584

Responses will vary. Be sure each response is a detail that supports the topic and is categorized correctly.

p. 585

Responses will vary. Be sure the detail sentences include vivid adjectives.

p. 586

Responses will vary. Be sure each sentence includes adjectives.

p. 587

¶ Don't you just love a parade? I like to see the band march (buy) *by* the uniforms shine with brass buttons and gold braid. The loud (musik) *music* always makes me want to clap and stamp my feet. i also like to see the floats. The floats with storybook characters are the best. the kings and queens in purple velvet are so beautiful○

p. 601

1. The writer was on a train.
2. The writer had visited his or her grandparents.
3. sight, sound, smell, taste, and touch
4. Answer may include any two of the following: cool glass window; loud final whistle, car rocked slowly from side to side; snuggly bear hugs; sweet buttermilk taste; hearty laugh, mint chewing gum; cozy seat; green hills and fresh country air
5. Be sure your child correctly summarizes the significant events in the story, paraphrasing as needed. Summaries should be organized in a thoughtful way, with the main ideas and important details clearly presented in order. Spelling, punctuation, capitalization, and grammer should be correct.

p. 606

1. A Long Night
2. Lateisha couldn't sleep.
3. Lateisha, Mother

p. 607

1. The Hole
2. a boy, tiny mice
3. The boy falls down a hole.
4. The mice show the boy a way out.

p. 608

Problem: Aunt Sally is in the kitchen.
How to Solve: Responses will vary. Accept all responses that tell a way to solve the problem.

p. 609

Responses will vary. Be sure responses include enough details to tell clearly what John sees.

p. 610

Arnold climbed the stairs. he was very tired. School had been (tuff) *tough* that day. The soccer game had been (tuffer) *tougher*.

Arnold got into bed. He lay down, but he could not fall asleep. he was thinking about (he) *the* soccer game and the goal he missed ○

Arnold felt himself kicking the ball into the goal. Suddenly, he felt cold and heard birds chirping. he looked down and saw that he had kicked off the blanket. The sun was up and it was morning. He had fallen asleep after all!

p. 621

1. They went to summer camp.
2. They changed into their swimsuits.
3. Juan was afraid to go off the diving board.
4. Danny convinced him to try it.
5. He was happy.
6. Be sure your child correctly summarizes the significant events in the story, paraphrasing as needed. Summaries should be organized in a thoughtful way, with the main ideas and important details clearly presented in order. Spelling, punctuation, capitalization, and grammar should be correct.

p. 626

1. Sewing on a button can be easy.
2. First, get a needle and thread.
3. needle, thread, button, piece of clothing

p. 627

Underline: This is a simple way to wrap a gift.
Circle: First, Next, Then, Last
Things you need: wrapping paper, scissors, tape

p. 628

Possible responses:
1. First, get a can of soup, a can opener, and a pot.
2. Next, open the soup can.
3. Then, pour the soup into the po[t]
4. Last, heat the soup.

p. 629

1. a
2. a
3. b

p. 630

2. Tran and Carlos go with them.
3. Carlos and Bob pack a lunch.
4. Bob and Jasmine sled all day.
5. Bob and Jasmine are tired.

p. 631

¶ sewing on a button can be ~~eazy~~ *easy*.

First, get a needle and thread. you

will also need the button and ~~peece~~ *piece*

of clothing ⊙ Choose a thread color

to match the clothing. next, thread

the needle ⊙ then, sew on the

button tightly. Last, make a knot in

the thread. Cut the thread ⊙

p. 641

1. 350 degrees
2. mix the batter with an electric mixer
3. 30 minutes
4. allow the cake to cool

TEST PREP

Letter answers are provided for each question. When the first choice is correct, the answer is A. When the second choice is correct, the answer is B. When the third or fourth choices are correct, the answers are C or D, respectively.

p. 648-649

1. A
2. C
3. D
4. A
5. A
6. B

p. 650-651

1. C
2. A
3. D
4. C
5. A
6. A

p. 652-653

1. D
2. B
3. D
4. C
5. C
6. C

p. 654-655

1. A
2. D
3. C
4. C
5. A
6. D

p. 656-657

1. B
2. C
3. D

p. 658-659

1. C
2. A
3. B
4. C
5. C

p. 660-661

1. B
2. D
3. B
4. C
5. A
6. B

p. 662-663

1. A
2. B
3. B
4. D
5. A

p. 664-665

1. D
2. A
3. A
4. C
5. B

p. 666-667

1. C
2. A
3. D
4. A
5. C
6. A
7. D

p. 668-669

1. A
2. C
3. B
4. C
5. A
6. B

p. 670-671

1. A
2. B
3. B
4. C

p. 672-673

1. B
2. A
3. B
4. B
5. C

p. 674-679

SA. C
1. B.
2. because it was about to rain
3. D
4. C
5. The mouse woke him up.
6. C
7. A
8. He misses Harry.
9. D
10. D
11. A
12. B
13. C
14. A
15. C
16. Students volunteer to help others and earn a volunteer pin.
17. A
18. B
19. C
20. D
21. A
22. For example: Dawn's Special Part

p. 680-683

SA. A
1. D
2. A
3. B
4. in the sun
5. C
6. C
7. A
8. They have big eyes.
9. D
10. D
11. For example: tell someone at camp about his adventure
12. B
13. B
14. C
15. C
16. B
17. C

p. 684

SA. A
1. D
2. B
3. C
4. smallest
5. A
6. B

p. 685

SA. A
1. B
2. I heard the telephone ring.

p. 686

SA. shine
1. not allowed
2. A
3. A
4. C

p. 687

SA. C
1. A
2. B
3. A
4. C
5. A
6. B
7. C
8. B

p. 688

SA. B
1. C
2. B
3. C
4. A
5. B
6. C
7. A
8. C

p. 689

SA. A
1. A
2. C
3. C
4. B
5. C
6. B
7. B
8. B

p. 690

SA. C
1. C
2. A
3. A
4. B
5. C
6. B
7. C
8. B

p. 691-694

1. D
2. A
3. C
4. A
5. D
6. B
7. D
8. I visited my aunt last week.
9. A
10. B
11. B
12. B
13. C
14. A
15. B
16. B
17. C
18. B
19. A
20. C
21. B
22. B

23. A
24. C
25. C
26. B
27. C
28. C
29. B
30. A
31. C
32. C
33. B
34. A
35. C
36. B

p. 696
Step 1. How much did Paul pay for three apples?
Step 2. First apple is 25¢, additional apples are 20¢ each.
Step 3. Add.
Step 4. 25¢ + 20¢ + 20¢ = 65¢
Step 5. Yes, because when you add the costs of the apples the total is 65¢.

p. 697
Step 1. To find Jenny's number.
Step 2. The number is less than 9 and greater than 5. It is odd.
Step 3. Use logical thinking.
Step 4. Only 6, 7, and 8 are greater than 5 and less than 9. Of these, only 7 is odd, so it is Jenny's number.
Step 5. Yes, because 7 is the only possible answer.

p. 698
SA. C
1. 9
2. D
3. B

p. 699
SA. C
1. A
2. A
3. 0
4. B

p. 700
SA. C
1. C
2. 25
3. B

p. 701
SA. C
1. 3
2. D

p. 702
SA. C
1. D
2. B
3. B

p. 703
SA. D
1. 6
2. B
3. A

p. 704
SA. 12 − 8 = ❑
1. 3 + 9 = ❑
2. C
3. 32
4. A

p. 705-707
SA. C
1. B
2. A
3. B
4. 25
5. C
6. B
7. E
8. A
9. C
10. D
11. C
12. D
13. 197
14. C

p. 708
SA. B
1. B
2. D
3. B
4. C
5. E
6. 34

p. 709-710
1. B
2. 35
3. C
4. C
5. A
6. E
7. C
8. D
9. B
10. D
11. C
12. A
13. D
14. B
15. 37
16. A
17. E

p. 711-717
1. C
2. C
3. D
4. D
5. 638
6. 80
7. B
8. B
9. A
10. C
11. D
12. B
13. B
14. 7
15. 30 minutes
16. D
17. C
18. D
19. D
20. A
21. B
22. May
23. D
24. D
25. B
26. C

p. 718-724
SA. A
1. C
2. B
3. C
4. to tell why she likes soccer
5. C
6. B
7. A
8. C
9. C
10. Mr. Elkhorn
11. C
12. C
13. B

p. 725-726
SA. C
1. B
2. B
3. C
4. C
5. B
6. B
7. B
8. B
9. A
10. B
11. C
12. C
13. A
14. B

p. 727-734
SA. A
1. C
2. My bike has a flat tire.
3. B
4. 25
5. are
6. C
7. A
8. B
9. The farm this summer.
10. C
11. A
12. ?
13. B
14. A
15. B
16. B
17. C
18. A
19. B
20. B
21. A

p. 735-741
SA. D
1. A
2. B
3. B
4. D
5. D
6. B
7. B
8. C
9. D
10. C
11. A
12. C
13. D
14. B
15. C
16. A
17. B
18. C
19. D
20. A
21. C
22. B
23. A
24. C
25. B
26. A

1. C
2. B
3. B
4. B
5. C
6. C
7. B
8. C
9. A
10. A
11. C
12. B
13. C
14. A
15. C
16. B
17. B
18. A
19. C
20. C
21. A
22. B
23. C
24. A
25. A
26. A
27. D
28. C
29. C
30. B
31. A
32. B
33. B
34. D
35. C
36. For example: Did you dip your cookie into your milk?
37. D
38. A
39. D
40. C
41. B
42. write
43. B
44. A

1. B
2. A
3. C
4. A
5. 33
6. B
7. 921
8. A
9. A
10. D
11. A
12. B
13. B
14. A
15. B
16. C
17. 2
18. C
19. Alex
20. B
21. C
22. A
23. A
24. C
25. B
26. C

SA. D
1. B
2. C
3. E
4. B
5. C
6. A
7. 197
8. 62
9. C
10. C
11. E
12. A
13. C
14. 7
15. B
16. C
17. B

1. C
2. B
3. A
4. C
5. A
6. C
7. A
8. C
9. B
10. C
11. C
12. B
13. A
14. C
15. B
16. C
17. A
18. C
19. B
20. C
21. ?
22. B
23. A
24. A
25. A
26. B
27. A
28. B
29. A